Hands-On Data Science with R

Techniques to perform data manipulation and mining to build smart analytical models using R

Vitor Bianchi Lanzetta
Nataraj Dasgupta
Ricardo Anjoleto Farias

Packt

BIRMINGHAM - MUMBAI

Hands-On Data Science with R

Commissioning Editor: Pravin Dhandre
Acquisition Editor: Joshua Nadar
Content Development Editor: Karan Thakkar
Technical Editor: Suwarna Patil
Copy Editor: Safis Editing
Project Coordinator: Namrata Swetta
Proofreader: Safis Editing
Indexer: Priyanka Dhadke
Graphics: Jisha Chirayil
Production Coordinator: Arvindkumar Gupta

First published: November 2018
Production reference: 1301118

Published by Packt Publishing Ltd.
Livery Place
35 Livery Street
Birmingham
B3 2PB, UK.

ISBN 978-1-78913-940-2

www.packtpub.com

Contributors

About the authors

Vitor Bianchi Lanzetta (`@vitorlanzetta`) has a master's degree in Applied Economics (University of São Paulo—USP) and works as a data scientist in a tech start-up named RedFox Digital Solutions. He has also authored a book called *R Data Visualization Recipes*. The things he enjoys the most are statistics, economics, and sports of all kinds (electronics included). His blog, made in partnership with Ricardo Anjoleto Farias (`@R_A_Farias`), can be found at ArcadeData dot org, they kindly call it R-Cade Data.

> *I'd like to thank God and my family, especially my caring parents, Naide and Carmo, and my wonderful sister, Gabriela. I love you all beyond measure.*

Nataraj Dasgupta is the vice president of advanced analytics at RxDataScience Inc. Nataraj has been in the IT industry for more than 19 years, and has worked in the technical and analytics divisions of Philip Morris, IBM, UBS Investment Bank, and Purdue Pharma. At Purdue Pharma, Nataraj led the data science division, where he developed the company's award-winning big data and machine learning platform. Prior to Purdue, at UBS, he held the role of Associate Director, working with high-frequency and algorithmic trading technologies in the foreign exchange trading division of the bank.

> *I'd like to thank my wife, Sara, for her caring support and understanding as I worked on the book at weekends and evenings, and to my parents, parents-in-law, sister, and grandmother for all their support, guidance, tutelage, and encouragement over the years. I'd also like to thank Packt, especially the editors, Tushar Gupta, and Karan Thakkar, and everyone else in the team, whose persistence and attention to detail has been exemplary.*

Ricardo Anjoleto Farias is an economist who graduated from the Universidade Estadual de Maringá in 2014. In addition to being a sports enthusiast (electronic or otherwise) and enjoying a good barbecue, he also likes math, statistics, and correlated studies. His first contact with R was when he embarked on his master's degree, and since then, he has tried to improve his skills with this powerful tool.

> *I am grateful to my family, mainly my parents, for their support during the difficult moments. I would also like to thank my friend and the book's co-author, Vitor Bianchi Lanzetta , who has taught me a lot, both academically and personally.*

About the reviewer

Doug Ortiz is the founder of Illustris, LLC and is an experienced enterprise cloud, big data, data analytics, and solutions architect who has architected, designed, developed, reengineered, and integrated enterprise solutions. His other areas of expertise include Amazon Web Services, Azure, Google Cloud, Business Intelligence, Hadoop, Spark, NoSQL databases, and SharePoint, to name but a few.

Huge thanks to my wonderful wife, Milla, to Maria, and Nikolay, and to my children, for all their support.

Packt is searching for authors like you

Table of Contents

Preface

Hands-on Data Science with R deals with the practical aspects of R development, more so than the theoretical. In other words, emphasis has been given on how to use R for different data science-related activities, such as machine learning and data mining, as well as topics in visualization, cloud computing, and others. Note that much of the book assumes some prior familiarity with R, such that it is intended for intermediate R users. While a number of introductory explanations, such as instructions for installing R Studio, have been provided, the reader may find some topics more advanced, which necessitates prior experience with R programming.

Who this book is for

If you are a budding data scientist keen to learn about the popular `pandas` library, or a Python developer looking to step into the world of data analysis, this book is the ideal resource to get you started. Some programming experience in Python will be helpful in terms of getting the most out of this book.

What this book covers

`Chapter 1`, *Getting Started with Data Science and R*, provides an introduction to the field of data science, its applicability in different industry domains, an overview of the machine learning process, and how to install R Studio in order to get started in R development. It also introduces the reader to programming in R, starting off at an intermediate level to facilitate an analysis of the HDI, published by the UN development program. The HDI signifies the level of economic development, including general public health, education, and various other societal factors, of a state.

`Chapter 2`, *Descriptive and Inferential Statistics*, introduces fundamental statistical analysis using R, including techniques to perform random sampling, hypothesis testing, and non-parametric tests. This chapter contains extensive examples of commands in R for performing common analysis, such as t-tests and z-tests, and includes utilization of some well-known statistical packages, such as HMISC in R.

`Chapter 3`, *Data Wrangling with R,* provides an introduction to packages available in R to slice and manipulate data. Packages that are available as part of the `tidyverse` set of packages, such as `dplyr`, and, more generally, the `apply` family of functions in R, have been introduced. The chapter is example-heavy, in that several examples have been provided to guide the reader on how to apply the functions in the respective packages

`Chapter 4`, *KDD, Data Mining, and Text Mining,* includes extensive discussions on the art of extracting information from unstructured data sources, such as websites and Twitter. KDD is a popular term in the data science community and this chapter does full justice to the topic by providing step-by-step examples so as to provide a holistic overview of the subject matter. Sections on web scraping, data transformation, and data visualization have been included. Examples on how to leverage packages such as `rvest` and `httr` in order to perform such operations are also discussed at length.

`Chapter 5`, *Data Analysis with R,* covers a general introduction to data types and data categories in R as they apply to machine learning, manipulating strings and dates, and charting with R. This chapter is essentially a consolidation of topics that are found elsewhere in the book, but in a more concise format. This chapter can hence be used as a standalone section of the book that does not depend on any other chapter and can be used to gain familiarity with the topics discussed.

`Chapter 6`, *Machine Learning with R, provides* a detailed overview of using R for predictive analytics, more generally known as machine learning. It starts out with linear regression, and gradually progresses to more in-depth topics in ML such as decision trees, random forest, and SVMs. Extensively worked-out, hands-on examples, along with visualizations, complement the theoretical discussions in this chapter. The chapter concludes with a discussion on neural networks, one of the most popular fields today in machine learning.

`Chapter 7`, *Forecasting and ML App* with R, includes an advanced R Shiny application, full with custom CSS style sheets, Google fonts, modified data table formats, and such like, for forecasting the revenue and sales of pharmaceutical medications in the UK using the NHS dataset. Such datasets are also known as real-world datasets in the sense that they contain actual data pertaining to physicians' prescribing activities. The application is fully reactive; that is, changing the controls on the frontend will immediately run the respective forecasting algorithm and update forecast tables. We have also used an algorithm known as Markov Chain Monte Carlo, which is a machine learning-based forecasting model provided as part of the Facebook package, Prophet.

`Chapter 8`, *Neural Networks and Deep Learning*, initiates a comprehensive discussion, along with hands-on examples, of using R for machine learning using two of the most popular algorithms—neural networks, and its more advanced variation, deep learning. Indeed, some of the most successful machine learning projects in the world today, such as self-driving cars and automated assistants such as Siri, are powered by deep learning. This chapter gives readers a unique and robust opportunity to delve into these areas and learn how they, too, can apply some of the same algorithms driving sensational successes in the field of machine learning today.

`Chapter 9`, *Markovian in R*, applies to more advanced users who are interested in learning more about Markov processes that involve finding latent (or hidden) data from information in datasets. This is essentially a part of a field known as Bayesian analysis, which allows machine learning practitioners to model states that are not directly visible. Markov models are used in fields such as natural language processing, and object recognition.

`Chapter 10`, *Visualizing Data*, provides a comprehensive introduction to various plotting libraries in R. In particular, libraries such as `ggplot2`, `rCharts`, and mapping libraries have been discussed at length. R is well known for its presentation-grade libraries that are capable of creating stunning, professional-grade visualizations. The chapter walks the reader through many of the plotting libraries that have made R a mainstay of the data visualization field.

`Chapter 11`, *Going to Production with R*, provides an introduction to the Shiny R package, a tool for the development of interactive applications. This chapter delves into how it works, how reactivity works, the basics of its template, how to build a basic application, and how to build one using a real dataset. If you want a package to present your data to people who are unfamiliar with the R language, maybe you should start by learning the Shiny App.

`Chapter 12`, *Large Scale Data Analytics with Hadoop*, covers Apache Spark, an engine for large-scale data processing, similar but not identical to Apache Hadoop. Since its focus is on processing, you can use it entirely from your RStudio console. This chapter teaches how to install and take your first steps on it with `sparklyr`, an R package that provides a backend to the `dplyr` package. In this way, you can use the `dplyr` functions to manipulate your big dataset into the Spark cluster.

`Chapter 13`, *R on Cloud*, takes an in-depth look at using AzureML on the Microsoft Azure (cloud) platform. Cloud computing has allowed companies across the world to transition from a traditional data center-oriented architecture to a cloud-based decentralized environment. Unsurprisingly, machine learning has become a major part of the success of the cloud due to the ease of deploying multi-node clusters for large-scale machine learning. AzureML is an easy-to-use web-based platform from Microsoft that allows even new data scientists to get a jump start on machine learning via a GUI-based interface.

`Appendix A`, *The Road Ahead*, introduces the reader to various resources on the web, such as blogs and forums to utilize and learn more about the field of R. The world of R is rapidly evolving, and in this chapter, we share some insights on the specific resources that will help seasoned data scientists stay abreast of all the developments in R today.

To get the most out of this book

Readers should have a basic knowledge of R and the Shiny app.

Download the example code files

You can download the example code files for this book from your account at `www.packt.com`. If you purchased this book elsewhere, you can visit `www.packt.com/support` and register to have the files emailed directly to you.

You can download the code files by following these steps:

1. Log in or register at `www.packt.com`.
2. Select the **SUPPORT** tab.
3. Click on **Code Downloads & Errata**.
4. Enter the name of the book in the **Search** box and follow the onscreen instructions.

Once the file is downloaded, please make sure that you unzip or extract the folder using the latest version of:

- WinRAR/7-Zip for Windows
- Zipeg/iZip/UnRarX for Mac
- 7-Zip/PeaZip for Linux

The code bundle for the book is also hosted on GitHub at `https://github.com/PacktPublishing/Hands-On-Data-Science-with-R`. In case there's an update to the code, it will be updated on the existing GitHub repository.

We also have other code bundles from our rich catalog of books and videos available at `https://github.com/PacktPublishing/`. Check them out!

Download the color images

We also provide a PDF file that has color images of the screenshots/diagrams used in this book. You can download it here: `https://www.packtpub.com/sites/default/files/downloads/9781789139402_ColorImages.pdf`.

Conventions used

There are a number of text conventions used throughout this book.

`CodeInText`: Indicates code words in text, database table names, folder names, filenames, file extensions, pathnames, dummy URLs, user input, and Twitter handles. Here is an example: "The `ggplot2` package is the most commonly used visualization package in R."

A block of code is set as follows:

```
life <- fread("ch1_life_exp.csv", header=T)

# View contents of life
head(life)
```

Bold: Indicates a new term, an important word, or words that you see on screen. For example, words in menus or dialog boxes appear in the text like this. Here is an example: "After logging in, search for the topic **Cost Management + Billing** in the left-hand menu, as shown in the following screenshot."

Warnings or important notes appear like this.

Tips and tricks appear like this.

Get in touch

Feedback from our readers is always welcome.

General feedback: If you have questions about any aspect of this book, mention the book title in the subject of your message and email us at `customercare@packtpub.com`.

Errata: Although we have taken every care to ensure the accuracy of our content, mistakes do happen. If you have found a mistake in this book, we would be grateful if you would report this to us. Please visit `www.packt.com/submit-errata`, selecting your book, clicking on the Errata Submission Form link, and entering the details.

Piracy: If you come across any illegal copies of our works in any form on the internet, we would be grateful if you would provide us with the location address or website name. Please contact us at `copyright@packt.com` with a link to the material.

If you are interested in becoming an author: If there is a topic that you have expertise in, and you are interested in either writing or contributing to a book, please visit `authors.packtpub.com`.

Reviews

Please leave a review. Once you have read and used this book, why not leave a review on the site that you purchased it from? Potential readers can then see and use your unbiased opinion to make purchase decisions, we at Packt can understand what you think about our products, and our authors can see your feedback on their book. Thank you!

For more information about Packt, please visit `packt.com`.

1
Getting Started with Data Science and R

"It is a capital mistake to theorise before one has data."
— Sir Arthur Conan Doyle, The Adventures of Sherlock Holmes

Data, like science, has been ubiquitous the world over since early history. The term data science is not generally taken to literally mean science with data, since without data there would be of science. Rather, it is a specialized field in which data scientists and other practitioners apply advanced computing techniques, usually along with algorithms or predictive analytics to uncover insights that may be challenging to obtain with traditional methods.

Data science as a distinct subject was proposed since the early 1960s by pioneers and thought leaders such as Peter Naur, Prof. Jeff Wu, and William Cleveland. Today, we have largely realized the vision that Prof. Wu and others had in mind when the concept first arose; data science as an amalgamation of computing, data mining, and predictive analytics, all leading up to deriving key insights that drive business and growth across the world today.

The driving force behind this has been the rapid but proportional growth of computing capabilities and algorithms. Computing languages have also played a key role in supporting the emergence of data science, primary among them being the statistical language R.

In this introductory chapter, we will cover the following topics:

- Introduction to data science and R
- Active domains of data science
- Solving problems with data science

- Using R for data science
- Setting up R and RStudio
- Our first R program

Introduction to data science

The term, data science, as mentioned earlier, was first proposed in the 1960s and 1970s by Peter Naur. In the late 1990s, Jeff Wu, while at the University of Michigan, Ann Arbor, proposed the term in a formal paper titled *Statistics = Data Science?*. The paper, which Prof. Wu subsequently presented at the seventh series of P.C. Mahalonobis Lectures at the Indian Statistical Institute in 1998, raised some interesting questions about what an appropriate definition of statistics might be in light of the tasks that a statistician did beyond numerical calculations.

In the paper Prof. Wu highlighted the concept of *Statistical Trilogy*, consisting of data collection, data modeling and analysis, and problem solving. The following sections reflected upon the future directions in which Dr. Wu raised the prospects of neural network models to model complex, non-linear relationships, the use of cross validation to improve model performance, and data mining of large-scale data among others. [Source: `https://www2.isye.gatech.edu/~jeffwu/presentations/datascience.pdf`].

The paper, although written more than 20 years ago, is a reflection of the foresight that a few academicians such as Dr. Wu had at the time, which has been realized in full, almost verbatim as it was propositioned back then, both in thought and practical concepts. A copy of Dr. Wu's paper is available at `https://www2.isye.gatech.edu/~jeffwu/presentations/datascience.pdf`.

Key components of data science

The practice of data science requires the application of three distinct disciplines to uncover insights from data. These disciplines are as follows:

- Computer science
- Predictive analytics
- Domain knowledge

The following diagram shows the core components of data science:

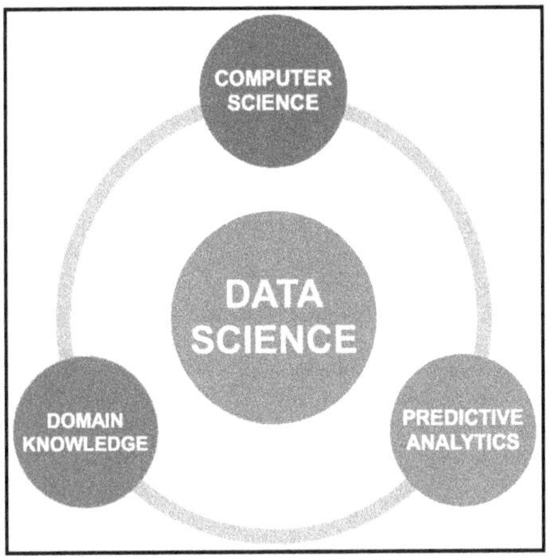

Computer science

During the course of performing data science, if large datasets are involved, the practitioner may spend a fair amount of time cleansing and curating the dataset. In fact, it is not uncommon for data scientists to spend the majority of their time preparing data for analysis. The generally accepted distribution of time for a data science project involves 80% spent in data management and the remaining 20% spent in the actual analysis of the data.

While this may seem or sound overly general, the growth of big data, that is, large-scale datasets, usually in the range of terabytes, has meant that it takes sufficient time and effort to extract data before the actual analysis takes place. Real-world data is seldom perfect. Issues with real-world data range from missing variables to incorrect entries and other deficiencies. The size of datasets also poses a formidable challenge.

Technologies such as Hadoop, Spark, and NoSQL databases have addressed the needs of the data science community for managing and curating terabytes, if not petabytes, of information. These tools are usually the first step in the overall data science process that precedes the application of algorithms on the datasets using languages such as R, Python and others.

Hence, as a first step, the data scientist generally should be capable of working with datasets using contemporary tools for large-scale data mining. For instance, if the data resides in a Hadoop cluster, the practitioner must be able and willing to perform the work necessary to retrieve and curate the data from the source systems.

Second, once the data has been retrieved and curated, the data scientist should be aware of the requirements of the algorithm from a computational perspective and determine if the system has the necessary resources to efficiently execute these algorithms. For instance, if the algorithms can be taken advantage of with multi-core computing facilities, the practitioner must use the appropriate packages and functions to leverage. This may mean the difference between getting results in an hour versus requiring an entire day.

Last, but not least, the creation of machine learning models will require programming in one or more languages. This in itself demands a level of knowledge and skill in applying algorithms and using appropriate data structures and other computer science concepts:

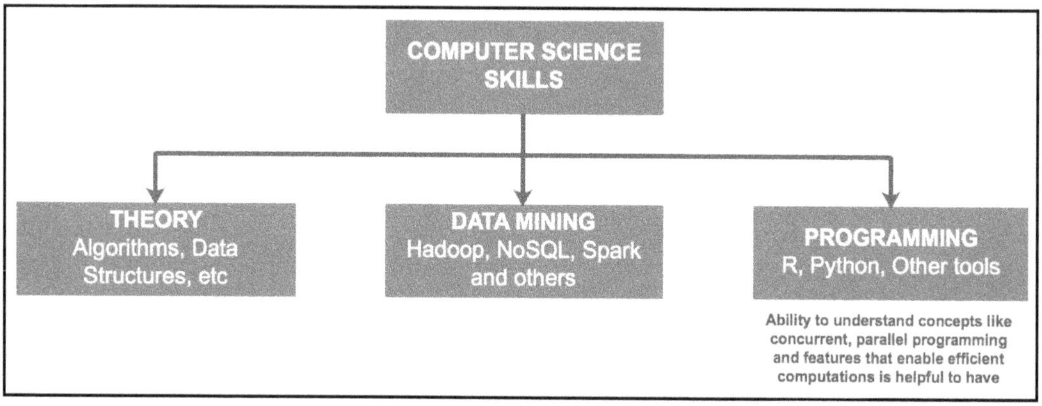

Predictive analytics (machine learning)

In popular media and literature, predictive analytics is known by various names. The terms are used interchangeably and often depend on personal preferences and interpretations. The terms predictive analytics, machine learning, and statistical learning are technically synonymous, and refer to the field of applying algorithms in machine learning to the data.

The algorithm could be as simple as a line-of-best-fit, which you may have already used in Excel, also known as linear regression. Or it could be a complex deep learning model that implements multiple hidden layers and inputs. In both cases, the mere fact that a statistical model, an algorithm was applied to generate a prediction qualifies the usage as a practice of machine learning.

In general, creating a machine learning model involves a series of steps such as the sequence:

1. Cleanse and curate the dataset to extract the cohort on which the model will be built.
2. Analyze the data using descriptive statistics, for example, distributions and visualizations.
3. Feature engineering, preprocessing, and other steps necessary to add or remove variables/predictors.
4. Split the data into a train and test set (for example, set aside 80% of the data for training and the remaining 20% for testing your model).
5. Select appropriate machine learning models and create the model using cross validation.
6. Select the final model after assessing the performance across models on a given (one or more) cost metric. Note that the model could be an ensemble, that is, a combination of more than one model.
7. Perform predictions on the test dataset.
8. Deliver the final model.

The most commonly used languages for machine learning today are R and Python. In Python, the most popular package for machine learning is scikit-learn (`http://scikit-learn.org`), while in R, there are multiple packages, such as random forest, **Gradient Boosting Machine** (**GBM**), kernlab, **Support Vector Machines** (**SVMs**), and others.

Although Python's scikit-learn is extremely versatile and elaborate, and in fact the preferred language in production settings, the ease of use and diversity of packages in R gives it an advantage in terms of early adoption and use for machine learning exercises.

> The **Comprehensive R Archive Network** (**CRAN**) has a task view page titled *CRAN Task View: Machine Learning & Statistical Learning* (`https://cran.r-project.org/web/views/MachineLearning.html`) that summarizes some of the key packages in use today for machine learning using R.

Popular machine learning tools such as TensorFlow from Google (`https://www.tensorflow.org`), XGBoost (`http://xgboost.readthedocs.io/en/latest/`), and H2O (`https://www.h2o.ai`) have also released packages that act as a wrapper to the underlying machine learning algorithms implemented in the respective tools.

It is a common misconception that machine learning is just about creating models. While that is indeed the end goal, there is a subtle yet fundamental difference between a model and a good model. With the functions available today, it is relatively easy for anyone to create a model by simply running a couple of lines of code. A good model has business value, while a model built without the rigor of formal machine learning principles is practically unusable for all intents and purposes. A key requirement of a good machine learning model is the judicious use of domain expertise to evaluate results, identify errors, analyze them, and further refine using the insights that subject matter experts can provide. This is where domain knowledge plays a crucial and indispensable role.

Domain knowledge

More often than data scientists would like to admit, machine learning models produce results that are obvious and intuitive. For instance, we once conducted an elaborate analysis of physicians, prescribing behavior to find out the strongest predictor of how many prescriptions a physician would write in the next quarter. We used a broad set of input variables such as the physicians locations, their specialties, hospital affiliations, prescribing history, and other data. In the end, the best performing model produced a result that we all knew very well. The strongest predictor of how many prescriptions a physician would write in the next quarter was the number of prescriptions the physician had written in the previous quarter! To filter out the truly meaningful variables and build a more robust model, we eventually had to engage someone who had extensive experience of working in the pharma industry. Machine learning models work best when produced in a hybrid approach—one that combines domain expertise along with the sophistication of models developed.

Active domains of data science

Data science plays a role in virtually all aspects of our day-to-day lives and is used across nearly all industries. The adoption of data science was largely spurred by the successes of start-ups such as Uber, Airbnb, and Facebook that rose rapidly and earned valuations of billions of dollars in a very short span of time.

Data generated by social media networks such as Facebook and Twitter, search engines such as Google and Yahoo!, and various other networks, such as Pinterest and Instagram led to a deluge of information about personal tastes, preferences, and habits of individuals. Companies leveraged the information using various machine learning techniques to gain insights.

For example, **Natural Language Processing** (**NLP**) is a machine learning technique used to analyse textual data on comments posted on public forums to extract users' interests. The users are then shown ads relevant to their interests generating sales from which companies earn ad revenue. Image recognition algorithms are utilized to automatically identify objects in an image and serve the relevant images when users search for those objects on search engines.

The use of data science as a means to not only increase user engagement but also increase revenue, has become a widespread phenomenon. Some of the domains in which data science is prevalent is given as follows. The list is not all-inclusive, but highlights some of the key industries in which data science plays an important role today:

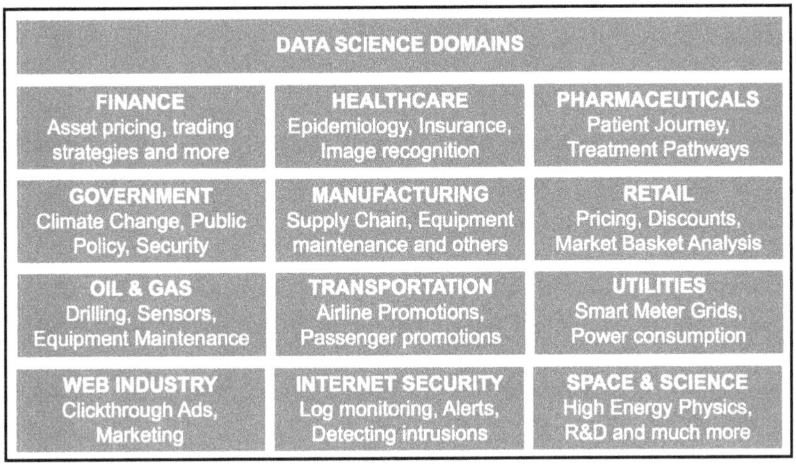
DATA SCIENCE DOMAINS
FINANCE
Asset pricing, trading strategies and more
HEALTHCARE
Epidemiology, Insurance, Image recognition
PHARMACEUTICALS
Patient Journey, Treatment Pathways
GOVERNMENT
Climate Change, Public Policy, Security
MANUFACTURING
Supply Chain, Equipment maintenance and others
RETAIL
Pricing, Discounts, Market Basket Analysis
OIL & GAS
Drilling, Sensors, Equipment Maintenance
TRANSPORTATION
Airline Promotions, Passenger promotions
UTILITIES
Smart Meter Grids, Power consumption
WEB INDUSTRY
Clickthrough Ads, Marketing
INTERNET SECURITY
Log monitoring, Alerts, Detecting intrusions
SPACE & SCIENCE
High Energy Physics, R&D and much more

A few of these domains have been discussed in the following sections.

Finance

Data science has been used in finance, especially in trading for many decades. Investment banks, especially trading desks, have employed complex models to analyse and make trading decisions. Some examples of data science as used in finance include:

- **Credit risk management**: Analyse the creditworthiness of a user by analyzing the historical financial records, assets, and transactions of the user
- **Loan fraud**: Identifying applications for credit or loans that may be fraudulent by analyzing the loan and applicant's characteristics

- **Market Basket Analysis**: Understanding the correlation among stocks and other securities and formulating trading and hedging strategies
- **High-frequency trading**: Analyzing trades and quotes to discover pricing inefficiencies and arbitrage opportunities

Healthcare

Healthcare and related fields such as pharmaceuticals and life sciences, have also seen a gradual rise in the adoption and use of machine learning. A leading example has been IBM Watson. Developed in late 2000s, IBM Watson rose to popularity after it won the *Double Jeopardy*, a popular quiz contest in the US in 2011. Today, IBM Watson is being used for clinical research and several institutions have published preliminary results of success. (Source: `http://www.ascopost.com/issues/june-25-2017/how-watson-for-oncology-is-advancing-personalized-patient-care/`). The primary impediment to wider adoption has been the extremely high cost of using the system with usually an uncertain return on investment. Companies that are generally well capitalized can invest in the technology.

More common uses of data science in healthcare include:

- **Epidemiology**: Preventing the spread of diseases and other epidemiology related use cases are being solved with various machine learning techniques. A recent example of the use of clustering to detect the Ebola outbreak received attention, being one of the first times that machine learning was used in a medical use case very effectively. (Source: `https://spectrum.ieee.org/tech-talk/biomedical/diagnostics/healthmap-algorithm-ebola-outbreak`).
- **Health insurance fraud detection**: The health insurance industry loses billions each year in the US due to fraudulent claims for insurance. Machine learning, and more generally, data science is being used to detect cases of fraud and reduce the loss incurred by leading health insurance firms. (Source: `https://www.sciencedirect.com/science/article/pii/S1877042812036099`).
- **Recommender engines**: Algorithms that match patients with physicians are used to provide recommendations based on the patients' symptoms and doctor specialties.
- **Image recognition**: Arguably, the most common use of data science in healthcare, image recognition algorithms are used for a variety of cases ranging from segmentation of malignant and non-malignant tumours to cell segmentation. (Source: `https://www.ncbi.nlm.nih.gov/pmc/articles/PMC3159221/`).

Pharmaceuticals

Although closely linked to the data science use cases in healthcare, data science use cases in pharma are geared toward the development of drugs, physician marketing, and treatment-related analysis. Examples of data science in pharma include the following:

- **Patient journey and treatment pathways**: Understanding the progression of diseases in patients and treatment or therapy outcomes is one of the prime examples of data science in pharma. Several companies have engaged in deep studies related to the development of such tools to understand not only the efficiency of drugs, but also how to best position and market their products. (Source: `https://kx.com/blog/use-case-rxdatascience-patient-journey-app/`).
- **Sales field messaging**: Using NLP, pharma companies analyse discussions between sales representatives and physicians during sales visits to improve their messaging content and better inform physicians on the potential risks and benefits of medications as needed. (Source: `https://www.aktana.com/blog/field-sales/power-personalization-using-advanced-machine-learning-drive-rep-engagement/`).
- **Biomarker analysis**: Machine learning for identifying biomarkers and their importance and/or relevance to diseases are used in clinical research such as cancer-related studies. (Source: `https://www.futuremedicine.com/doi/abs/10.2217/pme.15.5?journalCode=pme`).
- **Research and development**: The use of machine learning for identifying small and large molecules that treat diseases is another common application of data science in pharma. It is a challenging task and several large pharma companies have engaged teams to solve such use cases. (Source: `https://www.kaggle.com/c/MerckActivity`).

Government

Data science is used by state and national governments for a wide range of uses. These include topics in cyber security, voter benefits, climate change, social causes, and other similar use cases that are geared toward public policy and public benefits.

Some examples include the following:

- **Climate change**: One of the most popular topics among climate change proponents, there is extensive machine learning related work that is being conducted around the globe to detect and understand the causes of climate change. (Source: `https://toolkit.climate.gov`).
- **Cyber security**: The use of extremely advanced machine learning techniques for national cyber security is evident and well known all over the world, ever since such practices were disclosed by consultants at security firms a few years back. Security-related organizations employ some of the most advanced hardware and software stacks for detecting cyber threats and prevent hacking attempts. (Source: `https://www.csoonline.com/article/2942083/big-data-security/cybersecurity-is-the-killer-app-for-big-data-analytics.html`).
- **Social causes**: The use of data science for a wide range of use cases geared toward social good is well known due to several conferences and papers that have been organized and released respectively on the topic. Examples include topics in urban analytics, power grids utilizing smart meters, criminal justice. (Source: `https://dssg.uchicago.edu/data-science-for-social-good-conference-2017/agenda/`).

Manufacturing and retail

The manufacturing and retail industry has used data science to designing better products, optimize pricing, and design strategic marketing techniques. Some examples include the following:

- **Price optimization**: Generally related to the realm of linear programming, the challenge of price optimization, that is, pricing products, is now also being addressed with the help of machine learning. Dynamic pricing based upon market conditions, user preferences, and other factors are used as inputs to assess optimal pricing of products. (Source: `https://www.datasciencecentral.com/profiles/blogs/price-optimisation-using-decision-tree-regression-tree`).
- **Retail sales**: Retailers use algorithms to determine future sales forecasts, price discounts, and promotion sequences. (Source: `http://www.oliverwyman.com/our-expertise/insights/2017/feb/machine-learning-for-retail.html`).

- **Production capacity and maintenance**: In manufacturing, data science is being used to determine device maintenance requirements, equipment effectiveness, optimize production lines, and much more. The overall supply chain management is an area that has benefited and continues to earn profits from smart use of machine learning. (Source: `https://www.forbes.com/sites/louiscolumbus/2016/06/26/10-ways-machine-learning-is-revolutionizing-manufacturing/#51d4927228c2`).

Web industry

One of the earliest beneficiaries of data science was the web industry. Empowered by the collection of user-specific data from social networks, firms around the world employ algorithms to understand user behavior and generate targeted ads. Google, one of the earliest proponents of targeted ad marketing today, earns most of its revenue from ads, more than $95 billion in 2017. (Source: `https://www.statista.com/statistics/266249/advertising-revenue-of-google/`). The use of data science for web-related businesses is ubiquitous today and companies such as Uber, Airbnb, Netflix, and Amazon have successfully navigated and made full use of this complex ecosystem, generating not only huge profits but also added millions of new jobs directly or indirectly as a result.

- **Targeted ads**: Click through ads have been one of the prime areas of machine learning. By reading cookies saved on users' computers from various sites, other sites can assess the users interests and accordingly decide which ads to serve when they visit new sites. As per online sources, the value of internet advertising is over $1 trillion and has generated over 10 million jobs in 2017 alone. (Source: `https://www.iab.com/insights/economic-value-advertising-supported-internet-ecosystem/`).
- **Recommender engines**: Netflix, Pandora, and other movies and audio streaming services utilize recommender engines to understand which movies or music the viewer or listener would be interested in and make recommendations. The recommendations are often based on what other users with similar tastes might have already seen and leverage recommender algorithms such as collaborative, content-based, and hybrid filtering.
- **Web design**: Using A/B testing, mouse tracking, and other sophisticated techniques, web developers leverage data science to design better web pages such as landing pages and in general websites. A/B testing for instance allows developers to decide between different versions of the same web page and deploy accordingly.

Other industries

There are various other industries today that benefit from data science and as such, it has become so common that it would be impractical to list all, but at a high level, some of the others include the following:

- Oil and natural gas for oil production
- Meteorology for understanding weather patterns
- Space research for detecting and/or analyzing stars and galaxies
- Utilities for energy production and energy savings
- Biotechnology for research and finding new cures for diseases

In general, since data science, or machine learning algorithms are not specific to any particular industry, it is entirely possible to apply algorithms to creative use cases and derive business benefits.

Solving problems with data science

Data science is being used today to solve problems ranging from poverty alleviation to scientific research. It has emerged as the leading discipline that aims to disrupt the industry's status quo and provide a new alternative to pressing business issues.

However, while the promise of data science and machine learning is immense, it is important to bear in mind that it takes time and effort to realize the benefits. The return-on-investment on a machine learning project typically takes a fairly long time. It is thus essential to not overestimate the value it can bring in the short run.

A typical data science project in a corporate setting would require the collaborative efforts of various groups, both on the technical and the business side. Generally, this means that the project should have a business sponsor and a technical or analytics lead in addition to the data science team or data scientist. It is important to set expectations at the onset—both in terms of the time it would take to complete the project and the outcome that may be uncertain until the task has completed. Unlike other projects that may have a definite goal, it is not possible to predetermine the outcome of machine learning projects.

Some common questions to ask include the following:

- What business value does the data science project bring to the organization?
- Does it have a critical base of users, that is, would multiple users benefit from the expected outcome of the project?

- How long would it take to complete the project and are all the business stakeholders aware of the timeline?
- Have the project stakeholders taken all variables that may affect the timeline into account? Projects can often get delayed due to dependencies on external vendors.
- Have we considered all other potential business use cases and made an assessment of what approach would have an optimal chance of success?

A few salient points for successful data science projects are given as follows:

- Find projects or use cases related to business operations that are:
    - Challenging
    - Not necessarily complex, that is, they can be simple tasks but which add business value
    - Intuitive, easily understood (you can explain it to friends and family)
    - Takes effort to accomplish today or requires a lot of manual effort
    - Used frequently by a range of users and the benefits of the outcome would have executive visibility
- Identify **low difficulty–high value** (shorter) versus **high difficulty–high value** (longer)
- Educate business sponsors, share ideas, show enthusiasm (it's like a long job interview)
- Score **early wins on low difficulty–high value**; create minimum viable solutions, get management buy-in before enhancing them (takes time)
- Early wins act as a catalyst to foster executive confidence; and also make it easier to justify budgets, making it easier to move on to high difficulty—high value tasks

Using R for data science

Being arguably the oldest and consequently the most mature language for statistical operations, R has been used by statisticians all over the world for over 20 years. The precursor to R was the S programming language, written by John Chambers in 1976 in Bell Labs. R, named after the initials of its developers, Ross Ihaka and Robert Gentleman, was implemented as an open source equivalent to S while they were at the University of Auckland.

The language has gained immensely in popularity since the early 2000s, averaging between 20% to 30% growth on a year-on-year basis:

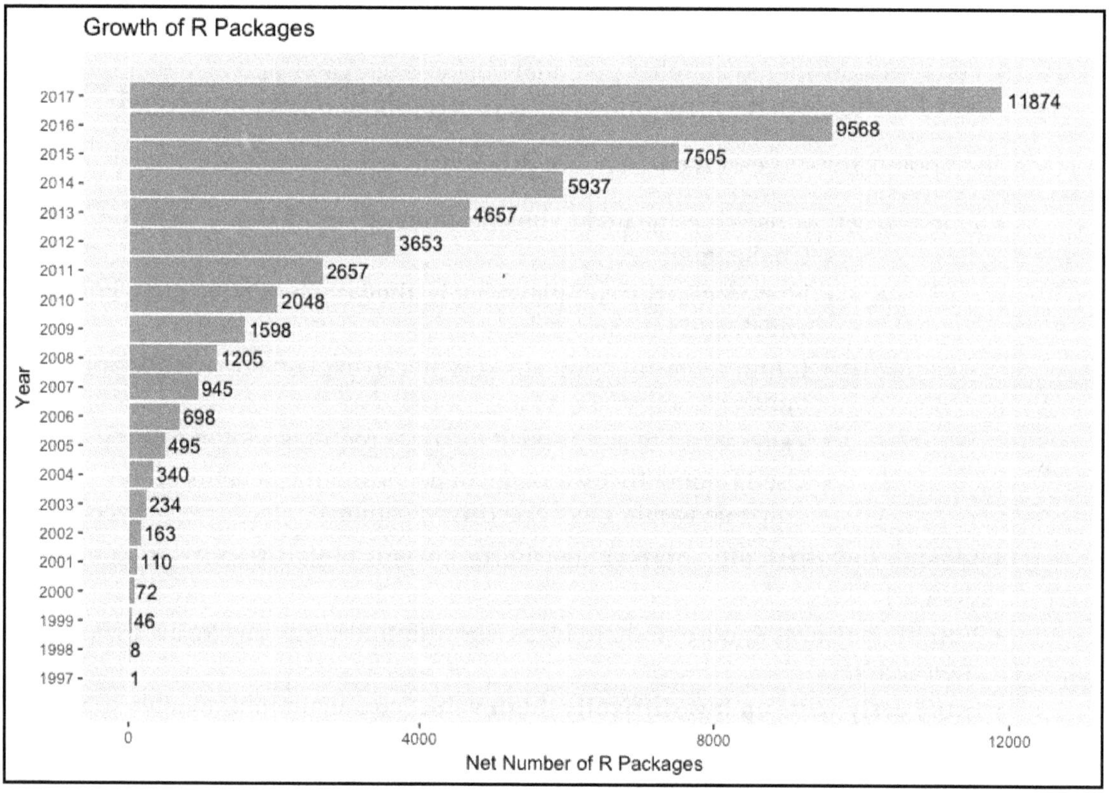

The growth of R packages

In 2018, there were more than 12,000 R packages, up from about 7,500 just 3 years before, in 2015.

A few key features of R makes it not only very easy to learn, but also very versatile due to the number of available packages.

Key features of R

The key features of R are as follows:

- **Data mining**: The R package, `data.table`, developed by Dowle and Srinivasan, is arguably one of the most sophisticated packages for data mining in any language provides R users with the ability to query millions, if not billions of rows of data. In addition, there is `tibble`, an alternative to `data.frame` developed by Hadley Wickham. Other packages from Wickham include, `plyr`, `dplyr` and `ggplot2` for visualization.
- **Visualizations**: The `ggplot2` package is the most commonly used visualization package in R. Packages such as `rcharts`, `htmlwidgets` have also become extremely popular in recent years. Most of these packages allow R users to leverage elegant graphics features commonly found in JavaScript packages such as D3. Many of them act as wrappers for popular JavaScript visualization libraries to facilitate the creation of graphics elements in R.
- **Data science**: R has had various statistical libraries used for research for many years. With the growth of data science as a popular subject in the public domain, R users have released and further developed both new and existing packages that allows users to deploy complex machine learning algorithms. Examples include `randomforest`, `gbm`.
- **General availability of packages**: The 12,000+ packages in R provide coverage for a wide range of projects. These include packages for machine learning, data science, and even general purpose needs such as web scraping, cartography, and even fisheries sciences. Due to this rich ecosystem that can cater to the needs of a wide variety of use cases, R has grown exponentially in popularity. Whether you are working with JSON files or trying to solve an obscure machine learning problem, it is very likely that someone in the R community has already developed a package that contains (or can indirectly fulfill) the functionality you need.
- **Setting up R and RStudio**: This book will focus on using R for data science related tasks. The language R, as mentioned, is available as an open source product from `http://r-project.org`. In addition, we will be installing RStudio—an IDE (a graphical user interface) for writing and running our R code as well as R Shiny, a platform that allows users to develop elegant dashboards.

Downloading and installing R is as follows:

1. Go to `http://r-project.org` and click on the **CRAN** (`http://cran.r-project.org/mirrors.html`):

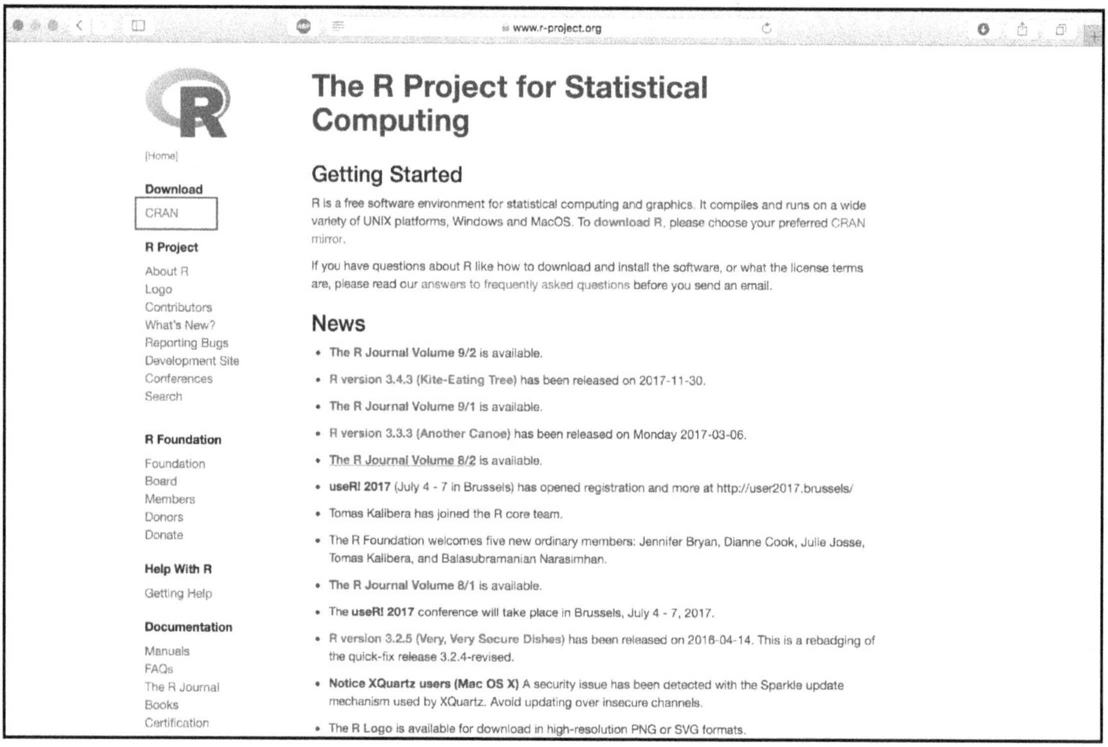

2. Select any one of the links in the corresponding page. These are links to *CRAN Mirrors*, that is, sites that host R packages and R installation files:

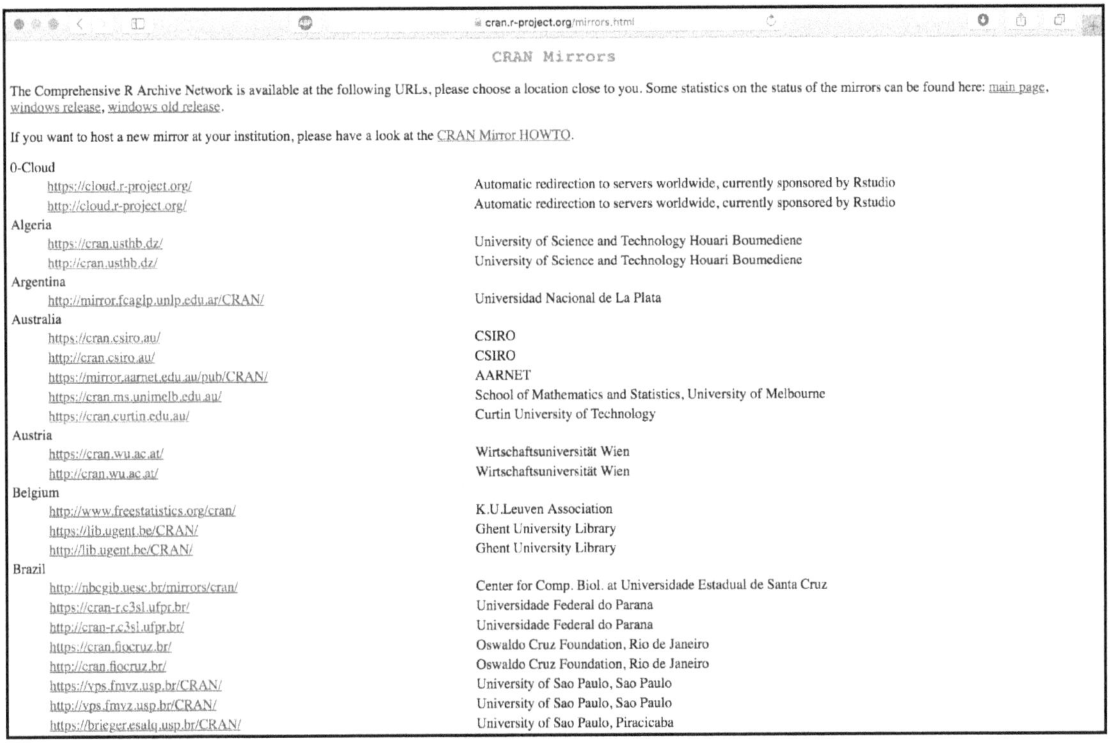

3. Once you select and click on the link, you'll be taken to a page with the links to download R for different operating systems, such as Windows, macOS, and Linux. Select the distribution that you need to start the download process:

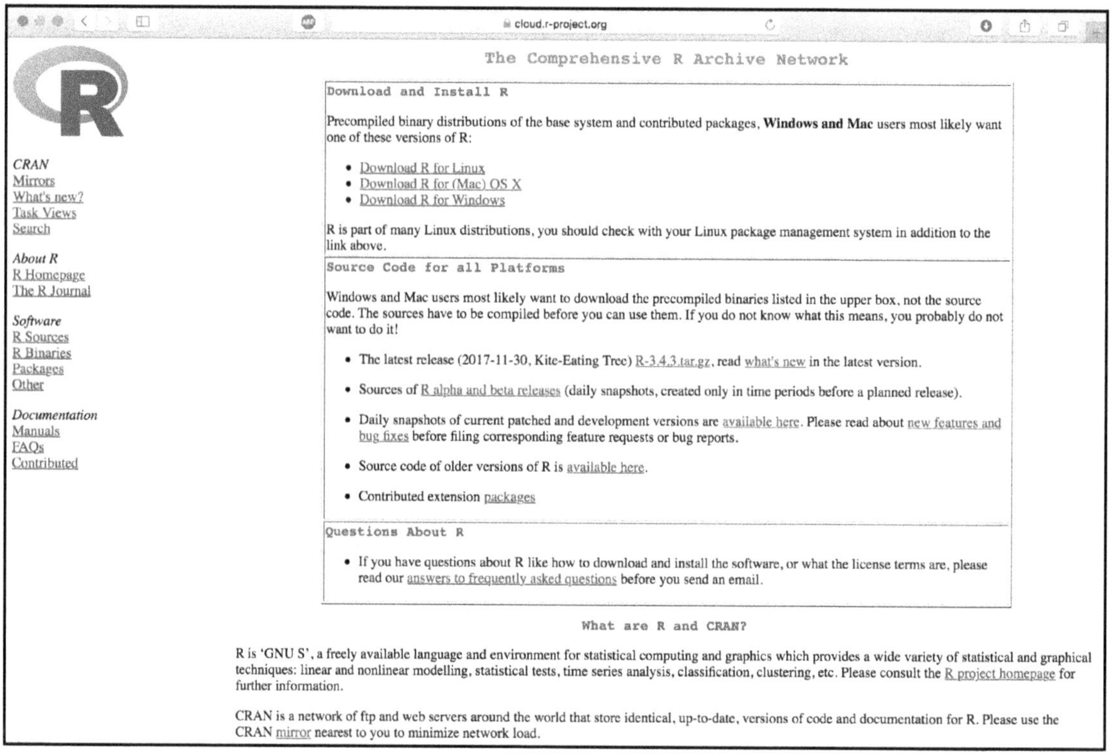

4. This is the R for macOS download page:

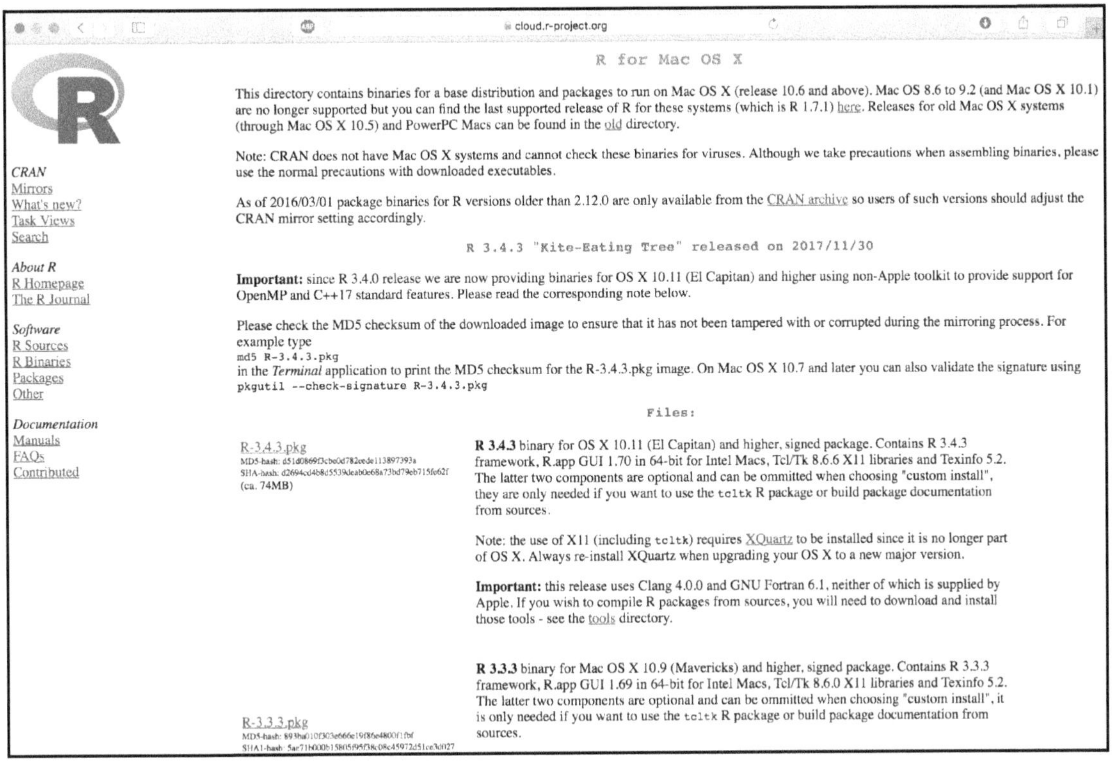

5. This is the R for Windows download page (click on **install R for the first time** if it is a new installation):

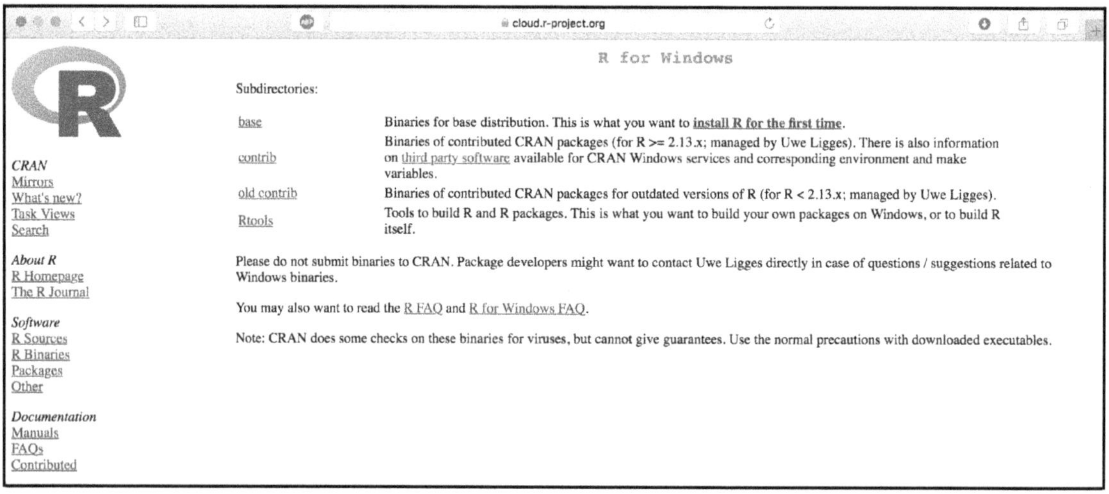

6. This is the R for Windows download page. Download and install the `.exe` file for R:

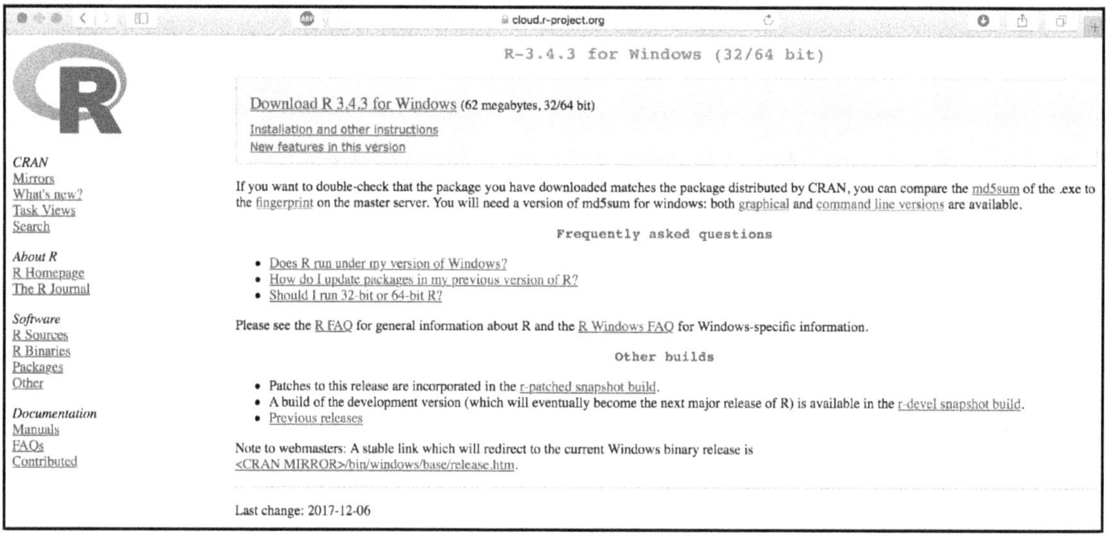

7. The R for macOS installation process will require you to download the `.dmg` file. Select the default options for installation if you do not intend to make any changes, such as installing in a different directory:

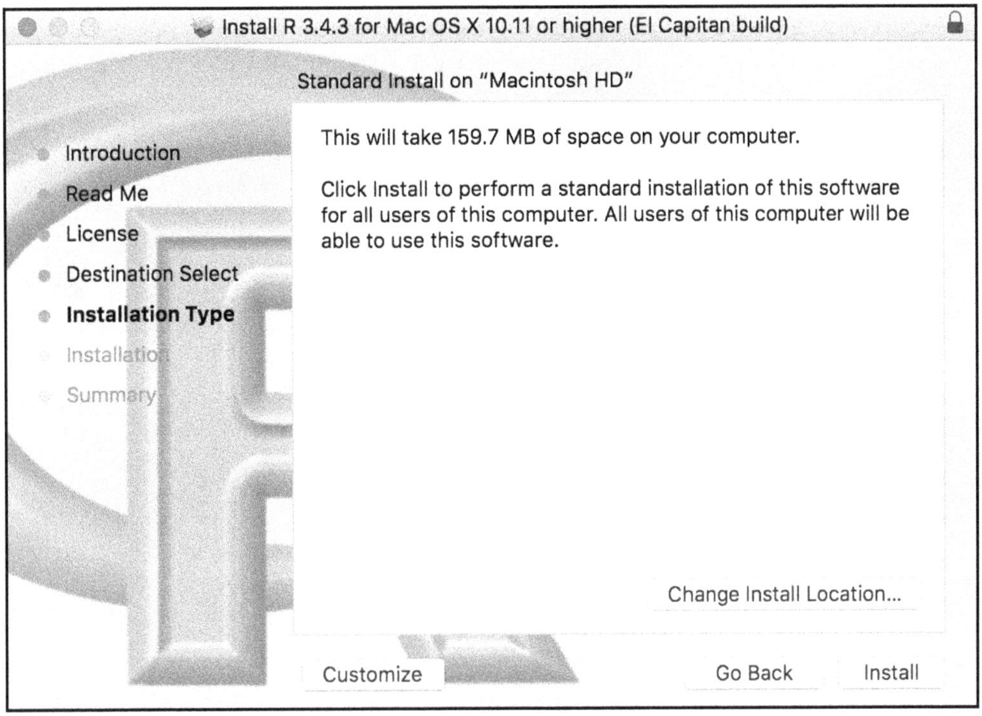

You will also need to download and install RStudio and R Shiny. RStudio is used as the frontend, which you'll use to develop your R code. As such, it is not necessary to use RStudio to write code in R as you can launch the R console from the desktop (Windows), but RStudio has a nicer and a more user-friendly interface that makes it easier to code in R.

8. Download RStudio and R Shiny from `https://www.rstudio.com`:

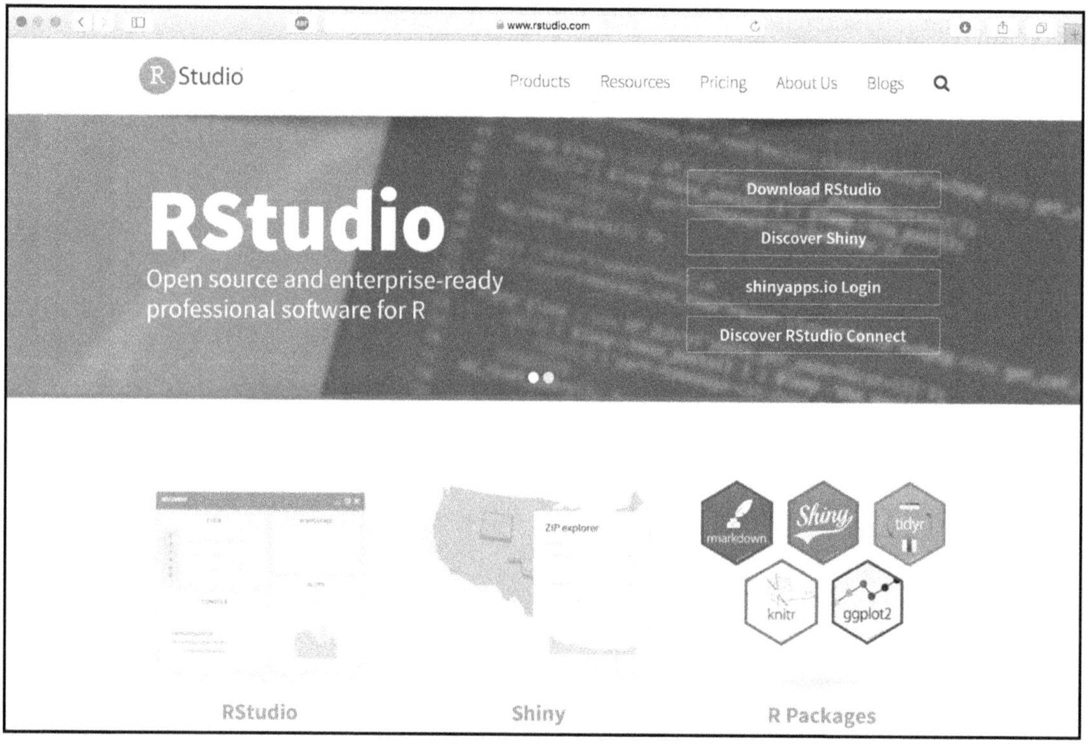

9. Click on **Products** in the top menu and select RStudio to download and install the software.

10. Download the open source version of RStudio. Note that there are other versions which are paid commercial versions of the software. For our exercise, we'll be using the open source version only. Download it from `https://www.rstudio.com/products/rstudio/download/`:

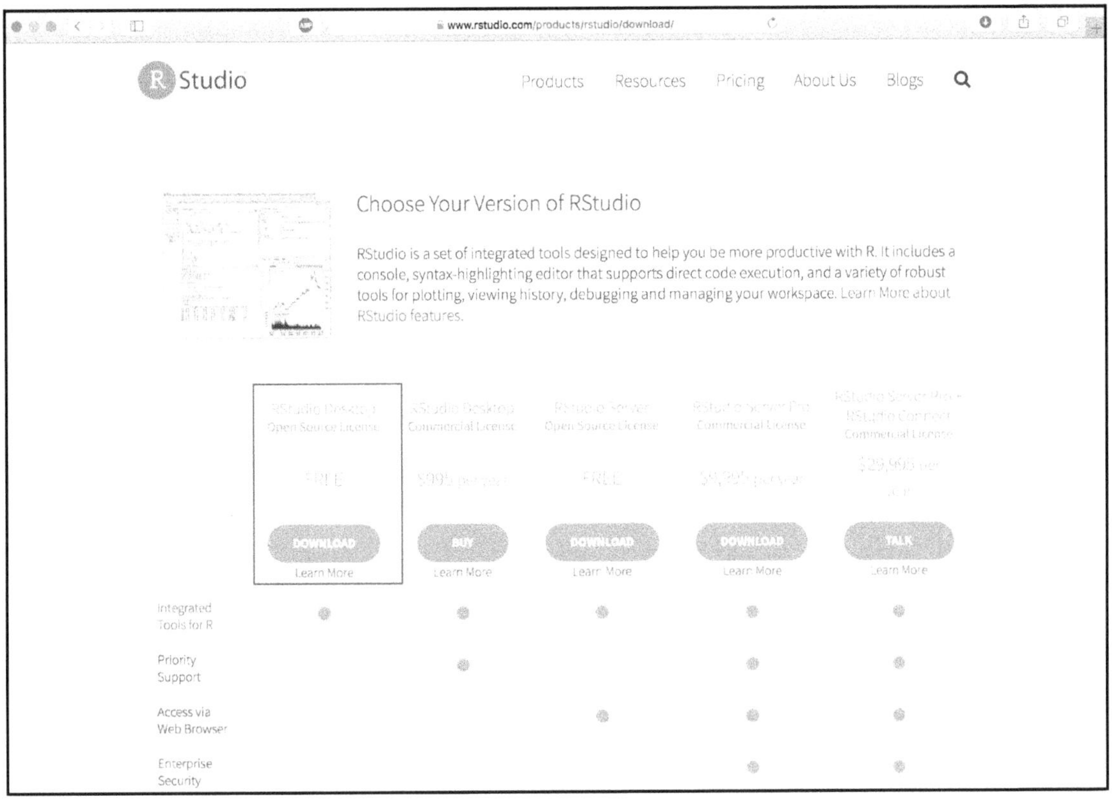

11. Once you have installed RStudio, launch the application. This will bring up the Following screenshot. There are four panels in RStudio. The first three are shown when you first launch RStudio:

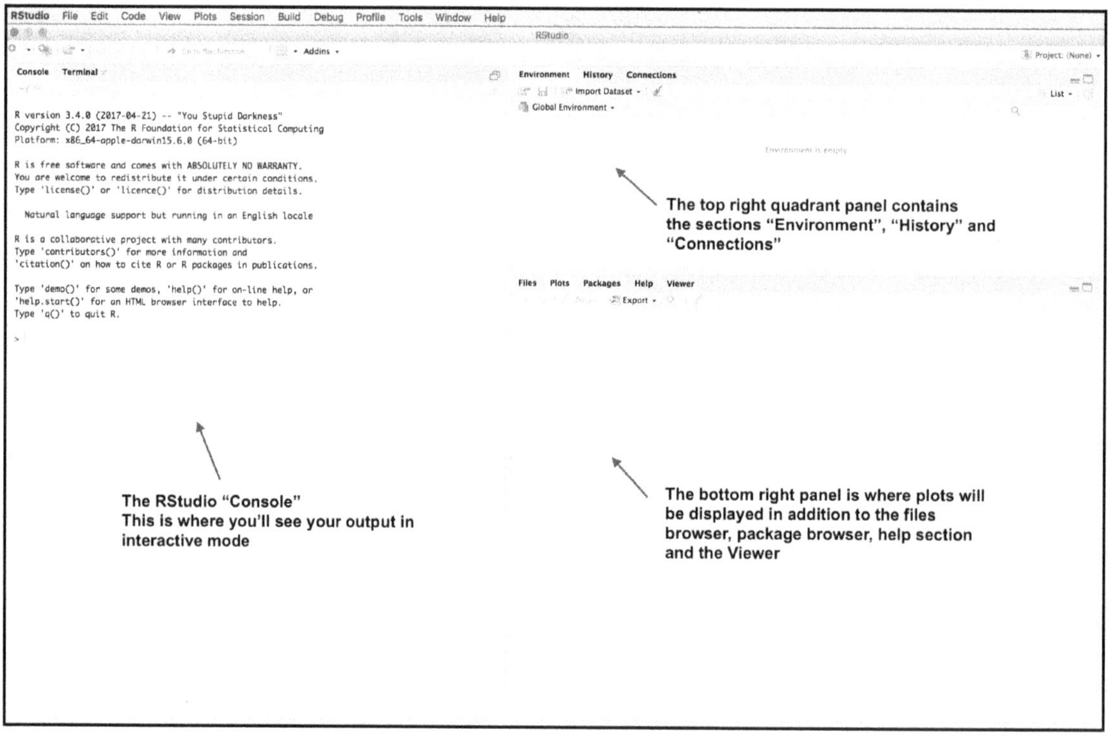

12. Click on **File** | **New File** | **R Script**. This will open a new panel. This is the section where you'll be writing your R code:

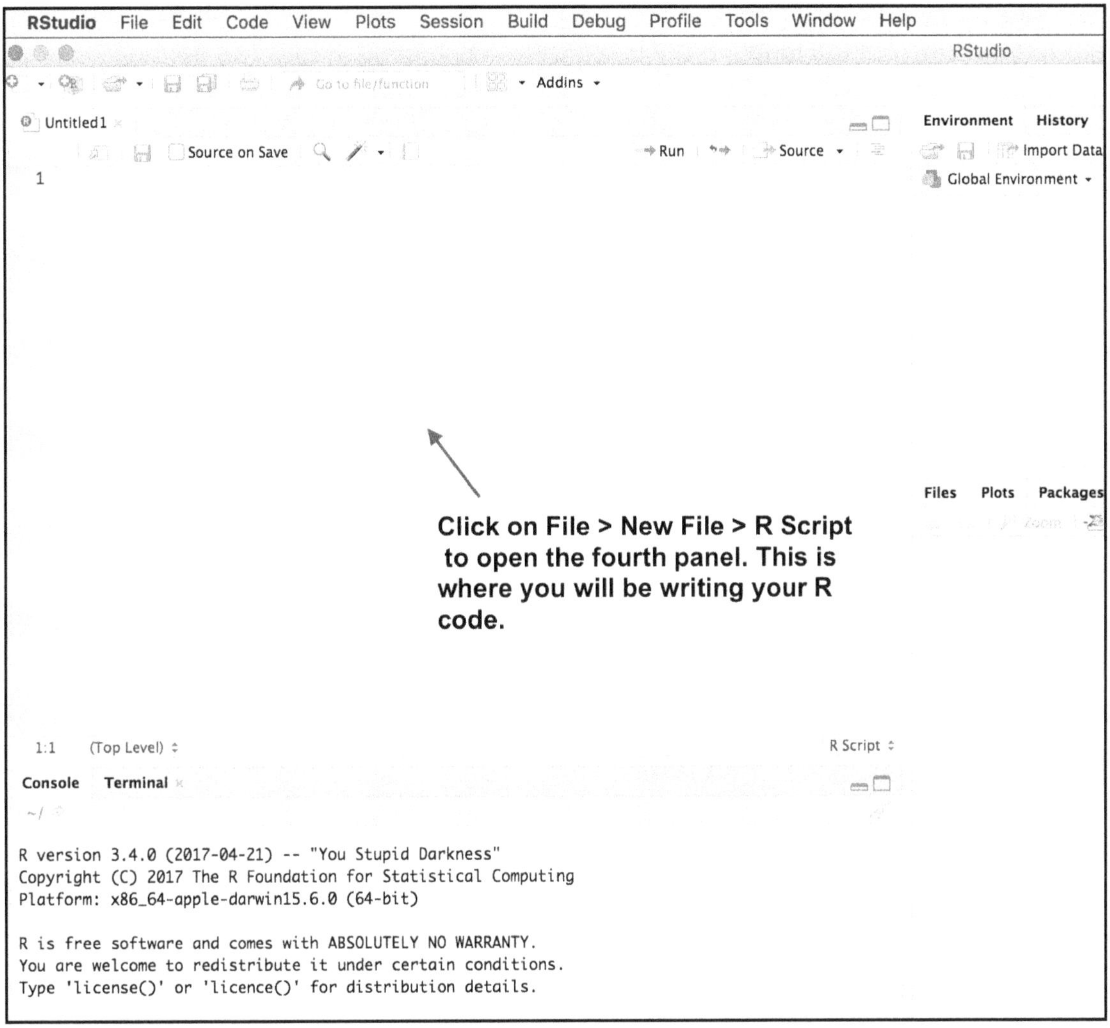

RStudio is a very mature interface for developing R code and has been in use for several years. You should familiarize yourself with the different features in RStudio as you'll be using the tool throughout the book.

Our first R program

In this section, we will create our first R program for data analysis. We'll use the human development data available from the United Nations development program. The initiative produces a **Human Development Index** (**HDI**) corresponding to each country, which signifies the level of economic development, including general public health, education, and various other societal factors.

Further information on HDI can be found at `http://hdr.undp.org/en/content/human-development-index-hdi`. The site also hosts an FAQ page that provides short summary explanations of the various characteristics of the program at `http://hdr.undp.org/en/faq-page/human-development-index-hdi`.

The following diagram from the UN development program's website summaries the concept at a high level:

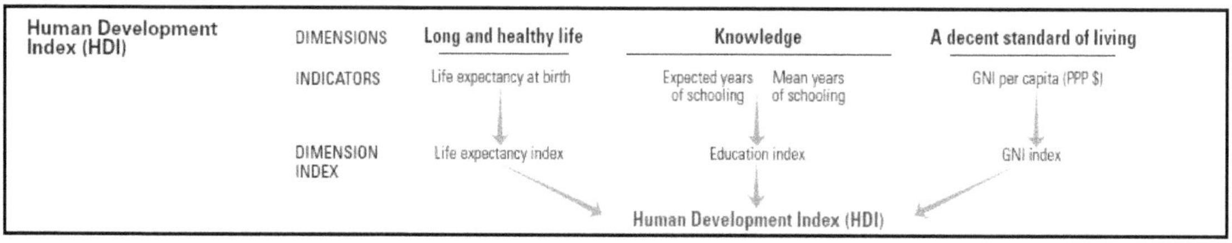

UN development index

In this exercise, we will be looking at the life expectancy and expected years of schooling on a per country per year basis starting from 1990 onward. Not all data is available for all countries, due to various geopolitical and other reasons that have made it difficult to obtain data for respective years.

The datasets for the HDP program have been obtained from `http://hdr.undp.org/en/data`.

In the exercises, the data has been cleaned and formatted to make it easier for the reader to analyse the information, especially given it is the first chapter of the book. Download the data from the Packt code repository for this book. Following are the steps to complete the exercise:

1. Launch RStudio and click on **File** | **New File** | **R Script**.
2. Save the file as `Chapter1.R`.

3. Copy the commands shown in the following script and save.
4. Install the required packages for this exercise by running the following command. First, copy the command into the code window in RStudio:

```
install.packages(c("data.table","plotly","ggplot2","psych"))
```

5. Then, place your cursor on the line and click on **Run**:

6. This will install the respective packages in your system. In case you encounter any errors, search on Google for the cause of the error. There are various online forums, such as Stack Overflow, where you can search for common errors and learn how to fix them. Since errors can depend on the specific configuration of your machine, we cannot identify all of them, but it is very likely that someone else might have experienced the same error conditions.

We have already created the requisite CSV files, and the following code illustrates the entire process of reading in the CSV files and analyzing the data:

```
# We'll install the following packages:
## data.table: a package for managing & manipulating datasets in R
## plotly: a graphics library that has gained popularity in recent year
## ggplot2: another graphics library that is extremely popular in R
## psych: a tool for psychmetry that also includes some very helpful
#statistical functions

install.packages(c("data.table","plotly","ggplot2","psych"))

# Load the libraries
# This is necessary if you will be using functionalities that are
#available outside
# The functions already available as part of standard R
```

```
library(data.table)
library(plotly)
library(ggplot2)
library(psych)
library(RColorBrewer)

# In R, packages contain multiple functions and once the package has
#been loaded
# the functions become available in your workspace
# To find more information about a function, at the R console, type #in
?function_name
# Note that you should replace function_name with the name of the
actual function
# This will bring up the relevant help notes for the function
# Note that the "R Console" is the interactive screen generally #found

# Read in Human Development Index File
hdi <- fread("ch1_hdi.csv",header=T) # The command fread can be used to
read in a CSV file

# View contents of hdi
head(hdi) # View the top few rows of the data table hdi
//
```

The output of the preceding code is as follows:

```
> head(hdi) # View the top few rows of the data table hdi
                Country Year   HDI
1:          Afghanistan 1990 0.295
2:              Albania 1990 0.635
3:              Algeria 1990 0.577
4:              Andorra 1990    NA
5:               Angola 1990    NA
6:  Antigua and Barbuda 1990    NA
```

Read the life expectancy file by using the following code:

```
life <- fread("ch1_life_exp.csv", header=T)

# View contents of life
head(life)
```

The output of the code file is as follows:

```
> head(life)
              Country Year LifeExp
1:        Afghanistan 1990    49.9
2:            Albania 1990    71.8
3:            Algeria 1990    66.7
4:            Andorra 1990    76.5
5:             Angola 1990    41.2
6: Antigua and Barbuda 1990    71.4
```

Read the years of schooling file by using the following code:

```
# Read Years of Schooling File
school <- fread("ch1_schoolyrs.csv", header=T)

# View contents of school
head(school)
```

The output of the preceding code is as follows:

```
> head(school)
              Country Year SchoolYrs
1:        Afghanistan 1990       2.6
2:            Albania 1990      11.6
3:            Algeria 1990       9.6
4:            Andorra 1990      10.8
5:             Angola 1990       3.8
6: Antigua and Barbuda 1990        NA
```

Now we will read the country information:

```
iso <- fread("ch1_iso.csv")

# View contents of iso
head(iso)
```

The following is the output of the previous code:

```
> head(iso)
          Country  Region        SubRegion
1:    Afghanistan    Asia    Southern Asia
2:  Åland Islands  Europe  Northern Europe
3:        Albania  Europe  Southern Europe
4:        Algeria  Africa  Northern Africa
5: American Samoa Oceania        Polynesia
6:        Andorra  Europe  Southern Europe
```

Here we will see the processing of the `hdi` table by using the following code:

```
# Use melt.data.table to change hdi into a long table format

hdi <- melt.data.table(hdi,1,2:ncol(hdi))

# Set the names of the columns of hdi
setnames(hdi,c("Country","Year","HDI"))

# Process the life table
# Use melt.data.table to change life into a long table format
life <- melt.data.table(life,1,2:ncol(life))
# Set the names of the columns of hdi
setnames(life,c("Country","Year","LifeExp"))

# Process the school table
# Use melt.data.table to change school into a long table format
school <- melt.data.table(school,1,2:ncol(school))
# Set the names of the columns of hdi
setnames(school,c("Country","Year","SchoolYrs"))

# Merge hdi and life along the Country and Year columns
merged <- merge(merge(hdi, life,
  by=c("Country","Year")),school,by=c("Country","Year"))

# Add the Region attribute to the merged table using the iso file
# This can be done using the merge function
# Type in ?merge in your R console
merged <- merge(merged, iso, by="Country")
merged$Info <- with(merged,
paste(Country,Year,"HDI:",HDI,"LifeExp:",LifeExp,"SchoolYrs:",
  SchoolYrs,sep=" "))

# Use View to open the dataset in a different tab
# Close the tab to return to the code screen
View(head(merged))
```

The output of the preceding code is as follows:

	Country	Year	HDI	LifeExp	SchoolYrs	Region	SubRegion	Info
1	Afghanistan	1990	0.295	49.9	2.6	Asia	Southern Asia	Afghanistan 1990 HDI: 0.295 LifeExp: 49.9 SchoolYrs...
2	Afghanistan	1991	0.300	50.6	2.9	Asia	Southern Asia	Afghanistan 1991 HDI: 0.3 LifeExp: 50.6 SchoolYrs: 2.9
3	Afghanistan	1992	0.309	51.4	3.2	Asia	Southern Asia	Afghanistan 1992 HDI: 0.309 LifeExp: 51.4 SchoolYrs...
4	Afghanistan	1993	0.305	52.0	3.6	Asia	Southern Asia	Afghanistan 1993 HDI: 0.305 LifeExp: 52 SchoolYrs: 3.6
5	Afghanistan	1994	0.300	52.6	3.9	Asia	Southern Asia	Afghanistan 1994 HDI: 0.3 LifeExp: 52.6 SchoolYrs: 3.9
6	Afghanistan	1995	0.324	53.1	4.2	Asia	Southern Asia	Afghanistan 1995 HDI: 0.324 LifeExp: 53.1 SchoolYrs...

Here is the code for finding summary statistics for each country:

```
mergedDataSummary <-
  describeBy(merged[,c("HDI","LifeExp","SchoolYrs")],
  group=merged$Country, na.rm = T, IQR=T)


# Which Countries are available in the mergedDataSummary Data Frame ?
names(mergedDataSummary)
mergedDataSummary["Cuba"] # Enter any country name here to view
#the summary information
```

The output is as follows:

```
> mergedDataSummary["Cuba"] # Enter any country name here to view the summary information
$Cuba
          vars  n  mean   sd median trimmed  mad   min   max range  skew kurtosis   se IQR
HDI          1 26  0.72 0.05   0.70    0.72 0.06  0.65  0.78  0.13  0.17    -1.77 0.01 0.1
LifeExp      2 26 77.21 1.68  77.25   77.24 2.30 74.60 79.60  5.00 -0.12    -1.52 0.33 3.0
SchoolYrs    3 26 13.69 2.00  13.05   13.54 1.70 11.30 17.70  6.40  0.68    -0.91 0.39 2.6
```

Useing `ggplot2` to view density charts and boxplots:

```
ggplot(merged, aes(x=LifeExp, fill=Region)) + geom_density(alpha=0.25)
```

The output is as follows:

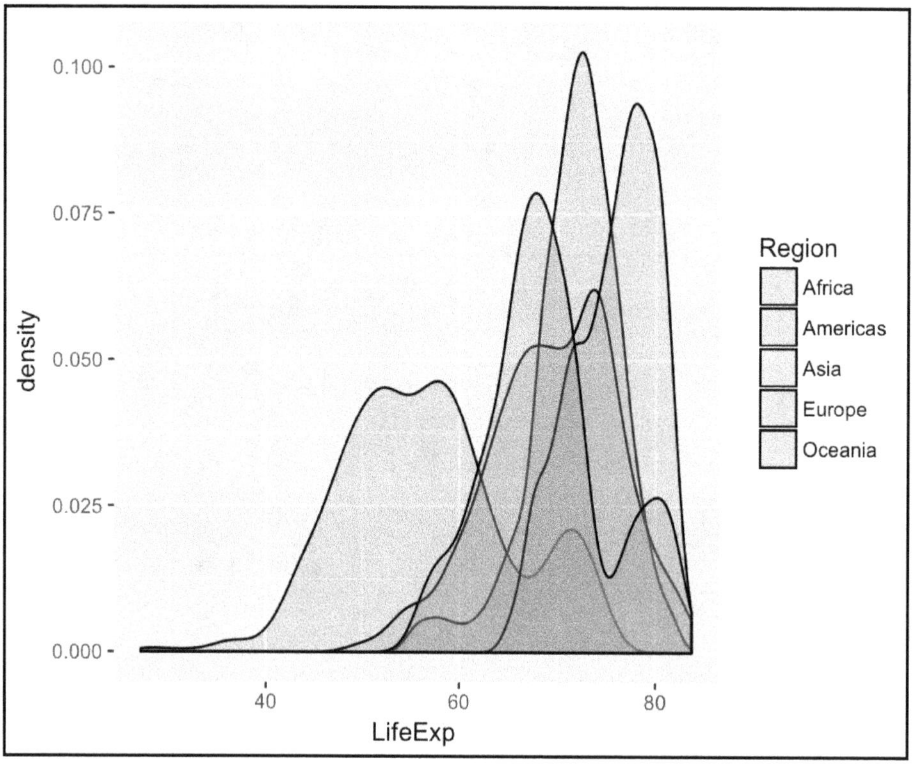

Now we will see what the result is for `geom_boxplot`:

```
ggplot(merged, aes(x=Region, y=LifeExp, fill=Region)) + geom_boxplot()
```

The output is as follows:

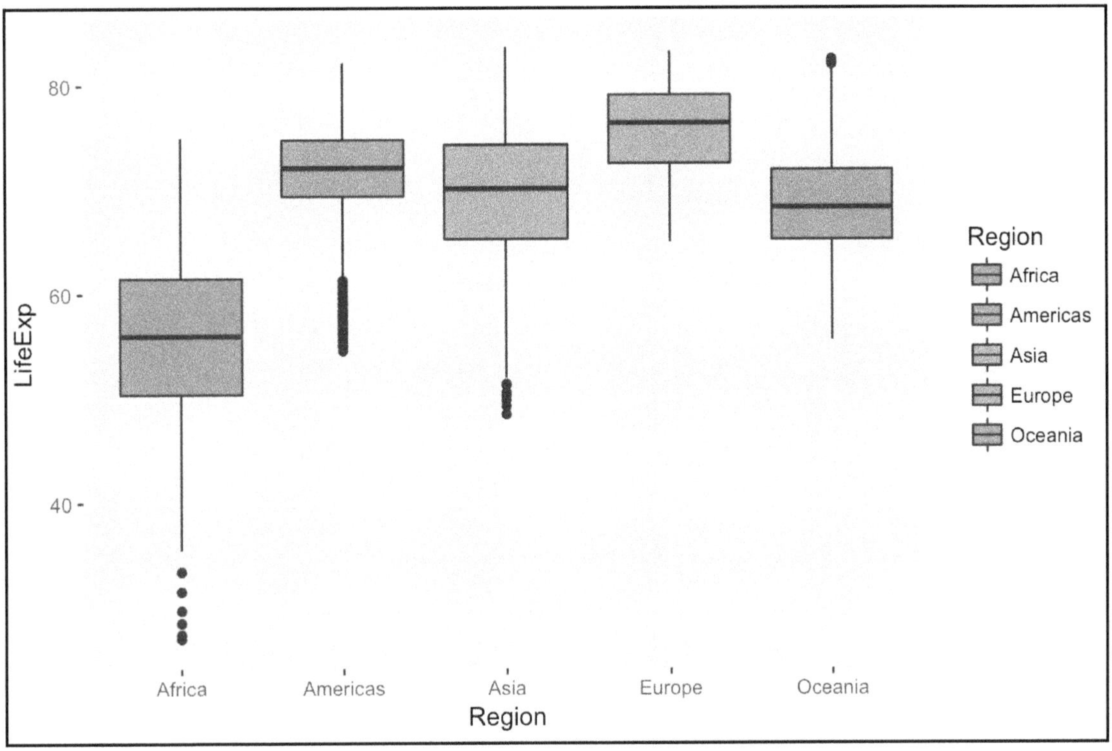

Create an animated chart using `plot_ly`:

```
# Reference: https://plot.ly/r/animations/
p <- merged %>%
  plot_ly(
    x = ~SchoolYrs,
    y = ~LifeExp,
    color = ~Region,
    frame = ~Year,
    text = ~Info,
    size = ~LifeExp,
    hoverinfo = "text",
    type = 'scatter',
    mode = 'markers'
  ) %>%
  layout(
    xaxis = list(
```

```
        type = "log"
      )
    ) %>%
    animation_opts(
      150, easing = "elastic", redraw = FALSE
    )

# View plot
p
```

The output is as follows:

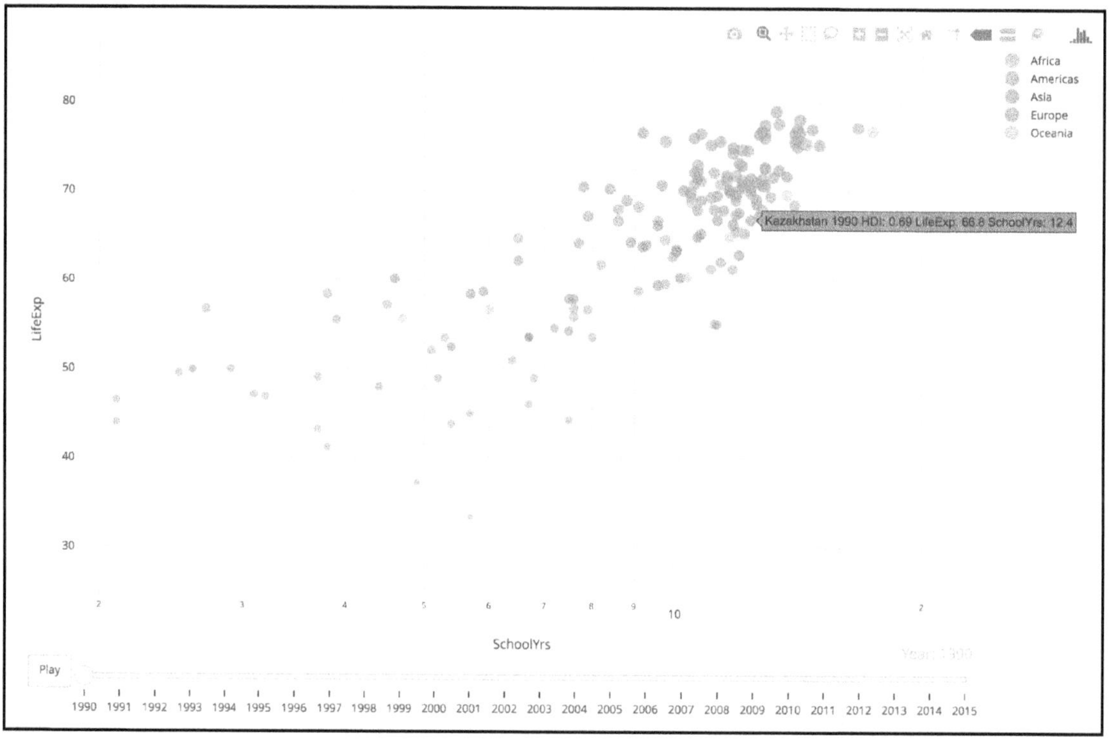

Creating a summary table with the average of `SchoolYrs` and `LifeExp` by `Region` and `Year` by using the following code:

```
mergedSummary <- merged[,.(AvgSchoolYrs=round(mean(SchoolYrs, na.rm =
  T),2), AvgLifeExp=round(mean(LifeExp),2)), by=c("Year","Region")]
  mergedSummary$Info <- with(mergedSummary,
  paste(Region,Year,"AvgLifeExp:",AvgLifeExp,"AvgSchoolYrs:",
  AvgSchoolYrs,sep=" "))
```

```
# Create an animated plot similar to the prior diagram
# Reference: https://plot.ly/r/animations/
ps <- mergedSummary %>%
  plot_ly(
    x = ~AvgSchoolYrs,
    y = ~AvgLifeExp,
    color = ~Region,
    frame = ~Year,
    text = ~Info,
    size=~AvgSchoolYrs,
    opacity=0.75,
    hoverinfo = "text",
    type = 'scatter',
    mode = 'markers'
    ) %>%
  layout(title = 'Average Life Expectancy vs Average School Years
    (1990-2015)',
         xaxis = list(title="Average School Years"),
         yaxis = list(title="Average Life Expectancy"),
         showlegend = FALSE)
# View plot
ps
```

Summary

In this section, we were introduced to R and in particular, data science with R. We learnt about the various applications of R across different industries and how R is being used across disciplines to solve a wide range of challenges. R has been growing at a tremendous rate, averaging 20% to 30% growth year-on-year, and today has over 12,000 packages.

We also downloaded and installed R and RStudio and wrote our very first program in R. The R program utilizes various libraries for both data analysis and charting. In the next chapter, we will work on descriptive and inferential statistics. We will learn about hypothesis testing, t-tests and various other measures in probability. While this chapter provided a high-level overview, in the next chapter, we will delve into more fundamental data science topics and see how you can use R to develop code and analyse data using R.

Quiz

1. What does the acronym CRAN stand for ?
    1. Comprehensive R Archive Network
    2. Common R Archive Nomenclature
    3. Categorical Regression And NLP
2. Which of the following options best describes Tensorflow?
    1. A machine learning package for Fluid Dynamics
    2. Tension Analysis for Fluid Dynamics
    3. A machine learning package from Google
3. Which of the following Algorithms is Netflix most likely to use to provide movie suggestions:
    1. Particle Swarm
    2. Genetic Algorithms for IMDB
    3. Recommender Engines

Answers:

Q1 - 1, Q2 - 3, Q3 - 3

2
Descriptive and Inferential Statistics

"To understand God's thoughts we must study statistics, for these are the measure of his purpose."

– Florence Nightingale

Instead of trusting gut feeling and guesses, data scientists trust data. Descriptive statistics are wonderful for introducing data and scavenging for insights. Statistical hypothesis testing is a great way to check how likely some behavior displayed by data is due to an actual trend or randomness. Although some key statistical concepts are recovered during the chapter, readers will greatly benefit from prior knowledge on probabilities and distributions. This chapter will discuss how to use R to draw descriptive analysis and test hypothesis.

The following topics are discussed in this chapter:

- Most commonly used descriptive measures
- How to summarize data with little effort
- How to set up a t-test
- How to design a function to run z-tests
- How to store and get your functions from the cloud
- How to use Fisher's exact test to run an A/B test

Measures of central tendency and dispersion

If you care to tackle a problem using the statistic's arsenal there are two tools to begin with: measures of central tendency and measures of variance. This is the starting point for most of the statistical problems. These measures are used in a thing that some would call descriptive analysis. A well done descriptive analysis may be all that you need, depending on the problem you have at hand. Think about the **force continuum** (and don't go straight to the **Megazord**—start small).

> Central tendency (or average) means typical/middle value from a distribution. This is an abstract concept and we can't really measure it. Yet there are estimates that try to translate this abstract concept into an actual measure. Arithmetic mean, median, and mode are all widespread and consolidated attempts.

Even if you got yourself stuck with a more complex problem, there is still room for descriptive analysis. A carefully drawn analysis will both appreciate and validate all the good work coming afterward. This section will introduce you to the measures of central tendency and variance. It will show you what they are made of as well as how to obtain them using R. Although base R is more than enough for this kind of action, there are packages that are able to do more with less—we will visit some of them.

Measures of central tendency

What if you had to describe the center of a distribution within a single number? Most people would appeal to one of these three estimators: mean, median, or mode. Those are probably the most popular measures of central tendency. Let's begin by sampling data from an arbitrary distribution. Get into your R console and try the following code:

```
set.seed(10)
small_sample <- rnorm(n = 10, mean = 10, sd = 5)
big_sample <- rnorm(n = 10^5, mean = 10, sd = 5)
```

The first line is setting the `seed` number to work with our **random number generator (RNG)**. Every time there's a need to rely on a pseudo-random process, the `set.seed()` function will make sure your code is reproducible (at least at some level). By setting it to `10` you will get the same numbers that I'm getting from the preceding code lines.

> **TIP:** Some people would advise you to set a new seed (with `set.seed()`) every single time you load a package.

The two last lines are sorting pseudo-random numbers from a normally distributed variable. Call the `rnom()` function to sort variables from a normal distribution. Choose the number of observations sorted by adjusting the `n` parameter. Modify the `mean` and `sd` parameters if you want a mean and standard deviation different from `0` and `1` respectively.

In the real world, you will hardly know for sure what underlying process is ruling your data, but here we do know beforehand that our numbers come from a normally distributed variable with a mean of `10` and a standard deviation of `5` units. We gathered two samples. The one called `small_sample` has only `10` observations, while `big_sample` sums up to *100,000* observations. Even though both come from similar distributions we will see how estimates behave with respect to sample sizes.

Calculating mean, median, and mode with base R

Altogether, the mean, median, and mode are the most popular measures of central tendency. They kind of tell us where the distribution is centered. The following code block shows how to calculate the first two of them:

```
mean(small_sample, na.rm = T)
# outputs [1] 7.546716
mean(big_sample, na.rm = T)
# outputs [1] 9.97051
median(small_sample, na.rm = T)
# outputs [1] 8.449614
median(big_sample, na.rm = T)
# outputs [1] 9.979968
```

> **TIP:** To keep it simple, the arithmetic mean is the sum of all values divided by the number of observations. Median is the middle observation (center) of a sorted sample and mode is the value (or values) that are most frequent in the dataset (if there is one).

The `mean()` and `median()` functions respectively return the mean and median from a set of numbers. If you have any NA at your set and you still want to compute the mean/median no matter what, the `na.rm = T` argument will prevent your function from crashing. This argument will demand the function remove NAs before handling the computation.

> TIP: Skip the `na.rm = T` argument if your data is not supposed to have any NAs. A warning will be displayed if any NA is found and you will notice that something may have gone wrong.

Given that the sample comes from continuous data, even with *100,000* observations, it's very unlikely for a single value to show up more than once. One or more modes are much more likely to show up if we looked into rounded samples. Base R does not have a fully dedicated function to calculate mode but we can easily wrap a function to do so. The next code block shows how to do it:

```
find_mode <- function(vals) {
  if(max(table(vals)) == min(table(vals)))
    'amodal'
  else
    names(table(vals))[table(vals)==max(table(vals))]
}
```

Modes can be also estimated for non-numeric distributions. A distribution can have no mode if all values can be seen as much as any other in the sample. Those are called `amodal` (with no mode). Now, we can now supply our recently crafted function (`find_mode`) with `big_sample`:

```
find_mode(big_sample)
# outputs [1] "amodal"
find_mode(round(big_sample))
# outputs [1] "10"
```

Even for big samples of continuous variables, there are considerable chances of not finding a mode. It's way easier to find one or more modes in a sample of integers. These are not the only central tendency measures available. A package called `psych` has functions that calculate harmonic and geometric means. The following code block demonstrates how to install `psych` and draw the calculations:

```
if(!require(psych)){ install.packages('psych')}
psych::harmonic.mean(big_sample)
# outputs [1] 7.419585
psych::geometric.mean(big_sample)
# outputs [1] 8.793195
# Warning message:
# In log(x) : NaNs produced
```

Let me break down the preceding code block:

- `if(!require(psych)){ install.packages('psych')}` can be read as if the `psych` package is not installed yet, install it
- `psych::harmonic.mean(big_sample)` tells R to calculate the harmonic mean from `big_sample` using the `harmonic.mean()` function of `psych`
- `psych::geometric.mean(big_sample)` asks for the `geometric.mean()` function of `psych` to calculate the geometric mean from `big_sample`

It would be most common for R users to load the entire package using either `library(psych)` or `require(psych)` and only then calling functions names (without saying from which package they came from).

> **TIP:** Using `library()` or `require()` to load packages will spare you some typing while making your code cleaner. On the other hand, calling a function by `<package name>::<function>` will make your code extensive but more explicit about what is being made, while also avoiding possible naming conflicts.

There are far more central tendency measures than those five presented until now. There is no one-size-fits-all kind of measure; different situations will benefit from different measures, but let's move on to next section.

Measures of dispersion

While measures of central tendency try to give an idea about where data is centered, measures of dispersion are meant to give a general idea about how data is distributed around the center. Standard deviation and variance are the most popular measures of dispersion. The square root of the variance equals the standard deviation. It's very easy to get both values with R:

```
sd(big_sample, na.rm = T)
# outputs [1] 5.01836
var(big_sample, na.rm = T)
# outputs [1] 25.18394
```

> **Info:** Keep in mind that these computations we've done so far are estimations from the (real) parameters, not parameters itself.

The `sd()` function estimates the standard deviation while `var()` estimates the variation. In most cases, we find ourselves with a DataFrame full of variables we want to analyze. One way out of this is to use a function that will quickly summarize the whole dataset. These functions usually work equally well both with vectors and DataFrame objects. The next section introduces a couple of them.

Useful functions to draw automated summaries

A very standard procedure whenever conducting data analysis with R is to get a glimpse of data. To input `head()` and `tail()` functions with a DataFrame is quite common among R users; people tend to use both to check whether data was correctly read. While the latter function will display the last few observations, the former will show you the first ones. That's useful, but not what we're looking for.

There is another function commonly called at the beginning of a data analysis process. It's called `summary()`. A short demonstration lies ahead:

```
summary(big_sample)
#    Min. 1st Qu. Median Mean 3rd Qu. Max.
# -11.317 6.586 9.980 9.971 13.345 32.341
```

This function works differently depending on what class of object you input it with. For both vectors and DataFrames, it will display central trend measures (median and mean) along with other useful information about how your variables are distributed (minimum value, maximum value, first quartile, and third quartile).

Some packages have similar functions. Let's make sure the `psych`, `Hmisc`, and `pastecs` packages are already installed:

```
pkgs <- c('psych','Hmisc','pastecs')
pkgs <- pkgs[!(pkgs %in% installed.packages())]
if(length(pkgs) != 0) {install.packages(pkgs)}
rm(pkgs)
```

Now, we can try some descriptive summaries from these packages:

```
psych::describe(big_sample)
Hmisc::describe(big_sample)
pastecs::stat.desc(big_sample)
```

Each of these functions will output a different set of information about data that has been input. I encourage the reader to try them all. Which of them do you like best?

This section has introduced you to some of the most popular measures of central tendency and dispersion. Those are not only used to draw descriptive analysis, but they are also used to handle inferences. It's hard to find any model that won't benefit from mean and variance (and standard deviation) at all.

> TIP: The average prediction given by the arithmetic mean is usually more accurate than predictions considered individually. This phenomenon is known as **Wisdom of the Crowd**.

With mean and standard deviation at hand, it's time to move on to inference. The inferences discussed next can be found under an umbrella called **statistical hypothesis testing**.

Statistical hypothesis testing

Imagine that you have estimated something about your data that you don't know for sure. Assuming that what you have imagined is true, what are the chances of getting the estimations that you found or even more extreme values? This is hypothesis testing. Statistical hypothesis testing (or simply, hypothesis testing, HT) is the name given to a set of well-known, practical methods used to make inferences with statistics. As long you have data and you're willing to make some inferences about it, the odds are that HT is the way to go. It can work out a great variety of real-world problems.

Although it's usually better to work with experimental data, it's also possible to statistically test hypotheses using observational data as well. Exhibit A: economists all over the world are doing it. A medical treatment's effectiveness, production quality (quality control), and guessing abilities can all be tested under the guidelines of HT. It's particularly easy to design a test to check whether that friend of yours has psychic powers or not. As Bob Rudis would say: in God we trust, all the others must bring data.

> TIP: Have you met Rudis? `https://rud.is/b/`.

This section is going to bring you data and the very popular tests known as the z-test, t-test, and A/B test. We will be also discussing the paradigm of hypothesis acceptance and how it has evolved over the years, but before going any further let's get to know concepts that are very likely to show up while doing any sort of HT:

- **Null hypothesis** (H_0): Generally assumed to be true at the test's start. Usually, it states values for the mean (μ) or variance (σ^2). Sometimes, it's phrased as a conclusion such as *the defendant is innocent* or *my friend can't read minds*, but what is truly being tested is some parameter.
- **Alternative hypothesis** (H_a): It's the counterpart of the null hypothesis. The great statistician Ronald Fisher stressed that an alternative hypothesis is always required. If the null hypothesis is rejected, it's rejected in favor of the alternative hypothesis. Out in the real world, there are consequences implied in rejecting or failing to reject the null hypothesis. It's always better to take consequences into account before deciding anything.
- **Type I error**: To reject the null hypothesis when it was actually true is to commit a type I error. Comparably, to accept the null hypothesis when it was actually false is to commit a type II error.
- **Significance level** (α): To put it simply, it's a threshold. It can be seen as the greatest probability of committing a type I error that the user is willing to risk in order to reject the null hypothesis. By the way, lower is better.

For the later concept, during the early days of modern statistics, researchers would fix it at a rigorous level (5% was a very popular number) and then infer something such as *we were able to reject the null hypothesis at 5% significance level* or *we failed to reject the null hypothesis given the significance level of 5%.*

Researchers prefer to say *we failed to reject the null hypothesis* instead of *we accepted the null hypothesis.*

Thumb rules such as *reject your null hypothesis if you can do it with at least 5% significance level* are still useful these days, but there are even more rigorous and reasonable approaches. Considering the likelihood of committing a type I error, an alternative approach estimates and calculates expected costs and revenues coming from going for one or an other hypothesis.

Using the alternative approach, a doctor is likely to prescribe deworming medicine to a patient if they suspect the person has worms rather than prescribe a medical exam. The exam is much more expensive than the medicine, while the former hardly shows any collaterals besides being inexpensive. This approach requires more work. For the moment, let's try the classic approach while running a t-test.

Running t-tests with R

Student's t-distribution was introduced by William Sealy Gosset under the pseudonym student (hence the name) while working at Guinness Brewery. The family of t-tests highly relies on the student's t-distribution in order to infer; in fact, t-test is the general name given to any HT for which the test statistic is assumed to follow a t-distribution. Although normal distributions are very popular and common, a rigorous approach would rather trust a t-distribution instead of the normal one whenever the population's standard deviation is unknown and a sample's estimation is trusted instead.

The t-test also assumes that your sample comes from a normally distributed variable.

In case you may be wondering how these distributions look, here is a visual explanation:

```
x <- seq(-4,4,.1)
par(lwd = 2)
plot(x, dnorm(x), type = 'l', ylab = 'density',
 main = 'prob. density distributions')
lines(x, dt(x, 5), col = '#e66101', lty = 2)
lines(x, dt(x, 10), col = '#5e3c99', lty = 3)
legend('topright',
 legend = c('normal','t-student (df = 5)', 't-student (df = 10)'),
 col = c('#000000','#e66101','#5e3c99'), lty = 1:3)
```

The last code block will generate a visual comparison across normal and t-student distributions' formats:

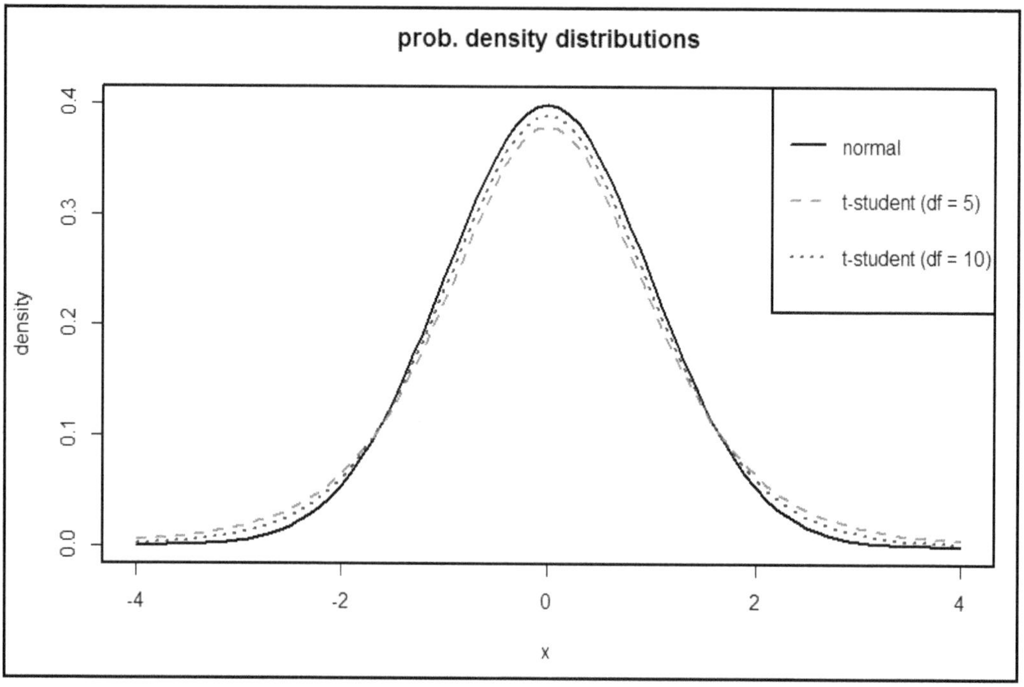

Figure 2.1: Normal and t-student probability density distributions formats

Both normal and t-student distributions are very similar; both are sort of bell-shaped. The thing is that t-student's distributions will depend on the degrees of freedom; greater degrees of freedom lead to t-student curves more similar to standardized normal curves. As you can see from the previous figure, normal curves are more concentrated around the center, while t-student curves have fatter tails.

> Some people would argue that for bigger samples there's no difference between assuming an underlying normal or t-distribution for the test statistic. On the other hand, a rigorous approach would only consider using a normal distribution (z-test) if the standard deviation is known.

Back in the early days of hypothesis testing, people would have to make several calculations by hand and then look at a table to see where the t statistic fit. The computations are now done by computer and there is no need to consult a table anymore, yet the core ideas and concepts remain the same. Given a sample (*X*) that is i.i.d. and follows a normal distribution with limited mean, μ, and unknown variance, so the following applies:

$$t = \frac{\bar{X} - \mu}{S/\sqrt{n}}$$

The value *t* will follow a Student's t-distribution with *n-1* degrees of freedom, where the following applies:

- n: Number of observations
- $\bar{X}$: Arithmetic mean (estimation)
- μ: Expected mean (parameter/true mean), stated by the null hypothesis
- S: A non-biased standard deviation estimator calculated from the sample as follows:

$$S = \sqrt{\frac{1}{n-1}\sum_{i=0}^{n}(X_i - \bar{X})^2}$$

That is how the test statistic is calculated; imagine computing all of these by hand. When Marley says *don't worry about a thing,* it's only because R will handle all of the computation for you. Once you are aware of what's going on, you can call `t.test()` to run the test for you. Let's run a simple mean test so we can walk through the output:

```
# set.seed(10)
# small_sample <- rnorm(n = 10, mean = 10, sd = 5)
# big_sample <- rnorm(n = 10^5, mean = 10, sd = 5)
t.test(big_sample, mu = 10, alternative = 'two.sided')
```

If you are missing the `big_sample` object, simply uncomment and run the first three lines of code. So, here we are. The `t.test()` function will run the test for us. The way it's designed, it will check the null hypothesis, that states that the true (populational) mean is equal to *10* against the alternative hypothesis that states that the true mean is not equal *10;* it's something like this:

$$H_0 : \mu = 10$$

$$H_a : \mu \neq 10$$

This is a simple t-test for the mean. A functions' first argument points towards the data. The mean assumed by the null hypothesis is declared into μ argument. A two-sided test asked by the `alternative = 'two.sided'` argument. Alternative inputs would be `'less'` or `'greater'`; both would ask for one-sided tests. Let's check the output we will get from the previous code:

```
#   One Sample t-test
#
# data: big_sample
# t = -1.8583, df = 99999, p-value = 0.06313
# alternative hypothesis: true mean is not equal to 10
# 95 percent confidence interval:
#   9.939406 10.001614
# sample estimates:
# mean of x
#   9.97051
```

R begins by telling us that it's a one sample t-test because, of course, two sample t-tests are also available. It goes on and tells us that the data tested comes from the `big_sample` data. Calculated statistic (`t`), degrees of freedom (`df`) and `p-value` are shown next. The p-value is the lowest level of confidence that allows us to reject the null hypothesis; for this case, it is 6,313%, so we failed to reject the null hypothesis at 5% level of confidence—which is good, given that the data came from a normal distribution with a mean equal to `10`.

Next comes the alternative hypothesis. Sometimes, it is useful to state your null hypothesis in terms of greater or less instead of not equal. Tweak the `alternative` argument to do so. In the following section, we can see the 95% confidence interval; be careful while interpreting this one. Given the alternative hypothesis, if repeated samples were taken and this same interval were calculated for all of them, 95% of the intervals would contain the populational mean. You can set a custom interval of your own by naming the `conf.level` argument. Last but not least, we have the mean of `x`. The output also told us that the sample estimated mean of `x` was `9.97051`.

Decision rule – a brief overview of the p-value approach

Just to be clear, the expected result from a hypothesis test is whether the researcher (you) is rejecting or failing to reject the null hypothesis. The heuristic adopted to go for one or the other is called the **decision rule**; basically, the rule used to either reject the null hypothesis or not.

The most common decision rule is to fix a limit to the significance level in advance. This limit can be seen as the greater probability of committing a type I error you're willing to risk; that is, the greater chance to reject the null hypothesis while it was actually right. Common numbers are 5% and 1% (these are usually arbitrary).

With your number at hand, you can check whether the p-value output by the test is greater or lower in comparison to this limit (which is the significance level, α). Let's say that you picked 5% and you get a p-value of *0.1* (10%); hence, you may say that you failed to reject the null hypothesis within 5% level of significance. But what if you get a p-value of *0.001* (0.1%)? You could even say that you were able to reject the null hypothesis within 1% level of significance. It's a good practice to show the actual p-value to the audience.

If your p-value is exactly equal to alpha, you may also fail to reject the null hypothesis.

In the immediately previous example, the p-value was *0.06313*; hence, we should fail to reject the null hypothesis within 5% level of significance. This means that we don't deny that the true mean could be equal to ten as our null hypothesis assumed. There may be more reasonable (and laborious) ways to set your significance level. 5% seems to be a widely adopted number among researchers in various fields and it's definitely a magical number.

The 5% level got very popular most probably because of Fisher's famous book, *Statistical Methods for Research Workers*, that showed tables for this level of significance.

Clearly stating your decision and showing the test statistic, p-value, and the confidence interval is probably the better way to go. You can also set your alpha based on the expected outcomes from not rejecting the H_0 while it's true versus rejecting it (while it's true). This may be challenging but pretty cool and goes very well with a thing called **test's power** (β).

Be careful

Previously, in the *Running t-tests with R* section, we used the bigger sample to run a t-test; but what about the smaller sample? Speaking of R, yes, we can run it. The next code block shows how, but you shouldn't trust a sample so small:

```
t.test(small_sample, mu = 10, alternative = 'two.sided')

#   One Sample t-test
#
# data: small_sample
# t = -2.2169, df = 9, p-value = 0.05384
# alternative hypothesis: true mean is not equal to 10
# 95 percent confidence interval:
#   5.043347 10.050084
# sample estimates:
# mean of x
#  7.546716
```

The test now came close to rejecting the null hypothesis with a 95% confidence level (and, as we already know, the sample does come from a normal distribution with a mean, μ, equal to `10`). This test is not all mighty powerful, I can assure you, but it's more trustworthy if you have lots of observations. Actually, you should be very cautious about making any kind of statistical inference using little data.

You can also test if two samples have the same mean (μ) using the t-test, using `t.test()`. To do so, name the `x` and `y` parameters and at least set `var.equal = T` to `t.test()`. The latter will make sure that the variance is considered the same for both samples. This equal variance thing is a necessary assumption for the simple two samples t-test, otherwise you're committing yourself to a Welch's t-test (feel free to do it if you will, it's probably better to a great variety of situations). There is also the possibility to set a custom confidence level by declaring the `conf.level` argument and to use a different alternative hypothesis with the `alternative` argument. A quick example can be found as follows:

```
t.test(x = small_sample, y = big_sample, var.equal = T)
```

Let me stress that you shouldn't run it with a sample as small as `small_sample`. Of course, R will run it, but nonetheless, speaking about the statistical point of view, this is very poor inference because it is based on very poor evidence (a small sample). So, keep in mind, these tests are assuming your data is coming from a normal distribution of unknown standard deviation, and really small samples could be problematic.

> **TIP:** One could try something like `plot(density(<variable>))` to check whether a variable resembles a normal distribution or not.

But what if you do know the populations' variance?

Running z-tests with R

If you are sure about it or at least have very good reasons to assume that you are right about the population's variance, you should use a z-test. Some would say that you could go strictly to a z-test if you have a big enough sample even if you're estimating your population's variance through sample—which is not assumed by z-tests.

There are mainly two reasons for that. First, as your sample gets bigger—given some conditions such as limited mean—your sample's estimations converge to the true values, and the true parameters; so, with a big enough sample, you have more reasons to believe that you really know the real parameters.

The other reason can be seen in *Figure 2.1*. With greater samples come greater degrees of freedom (these were actually Uncle Ben's last words to Peter Parker). The more degrees of freedom you have, the more your test distribution will look like a normal distribution. That is actually a consequence of reason number one, and you can visualize this by trying the following code:

```
x <- seq(-4,4,.1)
par(lwd = 2)
plot(x, dnorm(x), type = 'l', ylab = 'density',
     main = 'prob. density distributions')
lines(x, dt(x, 500), col = '#e66101')
```

Try to find the black line and fail! The black line is hiding behind the orange line. Both lines are matching. But, of course, if you could zoom in enough you would see there's still a small difference between these two lines; hence, I and some other people would argue that it's best to use the t-test no matter the sample's size (size doesn't matter—that's what she said). Practically, the difference you get from using one or another comes to be very small as your sample grows—it's up to you which one to use.

So, now that we discussed why/when we should use one instead of the other, we can go ahead and see how to practically run a z-test with R. There's no function like `t.test()` sitting there waiting for you to run a z-test right away—maybe R developers agree with me, t-tests are usually better. But you can easily wrap a function to calculate the test and drop the statistics for you.

Do you remember the formula for the t-test statistic? The only difference between the t-test statistic and z-test one is that, instead of trusting the estimator, *S*, for the standard deviation, you use the value that we assume you know and trust a standard normal distribution to make your decision. That's it, you are assuming that you know the true standard deviation and hence that your test statistic follows a standard normal distribution (that is, a normal distribution with mean zero and variance one). The formula gets to be this:

$$z = \frac{\bar{X} - \mu}{\sigma/\sqrt{n}}$$

The sigma in the equation is now accounting for the true value of the standard deviation that the test assumes you know (a very uncommon situation). Sigma is usually estimated in the exact same way that the t-test does, a very good reason to stick with t-test. Anyway, to walk through this test is also a good way to get to know the t-test better, given that everything remains the same and the only change is the distribution used to compare the statistic.

Usually, to use a z-test means you're comparing your test statistic with a standardized normal distribution and not that you actually know the standard deviation, sigma, for sure. Yet, if your sample is big enough, you're safe using a z-test.

A good way to start is to make a checklist of everything we might need to get this test done. We need:

1. `mu`, `sigma`, and `sample` to work as inputs
2. Calculate the test statistic
3. Define an alternative hypothesis
4. Calculate the p-value
5. Estimate a confidence interval

Let's start with steps one and two:

```
z.test <- function(sample, mu, sigma){
n <- length(sample)
xbar <- mean(sample, na.rm =T)
z <- (xbar - mu)/(sigma/sqrt(n))
cat('z = ', z,'\n')
}
```

Now we have a function that will output the test statistic if we input a sample, a hypothetical mean, and a standard deviation. We could elaborate on this function in order to output the p-value; this way we could put our decision rule to good use. The way the alternative hypothesis is set does affect how the p-value should be calculated; hence, the code is chaining some `if...else` statements to work things out. The code becomes lengthy but do not be afraid, read it calmly and I'm positive that you are getting it right:

```
z.test <- function(sample, mu, sigma, alternative = 'two.sided'){
  n <- length(sample)
  xbar <- mean(sample, na.rm =T)
  z <- (xbar - mu)/(sigma/sqrt(n))

  if(alternative == 'two.sided'){
    p.value <- 2*pnorm(-abs(z))
  }
  else if(alternative == 'greater'){
    p.value <- pnorm(z, lower.tail = F)
  }
  else if(alternative == 'less'){
    p.value <- pnorm(z)
  }
  else{stop('alternative is missepecified, accepted values are
             \'two.sided\',\'greater\' or \'less\'\n')}
  cat('z = ', z, ' obs. = ', n, ' p-value = ', p.value, '\n')
  cat('mean of x\n', xbar, '\n')
}
```

The preceding code is pretty lengthy but it's only due to the various unfoldings that might come from different ways of setting the alternative hypothesis. It's modular, though. The previous code can be split into three modules: a first module stores the mean, number of observations, and calculates test statistic (`z`); the second one calculates the p-value based on the alternative hypothesis chosen; and the last module prints a little summary.

Let's navigate through the `if` statements from the second module. By looking at one `if` statement at a time, we can get a better understanding of how p-values should be calculated with respect to the alternative hypothesis. The first `if` statement is the following:

```
if(alternative == 'two.sided'){
  p.value <- 2*pnorm(-abs(z))'
}
```

Two-sided tests (H_a: *mu* ≠ *mu₀*) consider both tails from the test's distribution as rejecting areas—areas for which you might reject the null hypothesis. These tests are trying to figure out how likely it would be to see a test statistic of `z` or even more extreme values if those samples were coming from a normally distributed variable with true mean equal (μ) and standard deviation equal σ.

The last chunk is looking for the negative version (left-hand version) of the test statistic (`-abs(z)`) and asking how likely it would be to find values equal or lower to this one within a standard normal distribution (the same distribution that our test statistic is assumed to follow). The `pnorm()` function is taking care of calculating this probability. Since the exact same probability may be found on the other extreme (the right-hand tail), our p-value is simply two times that probability; hence, p-value (`p.value`) is given by `2*pnorm(-abs(z))`.

A one-sided test could be selected by setting the alternative argument of `z.test()` either to `'greater'` or `'less'`. In case the former is selected, the following the `else if` statement will be called to use:

```
else if(alternative == 'greater'){
  p.value <- pnorm(z, lower.tail = F)
}
```

Declaring `alternative = 'greater'` is useful when the true mean being greater than some value is critical to the decision-making process. For example, if you're testing the concentration of a toxin in the bloodstream, you don't care if the level of toxin is too low, the important thing is to make sure that it's not too high.

For these cases, you will only reject your null hypothesis if you find extreme values on the right-hand side of the distribution, also known as the upper tail. The p-value is then the probability of finding the estimated test statistic (`z`) or even greater values if our assumptions were true. Such a probability is easily calculated by `pnorm(z, lower.tail = F)`. The `lower.tail = F` argument makes sure that we are looking for the probability of getting values equal or higher than `z` instead of the other way round.

> **TIP**
> You can also specify mean and standard deviation from the normal distribution you're looking for with `pnorm()`. Name and set values for the `mean` and `sd` arguments. Default values for those are respectively zero and one, which leads to a standardized normal distribution—the distribution that our test statistic is assumed to follow.

On the other hand, if the only thing that is critical to your decision-making process is whether the true mean is lower than some value, set `alternative = 'less'` when calling `z.test()`. The rejection area will now be sitting on the lower tail (left-hand side) of the test's distribution and is calculated by the following `if` statement (inside the `z.test()` function):

```
else if(alternative == 'less'){
  p.value <- pnorm(z)
}
```

This time, the p-value is showing the probability of getting a value equal or lower to `z` within the test distribution. Notice that we skipped the `lower.tail = F` argument so that `pnorm()` will only seek the probability of getting values equal or lower than `z`. After the p-value is properly computed, `z.test()` will output the test statistic (`z`), the number of observations, the p-value (which is useful to the previously described decision rule), and the estimated sample mean.

Elaborating a little longer

However, we could elaborate a little longer to get a more detailed summary that will also output the alternative hypothesis and the confidence interval. The following code block demonstrates how such a function can be created. Afterward, we will see how to keep this function close in order to easily call and use it later:

```
z.test <- function(sample, mu, sigma, conf.lvl = .95,
                   alternative = 'two.sided'){
  n <- length(sample)
  xbar <- mean(sample, na.rm =T)
  z <- (xbar - mu)/(sigma/sqrt(n))

  if(alternative == 'two.sided'){
    p.value <- 2*pnorm(-abs(z))
    alt <- 'not equal '
    err <- -qnorm((1-conf.lvl)/2)*sigma/sqrt(n)
    a <- xbar - err
    b <- xbar + err
  }
  else if(alternative == 'greater'){
```

```
    p.value <- pnorm(z, lower.tail = F)
    alt <- 'greater than '
    err <- qnorm(conf.lvl)*sigma/sqrt(n)
    a <- xbar - err
    b <- 'Inf'
  }
  else if(alternative == 'less'){
    p.value <- pnorm(z)
    alt <- 'less than '
    err <- qnorm(conf.lvl)*sigma/sqrt(n)
    a <- '-Inf'
    b <- xbar + err
  }
  else{stop('alternative is missepecified. Accepted values are',
            ' \'two.sided\',\'greater\' or \'less\'\n')}
  cat('z = ', z, ' obs. = ', n, ' p-value = ', p.value, '\n')
  cat('alternative hypothesis: true mean is ', alt , mu, '\n')
  cat(conf.lvl*100, ' percent confidence interval: \n')
  cat(a,' ',b, '\n')
  cat('mean of x\n', xbar, '\n')
}
```

Just like the later designation of `z.test()`, this function is lengthy but works in a very modular way. The first module estimates the arithmetic mean from the sample, storing the number of observations and calculating the test statistic, `z`. The second module calculates the p-value and confidence interval with respect to the assigned alternative hypothesis, while the third module simply prints the summary—which looks a lot like the summary given by `t.test()`.

> The concept of the confidence interval was introduced by Jerzy Neyman in 1937. It's very useful in the decision-making process (and remarkably misinterpreted).

Once we have designed our function, we can make it easily available for later use by doing a few things. First, save this code into a separate `.R` file, preferably somewhere where the path to it will be very short or in your working directory. I named mine `z_test.r` and stored it in the `C:/libr` directory—a personal library of R functions. So, the path in my computer that will lead to this file will be `'C:/libr/z_test.r'`. Now, I can use the `source()` function to run this file, thus making the `z.test()` function available at any time in the future:

```
source('C:/libr/z_test.r')
```

I would advise the reader to adopt a directory that requires little text to reach for these files. Intuitive names and logs are also advisable, to keep your personal library organized. It's also possible to group several functions into a single `.R` file (and run any kind of R codes from the console). There is, at least, one other way to work your personal library out and requires combining the `source()` and `url()` functions.

I find this second way pretty cool (I like to imagine that I'm constructing my own Arcana library in the clouds). It's mostly useful in order to keep a backup of your library or to make it remotely accessible (either for you or for other people). It consists basically of uploading your file through the cloud, sharing it, and accessing your file through a link; extra steps can make things better.

> Another piece of advice: keep both cloud and flash-drive backups of your codes and other kinds of important stuff. Sharing or not will only be a matter of how sensible the content is. If you happen to create great stuff that can't be found elsewhere, kindly consider publishing it as a package trough CRAN and GitHub.

If you seek to do something like that, the following steps may work as a sort of guide:

> If you want to see the magic happening, make sure to have internet access, remove `z.test()` from your environment with `rm(z.test)`, and run the code coming next.

1. Upload the file to a cloud. I prefer to use Dropbox, but only because I know how to ask for the raw file using nothing but the URL (this might be also possible with other services, I just don't know how to do it).
2. Select the file from the cloud and share it through a link. For example, I have this link: `https://www.dropbox.com/s/53l79kwklr9xnh3/z_test.R?dl=0`. Add `&raw=1` to its end in order to ask for the raw file (`https://www.dropbox.com/s/53l79kwklr9xnh3/z_test.R?dl=0raw=1`).
3. To improve things a little bit, you can shorten the URL using an URL shortener. Using **bit.do** I got: `http://bit.do/z_test`.
4. Combine `source()` and `url()` to read the file from the cloud, like this:

```
source(url('http://bit.do/z_test'))
```

5. Now you can compare the summary given by `z.test()` and `t.test()`:

```
t.test(big_sample, mu = 10)
z.test(big_sample, mu = 10, sigma = 5)
```

6. Notice that the p-value and confidence intervals are pretty close; that is explained by the sample size. Do not forget that `z.test()` will require a `sigma` parameter. The results are not so similar using the small sample:

```
t.test(small_sample, mu = 10)
z.test(small_sample, mu = 10, sigma = 5)
```

7. Given that these samples were generated from a normal distribution with mean equal `10` and a standard deviation of `5`, `z.test()` was more precise for the `small_sample` test in comparison to `t.test()`. The latter came pretty close to rejecting the null hypothesis, with 95% confidence level. This is only due to us knowing exactly what the standard deviation was for sure. But what if the standard deviation was unknown? What outcomes should we expect by trying an unbiased estimator rather than the true `sigma`? Let's have a look:

```
z.test(small_sample, mu = 10 , sigma = sd(small_sample))
# z = -2.216899 obs. = 10 p-value = 0.02663
# alternative hypothesis: true mean is not equal 10
# 95 percent confidence interval:
# 5.377763 9.715668
# mean of x
#  7.546716
```

Bad ones, of course. The actually true null hypothesis was rejected with a 5% significance level, leading us towards a type I error. Bottom line: if you do know population standard deviation, you should use a z-test; if you don't, you're better off with a t-test. Although, so far, this chapter only quickly mentioned how these tests could be used in real-life applications, the truth is they are very general tests that fit well in a great variety of real-life problems. Depending on what is to be tested, they could be working in the background of an A/B test, for example.

A/B testing – a brief introduction and a practical example with R

Unlike the other tests that we've seen so far, A/B tests do not rely on a unique test statistic and a unique distribution to derive inference; as a matter of fact, they could benefit from any test statistic and distribution. A/B testing is, rather, a name given to a broad technique used for versions comparison that will dictate things from how to sample all of the way to getting your p-value and confidence interval and making a decision. These tests are wildly popular in the field of web analytics, for very good reasons, but are not restricted to it.

These tests are capable of handling statistically based insights to a broad set of *is A better than B?* kind of problems. Will layout A attract more clicks than layout B? Will this color A be more profitable than color B? Would campaign A work better than campaign B? A/B tests tend to guide better than gut feeling and guesses. This section aims to introduce the reader to them.

The two versions of something you wish to test are called **control treatment** and **variant treatment**.

There are a couple of things that deserve a great deal of attention while addressing these tests. The first thing to decide is what we are looking for, in other words, the variable of interest. The variable of interest decides in which ways we want to check if version A does things better than B—adopting the perspective of web analytics, it could be click rate, revenue per paying user, or time spent on the website. The kind of variable chosen will rule which statistic test to use later (t-test, chi-square test, Fisher's exact test, and so on).

Once the variable is chosen, it's time to get samples. Samples of two or more versions must be gathered simultaneously. Speaking web, this is done by redirecting some traffic to one version and the other one to the alternative version. It's important to do this randomly.

Samples from control and variant treatments must have similar sizes. They must also be large enough to make inferences. The user must let the test run long enough to gather enough data, but not too long. There are mainly two reasonable arguments that will advise us not to let the test run for so long:

- **Economic argument**: If two versions are running simultaneously there is a great chance you are not getting optimal results
- **Statistical argument**: The population might change drastically during a test of a long duration; results might be coming from something other than what the test was designed to investigate

It's very common to get live results from tests like these as the samples keep growing. Some users would stop their tests once the results showed statistical significance and that's not a good way to go. Even A on A tests would reject the null hypothesis once in a while. Good practices may include minimal sample sizes and a time limit.

Once you get your test running, you can do the calculations with R and even determine if your sample is sufficiently large. Let's check this with an example. Imagine that you are running an A/B test on a website. You are testing if a green button (variant treatment) does better than a red one (control treatment). After running the test with the traffic split seemingly randomly between those two versions for one week, you get data about click rates:

	Clicks	**No-clicks**
Red button (control)	130	9870
Green button (variant)	170	9830

We can reproduce this table using R with the following code:

```
control <- c(130, 9870)
variant <- c(170, 9830)
tab <- rbind(control, variant)
```

Now the object tab holds the exact same table showing how many clicks each button received during the experiment. The red button had a click rate of 1.3%, while the green one did slightly better with 1.7%. What is the likelihood of these values showing up even though there is no real difference between them? Now, it's time to deliver these numbers to a Fisher's exact test, a test suitable to get comparisons from two proportions:

```
fisher.test(tab, alternative = 'less')
#   Fisher's Exact Test for Count Data
#
# data: tab
# p-value = 0.01156
# alternative hypothesis: true odds ratio is less than 1
# 95 percent confidence interval:
#  0.0000000 0.9296408
# sample estimates:
# odds ratio
#  0.7616196
```

The odds ratio will show how likely the red button is to be clicked in comparison with the green button. The null hypothesis will state that they're equally likely to be clicked, in other words, the odds ratio is equal one. Once I think that the green button does better, I set the test with an alternative hypothesis stating that the true odds ratio is less than one.

We got a p-value of `0.01156` (1156%), which is favorable to the alternative hypothesis—green is better. These tests also seek to minimize the chances of getting a type II error by improving what is called **statistical power**. Power is improved by sample sizes. There is an easy way to estimate how many observations per group we may need to achieve some power using R:

```
fisher.test(tab, alternative = 'less')
power.prop.test(p1 = 130/(130+9870), p2 = 170/(170+9830),
                power = 0.8, sig.level = 0.012,
                alternative = 'one')

#      Two-sample comparison of proportions power calculation
#
#               n = 17732.86
#              p1 = 0.013
#              p2 = 0.017
#       sig.level = 0.012
#           power = 0.8
#     alternative = one.sided
#
# NOTE: n is number in *each* group
```

The `p1` and `p2` arguments are input respectively with the click rates of the red and green buttons; `power` and `sig.level` ask for the minimal statistical power and significance level that we are looking for. `17732.86` observations per group are expected to be needed in order to achieve a power of 80% (a very popular number). Given that in the first week 10,000 observations per group were gathered, I would say that it is reasonable to let the experiment run for one more week in order to get even better results.

Summary

The intentions of this chapter were to introduce readers to measures of central tendency, dispersion, and statistical hypothesis testing. While the arithmetic mean, median, and mode are the most popular measures of central tendency, t-tests and z-tests may be the most popular statistical tests used. This chapter also taught you how to design your own function to run a z-test, and how to recover it from local files or the cloud. A/B tests were also covered.

In the next chapter, we will cover what data wrangling is and how to use it in R.

Quiz

1. Which of these tests assume that the standard deviation is unknown?
    - The great macaroni test
    - The z-test
    - The t-test
    - Every A/B test
2. Which of the following functions will give the probability of getting values equal or greater than one from a standardized normal distribution?
    - `qnorm(1, lower.tail = F)`
    - `pnorm(1, lower.tail = F)`
    - `pnorm(1)`
    - `t.test(1, alternative = 'less')`
3. Select the false statement:
    - A/B tests can be used to compare website versions
    - A/B tests can be only used by the web industry
    - Mean is a measure of central tendency
    - Z-tests assume that the standard deviation is known

Answers—executing the following code will give you the answers to the quiz questions:

```
set.seed(10)
round(runif(3,1,4))
```

3 Data Wrangling with R

"You can have data without information, but you cannot have information without data."
– Daniel Keys Moran

Data wrangling has been one of the core strengths of R, given its capabilities of relatively fast in-memory processing on demand and a wide array of packages that facilitate the fast data curation processes that data wrangling involves.

R is especially invaluable when working with datasets in excess of 1 million rows—the limit in Microsoft Excel—or when working with files that are in the order of gigabytes. Due to several easy-to-use functions for common day-to-day tasks such as aggregations, joins, and pivots, R is also arguably much simpler to use relative to some of the GUI-based tools that are available for similar tasks.

At a high level, the core categories of data wrangling with R include data extraction, data cleansing, data transformation, and data consolidation. This is a simplified categorization of the basic tenets of data wrangling and we'll delve deeper into these individual subject areas in the next few sections. The challenge emanates largely due to the fact that data comes in a range of data types and data formats from a diverse pool of data sources. Here, data type refers to the characteristics of the contents of the files, format refers to the file format in which data is delivered, and source refers to the systems from when you receive data. There is no common universal convention for these—the data may exist in a CSV file or a binary SAS file or be present in a database, each of which can have its own nuances and challenges.

In this chapter, we will cover the following topics:

- Introduction to data wrangling with R
- The foundational tools of data wrangling: `dplyr`, `data.table`, and others
- ETL with R data extraction

- ETL with R data transformation
- ETL with R data load
- Helpful data wrangling tools for everyday use
- Tutorial

Introduction to data wrangling with R

The effort required to perform data wrangling operations, also known as **data munging**, is an understated aspect to all data science activities. Online courses or web-based examples generally provide pre-cleansed datasets for end users. This may give the impression that real-world data is similar to that used for data mining exercises and/or courses. In fact, real-world data is seldom, if ever, anywhere close to the pristine datasets depicted in such courses.

Real-world data will very likely not be in the format you need for your machine learning activities, may contain inaccurate or missing data, have mixed data types in the same column (for example, numbers and characters in the price column), and pose a host of other challenges that few of us are prepared for at the onset.

Data types, formats, and sources

The three categorical characteristics of data are as follows:

- **Data types**: Data type generally refers to the type of the data in the respective column. R supports character, numeric (real or decimal), integer, logical, and complex numbers. When reading data in from CSV files, R automatically tries to determine the type of data in each column of the file. This might not always work as desired. For instance, a column with the prices of products may have a sign or text indicating the name of the currency (for example, USD/$ and GBP/£). Columns with text data may have unicode characters (for instance, Cyrillic or Greek) with accent marks. Reading data from an external structured data source such as a database may be slightly more precise because there may be dedicated packages such as RODBC that can interpret data types across heterogeneous data sources.

- **Data formats**: Datasets can come in a range of different formats—text files such as CSV files; tab delimited files; binary files such as Excel and SAS datasets; and external data sources such as databases, as explained earlier. Of these, CSV is one of the most portable cross-platform formats for storing data (it's simply the data separated by commas for each column). Tab-delimited and pipe-delimited are two of the other data formats that you may encounter during work. Binary files, such as Excel and SAS datasets, and external data sources represent the second and third types of data formats respectively. R also has its own binary formats, most notably, RDS, with which the user can store R objects natively in an R serialized format (using `readRDS` and `saveRDS`). Another option for storing R objects is `.RData` files, which are generally used to store a collection of objects (using save and load). In recent days, newer R binary formats have appeared. Feather is one such popular format that has shown impressive read/write I/O performance.
- **Data sources:** Data sources refer to the source system from which data is retrieved. In a commercial setting, datasets are generally stored either in the cloud or in-house servers. The datasets can be accessed as web-based downloads or more commonly directly from the servers as a shared folder (for example, in Windows). Data vendors transmit data either via FTP or, in the case of sensitive data, using physical hard drives. Wherever the data may be, we need a means to access the dataset in order to use it with our R programs. R has native connectors to extract data directly from web-based URLs, from Hadoop-based storage such as HDFS, from databases using database connectors, and much more:

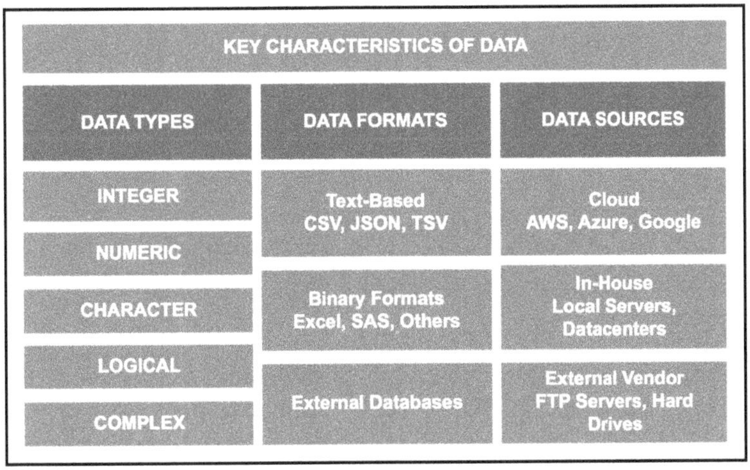

Data extraction, transformation, and load

The previous section looked at the high-level characteristics of data as defined by data types, formats and sources. Data **Extraction-Transformation-Load** (**ETL**) is a generic term that signifies the process of extracting (retrieving) data, applying transformations such as cleansing operations and aggregations, and finally loading the data onto a target system, if such is needed.

Basic tools of data wrangling

In this section, we're going to share some of the common data mining and aggregation operations that can be performed on `data.frame`, `dplyr`, and `data.table`.

First, we are going to learn how to use a few functions in Base R to perform basic manipulation operations. We'll then cover `dplyr` and `data.table`—two of the most well known and powerful packages in the R world today for managing data. `tibble` is an alternative to `data.frame` that is used widely in conjunction with `dplyr` and adheres more closely to how `data.frame` behave and uses the same conventions for slicing, indexing, and other operations as `data.frame`. The latter, `data.table`, uses a slightly different convention, but is extremely powerful, especially for handling large datasets.

Each of these sections, will in turn, cover the following:

- **Reading and writing**: How to read and write data from and to files, websites, and other sources
- **Analysis**: How to perform ad hoc data analysis such as aggregations and pivots

Although it is assumed that readers are familiar with R to some measure, we have nevertheless provided a brief example of `data.frame` and common operations on the same as a primer for new users.

The fundamental data structure used across R is called `data.frame("Data Frame")`. Many of you may be already familiar with the concept, and the following has been provided as a refresher.

A DataFrame is similar to a table or a spreadsheet consisting of rows and columns. Similar to spreadsheets, such as in Excel, each column has a header, known as the column name, and the data type in each column is the same; for example, a column of data type numeric cannot store characters. The general syntax of `data.frame` is represented as `dataframe[rows, columns]`, where `dataframe` is the name of the `data.frame` being referenced.

For instance, the `state` dataset in R contains several key characteristics of US states:

```
# Load the data for state
data(state)

state <- data.frame(state.x77) # Creating a data.frame from the matrix
state.x77

# View the first few rows of state
head(state)

# View First 3 rows
state[1:3,]

# View First 3 columns
state[,1:3]

# View First 3 rows and 3 columns
state[1:3,1:3]

# Create a new column
state$State <- row.names(state)

# Find matches using boolean operations
state[state$State == "Connecticut",]

state[state$Population > 1000 & state$Income > 2000,] # Find states with
Population > 1000 and Income > 2000
```

As we will be covering how to read and write CSV files in later sections, let us also see how we can create and read CSV-formatted text files. In order to save the `data.frame` state as a CSV file, we can use the `write.csv` command as follows:

```
# Saving the state data.frame as a CSV File
write.csv(x=state,file = "state.csv",row.names = F)

# The arguments were as follows:
# x = the name of the data.frame we want to save; file = the file we want
to save as; row.names=F means do not include the row names

# We can read/import the file back to see what it contains
read.csv("state.csv")
```

Note the difference—the original `data.frame` state contained row names, whereas the saved CSV file doesn't because of the options we had selected. Both `write.csv` and `read.csv` take several other options that you can view by running `?write.csv` and `?read.csv` in the R console respectively:

Data Frame

COLUMN NAMES (colnames or names)

	Population	Income	Illiteracy	Life Exp	Murder	HS Grad	Frost	Area
Alabama	3615	3624	2.1	69.05	15.1	41.3	20	50708
Alaska	365	6315	1.5	69.31	11.3	66.7	152	566432
Arizona	2212	4530	1.8	70.55	7.8	58.1	15	113417
Arkansas	2110	3378	1.9	70.66	10.1	39.9	65	51945
California	21198	5114	1.1	71.71	10.3	62.6	20	156361
Colorado	2541	4884	0.7	72.06	6.8	63.9	166	103766
Connecticut	3100	5348	1.1	72.48	3.1	56.0	139	4862
Delaware	579	4809	0.9	70.06	6.2	54.6	103	1982
Florida	8277	4815	1.3	70.66	10.7	52.6	11	54090
Georgia	4931	4091	2.0	68.54	13.9	40.6	60	58073
Hawaii	868	4963	1.9	73.60	6.2	61.9	0	6425
Idaho	813	4119	0.6	71.87	5.3	59.5	126	82677
Illinois	11197	5107	0.9	70.14	10.3	52.6	127	55748
Indiana	5313	4458	0.7	70.88	7.1	52.9	122	36097

ROWNAMES (row.names())

Using base R for data manipulation and analysis

Base R provides some extremely helpful functions for day-to-day data analysis. Some such examples have been provided in this section, but are by no means exhaustive. Further details will be available in subsequent chapters, but the corresponding information is intended to provide a general overview of some of base R's capabilities. The structure of a DataFrame can be viewed using the `str` command.

You can view the structure of `data.frame` using the `str` command. This is often the first starting point (after reading a file if applicable) in order to see what your dataset looks like:

```
# View the structure of the state data.frame
str(state)
```

The output is as follows:

```
> str(state)
'data.frame':	50 obs. of  9 variables:
 $ Population: num  3615 365 2212 2110 21198 ...
 $ Income    : num  3624 6315 4530 3378 5114 ...
 $ Illiteracy: num  2.1 1.5 1.8 1.9 1.1 0.7 1.1 0.9 1.3 2 ...
 $ Life.Exp  : num  69 69.3 70.5 70.7 71.7 ...
 $ Murder    : num  15.1 11.3 7.8 10.1 10.3 6.8 3.1 6.2 10.7 13.9 ...
 $ HS.Grad   : num  41.3 66.7 58.1 39.9 62.6 63.9 56 54.6 52.6 40.6 ...
 $ Frost     : num  20 152 15 65 20 166 139 103 11 60 ...
 $ Area      : num  50708 566432 113417 51945 156361 ...
 $ State     : chr  "Alabama" "Alaska" "Arizona" "Arkansas" ...
```

Applying families of functions

The `apply` family of functions allow users to easily apply custom vector functions on matrices, lists, and other R data structures. Operations such as summing by rows and columns or more complex ones, such as functions with conditional logic, can be applied using `apply` commands. These are extremely convenient, not only from an ease-of-use perspective but also from a performance standpoint. In general, vectorised operations will almost always be faster and more efficient than looping, such as with for-next loops in R:

```
# apply

# Usage
#
# apply(X, MARGIN, FUN, ...)
# Arguments
#
# X: an array, including a matrix.
# MARGIN: a vector giving the subscripts which the function will be applied
over. E.g., for a matrix 1 indicates
# rows, 2 indicates columns, c(1, 2) indicates rows and columns. Where X
has named dimnames, it can be a
# character vector selecting dimension names.

apply(state[,-ncol(state)], 2, sum) # Sum of all values in the numeric
columns
apply(state[,-ncol(state)], 2, mean) # Mean of all values in the numeric
columns
```

The output is as follows:

```
> apply(state[,-ncol(state)], 2, mean) # Mean of all values in the numeric columns
Population     Income Illiteracy   Life.Exp     Murder    HS.Grad      Frost       Area
 4246.4200  4435.8000     1.1700    70.8786     7.3780    53.1080   104.4600 70735.8800
```

`lapply`, which belongs to the `apply` family of functions, is used to the `apply` functions on lists in R:

```
# lapply - list apply which is similar to apply, but can be also used for
other R object types
## Produces the output as a list
lapply(state[,-ncol(state)], function(x) {list(MIN=min(x), MAX=max(x),
MEAN=mean(x))})
```

The output is as follows:

```
> lapply(state[,-ncol(state)], function(x) {list(MIN=min(x), MAX=max(x), MEAN=mean(x))})
$Population
$Population$MIN
[1] 365

$Population$MAX
[1] 21198

$Population$MEAN
[1] 4246.42


$Income
$Income$MIN
[1] 3098
```

`sapply`—it provides the same functionality as `lapply` but, instead of a list output, `sapply` returns the result as a vector:

```
# sapply - simplifies the output (eg., produce a vector instead of a list)
sapply(state[,-ncol(state)], function(x) {list(MIN=min(x), MAX=max(x),
MEAN=mean(x))})
```

The output of the preceding code is as follows:

```
> sapply(state[,-ncol(state)], function(x) {list(MIN=min(x), MAX=max(x), MEAN=mean(x))})
     Population Income Illiteracy Life.Exp Murder HS.Grad Frost  Area
MIN  365        3098   0.5        67.96    1.4    37.8    0      1049
MAX  21198      6315   2.8        73.6     15.1   67.3    188    566432
MEAN 4246.42    4435.8 1.17       70.8786  7.378  53.108  104.46 70735.88
```

Aggregation functions

If, say, we were interested in finding the aggregate values of each `Region` of the US, we could use `aggregate` to find the cumulative values on a per region basis. To find the min, max, and mean of each column aggregated by `region`, we will first add the region value to our DataFrame:

```
# aggregate

state$Region <- state.region
ncol(state)
aggregate(state[,-c(9,10)], by=list(state$Region), mean, na.rm = T)
```

Following is the output:

```
> aggregate(state[,-c(9,10)], by=list(state$Region), mean, na.rm = T)
        Group.1 Population   Income Illiteracy Life.Exp    Murder  HS.Grad    Frost      Area
1     Northeast   5495.111 4570.222   1.000000 71.26444  4.722222 53.96667 132.7778  18141.00
2         South   4208.125 4011.938   1.737500 69.70625 10.581250 44.34375  64.6250  54605.12
3 North Central   4803.000 4611.083   0.700000 71.76667  5.275000 54.51667 138.8333  62652.00
4          West   2915.308 4702.615   1.023077 71.23462  7.215385 62.00000 102.1538 134463.00
```

Merging DataFrames

R also provides a built-in command, `merge`, in order to join DataFrames. Let us create a separate DataFrame with the geographic location of the center of each state (`Latitude` and `Longitude`):

```
state2 <- data.frame(State=state.name, Latitude=state.center$y,
Longitude=state.center$x)

# The syntax for merge is as follows:

## S3 method for class 'data.frame'
```

```
# merge(x, y, by = intersect(names(x), names(y)),
#       by.x = by, by.y = by, all = FALSE, all.x = all, all.y = all,
#       sort = TRUE, suffixes = c(".x",".y"),
#       incomparables = NULL, ...)

# Arguments

# x and y = the DataFrames we want to merge
# by = the column names by which we want to perform the merge

# Note that since this can be different (if say the same column had
different names in different DataFrames), we can use by.x and by.y to
specify the corresponding name of the column across the 2 DataFrames

# all = whether to keep rows that did not match in either in x or y
# Using all=T means keep all rows of both the DataFrames even if there was
no match

merged <- merge(state, state2, by="State", all=T)
merged
```

Output is as follows:

Common Key (State)
merge(state,state2,by="State",all=T)
state data.frame | **state2 data.frame**

State	Population	Income	Illiteracy	Life.Exp	Murder	HS.Grad	Frost	Area	Region	Latitude	Longitude
Alabama	3615	3624	2.1	69.05	15.1	41.3	20	50708	South	32.5901	-86.7509
Alaska	365	6315	1.5	69.31	11.3	66.7	152	566432	West	49.2500	-127.2500
Arizona	2212	4530	1.8	70.55	7.8	58.1	15	113417	West	34.2192	-111.6250
Arkansas	2110	3378	1.9	70.66	10.1	39.9	65	51945	South	34.7336	-92.2992
California	21198	5114	1.1	71.71	10.3	62.6	20	156361	West	36.5341	-119.7730
Colorado	2541	4884	0.7	72.06	6.8	63.9	166	103766	West	38.6777	-105.5130
Connecticut	3100	5348	1.1	72.48	3.1	56.0	139	4862	Northeast	41.5928	-72.3573
Delaware	579	4809	0.9	70.06	6.2	54.6	103	1982	South	38.6777	-74.9841

New rows and columns can be added using the `rbind` and `cbind` functions.

For example, if, say, we create two DataFrames using a subset of the `state` DataFrame, we can combine them as follows:

```
# Using cbind to combine 2 separate data.frame of 2 columns each
state0 <- state[,c(1:2)]
state1 <- state[,c(3:4)]

dim(state0)
dim(state1)

state01 <- cbind(state0,state1)
state01
```

```
# Population Income Illiteracy Life.Exp
# Alabama                3615   3624         2.1     69.05
# Alaska                  365   6315         1.5     69.31
# Arizona                2212   4530         1.8     70.55
# Arkansas               2110   3378         1.9     70.66

# Using rbind to combine 2 separate data.frame of 2 rows each
state0 <- state[c(1:2),]
state1 <- state[c(3:4),]

dim(state0)
dim(state1)

state01 <- rbind(state0,state1)
state01
```

Output is as follows:

```
> state01
        Population Income Illiteracy Life.Exp Murder HS.Grad Frost   Area   State Region
Alabama       3615   3624        2.1    69.05   15.1    41.3    20  50708 Alabama  South
Alaska         365   6315        1.5    69.31   11.3    66.7   152 566432  Alaska   West
```

Using tibble and dplyr for data manipulation

`tibble` is a recent development. It is essentially a more user-friendly version of DataFrames. For example, when you view `data.frame` in R, it will attempt to print as many rows as your console supports until it reaches the `max.print` value, at which point you'll get the following message:

```
getOption("max.print") -- omitted 99000 rows
```

`tibble`, on the other hand, will show only the first few rows by default and adjust the viewable columns based on your viewable area on the screen.

To use `tibble`, and other related functionalities, install the `tidyverse` package as follows:

```
install.packages("tidyverse")
library("tidyverse")
```

The output of `library("tidyverse")` is as follows:

```
> library("tidyverse")
— Attaching packages ————————————————
✔ ggplot2 2.2.1     ✔ purrr   0.2.4
✔ tibble  1.3.4     ✔ dplyr   0.7.4
✔ tidyr   0.8.0     ✔ stringr 1.3.0
✔ readr   1.1.1     ✔ forcats 0.2.0
```

Let us create `tibble` of the `state` DataFrame that we have used thus far:

```
tstate <- as_tibble(state.x77)
tstate$Region <- state.region
```

Before getting into the details of `dplyr`, it would help to get familiarized with a commonly used notation in R called `pipe`, which is represented as `%>%`. This notation has been a recent development.

Pipes allow the developer to pass the output of one function in the input of a subsequent function successively. For instance, suppose we wanted to find `Region` with the highest income from our `state` dataset.

One way to find the region with the maximum income would be to aggregate by `Region` and then find `Region` corresponding to the highest value, as follows:

```
step1 <- aggregate(tstate[,-c(9)], by=list(state$Region), mean, na.rm = T)
step1
```

The output is as follows:

```
> step1
        Group.1 Population   Income Illiteracy Life Exp    Murder  HS Grad    Frost      Area
1     Northeast   5495.111 4570.222   1.000000 71.26444  4.722222 53.96667 132.7778  18141.00
2         South   4208.125 4011.938   1.737500 69.70625 10.581250 44.34375  64.6250  54605.12
3 North Central   4803.000 4611.083   0.700000 71.76667  5.275000 54.51667 138.8333  62652.00
4          West   2915.308 4702.615   1.023077 71.23462  7.215385 62.00000 102.1538 134463.00
```

```
step2 <- step1[step1$Income==max(step1$Income),]
step2
```

```
> step2
  Group.1 Population   Income Illiteracy Life Exp   Murder HS Grad    Frost   Area
4    West   2915.308 4702.615   1.023077 71.23462 7.215385      62 102.1538 134463
```

This can, however, be greatly simplified using the `%>%` pipe operator, as follows:

```
tstate %>% group_by(Region) %>% summarise(Income = mean(Income)) %>%
filter(Income == max(Income))

# # A tibble: 1 x 2
# Region   Income
# <fctr>    <dbl>
#   1   West 4702.615
```

It is also possible to summarize all of the column values at once using `summarise_all` and find the row corresponding to the max income, as in the prior example:

```
tstate %>% group_by(Region) %>% summarise_all(funs(mean)) %>% filter(Income
== max(Income))
```

The output is as follows:

```
# A tibble: 1 x 9
  Region Population   Income Illiteracy `Life Exp`   Murder `HS Grad`    Frost   Area
  <fctr>      <dbl>    <dbl>      <dbl>      <dbl>    <dbl>     <dbl>    <dbl>  <dbl>
1   West   2915.308 4702.615   1.023077   71.23462 7.215385        62 102.1538 134463
```

Basic dplyr usage

We have already used some `dplyr` commands in the previous section and, here, we'll be looking at the standard functions. `dplyr` provides a set of useful verbs that can be used in conjunction with one another (using the pipe operator or otherwise) to produce the final result.

These verbs are set out in the following list:

- `sample_n` and `sample_frac`: To extract random values
- `summarise`: To aggregate values
- `mutate`: To add new variables
- `arrange`: To sort the dataset
- `filter`: To filter the data and extract relevant rows
- `Select`: To select columns from the dataset

Using select

The verb `select`, which is part of the `dplyr` package (installed automatically when the `tidyverse` package is installed), can be used to select and rename columns from a dataset, as follows:

```
# dplyr Verbs
# select

# Add the state name to the tstate dataset
tstate$Name   <- state.name

select(tstate, Income, Frost, Area) # selecting specific columns

# # A tibble: 50 x 3
# Income Frost   Area
# <dbl> <dbl>  <dbl>
#   1   3624    20  50708
# 2   6315   152 566432

select(tstate, Population:Illiteracy) # selecting a range of columns

# # A tibble: 50 x 3
# Population Income Illiteracy
# <dbl>  <dbl>      <dbl>
#   1       3615   3624        2.1
# 2        365   6315        1.5
# 3       2212   4530        1.8

select(tstate, -c(Population:Illiteracy)) # excluding a range of columns

# # A tibble: 50 x 7
# `Life Exp` Murder `HS Grad` Frost   Area    Region        Name
# <dbl>  <dbl>     <dbl> <dbl>  <dbl>    <fctr>       <chr>
#   1      69.05   15.1      41.3    20  50708     South     Alabama
# 2      69.31   11.3     66.7   152 566432     West     Alaska
# 3      70.55    7.8     58.1    15 113417     West    Arizona

rename(tstate, Pop=Population) # renaming specific columns and selecting
all columns

# # A tibble: 50 x 10
# Pop Income Illiteracy `Life Exp` Murder `HS Grad` Frost   Area    Region
Name
# <dbl>  <dbl>      <dbl>      <dbl>  <dbl>     <dbl> <dbl>  <dbl>
<fctr>       <chr>
#   1  3615   3624        2.1      69.05   15.1      41.3    20  50708
South     Alabama
```

```
# 2   365   6315         1.5       69.31   11.3       66.7    152 566432
West      Alaska
#
```

You can also use helper functions such as `starts_with`, `ends_with` to select only specific columns matching a criteria, as follows:

```
select(tstate, starts_with("P"))

# # A tibble: 50 x 1
# Population
# <dbl>
#   1       3615
#

select(tstate, ends_with("n"))

# # A tibble: 50 x 2
# Population    Region
# <dbl>    <fctr>
#   1       3615     South
# 2        365      West
#
```

Filtering with filter

The `filter` verb can be used to extract a subset of rows matching the filter criteria, as shown:

```
# Filter states with < 1% Illiteracy (i.e., > 99% literacy)
filter(tstate, Illiteracy < 1) # Equivalently -> filter(tstate, (100 -
Illiteracy) > 99)

# Filter states with < 1% Illiteracy and Income > the mean Income of all
states
# We will apply the AND condition using &

filter(tstate, Illiteracy < 1 & Income > mean(Income))

# This is the same as using , (comma), multiple parameters are treated as
AND

identical(filter(tstate, Illiteracy < 1 & Income >
mean(Income)),filter(tstate, Illiteracy < 1, Income > mean(Income)))
# [1] TRUE

# Filter states with Income > the mean Income of all states OR HS
```

```
Graduation Rate > 60%
# We will apply the OR condition using |

filter(tstate, Income > mean(Income) | `HS Grad` > 60)

# Filter for states in the West Region and the above condition (Income >
the mean Income of all states OR HS Graduation Rate > 60%)

filter(tstate, (Income > mean(Income) | `HS Grad` > 60) & Region=="West")

# Other related verbs include filter_all, filter_if and filter_at
# An example for each is given below

# Print names of all numeric column
filter_all(tstate, all_vars(class(.)=="numeric"))


# Filter if ALL row values > 1 using all_vars
select_if(tstate, is.numeric) %>% filter_all(all_vars(. > 1)) # When all
vars > 1

# Filter if ANY row values > 4000 using any_vars
select_if(tstate, is.numeric) %>% filter_all(any_vars(. > 4000)) # When any
vars > 4000
```

There are various other ways that `filter` can be used and more details can be found at the online resources for the same.

Using arrange for sorting

Using `arrange` method is used to sort datasets as shown as follows:

```
# Sort the dataset in descending order of Income (high to low)
arrange(tstate, desc(Income))

# Sort by Region and Illiteracy (within Region)
arrange(tstate, Region, desc(Income))

## Mutate
# The verb mutate is used to add new columns to a dataset, most commonly to
represent a calculated value

# For instance to find population on a per square mile basis:
mutate(tstate, pop_per_sq_mile = Population/Area)
```

If you want to keep only the newly created variable, use `transmute`, as shown:

```
transmute(tstate, pop_per_sq_mile = Population/Area)
# # A tibble: 50 x 1
# pop_per_sq_mile
# <dbl>
#   1     0.0712905261
# 2    0.0006443845
# 3    0.0195032491
```

Summarise

The `summarise` verb is used to obtain aggregate values, generally over a grouped variable.

The following highlights some of the common operations using `summarise`. Generally, `summarise` is preceded by a `group_by` operation, that is, the summary is performed over grouped variables, as shown:

```
# In the example below:
# 1) We sorted the DataFrame by State Name using arrange
# 2) We applied a group-by using Region, i.e., all resulting values would
be aggregated using Region
# 3) We calcuated the values for total rows using n(), the unique states
belonging to each region using n_distinct
#   the max & mean literacy using max and mean respectively
#

tstate %>% arrange(Name) %>% group_by(Region) %>%
  summarise(total_rows = n(), first_state = first(Name),
unique_states = n_distinct(Name), max_literacy = max(100-Illiteracy),
mean_literacy = mean(100-Illiteracy, na.rm=T))
```

The output is as follows:

```
# A tibble: 4 x 6
         Region total_rows first_state unique_states max_literacy mean_literacy
         <fctr>      <int>       <chr>         <int>        <dbl>         <dbl>
1     Northeast          9 Connecticut             9         99.4      99.00000
2         South         16     Alabama            16         99.1      98.26250
3 North Central         12    Illinois            12         99.5      99.30000
4          West         13      Alaska            13         99.5      98.97692
```

Sampling data

Sampling can be done with `sample_n` and `sample_frac`. Both `sample_n` and `sample_frac` allows the user to select random samples (by count or fraction respectively) from the given dataset. It is primarily a wrapper to gather random samples using `sample.int`, as shown:

```
sample_n(tstate, 10) # To select 10 random rows
```

The output of the preceding code is as follows:

```
> sample_n(tstate, 10) # To select 10 random rows
# A tibble: 10 x 10
   Population Income Illiteracy `Life Exp` Murder `HS Grad` Frost  Area        Region          Name
        <dbl>  <dbl>      <dbl>      <dbl>  <dbl>     <dbl> <dbl> <dbl>        <fctr>         <chr>
 1        637   5087        0.8      72.78    1.4      50.3   186 69273 North Central  North Dakota
 2        868   4963        1.9      73.60    6.2      61.9     0  6425          West        Hawaii
 3       3806   3545        2.8      68.76   13.2      42.2    12 44930         South     Louisiana
 4       3387   3712        1.6      70.10   10.6      38.5    95 39650         South      Kentucky
 5      18076   4903        1.4      70.55   10.9      52.7    82 47831     Northeast      New York
 6       4767   4254        0.8      70.69    9.3      48.8   108 68995 North Central      Missouri
 7       4981   4701        1.4      70.08    9.5      47.8    85 39780         South      Virginia
 8       2341   3098        2.4      68.09   12.5      41.0    50 47296         South   Mississippi
 9       1203   4022        0.6      72.90    4.5      67.3   137 82096          West          Utah
10       1799   3617        1.4      69.48    6.7      41.6   100 24070         South West Virginia
```

```
sample_frac(tstate, 0.10) # To select 10% of the rows at random, i.e.,
# 5 rows out of 50
```

The tidyr package

The last package that deserves mention here is `tidyr`. The package provides a few helpful functions to convert wide tables into long and vice versa. Consequently, it can be used effectively for creating long tables and pivoting values based on column data.

The `gather` function allows the creation of key-value pairs by flattening the columns into a key column with the corresponding measurements in a value column.

> TIP: Note that columns can be prevented from being flattened by simply passing a—sign before the name of the column

Converting wide tables into long tables

In order to keep only the `Region` and `Name` column and convert everything else into a key-value pair, run:

```
gathered <- gather(tstate, "Keys", "Values", -Region, -Name) %>%
arrange(Region) # Note that arrange has been used only for aesthetic
purposes

gathered

# # A tibble: 400 x 4
# Region           Name       Keys Values
# <fctr>          <chr>      <chr>  <dbl>
#   1 Northeast   Connecticut Population   3100
# 2 Northeast          Maine Population   1058
# 3 Northeast Massachusetts Population   5814
# 4 Northeast New Hampshire Population    812
# 5 Northeast    New Jersey Population   7333
```

Converting wide tables into long tables

The opposite of `gather()` is `spread()`, which converts a long table into a wide table by converting the values in the key column into column headers, as shown:

```
spread_df <- spread(gathered, "Keys", "Values")
spread_df # Note that this in essence restores the original look alignment
of the table

# # A tibble: 50 x 10
# Region           Name  Area Frost `HS Grad` Illiteracy Income `Life Exp`
Murder Population
# <fctr>          <chr> <dbl> <dbl>     <dbl>      <dbl>  <dbl>      <dbl>
<dbl>      <dbl>
#   1 Northeast   Connecticut  4862   139      56.0        1.1   5348
72.48    3.1       3100
# 2 Northeast          Maine 30920   161      54.7        0.7   3694
70.39    2.7       1058
# 3 Northeast Massachusetts  7826   103      58.5        1.1   4755
71.83    3.3       5814

## unite
## The unite function is used to merge two or more variables
unite(tstate, "NewColumn", "Region","Name") %>% select(NewColumn)
```

```
# # A tibble: 50 x 1
# NewColumn
# <chr>
#   1         South_Alabama
# 2           West_Alaska
# 3          West_Arizona
# 4        South_Arkansas
```

Joining tables

Finally, there are a few helpful functions to merge `tibble`. Various types of joins are supported—for example, `inner_join`, `left_join`, and `right_join`. The main difference among these is related to which rows are kept from two `tibble` in the event there is no match.

An example of `left_join` has been provided here for reference. More exhaustive treatment of these join types is available online:

```
astate <- tibble(Name=state.name, Abbr=state.abb)
astate

tstate %>% left_join(astate, by="Name")
```

The output of the preceding code is as follows:

```
# A tibble: 50 x 11
   Population Income Illiteracy `Life Exp` Murder `HS Grad` Frost   Area    Region        Name  Abbr
        <dbl>  <dbl>      <dbl>      <dbl>  <dbl>     <dbl> <dbl>  <dbl>    <fctr>       <chr> <chr>
 1       3615   3624        2.1      69.05   15.1      41.3    20  50708     South     Alabama    AL
 2        365   6315        1.5      69.31   11.3      66.7   152 566432      West      Alaska    AK
 3       2212   4530        1.8      70.55    7.8      58.1    15 113417      West     Arizona    AZ
 4       2110   3378        1.9      70.66   10.1      39.9    65  51945     South    Arkansas    AR
 5      21198   5114        1.1      71.71   10.3      62.6    20 156361      West  California    CA
 6       2541   4884        0.7      72.06    6.8      63.9   166 103766      West    Colorado    CO
 7       3100   5348        1.1      72.48    3.1      56.0   139   4862 Northeast Connecticut    CT
 8        579   4809        0.9      70.06    6.2      54.6   103   1982     South    Delaware    DE
 9       8277   4815        1.3      70.66   10.7      52.6    11  54090     South     Florida    FL
10       4931   4091        2.0      68.54   13.9      40.6    60  58073     South     Georgia    GA
# ... with 40 more rows
```

TIP: Note that the `Abbr` column has been added on the right.

dbplyr – databases and dplyr

One of the most interesting characteristics of `dplyr` is that it is possible, with `dbplyr`, to work with an external table stored in a database as if it were an R DataFrame. In other words, by defining a connection to a database, the same `dplyr` code that was developed on a DataFrame can be applied to an external table.

> **TIP:** The capabilities of `dbplyr` have been extremely popular within enterprises where the tables may be too large to store on disk. The analytics department can access and analyse data stored in databases such as AWS Redshift, Oracle, and many others using standard R code (`dplyr`).

Further information on `dbplyr` can be found on CRAN at: `https://cran.rproject.org/web/packages/dbplyr/vignettes/dbplyr.html`.

Using data.table for data manipulation

One of the most efficient packages for data mining and manipulation in R is `data.table`. Developed by Matt Dowle and Arun Srinivasan, `data.table` has consistently outperformed other contemporary R packages in general day-to-day data analysis operations.

The only caveat to using `data.table` is the fact that its behavior is slightly different from `data.frame` in terms of the syntax used for subsetting and other operations. That said, the benefits of using `data.table` greatly outweighs the slightly extra effort required to learn the package.

`data.table` can be installed using the following code:

```
install.packages("data.table")
library(data.table)
```

The general form of `data.table` operations is as follows:

```
dt[i, j, by]
```

And the following applies:

- `dt` is the name of `data.table`
- `i` is the condition or rows by which `data.table` is being subset
- `j` represents the calculations or columns to be produced
- `by` represents the group-by aggregates

We can create a new `data.table` using the `data.table` function as follows:

```
dstate <- data.table(state.x77,State=row.names(state.x77))
```

Note that the column, `state`, has been added as `data.table` do not have row names (uses row indices instead).

An interesting aspect of `data.table` is that operations can occur by reference without the need for copying the data. In base R, operations such as renaming columns may require copying the entire `data.frame`. By avoiding such steps and along with several other optimizations, `data.table` provides an immense improvement in performance over most of the other data manipulation solutions in R today.

To select the first three rows, use the following:

```
dstate[3:5]
```

To select the rows where `Income > 5000` use the following:

```
dstate[Income > 5000]
```

To select the rows where `` Income > 5000 & `HS Grad` > 60 `` use the following:

```
dstate[Income > 5000 & `HS Grad` > 60]
```

To select the columns `Population`, `Income`, `Frost`, and `State` where `Income > 5000`, use the following:

```
dstate[Income > 5000, list(Population, Income, Frost, State)]
```

Note that we can also use the `.` notation in order to return the results as `data.table`, as shown:

```
dstate[Income > 5000, .(Population, Income, Frost, State)]
```

As stated before, the j value can also be used in order to perform calculations. For example, if instead of just returning the individual values for Population, Income, and Frost we wanted to get the mean of each, we can instead use the following:

```
dstate[Income > 5000, .(Mean_Pop=mean(Population), Mean_Inc=mean(Income),
Mean_Frost=mean(Frost))]
```

The .N notation can be used in order to get counts, as follows:

```
dstate[Income > 5000, .(Count=.N, Mean_Pop=mean(Population),
Mean_Inc=mean(Income), Mean_Frost=mean(Frost))]
```

Note that this manner of making selections is different from that in data.frame where variables are quoted. In data.table, we can use the variable names as is. There is a way by which we can also refer to the columns or subset it using the data.frame [row, column] method by using with.

For example, to select the columns, Population, Income, and State where Income > 5000 using the data.frame method, we can use the following:

```
dstate[Income > 5000, c("Population","Income","State"), with=F]
```

We can also use : (colon) to select a range of columns. For instance, to select the first three rows of all of the columns from HS Grad to State, we can use the following:

```
dstate[1:3,'HS Grad':State]
```

Grouping operations

In data.table, we can perform grouping operations using the by notation. Let us first add a new column with the Region names to data.table.

Adding a column

We can do so using the := notation. This is a notation that is already available in R, but generally not used. It allows the update to happen in-place. In other words, it avoids making a copy of the dataset in order to add a new column, as shown:

```
dstate[,Region:=state.region]
dstate[1:3] # We can see that the Region column has been added
```

We can use := to add multiple columns.

For instance, to add the division and abbrevation of each state, we can use the following:

```
dstate[,c("Division","Abb"):=.(state.division, state.abb)]
dstate[1:3] # We can see that the new columns, Division and Abb have been
added
```

To find the sum of `Population` grouped by `Region`, we can use the following:

```
dstate[,.(Sum_Pop=sum(Population)),by=Region]
```

To find the sum of `Population` grouped by `Region` and `Division`, we can use the following:

```
dstate[,.(Sum_Pop=sum(Population)),by=.(Region,Division)]
```

Notice that we always use the `.` notation when performing such operations. `data.table` is in essence, a *list of lists*, that is, each column is a list. Hence, in order to group by a column, instead of using the `c()` notation (which represents vectors), we use `.` or `list()`.

If we had to perform an operation across multiple columns, we can use the inbuilt `.SD` symbol (which stands for subset of data). For instance, to find the first row corresponding to each region, we can use `.SD` with `head()` as follows:

```
dstate[,head(.SD,1), by=.(Region)]
```

We can also modify the `.SD` symbol to operate on only a fixed set of columns. For example, to find the maximum of `Population` and `Income` grouped by `Region` using `.SD`, we can use it in conjunction with `lapply()` to run the `max()` function for each column specified in `.SD` as shown:

```
dstate[,lapply(.SD,max), by=.(Region), .SDcols=c("Population","Income")]
```

To perform the same operation as shown previously and add the minimum per `Region`, we can use the following:

```
dstate[,c(lapply(.SD, max), lapply(.SD, min)), by=.(Region),
.SDcols=c("Population","Income")]
```

Ordering columns

We can order the rows by using `order()` as the `j` value in `data.table` as follows:

```
dstate[order(Region)]
```

We can order using multiple columns by just adding them to `order()` as shown:

```
dstate[order(Region, State)] # Ascending Region, Ascending State
dstate[order(Region,-State)] # Ascending Region, Descending State
 ## Joining tables using data.table
```

`data.table` includes a very useful function called `setkey()` and `setkeyv()`. There are other `set*` functions that, when used along with `:=`, modify the object by reference. It is also extremely useful when merging tables, as discussed next.

To query the table by `Region`, we can set `Region` as `key` and query by simply using the value of `Region`:

```
setkey(dstate,Region)
key(dstate) # Check if the table is keyed
# [1] "Region"

dstate[.("West")] # View all entries with Region "West"
```

We can also set multiple keys. For instance, to set both `Region` and `Division` as `key` we use the following code:

```
setkey(dstate,Region,Division)

key(dstate)
dstate[.("West","Mountain")] # View all entries with Region "West" and
Division "Mountain"
```

Notice that the keys are being passed as the `i` value in the corresponding `data.table` notation as we are subsetting the table. We can use this in conjunction with the `j` value to return only specific columns, as shown:

```
dstate[.("West","Mountain"),.(Mean=mean(Area))] # Find the Mean Area for
Region "West" and Division "Mountain"

dstate[.("West"),.(Mean=mean(Area)), by = Division] # Find the Mean Area
for Region "West" group-ed by Division

# A couple of addition arguments, mult and nomatch allows the user to
specify the behaviour if multiple matches or no matches are found

dstate[.("West","Mountain"),mult="first"]

dstate[.("West",c("Mountain","InvalidEntry")),nomatch=0L] # Skips no
matches
```

What is the advantage of searching using key by?

The primary advantage of using keys is that the sorting is based on a binary search. This means that, instead of scanning the entire column, it is possible to complete the search in log-time, which can be extremely powerful in practice. It is also very memory efficient, hence improving the overall performance of the query from a systems or resource needs standpoint.

Creating new columns in data.table

New columns can be created in `data.table` using the `:=` notation, as shown:

```
dstate[,IncomeGreaterThan5000:=Income>5000] # We will add a column
IncomeGreaterThan5000 in-place using :=

# Adding multiple columns

dstate[,c("IncomeGreaterThan5000","AreaLessThan5000"):=list(Income>5000,Are
a<5000)] # We will add a column IncomeGreaterThan5000 in-place using :=

# alternatively, we can also use `:=`

dstate[,`:=`(IncomeGreaterThan5000=Income>5000,AreaLessThan5000=Area<5000)]
# We will add a column IncomeGreaterThan5000 in-place using :=
```

Deleting a column

Columns can likewise be deleted using `:=NULL`, as follows:

```
dstate[,IncomeGreaterThan5000:=NULL]

## We can delete multiple columns as well
dstate[,c("AreaLessThan5000","Abb","Division"):=NULL]
```

Pivots on data.table

Pivot operations on `data.table` can be performed using the `melt` and `cast` functions.

The melt functionality

The `data.table::melt` function is used to convert a wide table into a long table, that is, the columns are collapsed into a key and value relationship.

If, say, we wanted to convert the dstate table into a long table consisting of a column with State, Region, Income, and Area as the values, we could use:

```
dmelted <- data.table::melt(dstate, id.vars=c("State","Region"),
measure.vars=c("Income","Area"))
dmelted
```

An easy way to remember this is that id.vars are the columns that will remain constant, in this case, State, Region, and measure.vars indicate the columns that will be collapsed as shown as follows:

```
#              State      Region variable  value
# 1:     Connecticut   Northeast   Income   5348
# 2:           Maine   Northeast   Income   3694
# 3:   Massachusetts   Northeast   Income   4755
# 4:   New Hampshire   Northeast   Income   4281
# 5:    Rhode Island   Northeast   Income   4558
# 6:         Vermont   Northeast   Income   3907
# 7:      New Jersey   Northeast   Income   5237
```

We can convert this back into a wide table, simply by using the dcast functionality, as follows:

```
data.table::dcast(dmelted, State + Region ~ variable, value.var="value")
```

Read literally, this means keeping the State and Region columns constant, un-collapsing the column named variable with values corresponding to the value column.

Reading and writing files with data.table

For reading and writing files—for example, CSV files—there is no other function as fast and efficient as fread and fwrite in R as of today. Let us first see how to read and write CSV files as shown as follows:

```
# fwrite: Writing csv files
# Check the help file for fwrite as it includes numerous options that can
be passed to the fwrite function.

?fwrite
```

The simplest way to use fwrite is to pass the name of the data.table or data.frame as the first argument followed by the name of the file you'd like to create, as follows:

```
fwrite(dstate, file="dstate.csv") # Save data.table dstate into the csv
file dstate.csv
```

```
# Note that we can change the separator using the sep argument (eg.,
sep="|)

# To read back the file, simply use fread(filename)
fread("dstate.csv")

# Similar to fwrite, the function fread can accept several other helpful
arguments as can be seen from ?fread
```

A special note on dates and/or time

Parsing date-time values in any platform can be a tedious operation, not least because of the various formats in which dates and times can be written.

The `lubridate` package makes it easy for anyone to work with dates and times in R. In addition, `data.table` also includes several helpful functions in order to work with date and time values:

```
Install.packages("lubridate")
library(lubridate)
```

We can create a sample table with dates and times as follows:

```
tdate <- data.frame(dt=(as.POSIXct("2010-03-18 19:08:10 EDT")) + 1000000 *
runif(1000,-100,100), value=sample(LETTERS,1000,T))

head(tdate)

str(tdate)
```

Note that the `dt` column is already defined as of class `POSIXct`. However, in general, when reading date times from files, they may instead get read in as strings. We'll create a separate column, called `dts`, where the column `dt` will be cast to string, as shown:

```
tdate$dts <- as.character(tdate$dt)
str(tdate)
```

The `lubridate` package provides an easy method to translate the character column into dates and times, as in the following:

```
ymd_hms(tdate$dts[1:3]) # The character values in dts are read in as
dates/times
# [1] "2012-02-25 01:15:02 UTC" "2007-03-01 15:18:32 UTC" "2011-09-19
13:34:47 UTC"
```

```
class(tdate$dts[1:5])
# [1] "character"

class(ymd_hms(tdate$dts[1:5]))
# [1] "POSIXct" "POSIXt"
```

In general, it is possible to interpret any string as a date and time using `ymd` and `hms` notations, as shown:

```
# For example:

ymd(20190420) # Change 20190420 into year 2014, month 04 and date 20
mdy(04202019)
dym(20201904)
dmy(20042020)

# We can verify whether they are equivalent using identical
identical(ymd(20190420),mdy(0420201))

identical(ymd(20190420),dym(20201904))
```

Once the data type is interpreted as date and time, we can then use other operations, such as extracting only parts of the date and time values, as shown:

```
tdate$dts[1:3]
# [1] "2012-02-25 01:15:02" "2007-03-01 15:18:32" "2011-09-19 13:34:47"

ymd_hms(tdate$dts[1:3])
# [1] "2012-02-25 01:15:02 UTC" "2007-03-01 15:18:32 UTC" "2011-09-19
13:34:47 UTC"

year(ymd_hms(tdate$dts[1:3]))
# [1] 2012 2007 2011

month(ymd_hms(tdate$dts[1:3]))
# [1] 2 3 9

day((ymd_hms(tdate$dts[1:3])))
# [1] 25  1 19

yday((ymd_hms(tdate$dts[1:3]))) #nth day of the year y
# [1]  56  60 262

wday((ymd_hms(tdate$dts[1:3]))) # Weekday
# [1] 7 5 2

wday((ymd_hms(tdate$dts[1:3])), label=T) # Weekday
# [1] Sat Thu Mon
```

```
ymd(20190420) + days(10)
# [1] "2019-04-30"

ymd(20190420) + months(2)
# [1] "2019-06-20"

ymd(20190420) + years(2)
# [1] "2021-04-20"

# Lubridate also includes functions to perform simple date/time
calculations such as,

my_birthday <- ymd("20010101")

# The standard difftime object (obtained when subtracting dates/times) can
be a bit difficult to interpret
today() - my_birthday
# Time difference of 6299 days

class(today() - my_birthday)
# [1] "difftime"
```

The `lubridate` package includes useful functions named `d*` such as `dseconds`, `ddays`, and `dhours` that make it easier to interpret `difftime` values, as shown:

```
as.duration(today() - my_birthday)
# [1] "544233600s (~17.25 years)"
```

Further details can be found at `http://r4ds.had.co.nz/dates-and-times.html`.

Note that we can also use `data.table` in order to work on date and time values. Common date and time functions in `data.table` include the following:

```
IDateTime(x, ...)

# second(x)
# minute(x)
# hour(x)
# yday(x)
# wday(x)
# mday(x)
# week(x)
# isoweek(x)
# month(x)
```

```
# quarter(x)
# year(x)
```

The feature was still experimental at the time of writing and details can be found at https://www.rdocumentation.org/packages/data.table/versions/1.10.4-2/topics/IDateTime.

Miscellaneous topics

In this section, we will look at a few other data-related topics. The following will be covered:

- Checking data quality
- Reading binary files: Excel, SAS, and other data sources
- On-disk formats
- Working with web data

Checking data quality

There are several inbuilt functions as well as packages for checking the quality of data in R. The most commonly used among them is the `summary` function in base R:

```
## Packages Used:
## psych, pastecs, dataMaid, daff

# install.packages(c("psych","pastecs","dataMaid","daff"))

state <- data.frame(state.x77)
state$State <- row.names(state)
state


summary(state)
```

The output of the preceding code is as follows:

```
> summary(state)
  Population        Income       Illiteracy       Life.Exp         Murder
 Min.   :  365   Min.   :3098   Min.   :0.500   Min.   :67.96   Min.   : 1.400
 1st Qu.: 1080   1st Qu.:3993   1st Qu.:0.625   1st Qu.:70.12   1st Qu.: 4.350
 Median : 2838   Median :4519   Median :0.950   Median :70.67   Median : 6.850
 Mean   : 4246   Mean   :4436   Mean   :1.170   Mean   :70.88   Mean   : 7.378
 3rd Qu.: 4968   3rd Qu.:4814   3rd Qu.:1.575   3rd Qu.:71.89   3rd Qu.:10.675
 Max.   :21198   Max.   :6315   Max.   :2.800   Max.   :73.60   Max.   :15.100
    HS.Grad          Frost             Area            State
 Min.   :37.80   Min.   :  0.00   Min.   :  1049   Length:50
 1st Qu.:48.05   1st Qu.: 66.25   1st Qu.: 36985   Class :character
 Median :53.25   Median :114.50   Median : 54277   Mode  :character
 Mean   :53.11   Mean   :104.46   Mean   : 70736
 3rd Qu.:59.15   3rd Qu.:139.75   3rd Qu.: 81162
 Max.   :67.30   Max.   :188.00   Max.   :566432
```

```
library(psych)
describe(state)
```

The output of the preceding code is as follows:

```
> describe(state)
           vars  n     mean       sd   median  trimmed      mad     min      max     range  skew kurtosis       se
Population    1 50  4246.42  4464.49  2838.50  3384.28  2890.33  365.00  21198.0  20833.00  1.92     3.75   631.37
Income        2 50  4435.80   614.47  4519.00  4430.07   581.18 3098.00   6315.0   3217.00  0.20     0.24    86.90
Illiteracy    3 50     1.17     0.61     0.95     1.10     0.52    0.50      2.8      2.30  0.82    -0.47     0.09
Life.Exp      4 50    70.88     1.34    70.67    70.92     1.54   67.96     73.6      5.64 -0.15    -0.67     0.19
Murder        5 50     7.38     3.69     6.85     7.30     5.19    1.40     15.1     13.70  0.13    -1.21     0.52
HS.Grad       6 50    53.11     8.08    53.25    53.34     8.60   37.80     67.3     29.50 -0.32    -0.88     1.14
Frost         7 50   104.46    51.98   114.50   106.80    53.37    0.00    188.0    188.00 -0.37    -0.94     7.35
Area          8 50 70735.88 85327.30 54277.00 56575.72 35144.29 1049.00 566432.0 565383.00  4.10    20.39 12067.10
State*        9 50      NaN       NA       NA      NaN       NA     Inf     -Inf      -Inf    NA       NA       NA
```

You can also use `describe.by` to get summary information on a per group basis, as shown:

```
describe.by(state,state$State)
```

The following is the output:

```
 Descriptive statistics by group
group: Alabama
           vars n     mean sd   median trimmed mad      min      max range skew kurtosis se
Population    1 1  3615.00 NA  3615.00  3615.00   0  3615.00  3615.00     0   NA       NA NA
Income        2 1  3624.00 NA  3624.00  3624.00   0  3624.00  3624.00     0   NA       NA NA
Illiteracy    3 1     2.10 NA     2.10     2.10   0     2.10     2.10     0   NA       NA NA
Life.Exp      4 1    69.05 NA    69.05    69.05   0    69.05    69.05     0   NA       NA NA
Murder        5 1    15.10 NA    15.10    15.10   0    15.10    15.10     0   NA       NA NA
HS.Grad       6 1    41.30 NA    41.30    41.30   0    41.30    41.30     0   NA       NA NA
Frost         7 1    20.00 NA    20.00    20.00   0    20.00    20.00     0   NA       NA NA
Area          8 1 50708.00 NA 50708.00 50708.00   0 50708.00 50708.00     0   NA       NA NA
State*        9 1      NaN NA       NA      NaN  NA      Inf     -Inf  -Inf   NA       NA NA
---------------------------------------------------------------------------------------------
group: Alaska
           vars n     mean sd   median trimmed mad      min      max range skew kurtosis se
Population    1 1   365.00 NA   365.00   365.00   0   365.00   365.00     0   NA       NA NA
Income        2 1  6315.00 NA  6315.00  6315.00   0  6315.00  6315.00     0   NA       NA NA
```

Or, for a comprehensive statistical description, you can use `stat.desc` from `pastecs`, as shown:

```
library(pastecs)
stat.desc(state)
```

The output of the preceding code is as follows:

```
> stat.desc(state)
               Population       Income Illiteracy     Life.Exp      Murder      HS.Grad        Frost         Area State
nbr.val      5.000000e+01 5.000000e+01 50.0000000 5.000000e+01  50.0000000   50.0000000   50.0000000 5.000000e+01    NA
nbr.null     0.000000e+00 0.000000e+00  0.0000000 0.000000e+00   0.0000000    0.0000000    1.0000000 0.000000e+00    NA
nbr.na       0.000000e+00 0.000000e+00  0.0000000 0.000000e+00   0.0000000    0.0000000    0.0000000 0.000000e+00    NA
min          3.650000e+02 3.098000e+03  0.5000000 6.796000e+01   1.4000000   37.8000000    0.0000000 1.049000e+03    NA
max          2.119800e+04 6.315000e+03  2.8000000 7.360000e+01  15.1000000   67.3000000  188.0000000 5.664320e+05    NA
range        2.083300e+04 3.217000e+03  2.3000000 5.640000e+00  13.7000000   29.5000000  188.0000000 5.653830e+05    NA
sum          2.123210e+05 2.217900e+05 58.5000000 3.543930e+03 368.9000000 2655.4000000 5223.0000000 3.536794e+06    NA
median       2.838500e+03 4.519000e+03  0.9500000 7.067500e+01   6.8500000   53.2500000  114.5000000 5.427700e+04    NA
mean         4.246420e+03 4.435800e+03  1.1700000 7.087860e+01   7.3780000   53.1080000  104.4600000 7.073588e+04    NA
SE.mean      6.313744e+02 8.689917e+01  0.0862010 1.898431e-01   0.5220626    1.1422600    7.3512020 1.206710e+04    NA
CI.mean.0.95 1.268794e+03 1.746304e+02  0.1732274 3.815040e-01   1.0491240    2.2954574   14.7727936 2.424975e+04    NA
var          1.993168e+07 3.775733e+05  0.3715306 1.802020e+00  13.6274653   65.2378939 2702.0085714 7.280748e+09    NA
std.dev      4.464491e+03 6.144699e+02  0.6095331 1.342394e+00   3.6915397    8.0769978   51.9808481 8.532730e+04    NA
coef.var     1.051354e+00 1.385252e-01  0.5209685 1.893934e-02   0.5003442    0.1520863    0.4976149 1.206280e+00    NA
```

Among other utilities, a more recent package, called `dataMaid`, makes is easy to capture a high-level comparison of all of the data contained in the dataset using a one-line command, as follows:

```
library(dataMaid)
makeDataReport(state)
```

The output of the preceding code is as follows:

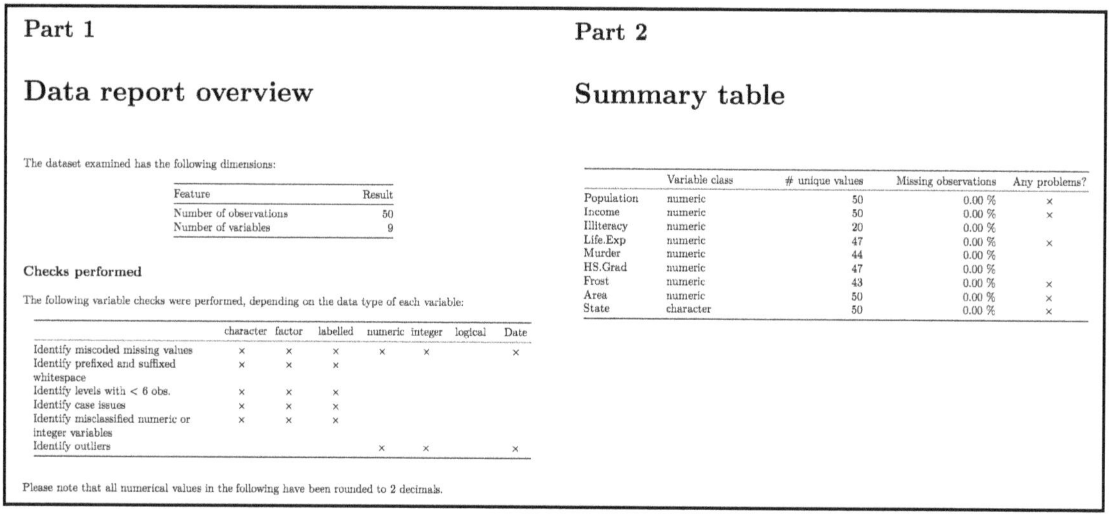

Part 1

Data report overview

The dataset examined has the following dimensions:

Feature	Result
Number of observations	50
Number of variables	9

Checks performed

The following variable checks were performed, depending on the data type of each variable:

	character	factor	labelled	numeric	integer	logical	Date
Identify miscoded missing values	×	×	×	×	×		×
Identify prefixed and suffixed whitespace	×	×	×				
Identify levels with < 6 obs.	×	×	×				
Identify case issues	×	×	×				
Identify misclassified numeric or integer variables	×	×	×				
Identify outliers				×	×		×

Please note that all numerical values in the following have been rounded to 2 decimals.

Part 2

Summary table

	Variable class	# unique values	Missing observations	Any problems?
Population	numeric	50	0.00 %	×
Income	numeric	50	0.00 %	×
Illiteracy	numeric	20	0.00 %	
Life.Exp	numeric	47	0.00 %	×
Murder	numeric	44	0.00 %	
HS.Grad	numeric	47	0.00 %	
Frost	numeric	43	0.00 %	×
Area	numeric	50	0.00 %	×
State	character	50	0.00 %	×

We often need to find differences in datasets when some information changes. This can be done on an iterative basis by inspecting individual columns and so on, but a new package called `daff` can now be used to get very nice visual renderings of the changes, in a similar fashion to how you may have seen them on sites such as GitHub and elsewhere:

```
library(daff)
state <- data.frame(state.x77)
state2 <- state
identical(state, state2)

state2$Population <- state2$Population+1
diff_data(state,state2)
```

The output of the preceding code is as follows:

```
> diff_data(state,state2)
Daff Comparison: 'state' vs. 'state2'
  First 6 and last 6 patch lines:
      @:@         A:A    B:B       C:C     D:D    E:E     F:F   G:G    H:H
1          @@  Population Income Illiteracy Life.Exp Murder HS.Grad Frost   Area
2      1:1  ->  3615->3616   3624       2.1   69.05   15.1    41.3    20  50708
3      2:2  ->    365->366   6315       1.5   69.31   11.3    66.7   152 566432
4      3:3  ->  2212->2213   4530       1.8   70.55    7.8    58.1    15 113417
5      4:4  ->  2110->2111   3378       1.9   70.66   10.1    39.9    65  51945
6      5:5  -> 21198->21199  5114       1.1   71.71   10.3    62.6    20 156361
...    ...  ...        ...    ...       ...     ...    ...     ...   ...    ...
47   45:45  ->    472->473   3907       0.6   71.64    5.5    57.1   168   9267
48   46:46  ->  4981->4982   4701       1.4   70.08    9.5    47.8    85  39780
49   47:47  ->  3559->3560   4864       0.6   71.72    4.3    63.5    32  66570
50   48:48  ->  1799->1800   3617       1.4   69.48    6.7    41.6   100  24070
51   49:49  ->  4589->4590   4468       0.7   72.48      3    54.5   149  54464
52   50:50  ->    376->377   4566       0.6   70.29    6.9    62.9   173  97203
```

```
diff_info <- diff_data(state,state2)
render_diff(diff_info)
```

The output of the preceding code is as follows:

'state' vs. 'state2'

2018-04-01 19:05:29

	#	Modified	Reordered	Deleted	Added
Rows	50	49	1	1	1
Columns	8	0	0	0	0

@:@		A:A	B:B	C:C	D:D	E:E	F:F	G:G	H:H
	@@	**Population**	**Income**	**Illiteracy**	**Life.Exp**	**Murder**	**HS.Grad**	**Frost**	**Area**
1:1	⇒	3615 → 3616	3624	2.1	69.05	15.1	41.3	20	50708
2:2	⇒	365 → 366	6315	1.5	69.31	11.3	66.7	152	566432
3:3	⇒	2212 → 2213	4530	1.8	70.55	7.8	58.1	15	113417
4:4	⇒	2110 → 2111	3378	1.9	70.66	10.1	39.9	65	51945
5:5	⇒	21198 → 21199	5114	1.1	71.71	10.3	62.6	20	156361
6:6	⇒	2541 → 2542	4884	0.7	72.06	6.8	63.9	166	103766
7:7	⇒	3100 → 3101	5348	1.1	72.48	3.1	56	139	4862
8:8	⇒	579 → 580	4809	0.9	70.06	6.2	54.6	103	1982
9:9	⇒	8277 → 8278	4815	1.3	70.66	10.7	52.6	11	54090
10:10	⇒	4931 → 4932	4091	2	68.54	13.9	40.6	60	58073
11:11	⇒	868 → 869	4963	1.9	73.6	6.2	61.9	0	6425
-:12	+++	814	4119	0.6	71.87	5.3	59.5	126	82677
13:13	⇒	11197 → 11198	5107	0.9	70.14	10.3	52.6	127	55748
14:14	⇒	5313 → 5314	4458	0.7	70.88	7.1	52.9	122	36097
15:15	⇒	2861 → 2862	4628	0.5	72.56	2.3	59	140	55941
16:16	⇒	2280 → 2281	4669	0.6	72.58	4.5	59.9	114	81787
17:17	⇒	3387 → 3388	3712	1.6	70.1	10.6	38.5	95	39650

You can also patch the data using `patch_data` and merge datasets using `merge_data`. More information can be found on the developer's website.

Reading other file formats – Excel, SAS, and other data sources

R can be used to read (and write) files in various formats other than the native RDS, `.RData`, and text files. In particular, there are mature R connectors for Excel, SAS, and various other third-party platforms.

The most commonly used package in R for reading files in other formats is `foreign`. As per its description in CRAN, the library can be used to read files in S, SPSS, Stata, SAS, Weka, and other formats.

The package, `SASxport`, is commonly used to read and write files in SAS and is quite mature.

There are also various packages for reading Microsoft Excel files such as `XLConnect`, `xlsx`, and `gdata`. Many of them rely on Java in order to process the files and installation may be slightly more complex or error-prone. A more recent package, called `readxl`, which is part of the `tidyverse` group of packages, utilizes the `libxls` library in C and `RapidXML` in C++ in order to read and write `.xls` and `.xlsx` files respectively.

Among the popular text-based formats, the `RJSON` and `jsonlite` packages can be used to read JSON.

Miscellaneous database connectors exist in R. Examples include RODBC, ODBC, ROracle, and others. As noted earlier, `dbplyr` is perhaps the most frequently used connector today due to its ability to apply `dplyr` code on data stored natively in an external database. It does so by creating a SQL expression equivalent to the R `dplyr` code.

Finally, it is also possible to store data in the raw binary format using the `readBin` and `writeBin` functions.

On-disk formats

R creates and stores data in memory. This means that, if the size of your dataset exceeds the amount of available memory, it will not be feasible to read and write the corresponding data.

There are, however, a few tools that can save and operate on data stored locally on disk using R. A few of them have been mentioned for reference:

Package	Use
`bigmemory`	Can store and manipulate massive matrices and create the `big.matrix` objects
`bigtabulate`	Used for `table`, `tapply`, and other operations on the `big.matrix` objects
`biganalytics`	Extends the big memory package and adds functionality such as large-scale k-means and other analytical functions
`biglm`	Used for generalized linear modeling on large datasets
`bigstatsr`	Used for statistical analysis of large matrices (under development at the time of writing) and available at: `https://github.com/cran/bigstatsr`
`ff`	Used for storing large datasets on disk
`SparkR`	R connector to Spark

While other connectors also exist, the preceding are some of the more common ones that you will encounter today.

Working with web data

R can directly access data stored as `.csv` files (and/or other formats) from the web. It is as simple as passing the URL to the `fread` function.

For example, the following loads data directly from the web into `flights_extra`:

```
flights_extra <- fread("http://ourairports.com/data/airports.csv")
```

There are also dedicated packages to work with web pages. One such example is `httr` as shown as follows:

```
install.packages("httr")

library(httr)

rxds <- GET("http://www.rxdatascience.com")

rxds

# View the HTTP headers
headers(rxds)

# View the content
```

```
content_rxds <- content(rxds, "text")

substr(content_rxds,1,500)

# Use parsers
str(content(rxds, "parsed"))
```

Web APIs

When you need to download more detailed information/data from sites, most often the website may have an API—it is a means to access data in a controlled manner. An API allows the user to specify simple URLs suffixed with queries to retrieve only the necessary fields/information.

Most APIs require users to sign up for an account and register a token. The token is generally application specific and each application can get its own token that will enable more granular control such as number of requests and throttling. Having an application token also prevents your applications from getting restricted as the site may not know your identity and, if there are a sufficiently high number of requests, block access to the resources.

Examples of APIs can be found at the following link: `http://ropengov.github.io/projects/`.

Examples of open data can be found at the following links: `https://dev.socrata.com/docs/endpoints.html` and `https://cran.r-project.org/web/packages/RSocrata/index.html`:

```
# Example of a Web API Call

install.packages("RSocrata")

library(RSocrata)

datasets <- ls.socrata("https://soda.demo.socrata.com")

names(datasets)

# View the datasets

data.frame(datasets$title, datasets$identifier)

# Simple download

population <-
```

```
read.socrata("https://soda.demo.socrata.com/api/views/irft-er6i")

# Using App Tokens

# ** This needs to be set up, create an account at
https://opendata.socrata.com/login **

token <- YOUR_TOKEN

population <-
read.socrata("https://soda.demo.socrata.com/api/views/irft-er6i", app_token
= token)

head(population)

# Using ID/Password

# ** This needs to be set up, create an account at
https://opendata.socrata.com/login **

email <- Sys.getenv("SOCRATA_EMAIL", "Your_Registered_Email_Address")

password <- Sys.getenv("SOCRATA_PASSWORD", "Your_Password")

privateURL <- "https://soda.demo.socrata.com/resource/a9g2-feh2.csv" #
dataset

# Uncomment the following line once you have set up your id and password

read.socrata(url = privateURL, email = email, password = password)
```

The following section highlights a very simple use case of an API along with R. The topic is vast as there are thousands, if not millions of APIs on the web.

For further reading, see `https://www.rstudio.com/resources/videos/using-web-apis-from-r/`, which discusses the Twitter API, open movie database API, and others.

Tutorial – looking at airline flight times data

This is a general tutorial aimed at finding interesting snippets of information from Flights data available in the `nycflights13` package.

The dataset contains *On-time data for all flights that departed NYC (i.e. JFK, LGA or EWR) in 2013* as per its description:

```
# First, install the package if you haven't already

install.packages("nycflights13")
library(nycflights13)
library(data,table)

flights <- data.table(nycflights13::flights)
flights

# Get descriptive information about the dataset
describe(flights)
```

The output of the preceding code is as follows:

```
> describe(flights)
               vars      n    mean      sd median trimmed     mad  min  max range  skew kurtosis   se
year              1 336776 2013.00    0.00   2013 2013.00    0.00 2013 2013     0   NaN      NaN 0.00
month             2 336776    6.55    3.41      7    6.56    4.45    1   12    11 -0.01    -1.19 0.01
day               3 336776   15.71    8.77     16   15.70   11.86    1   31    30  0.01    -1.19 0.02
dep_time          4 328521 1349.11  488.28   1401 1346.82  634.55    1 2400  2399 -0.02    -1.09 0.85
sched_dep_time    5 336776 1344.25  467.34   1359 1341.60  613.80  106 2359  2253 -0.01    -1.20 0.81
dep_delay         6 328521   12.64   40.21     -2    3.32    5.93  -43 1301  1344  4.80    43.95 0.07
arr_time          7 328063 1502.05  533.26   1535 1526.42  619.73    1 2400  2399 -0.47    -0.19 0.93
sched_arr_time    8 336776 1536.38  497.46   1556 1550.67  618.24    1 2359  2358 -0.35    -0.38 0.86
arr_delay         9 327346    6.90   44.63     -5   -1.03   20.76  -86 1272  1358  3.72    29.23 0.08
carrier*         10 336776    9.00    0.00      9    9.00    0.00    9    9     0   NaN      NaN 0.00
flight           11 336776 1971.92 1632.47   1496 1830.51 1608.62    1 8500  8499  0.66    -0.85 2.81
tailnum*         12 334264     NaN      NA     NA     NaN      NA  Inf -Inf  -Inf    NA       NA   NA
origin*          13 336776     NaN      NA     NA     NaN      NA  Inf -Inf  -Inf    NA       NA   NA
dest*            14 336776     NaN      NA     NA     NaN      NA  Inf -Inf  -Inf    NA       NA   NA
air_time         15 327346  150.69   93.69    129  140.03   75.61   20  695   675  1.07     0.86 0.16
distance         16 336776 1039.91  733.23    872  955.27  569.32   17 4983  4966  1.13     1.19 1.26
hour             17 336776   13.18    4.66     13   13.15    5.93    1   23    22  0.00    -1.21 0.01
minute           18 336776   26.23   19.30     29   25.64   23.72    0   59    59  0.09    -1.24 0.03
time_hour*       19 336776     NaN      NA     NA     NaN      NA  Inf -Inf  -Inf    NA       NA   NA
```

We can also get descriptive information on a per NYC Airport basis:

```
# There are 3 major airports in the nycflights13 dataset

flights[,c(unique(origin))]
# [1] "JFK" "EWR" "LGA"

# Using describe.by, we can get descriptive information on each of them
describe.by(flights, flights$origin)
```

The output of the preceding code is as follows:

```
 Descriptive statistics by group
group: EWR
               vars      n    mean      sd median trimmed     mad  min  max range  skew kurtosis   se
year              1 120835 2013.00    0.00   2013 2013.00    0.00 2013 2013     0   NaN      NaN 0.00
month             2 120835    6.49    3.42      6    6.49    4.45    1   12    11  0.01    -1.19 0.01
day               3 120835   15.70    8.76     16   15.68   11.86    1   31    30  0.01    -1.18 0.03
dep_time          4 117596 1336.70  487.01   1341 1331.47  618.24    1 2400  2399  0.02    -1.14 1.42
sched_dep_time    5 120835 1322.47  465.37   1330 1318.27  594.52  106 2345  2239  0.01    -1.21 1.34
dep_delay         6 117596   15.11   41.32     -1    5.51    7.41  -25 1126  1151  4.15    30.97 0.12
arr_time          7 117445 1491.88  529.05   1522 1510.27  612.31    1 2400  2399 -0.40    -0.27 1.54
sched_arr_time    8 120835 1527.98  486.89   1542 1535.15  596.01    1 2359  2358 -0.22    -0.63 1.40
arr_delay         9 117127    9.11   45.53     -4    0.83   20.76  -86 1109  1195  3.35    21.99 0.13
carrier*         10 120835    9.00    0.00      9    9.00    0.00    9    9     0   NaN      NaN 0.00
flight           11 120835 2373.51 1746.61   1637 2309.54 1879.94    1 6181  6180  0.32    -1.45 5.02
tailnum*         12 120229     NaN      NA     NA     NaN      NA  Inf -Inf  -Inf    NA       NA   NA
origin*          13 120835     NaN      NA     NA     NaN      NA  Inf -Inf  -Inf    NA       NA   NA
dest*            14 120835     NaN      NA     NA     NaN      NA  Inf -Inf  -Inf    NA       NA   NA
air_time         15 117127  153.30   93.34    130  143.20   71.16   20  695   675  1.11     1.18 0.27
distance         16 120835 1056.74  730.22    872  974.42  508.53   17 4963  4946  1.23     1.78 2.10
hour             17 120835   12.95    4.65     13   12.91    5.93    1   23    22  0.02    -1.22 0.01
minute           18 120835   27.24   18.15     29   26.89   22.24    0   59    59  0.07    -1.07 0.05
time_hour*       19 120835     NaN      NA     NA     NaN      NA  Inf -Inf  -Inf    NA       NA   NA
---------------------------------------------------------------------------------------------------
group: JFK
               vars      n    mean      sd median trimmed     mad  min  max range  skew kurtosis   se
year              1 111279 2013.00    0.00   2013 2013.00    0.00 2013 2013     0   NaN      NaN 0.00
month             2 111279    6.50    3.41      7    6.50    4.45    1   12    11  0.00    -1.18 0.01
day               3 111279   15.73    8.79     16   15.73   11.86    1   31    30  0.00    -1.19 0.03
dep_time          4 109416 1398.57  505.53   1500 1403.10  630.11    1 2400  2399 -0.17    -1.02 1.53
sched_dep_time    5 111279 1401.93  482.27   1459 1403.55  636.04  540 2359  1819 -0.11    -1.20 1.45
dep_delay         6 109416   12.11   39.04     -1    3.07    5.93  -43 1301  1344  5.45    64.43 0.12
arr_time          7 109284 1520.07  579.09   1625 1565.91  690.89    1 2400  2399 -0.66    -0.08 1.75
sched_arr_time    8 111279 1564.98  544.69   1647 1599.73  641.97    1 2359  2358 -0.64     0.00 1.63
arr_delay         9 109079    5.55   44.28     -6   -2.03   20.76  -79 1272  1351  3.99    38.99 0.13
carrier*         10 111279    9.00    0.00      9    9.00    0.00    9    9     0   NaN      NaN 0.00
flight           11 111279 1365.75 1376.74    801 1181.75 1009.65    1 5765  5764  1.05     0.10 4.13
tailnum*         12 110370     NaN      NA     NA     NaN      NA  Inf -Inf  -Inf    NA       NA   NA
origin*          13 111279     NaN      NA     NA     NaN      NA  Inf -Inf  -Inf    NA       NA   NA
dest*            14 111279     NaN      NA     NA     NaN      NA  Inf -Inf  -Inf    NA       NA   NA
air_time         15 109079  178.35  113.79    149  172.81  139.36   21  691   670  0.49    -0.75 0.34
distance         16 111279 1266.25  896.11   1069 1229.73 1138.64   94 4983  4889  0.48    -0.67 2.69
hour             17 111279   13.74    4.80     14   13.77    5.93    5   23    18 -0.11    -1.22 0.01
minute           18 111279   27.50   19.36     30   27.24   22.24    0   59    59  0.00    -1.26 0.06
time_hour*       19 111279     NaN      NA     NA     NaN      NA  Inf -Inf  -Inf    NA       NA   NA
---------------------------------------------------------------------------------------------------
group: LGA
               vars      n    mean      sd median trimmed     mad  min  max range  skew kurtosis   se
```

```
flights_extra <- fread("http://ourairports.com/data/airports.csv")
```

```
# Extract the columns name, iata_code and region for only those entries
where the IATA code exists
flights_extra2 <- flights_extra[!iata_code=="",.(dest_name=name,
dest=iata_code, region=iso_region)]
flights_extra2

setkey(flights, dest)
setkey(flights_extra2, dest)

# The table, flights does not contain the names of the destination airport.
Using the data from the flights_extra2 DataFrame, we'd like to add the
respective information to the flights data
# We can do this using the "merge" function or the in-built functionality
of data.table which lets us subset using the key columns

flights2 <- flights_extra2[flights]
flights2

# Find the maximum, minimum and average of flight timings between JFK and
any other airport, ordered by the highest AvgTime (descending)

flights3 <- flights[,.(MaxTime=max(air_time, na.rm = T),
MinTime=min(air_time, na.rm = T), AvgTime=mean(air_time, na.rm = T)),
by=c("origin", "dest")]
flights3 <- merge(flights3, flights_extra2[,.(dest, dest_name)], by =
"dest")
flights3[order(-AvgTime)]

# From this we can see that the flight with the longest average duration
(498 minutes) is between JFK/EWR and Daniel K Inouye International Airport
in Honolulu
```

```
> flights3[order(-AvgTime)]
     dest origin MaxTime MinTime   AvgTime                              dest_name
  1:  HNL    JFK     691     580 623.08772      Daniel K Inouye International Airport
  2:  HNL    EWR     695     562 612.07521      Daniel K Inouye International Airport
  3:  ANC    EWR     434     388 413.12500   Ted Stevens Anchorage International Airport
  4:  SFO    JFK     490     301 347.40363          San Francisco International Airport
  5:  SJC    JFK     396     305 346.60671 Norman Y. Mineta San Jose International Airport
 ---
225:  PHL    JFK      61      21  30.83687                                  Erase Me 19
226:  PHL    EWR      39      21  28.66667           Philadelphia International Airport
227:  PHL    EWR      39      21  28.66667                                  Erase Me 19
228:  BDL    EWR      56      20  25.46602                Bradley International Airport
229:  LGA    EWR    -Inf     Inf       NaN                            La Guardia Airport
```

Finding the average delays between all airports can be as follows:

```
flights4 <- flights[,.(MeanDelay=mean(arr_delay+dep_delay, na.rm=T)),
by=c("origin","dest")][order(-MeanDelay)]

# origin dest MeanDelay
# 1:    EWR  TYS  82.80511
# 2:    EWR  CAE  78.94681
# 3:    EWR  TUL  68.54762
# 4:    EWR  OKC  59.80000
# 5:    EWR  JAC  59.73684

# Since the flights_extra2 is keyed on "dest" airport code, we can very
easily extract the names of the airports (and join it with the respective
table) by using the tablename[key] method as follows:

setkey(flights4, dest)
flights_extra2[flights4][order(-MeanDelay)]

# > flights_extra2[flights4][order(-MeanDelay)]
#     dest_name dest region origin MeanDelay
# 1:  McGhee Tyson Airport  TYS  US-TN    EWR  82.80511
# 2:  Columbia Metropolitan Airport  CAE  US-SC    EWR  78.94681
# 3:  Tulsa International Airport  TUL  US-OK    EWR  68.54762
# 4:  Will Rogers World Airport  OKC  US-OK    EWR  59.80000


# From this, we can see that the highest average delay was between EWR
(Newark) and McGhee Tyson airport in Tennessee (82 minutes)

# To see which of the NYC Airports is the busiest, we can use:

flights[,.(total_flights=.N, total_distance_flown=sum(distance),
total_air_time=sum(air_time, na.rm = T)), by=origin]

# origin total_flights total_distance_flown total_air_time
# 1:    JFK        111279             140906931        19454136
# 2:    EWR        120835             127691515        17955572
# 3:    LGA        104662              81619161        11916902

# This shows that even though JFK has comparatively lesser flights than
EWR, it has a much higher total_distance_flown and total_air_time

# In order to check which airlines have the best overall performance, we
can perform a group-by operation using the carrier code

# Notice that mix dplyr code along with data.table as follows
```

```
flights[,.(TotalFlights = .N, AvgDelay=mean(arr_delay+dep_delay, na.rm=T)),
by=carrier][order(AvgDelay)] %>% left_join(nycflights13::airlines)

# > flights[,.(TotalFlights = .N, AvgDelay=mean(arr_delay+dep_delay,
na.rm=T)), by=carrier][order(AvgDelay)] %>%
left_join(nycflights13::airlines)

# Joining, by = "carrier"
# carrier TotalFlights  AvgDelay                      name
# 1       AS          714 -4.100141      Alaska Airlines Inc.
# 2       HA          342 -2.014620    Hawaiian Airlines Inc.
# 3       US        20536  5.874288          US Airways Inc.
# 4       AA        32729  8.933421    American Airlines Inc.
# 5       DL        48110 10.868291      Delta Air Lines Inc.
# 6       VX         5162 14.521110            Virgin America
# 7       UA        58665 15.574920     United Air Lines Inc.
```

This shows the best on-time performance is that of Alaska Airlines followed by Hawaiian, US Airways, American Airlines, and Delta. We can combine output also with `ggplot2` to make nice looking charts:

```
flights[,.(TotalFlights = .N, AvgDelay=mean(arr_delay+dep_delay, na.rm=T)),
by=carrier][order(AvgDelay)] %>% left_join(nycflights13::airlines) %>%
arrange(desc(AvgDelay)) %>% rename(Airline=name) %>%
ggplot(aes(x=reorder(Airline, -AvgDelay),y=AvgDelay, fill=Airline)) +
geom_bar(stat="identity") + geom_text(aes(label=round(AvgDelay)),
vjust=1.6, color="white", size=4) + theme(axis.text.x = element_text(angle
= 75, hjust = 1, size = 12)) + labs (title = "Average Airline Delays from
NYC", x = "Airline", y = "Average Delay (Minutes)")
```

We have explored a few different ways we can manipulate datasets using `data.table` and `dplyr`. The intention of providing these examples is primarily to familiarize the user with the ways in which the packages can be used. The best resource for learning about data.table and `dplyr` can be found on Stack Overflow (search for any `data.table` or `dplyr` question and there is usually a link to questions on Stack Overflow that might already have an answer).

Summary

In this chapter, we looked at the various ways in which `data.table` and `dplyr` can be used. We covered the basics of loading data from various data sources, performing basic subsetting, grouping, pivoting, and other operations from both the data.table and `dplyr` perspective. We saw that both packages offer a high level of versatility—`data.table` is much faster than `dplyr` and is extremely useful for large-scale datasets but it comes at the expense of learning a new syntax. `dplyr`, on the other hand, is relatively slower than `data.table` but it provides a high level of simplicity and ease of downstream analysis.

In the next chapter, we will discuss data mining techniques for both structured data that conform to a clearly defined schema and unstructured data that exists in the form of natural language text. Specific topics include pattern discovery, clustering, text retrieval, text mining, and analytics and data visualization will also be addressed.

Quiz

1. **Quiz-tion**: What is the output of the command `lapply` from the `apply` family of functions
    1. List
    2. Matrix
    3. A list and a matrix
2. **Quiz-tion:** Which of the following options best describes the functionality of `fread` in `data.table`?
    1. To load functions from a file
    2. To load a delimited file
    3. To load comma-separated (csv) files with embedded R functions

3. **Quiz-tion:** Many `data.table` functions (set functions) are applied in-place, that is, the functions modify the object without creating a duplicate copy. How can we ensure that our original `data.table` remains unchanged when applying such operations?
    1. Create a copy of the `data.table` using the `make.data.table` command
    2. Create a copy using the copy command in `data.table`
    3. This is not possible due to restrictions in `data.table`. Use `data.frame` instead

Answers:
Q1 - 1, Q2 - 2, Q3 - 2

4
KDD, Data Mining, and Text Mining

"Certainty of death. Small chance of success. What are we waiting for?"
- Gimli, son of Gloin

Aside from being a buzzword, **data mining** is the analysis step from **Knowledge Discovery in Databases** (**KDDs**), which is concerned with uncovering hidden patterns from huge unstructured datasets. The term data mining doesn't define a single method, but a broad collection of used methods. Those methods range from linear regressions and clustering techniques, all the way to visualizations, random forests, and artificial intelligence methods.

You may have already noticed, but it's not that easy to set apart what data mining is from data science. I mostly think about data mining as something that data scientists are doing to big data (another buzzword). That said, practically any benefits coming from data science can be somehow directly related to data mining. Thriving data mining applications can be seen through finances, health industry, retail, marketing, astronomy, and web industries.

Although data mining is not restricted to a single method or data type, this chapter is dedicated to text data. Mining through text is known as **text mining**. We will use a text mining framework to go through tweets to check what the R community is talking about. By doing this, we will seek insights that could lead to skill improvements.

In this chapter, we will look at the following topics:

- How to get yourself a dwarf name
- The steps in the KDD process
- R tools to retrieve text from the web
- Some nuts and bolts of using the `rtweet` package
- Analytical tools for analyzing text
- How to visualize the results

How can you get from a complex dataset to an insightful report? Data mining is used to discover and extract patterns from datasets. Adopt a dwarf nickname and grab a suitable data-pick axe because we are totally doing this—we are mining data!

Good practices of KDD and data mining

Although the practices that are about to be discussed are associated with KDD and data mining, they are not restricted to them, and I believe that the vast majority can be easily extrapolated to other contexts.

Since its origin, humankind has been taking advantage (and sometimes being misguided) from its strong pattern recognition capabilities. We humans can now gather and store far more data than our natural abilities are capable of making sense of. We also developed tools and methods to deal with this data overload. KDD is one of these tools—it's an interactive, iterative, stage-wise approach that's used to make sense out of big and unstructured databases.

Stages of KDD

KDD can be split into stages. Seven of these are named and briefed ahead. Keep in mind that a well-conducted KDD process may require these stages to be looped once in a while:

1. **Understanding**: First, you have to understand your problem. Gather prior knowledge, understand challenges, limitations, and how the problem is generally dealt with (or not). Additionally, seeking inspiration in different places is advised. It's also important to set goals from the customer's viewpoint.
2. **Data selection**: In this stage, you look up data. Gather samples for training (discovery), test, and validation. How to sample and sample sizes are key decisions at this step. A well-designed and conducted sampling process can be the difference between meaningful and unmeaningful results.
3. **Data cleaning and preprocessing**: Usually, you may investigate outliers, typos, and noises, and deal with them. Preprocessing is often required. While **Natural Language Processing** (**NLP**) will require texts to be turned into vectors before trying to model it, image and video-related problems might require you to turn frames into tensors.
4. **Data reduction and transformation**: Consists of using data reduction and transformation techniques. By using fewer (and/or better) features, we can speed things up while avoiding some traps that will culminate in unmeaningful patterns, such as overfitting.

5. **Exploratory analysis and model selection**: The exploratory analysis objectively looks for a deeper understanding of the problem. Plus, you can pre-select many models you might find useful and drive some of the exploratory analysis toward failing as many as you can; check whether the assumptions hold under the noted conditions. By the end of this stage, one or more models that are highly likely to hand useful insights are expected to be selected. Thinking of ways to combine them is a plus. Failing model selection is OK; revisit prior stages if that is the case.
6. **Data mining**: It's time to put your decisions at stake. Fit your models as best as you can, and make things scalable. Seek patterns and check consistently to see whether they are valid.
7. **Interpretation, evaluation, and delivery**: Results can look so intuitive that they request neither interpretation nor evaluation, but they always do. Score the results and ask yourself what they really mean. Failing this stage can put all of your previously done work at risk. Delivering something might be needed; it could be as simple as a figure, a report, or an entire application.

Although seven stages were listed, there is no strict rules for this. You might tag both stages 5 and 6 as data mining. Others may find that all these stages are data mining itself.

Stage-wise division makes KDD a good candidate for teamwork. These seven stages might be seen as the basic structure of KDD; each of these stages will benefit from different abilities and skills. Usually, great advantages are sourced from sharp skills in statistics, R, and SQL. Python and Linux are also useful.

To be honest, the limits across KDD, data science itself, and data mining are not fully agreed among data people in general. Data science is a much younger field when compared to some of its pioneers—statistics and programming. Nowadays, it's most common to call data mining the entire KDD process, which is well accepted as being a practical tool for data science.

There is no right or wrong. Yet, it's good to know what these terms could mean. Now that we have a broad view on KDD, it's time to check some quick tips. The ones coming next are divided into 4 bullet points and even though they are not restricted to KDD or data ming, they are very likely to improve the results coming from them. Let's check them out:

- Write down your biases and face them—writing them down will make them much clearer and consequently easier to avoid
- Keep research notes—revisiting them later might be needed as you face the same problem over and over

- Stay loyal to statistics and good practices—data dredging is the name given to the reckless, seemly random, unreasonable examination of data which rarely leads to meaningful results. On the other hand, staying loyal to statical principles and good practices never fails
- Validate extensivenly—peer review, cross-validation, and double checks are a few ways that one can be more asure about its results. Sometimes, bugs can be mistaken for discoveries.

Once we acknowlodge the theory sorounding data mining and KDD, it's time to get hands dirty with practical stuff. The first task to do with R is to get ourselves a dwarf name. Dwarves are well-known for their mining abilities and so may you after you are done with this chapter.

Scraping a dwarf name

As silly as it is, I am not moving forward until I have a dwarf name of my own. I am not positive about getting this one directly from the web browser, either. We can do this using the R console alone. This section shows how. The first thing to do is find a website that will generate dwarf names for us. I picked the following one (`http://www.rdinn.com/generators/1/dwarven_name_generator.php?`):

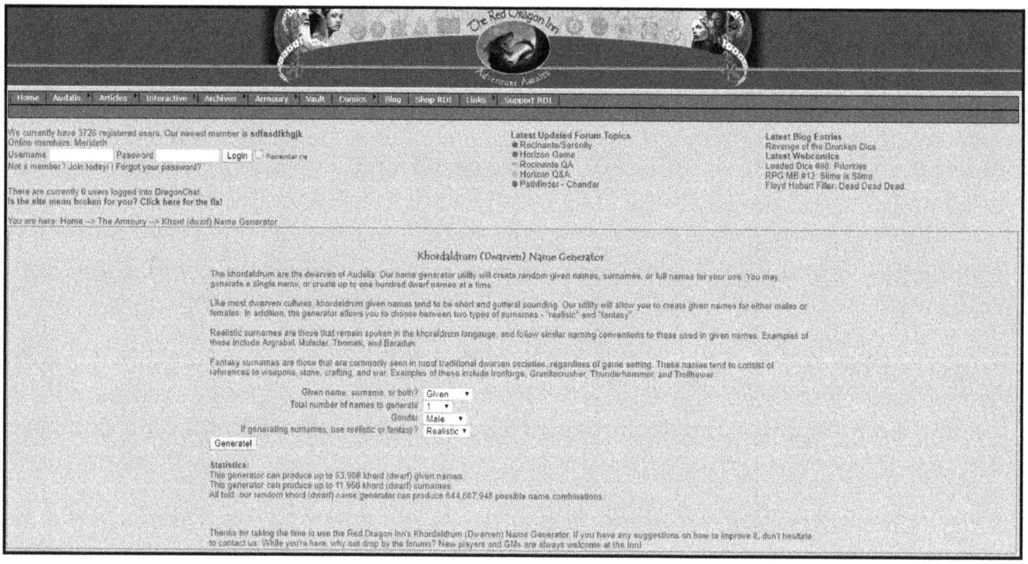

Figure 4.1: The Red Dragon Inn's dwarven name generator

The Red Dragon Inn will generate dwarf names, given four parameters:

- Name, surname, or both
- Total number of names to generate
- Gender
- Realistic or fantasy

Web pages usually communicate with users through a well-known protocol (HTTP). All we have to do is to open browser developer tools while requesting a name, so we can understand what kind of request is done and how. For Windows users, developer tools for Chrome can be accessed by pressing *Ctrl* + *Shift* + *I*. I asked for both names, only one male fantasy name with my developer tools wide open. Here is what I got:

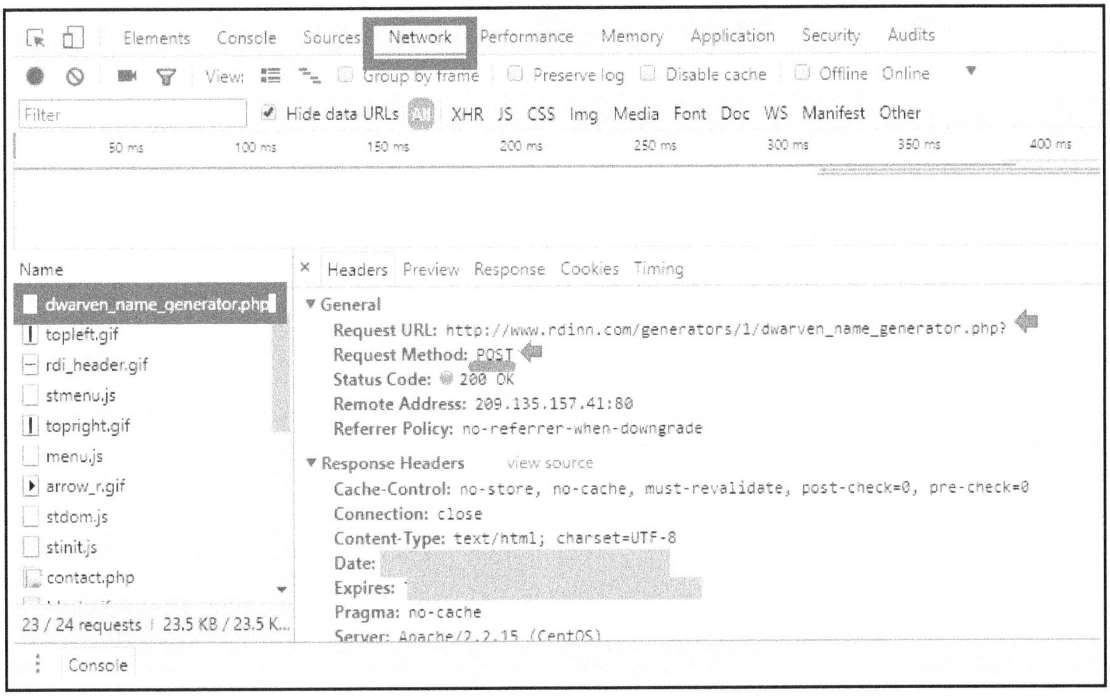

Figure 4.2: POST request

The first thing to seek is the request that will lead us to the dwarf name. There, we can check the **Request URL** and **Request Method** (`POST`). The `POST` method will send some information to the server, and we can get that if we scroll down the headers:

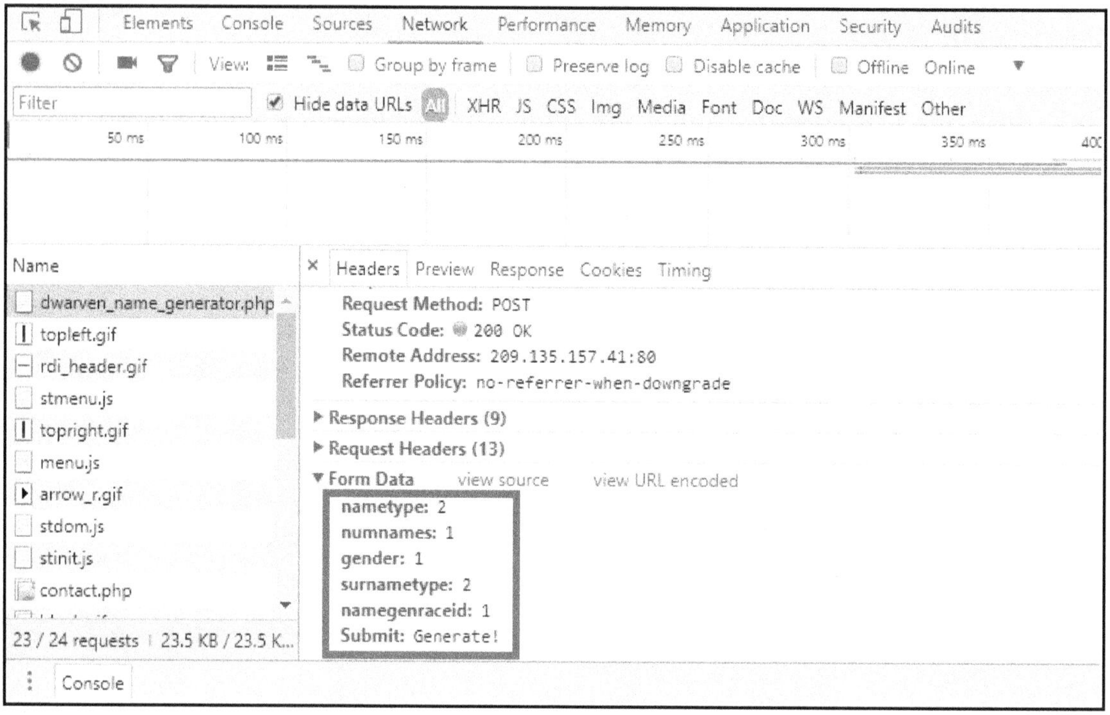

Figure 4.3: Form data

As you may have already imagined, this information tells the server what kind (and how many) names do we want. We can do a very similar `POST` request through R, just like the following code is doing:

```
if(!require(httr)){install.packages('httr')}
library(httr)

form_dt <- list(
  nametype = 2,
  numnames = 1,
  gender = 1, # replace with 2 for girls name
  surnametype = 2,
  namegenraceid = 1
)
```

```
url <- 'http://www.rdinn.com/generators/1/dwarven_name_generator.php'
post <- POST(url, body = form_dt, verbose())
page <- content(post, as = 'text')
```

Now, I ended up with a very long string called `page`. If you could find patterns between the generated name, we could easily extract it using the `substr()` function. The following code is using these patterns to extract the dwarf name from this very long string:

```
pattern_1 <- '<td width=\"25%\">'
pattern_2 <- '</td><td> </td><td> </td><td> '

dwarven_name <- substr(page,
                       start = regexpr(pattern_1,page) + nchar(pattern_1),
                       stop = regexpr(pattern_2, page) - 1)
dwarven_name
# I got:
# [1] "Thorru Steelmaul"
```

That is my new data miner name, `Thorru Steelmaul`—don't you dare create a Tibia character named `Thorru Steelmaul`. Here is what all this code has done. First, we make sure to have the `httr` package installed and ready for action using an `if...else` statement. After we loaded the package using `library()`, a list named `form_dt` was created carrying all that we looked for in a dwarf name (as I correctly guessed, the `Submit` variable displayed by Chrome's developer tools was kind of useless).

Using the `httr::POST()` function, we were able to make a `POST` request to the website. The result was stored in a variable named `post`. Later, this variable was called to extract the content from this request—the function to do it was `httr::content()`. Notice that we asked for a text output with the `as = 'text'` argument. We basically got a string with the HTML code from the page given as a response to the `POST` request.

Next, I looked for patterns around the outputted name—it's easier to do this inside developer tools (**Response** tab). The `substr()` function took care of extracting a substring from our huge string, `page`. To properly do this, we had to input the function with the big string, the character position to start the subsetting, and the character position to stop it.

Here lies a little trick. After I found the pattern code surrounding the dwarf name, I used the `regexpr()` function to return the position from this patterns. The `start` pattern was summed with the number of characters, so that it would not include the `start` pattern itself. The `stop` pattern was subtracted by one, and this way the pattern itself is not included.

> **TIP**
> You can try `source(url('http://bit.do/dwarven_name'))` and then `dwarven_name(gender = 1)` if you want a boy's name or `dwarven_name(gender = 2)` if you seek a girl's name. Let me stress that these numbers make reference to an evolution scale. Women are way more evolved than men (two times more evolved at least). Also, as cool as it sounds to name your kids using this function, please don't.

This section was absolutely necessary. It was painful to write, but totally worth it. A bunch of sailors will tell you that it is bad luck to do data mining without a proper dwarf name. From now on, you can call me `Thorru Steelmaul`—sounds badass. Jokes aside, this section introduced the `httr` package, which can be used to retrieve text from the web. Retrieving text from the web is essential to social media text mining, and it's also useful to practice and other kinds of text mining because you can get a lot of data from it. The next section is dealing with it.

Retrieving text from the web

There are numerous ways to retrieve text from the web. The previous section used the **Hypertext Transfer Protocol** (**HTTP**) through the `httr` package to retrieve text from the web. A combination of `substr()` and `regexpr()` was then used to extract only a small piece of information from it.

This section will show you how to retrieve text from the web using two different packages:

- `rvest`: This can easily perform common web scrapping tasks
- `rtweet`: It works with Twitter's web API to gather data

There are numerous ways to use data gathered this way. To name a few, it could be used to develop stock trading, marketing strategies, train chatbots, run sentiment analysis, seeks candidates for a job, or phrase click baits. Our final goal in this chapter will be to check which packages are most tweeted by the R community. Before going any further, there is a very important point to go through: law.

Legality of web scraping

The reason I wanted to talk about the law is that some people, especially beginners, fail to take it into account whenever practicing web crawling and/or scraping. Failing to recognize legal from illegal is very dangerous. Think about it. Becoming an outlaw is not something people are willing to do.

It's impossible to tell whether scrapping is legal or illegal; these things are always changing from time to time and from country to country. Generally, web scraping is not illegal; what you do with that could be. Take time to do some research on your own. Consider not just the kinds of data you are going to retrieve, but also what you're going to do with it. Seeking specialized advice is always the best solution.

Records exist of people being prosecuted or investigated by doing web scraping. Aaron Swartz was. Even if you don't have evil intentions—it's very hard to say that Aaron Swartz did—you should always be careful about what you are doing, especially if it's something disruptive.

Ethics are very important, too. Crafting a neural network that's capable of generating click bait is OK if you only want to practice or learn, but you shouldn't do it if your intention is to put those click baits to use. Moving ahead, it's time to check the gorgeous `rvest`.

Web scraping made easy with rvest

By now, I hope you do agree on the importance of understanding something about HTML and HTTP. Now, it's time to trust a query language of greater importance on text mining, **XPath**. Imagine that you have to navigate through a web page. Looking at the page, you can easily locate the content you are aiming for. How do you tell the computer to look at this same content?

XPath will help you to find and retrieve only some specific content that you are targeting at a web page. Let's say that you want to know all the packages available at CRAN, but calling `available.packages()` is too easy for you. You want to scrape this content directly from CRAN's web page using `rvest`.

Follow to the CRAN web page right into the packages list (`https://cran.r-project.org/web/packages/available_packages_by_name.html`). Navigate it with your browser. You may find something similar to the following screenshot:

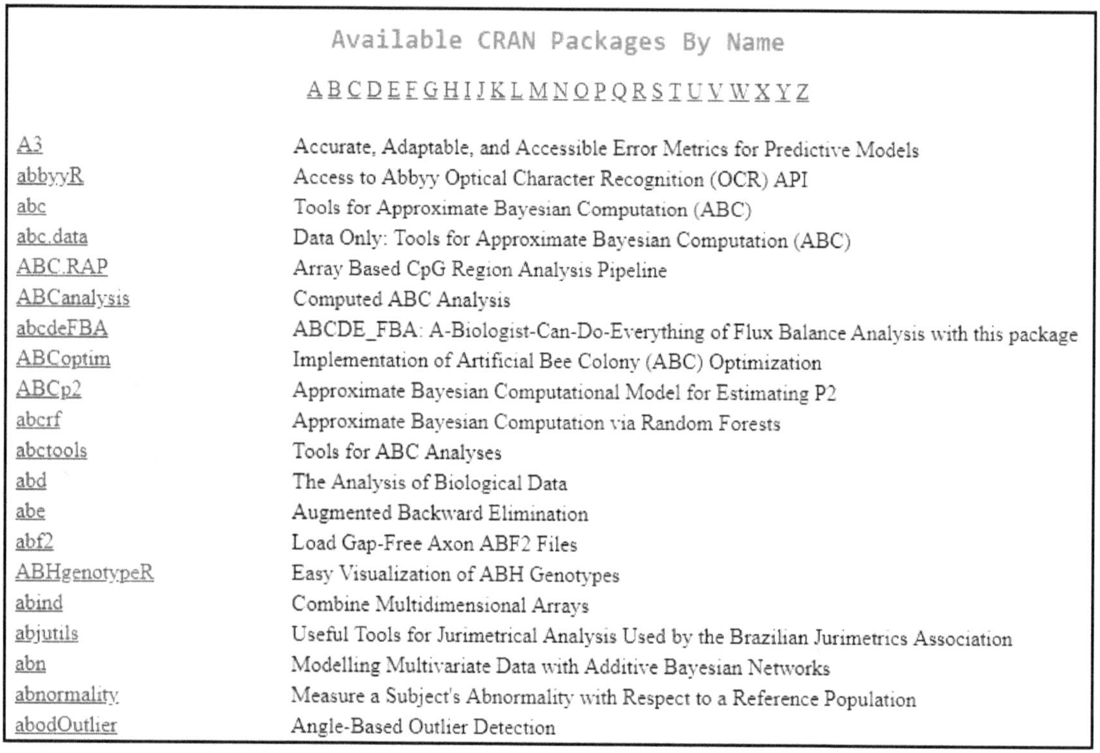
Available CRAN Packages By Name

A B C D E F G H I J K L M N O P Q R S T U V W X Y Z

A3	Accurate, Adaptable, and Accessible Error Metrics for Predictive Models
abbyyR	Access to Abbyy Optical Character Recognition (OCR) API
abc	Tools for Approximate Bayesian Computation (ABC)
abc.data	Data Only: Tools for Approximate Bayesian Computation (ABC)
ABC.RAP	Array Based CpG Region Analysis Pipeline
ABCanalysis	Computed ABC Analysis
abcdeFBA	ABCDE_FBA: A-Biologist-Can-Do-Everything of Flux Balance Analysis with this package
ABCoptim	Implementation of Artificial Bee Colony (ABC) Optimization
ABCp2	Approximate Bayesian Computational Model for Estimating P2
abcrf	Approximate Bayesian Computation via Random Forests
abctools	Tools for ABC Analyses
abd	The Analysis of Biological Data
abe	Augmented Backward Elimination
abf2	Load Gap-Free Axon ABF2 Files
ABHgenotypeR	Easy Visualization of ABH Genotypes
abind	Combine Multidimensional Arrays
abjutils	Useful Tools for Jurimetrical Analysis Used by the Brazilian Jurimetrics Association
abn	Modelling Multivariate Data with Additive Bayesian Networks
abnormality	Measure a Subject's Abnormality with Respect to a Reference Population
abodOutlier	Angle-Based Outlier Detection

Figure 4.4: CRAN web page

Using Chrome's developer tools, we can get the address that covers the content we wish for. Open the developer tools (*Ctrl* + *Shift* + *I* for Windows's users) and follow these steps:

1. Click the **Select an element in the page to inspect** icon (or press *Ctrl* + *Shift* + *C* for Windows and Ubuntu users).
2. Hover the mouse over the area with the content you want. Once the desirable content gets highlighted, just left-click it.
3. A line at the **Elements** tab will be highlighted; right-click it.
4. Select **Copy**.
5. Select **Copy XPath**.
6. Here we have got `/html/body/table`. Although this seems like a lot of steps, all of them are very simple. They are illustrated in the following screenshot:

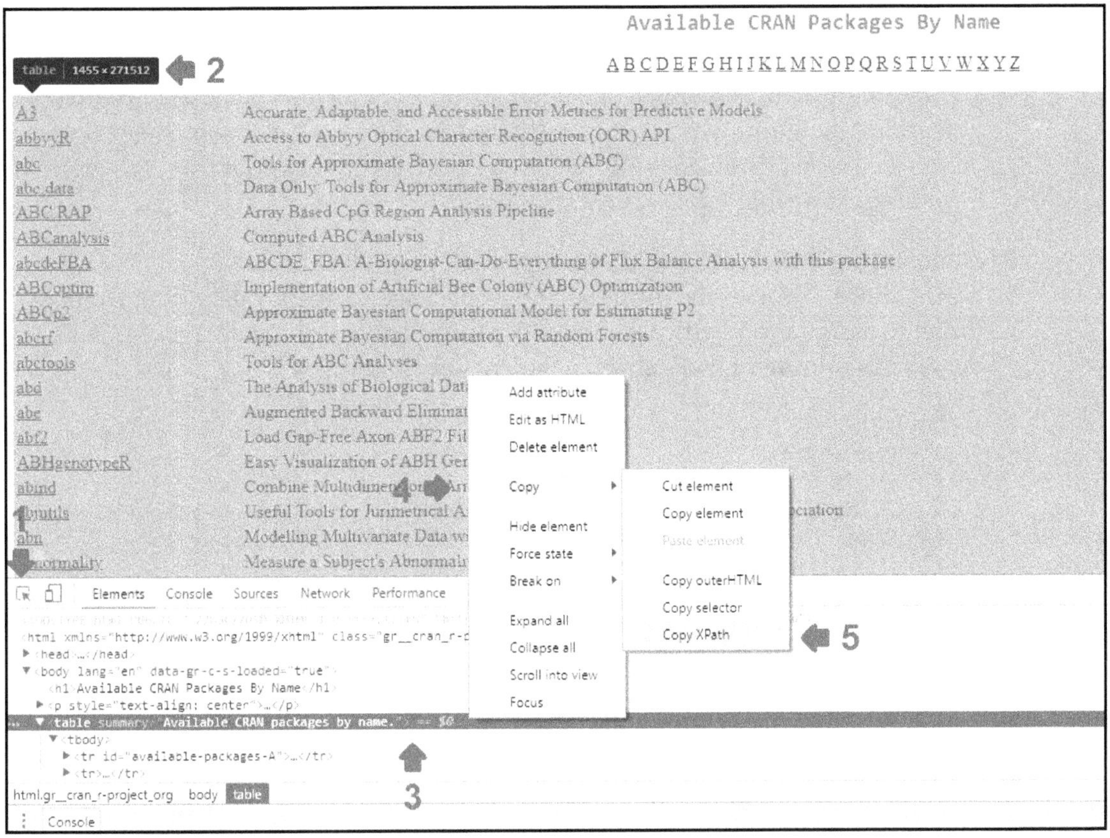

Figure 4.5: Getting the XPath

7. With `xpath` at hand, we can draw some R code, just like this:

```
if(!require(rvest)){install.packages('rvest')}
library(rvest)

url <-
'https://cran.r-project.org/web/packages/available_packages_by_name
.html'
xpath <- '/html/body/table//a'
dt <- read_html(url) %>%
  html_nodes(xpath = xpath)
```

The preceding code will look for the `rvest` package and try to install it in case it's missing. Following this, we store the web page address (`url`) and the XPath (`xpath`) as strings. The latter string is a little bit tricky. The XPath I originally found was `/html/body/table/tbody/a`. For some reason, `rvest` won't deal well with the `tbody` part, so I removed it from the original string, and what I got was `/html/body/table//a`.

8. After storing both URL and XPath, pipe the `read_html()` and `html_nodes()` functions from the `rvest` package to get our data (`dt`). Do not forget to assign the XPath string into its proper argument inside `html_noces()`, the `xpath` argument. Let's check what we got from this:

```
head(dt)
# {xml_nodeset (6)}
# [1] <a href="../../web/packages/A3/index.html">A3</a>
# [2] <a href="../../web/packages/abbyyR/index.html">abbyyR</a>
# [3] <a href="../../web/packages/abc/index.html">abc</a>
# [4] <a href="../../web/packages/abc.data/index.html">abc.data</a>
# [5] <a href="../../web/packages/ABC.RAP/index.html">ABC.RAP</a>
# [6] <a
href="../../web/packages/ABCanalysis/index.html">ABCanalysis</a>
```

As we can see, package names are in between the <a href="..."..> </a> command.

9. This is a way to set hyperlinks using HTML. To erase these unintended texts, we can use regex reference at the `gsub()` function:

```
dt <- dt %>%
  gsub(pattern = '<(.[^>]*)>',
       replacement = '')
```

Using regular expressions, we could use `gsub()` to cut off all the text that fitted inside <>.

A pretty useful cheat sheet for regular expressions in R can be found in the RStudio page (`https://www.rstudio.com/wp-content/uploads/2016/09/RegExCheatsheet.pdf`). Simply Google `regex r cheat sheet` if this link isn't useful.

10. If you examine the `dt` object again, we will see that only package names remain:

```
head(dt)
# [1] "A3" "abbyyR" "abc" "abc.data" "ABC.RAP" "ABCanalysis"
```

11. We could then compare that packages that we got by web scraping with the list that R gives using the `setdiff()` function:

```
r_list <- available.packages()[,'Package']
setdiff(r_list,dt)
setdiff(dt,r_list)
```

    The first line is storing all the packages' names coming from the `available.packages()` function into an object called `r_list`, a list of packages given by R. The following lines are respectively returning the packages that are into `r_list` but not in `dt`, and the packages that are in `dt` but not into `r_list`.

If you care enough to install a package from `r_list` that is missing in `dt`, everything will go fine. That's because R will get it from another repository rather than CRAN. On the other hand, if you try to install a package returned by `setdiff(dt,r_list)`, it will not work. These packages are from older versions of R and might not be available for the current one.

This section was meant to give a quick overview of the general way text can be retrieved from the web using the `rvest` package. Along the way, XPath and alternative ways to manipulate strings were introduced. Next, we will see how to retrieve text from Twitter using R.

Retrieving tweets from R community

Twitter has a web API that can be used to retrieve text (tweets) from it. A package named `rtweet` provides an interface to use it. Once we get used to it, it is very easy to scrape tweets. In this section, we are going to use `rtweet` to check what packages the R community tweet about, specifically which packages they talk about that most so that we can see whether we know about them. Make sure that `rtweet` is properly installed with the following code line:

```
if(!require(rtweet)){install.packages('rtweet')}
```

Using the `rtweet` package, along with some others that might aid us in the data cleaning process, we will count how many times R packages were mentioned using the `rstats` hashtag over 15,000 tweets. Besides internet connection, the proper use of `rtweet` also demands an authorization token and consequently a Twitter account. Most of the code will be reproducible at some level, but you need to set a token and an application for yourself.

Creating your Twitter application

While logged in to your Twitter account, the first thing to do is create a specific application to get the authorization token. Follow these steps to get it done:

1. Go to `https://apps.twitter.com` and create an application.
2. Provide a name (mine is `Thorru Steelmaul`), a website (it could be your blog or Twitter, mine is `http://arcadedata.org`), and a description.
3. Set the callback URL as `http://127.0.0.1:1410`.
4. Check whether you agree with the developer's policy and hit the **Create** button.
5. All the information you need to set up an authorization token will be lying in the **Keys and Access Tokens** tab, right under the big bold application's name. The following screenshot shows you where to look for it:

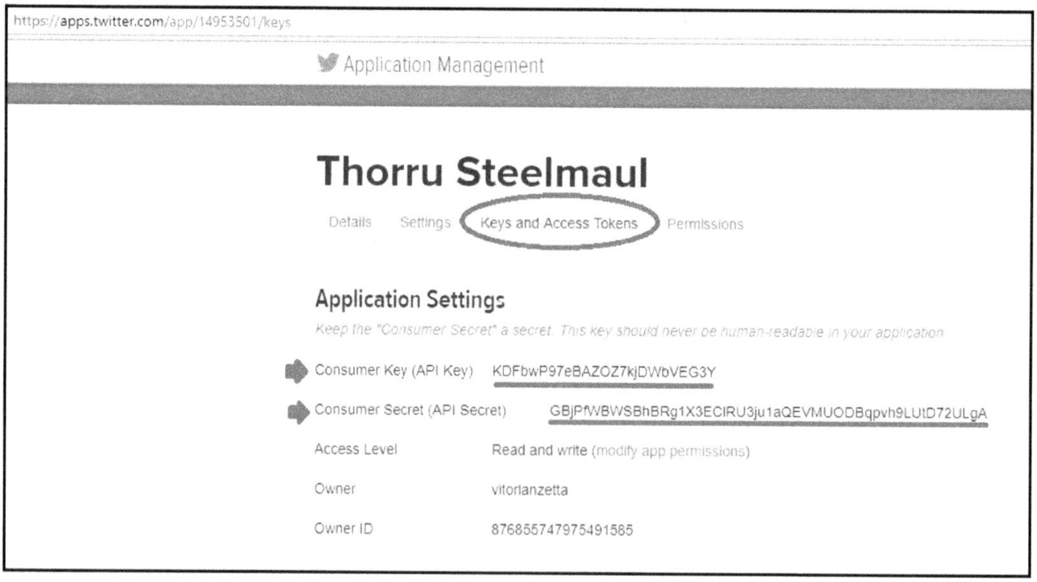

Figure 4.6: API Key and API Secret

Let me stress that my key and secret won't work for you because I changed it already.

6. For you to set the authorization token at your end, you need to call the `create_token()` function from the `rtweet` package using all of this information (app name, **API Key**, and **API Secret**). Notice that you will need to modify some of the code coming next to set the token for you:

```
library(rtweet)

my_token <- create_token(
  app = '*YOUR* APP NAME',
  consumer_key = '*YOUR* API Key',
  consumer_secret = '*YOUR* API Secret')
```

8. After properly running this code, a browser window should pop up, asking you to authorize the application. Then, as soon as you authorize, the following message will appear on that same window: **Authentication complete. Please close this page and return to R**.
9. With a token, we are ready to use `rtweet` package to interact with the API. The API is kind of tricky. You will notice that whenever you're querying for tweets, what you get is not always exactly what you asked for. The usual reasons for this to happen would go more or less like this:
    - There are not many tweets about what you are querying
    - A few extra tweets are returned because the interface will pull the max number of tweets per request, which is 100
    - The search API of Twitter does not index everything, only texts from the past six to nine days are returned
    - The API rate limits of 18,000 tweets won't allow you to dig more until it resets—it takes 15 minutes

Regarding point number two, the package is trying to avoid waste. It is doing the lowest number of requests (pulling the most of each per request) to get at least what you wanted—if there are that many tweets out there. For point number three, there is not much we are able to do. Building a web crawler may do it, but I am not at all positive about whether this would put you in trouble. Point number four has some turnarounds, but they are time-consuming.

Fetching the number of tweets

Depending on how many tweets you wish for, it could take many days and hours to get it. The query we are about to conduct may take only a few minutes. Using the `beepr` package, it's possible to trigger an alarm once the query is complete:

```
if(!require(beepr)){install.packages('beepr')}
library(beepr)
```

Given point number three, you might not be able to reproduce the results that I got myself. Yet, I encourage you to try the codes and compare the results; that's a great way to get some practice. Let's get started with `search_tweets2()`:

```
tweets_dt <- search_tweets2(q = '#rstats',
                            n = 20000,
                            include_rts = T,
                            tweet_mode = 'extended',
                            retryonratelimit = T,
                            token = my_token)

for(i in 0:2){beep(5); Sys.sleep(3)}
```

The previous code will collect tweets that have `#rstats` (`q` parameter) by using `search_tweets2()` and will store those in a DataFrame named `tweets_dt`. There is also a function called `search_tweets()`, the first of its kind. The former shows a small advantage by enabling you to directly pass arguments to the API; the `text_mode` argument can be found inside the API's documentation.

The default `tweet_mode` is `extended` and won't change our outcome. Yet, this is a way to introduce how parameters from the API can be inputted into `search_tweets2()`.

The code asked for 20,000 tweets, but I ended up with only 15,999; that is explained by point number three. Arguments `include_rts = T` and `retryonratelimit = T` are respectively asking `search_tweets2()` to also query retweets and also to continue after 15 minutes if the rate limit is reached. The last line will trigger an alarm that will repeat three times in a row, with a 3 seconds interval between each `beep`.

TIP

Setting an alarm with `beepr::beep()` is great to get you time to do other stuff while waiting for some time-consuming code to run. There are plenty of options for sounds; my favorite is `beep(5)`, which plays the treasure sound from Zelda's game.

Our recently created DataFrame with Twitter data (`tweets_dt`) has `42` variables. You can check how many observations and variables you got using the following code:

```
dim(tweets_dt)
# [1] 15999 42
names(tweets_dt)
```

The last line outputs all of the variables' names. We used the `search_tweets2()` function given by `rtweet` to collect information about tweets related to `#rstats`. There are a bunch of other functions that are often called to collect Twitter data:

- `get_timeline()`: Used to get the user's timeline
- `stream_tweets()`: Collects a live stream of Twitter data
- `post_tweet()`: Post tweets from your console
- `save_as_csv()`: Easily saves Twitter data that's created by `rtweet`
- `read_twitter_csv()`: Easily reads Twitter data, saved as a `.csv`

For the whole documentation, follow `https://cran.r-project.org/web/packages/rtweet/rtweet.pdf`. I put a similar CSV file out on the internet. If you want to get the exactly same results that I am getting, try this: `tweets_dt <- read_twitter_csv(url('http://bit.do/rstats4life'))`. Don't forget to load the `rtweet` package.

So far, we briefly discussed what KDD and data mining could mean. We also learned about some ways to retrieve text from the web using three different packages: `httr`, `rvest`, and `rtweet`. Now, it's time to move further, clean the data, and transform it in an insightful way.

Cleaning and transforming data

In `Chapter 3`, *Data Wrangling with R,* we approached the topic of data cleaning (**munging**). Data cleaning is so important that the majority of data scientists spend most of their work time cleaning and preparing data. The last session, *What is the R community tweeting about?,* gave us a DataFrame with `15999` rows and `42` columns. That is raw data. This session will clean and transform it.

Our initial goal was to check which packages the R community is talking about on Twitter. There are three variables we will use to achieve the final goal.

The variable `text` can be truncated when there is a retweet. When that is the case, check `retweet_text`, which won't be truncated. The `quoted_text` variable also brings useful information. To unite all the useful information into a single object, we can use the following code:

```
quotes <- tweets_dt$is_quote
rts <- tweets_dt$is_retweet

dt <- c(tweets_dt$quoted_text[quotes],
        tweets_dt$retweet_text[rts],
        tweets_dt$text[!rts])
```

The objects `quotes` and `rts` are storing `FALSE` and `TRUE`. The former will tell you whether the tweet is a quote, while the latter will signal a retweet. Next, the code block is creating the `dt` object, which holds all of the non-truncated text retrieved by `search_tweets2()` that might contain package names.

If you bother to run `class(dt)`, you will notice that `dt` is, in fact, a character. We need to unnest the words from the strings. Use `tidytext` for this task. This package won't work well with a vector of characters. A DataFrame is a more suitable object. Conversion can be made as follows:

```
dt <- data.frame(tweets = dt,
                 stringsAsFactors = F)
```

Now, `dt` is a DataFrame with a single column named `tweets`. Do not fail to set `stringAsFactors = F`, which will avoid the strings being interpreted as factors.

TIP

Strings accidentally being converted to factors is a major cause of errors in R for both newbies and experienced users as well. Users hardly notice when a variable is unintentionally converted to a factor—functions such as `data.frame()` and `read.csv()` will interpret strings as factors by default. On the other hand, the conscious use of factors is very useful.

To finally get that data cleaned, let's combine the methods from the `dplyr` and `tidytext` packages. Make sure you have both installed and loaded:

```
if(!require(dplyr)){install.packages('dplyr')}
if(!require(tidytext)){install.packages('tidytext')}
library(dplyr); library(tidytext)
```

The following code will clean and transform the data:

```
pkgs <- row.names(available.packages())

clean_dt <- dt %>%
  unnest_tokens(word, tweets,
                to_lower = F) %>%
  filter(word %in% pkgs) %>%
  count(word, sort = T)
```

After saving all of the available packages into a single object named `pkgs`, several functions are chained through pipes (`%>%`) to clean and transform `dt` into a format that will later be helpful to the analysis I am thinking about. Functions from `dplyr` and `tidytext` were used to clean and transform the dataset. The following bullets are meant to explain how the latter code block worked out:

- `dt` was piped to `unnest_tokens()` from `tidytext`—the object piped (`dt`) through `tidytext::unnest_tokens()`, which is a DataFrame derived subsets of `tweets_dt` (a tibble). Once we make sure that our strings were not taken as factors, `unnest_tokens()` can receive them and split words. We only had to tell the function how to name the column that will receive the words (`word`) and where to find the texts (`tweets` column). The `to_lower = F` argument is also of great importance given that packages in R are case sensitive.
- The outcome from `unnest_tokens()` is then piped through the `dplyr` packages' `filter()`; this function is filtering the unnested words. Only packages names (`pkgs`) are being kept.
- The filtered data is now counted by `dplyr` packages' `count()`—the pipes made sure to carry the filtered, unnested data to `count()`. Argument `sort = T` is asking the outcome to be sorted; that is, the packages' names are listed from the ones that most popped up, to the ones that less appeared.

We can check the top 10 cited packages with the following code:

```
> head(clean_dt, 10)
# A tibble: 10 x 2
#   word n
#   <chr> <int>
# 1 ggplot2 481
# 2 here 479
# 3 not 477
# 4 available 384
# 5 useful 364
# 6 maps 363
# 7 tutorial 351
```

```
# 8 files 322
# 9 tidyverse 316
#10 dplyr 296
```

Although `here`, `not`, `available`, and `useful` are real packages that are available for my current version of R, I am not sure that people using these words were talking about the packages—at least not every single time. There are several ways we could address those. Doing nothing is always an option. Another one would be to apply a discount rate on packages that are named after pretty common words or arbitrarily subtracting theses common words.

> **TIP**
> Package `here` constructs paths to projects' files. The not from the `not` package stands for **Narrowest-Over-Threshold** (**NOT**) change-point detection.

Each alternative comes with pros and cons—choose wisely. I am going for the third option:

```
clean_dt <- clean_dt[-(2:8),]
head(clean_dt, 10)
# A tibble: 10 x 2
#   word n
#   <chr> <int>
# 1 ggplot2 481
# 2 tidyverse 316
# 3 dplyr 296
# 4 population 242
# 5 shiny 221
# 6 ggfortify 192
# 7 purrr 191
# 8 fun 165
# 9 blogdown 146
#10 tables 137
```

This result sounds more reasonable. I am not sure about `fun` and `tables` being cited as packages every single time either, but I am keeping them. Let me stress that the process that I used could be called everything but rigorous. The only benefit that I got from this was not overextending myself while getting a result that sounds OK.

There are several things that would account for a more careful and rigorous way to deal with this problem. Here is one brief example:

1. Collect tweets from the hashtag `#PyData`.
2. Throw away tweets that also comes with `#RStats`.

3. Clean the dataset filtering by a dictionary (`rcorpora` maybe) and then filter based on package names. Only packages named after common words might appear.
4. Count how many times those words appeared.
5. Check the proportion of these words and compare them to what you got.

I am sure you can do this. It would be a great way to exercise your R coding skills. We have now finished cleaning data. Let's move on and do some analysis.

Looking for patterns – peeking, visualizing, and clustering data

This is the analysis step. Some people would refer it as the actual data mining, or, in this case, text mining. For other people, we have been doing text mining for a long time now. Terminology aside, we have a clean and transformed dataset (`clean_dt`) that very much speaks for itself.

The features displayed by the tibble might be useful for some people already. It is for me, as I can drive my studies and seek some more R adventures. Yet, the analysis could be deepened with no troubles; data mining is never about getting enough knowledge, but about maximizing the amount of insight we can get given our computing and time constraints.

As you get skilled and experienced, you can get and deliver more out from it. In this section, we will depart from our clean dataset to do the following:

- Draw some descriptive analysis
- Learn cool ways to visualize this kind of data
- Fit hierarchical clustering (and visualize it again!)

Hands on deck, sailor.

Peeking data

We already saw a couple of things in data, such as the first ten rows. There is more to look at. Let's check the dimensions we've got:

```
dim(clean_dt)
# [1] 951   2
```

We got 951 mentions to R packages after withdrawing seven observations. Let's check the last 10 observations:

```
tail(clean_dt, 10)
# A tibble: 10 x 2
#   word n
#   <chr> <int>
# 1 wpp2017 1
# 2 wrapr 1
# 3 WufooR 1
# 4 xgboost 1
# 5 XR 1
# 6 xray 1
# 7 XRJulia 1
# 8 xtractomatic 1
# 9 ZeBook 1
#10 zipfextR 1
```

A summary could also be useful:

```
summary(clean_dt)
#      word n
# Length:951          Min.   : 1.00
# Class :character  1st Qu.: 1.00
# Mode  :character  Median : 2.00
#                   Mean   : 10.58
#                   3rd Qu.: 7.00
#                   Max.   :481.00
```

Given that the first quarter was one, the median was two, and the third quarter was seven, it's not incorrect to infer that most packages were cited only once or twice. This little effort of calling the `summary()` function gave us additional information that turned out to be useful—now we know that quite a few packages are very popular in the tweets while a bunch of other ones are not so much.

By calling `clean_dt[1,]`, I got the most-cited package: `ggplot2`. There is a very good reason for this. Visualizing is a wonderful way to look for insights and to convince your audience. As soon as I get the results from the models, I try to tell the whole history using three to five plots.

TIP

Writing an article around three to five plots that tell the whole history really well is a wonderful way to do it.

`ggplot2` is capable of building wonderful plots with only a few lines. Additionally, there are many supplemental packages built on top of it. In the search for more knowledge on data, we are about to use `ggplot2` to craft some visualizations.

Visualizing data

There are some points to go through before crafting a visualization. If your figure is meant to be part of an exploratory analysis for yourself only, you might not work so hard into details such as the font's family and size; the ugly default settings given by base R graphing are enough. On the other hand, if you wish to publish your figure, you may want to pay a great deal of attention to details.

TIP

No matter what tool you use, production-grade plots require a great deal of work.

Another question to ask is, what kind of data do you have at hand? How many variables do you wish to represent? Are they discrete or continuous? Is there an underlying logical ordering for them? If we are talking time series, data could make more sense if presented chronologically. Many things need to be thought about while you design plots. You are very likely to develop preferences of your own while you become experienced.

TIP

No matter how good you are, there is always room for improvement. Carefully look for novel ways to improve what you have been doing, even if it's good already.

The two visualizations that I like the most when displaying the Twitter ranks are called **lollipop plots** and word clouds. Both can be done using R. We are about to breed both. The lollipops are a neat and clean way to show the difference between the most tweeted words; `ggplot2` can be used to convey such a visualization. Install it using `install.packages()`:

```
if(!require(ggplot2)){install.packages('ggplot2')}
```

We can use factors to rule an order to the lollipops we are about to draw:

```
clean_dt$word <- factor(clean_dt$word,
                        levels = rev(clean_dt$word))
```

Using `ggplot2`, it's possible to layer-wise conjure a lollipop plot:

```
library(ggplot2)

ggplot(data = clean_dt[1:10,], aes(x = n, y = word)) +
  geom_segment(linetype = 'dashed',
               size = .1,
               aes(yend = word,
                   x = min(n) - 50,
                   xend = n)) +
  geom_point(size = 17, color = '#e66101') +
  geom_text(aes(label = n), size = 6) +
  coord_cartesian(xlim = c(120, 500))
```

As a result, the following figure is generated:

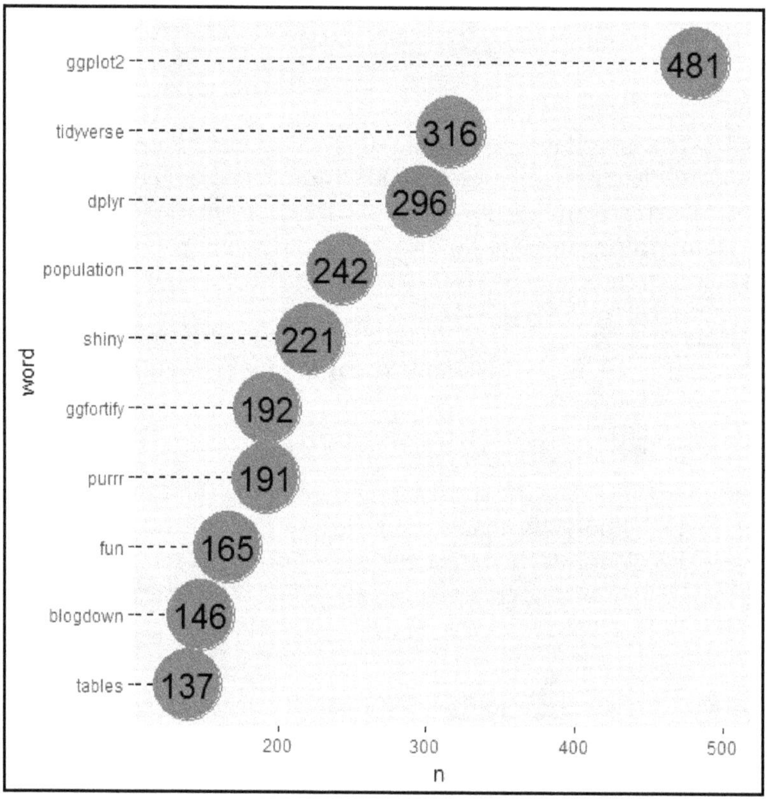

Figure 4.7: Lollipop plot, top 10 Twitter mentioned R packages between March 11, 2018 and March 21, 2018

The previous code may not be as friendly as you would expect, but read it layer by layer, and I am sure you will understand what is happening with a little aid from `ggplot2`'s documentation. Aside from one being a visualization, both *Figure 4.6* and object `clean_dt` displays an analysis called **term frequency analysis**.

There is another visualization that is very useful to display this kind of data: **word clouds**. Word clouds are the main concern from the `wordcloud` package. Perform a simple check or install drill with the following code:

```
if(!require(wordcloud)){install.packages('wordcloud')}
if(!require(tm)){install.packages('tm')}
```

Although the methods to craft the word cloud visualization come from the `wordcloud` package itself, missing the `tm` package sometimes causes trouble. The previous code also seeks and installs the latter. Once we have done that, we can proceed to conjure a word cloud. Setting a seed number generator with `set.seed()` is not necessary, but it will make your results reproducible.

TIP

For graphics that rely on a seed number generator, if you need it to be absolutely amazing, try a bunch of seeds and then choose the one that you liked the most.

The function `par()` is used to set general graphical parameters for methods related to the base `plot()`. Next, the comment shows how it can be used to set smaller margins. Uncomment and run the following code in your word cloud to spread over the margins:

```
#par(mar = rep(0,4))
library(wordcloud)
set.seed(10)
wordcloud(word = clean_dt$word, freq = clean_dt$n, random.order = F,
          rot.per = .35, scale = c(5,.5), max.words = 50,
          colors = c('#e66101','#fdb863','#b2abd2','#5e3c99'))
```

This is how the `wordcloud` package can be used to craft a word cloud. The result is displayed in the following figure. Before getting to it, let's navigate through the arguments that are used as input the `wordcloud()` function:

- `word`: A vector of words to be printed into the word cloud
- `freq`: The number of times each word appeared
- `random.order`: If you want the words that most appear to be printed first, set this argument to `FALSE` (or simply `F`)

- `rot.per`: Pick the probability of a word to be printed vertically; the way I did, about 35% of the words were printed vertically
- `scale`: A two-element vector ruling the size range of the words
- `max.words`: The maximum number of words to be printed
- `colors`: A color palette used to fill the words

It's much more fun to look at the results in the preceding figure than to look at a list of the most frequent 50 words; don't you agree? Following is the word cloud for R packages:

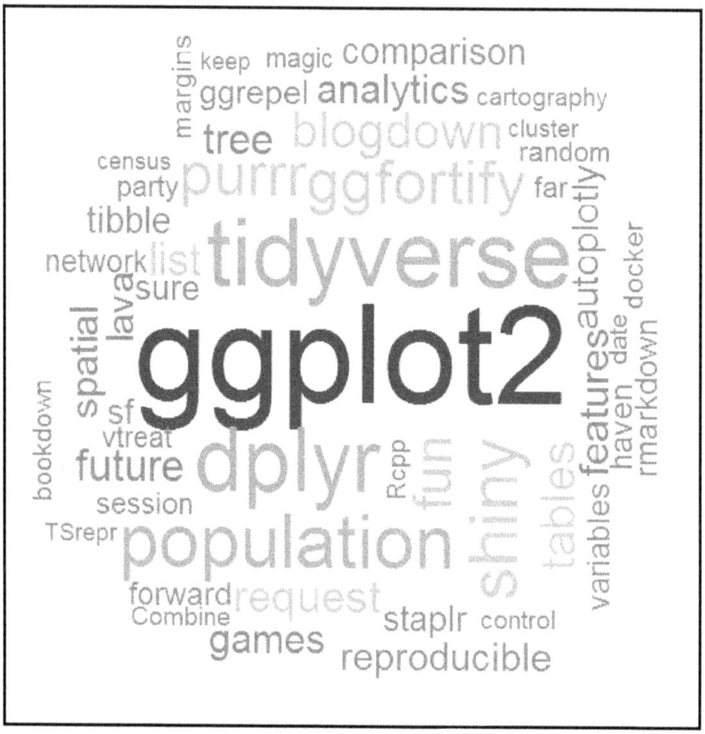

Figure 4.8: R packages word cloud

Notice how we still got many names that could be mistaken as R packages, as they refer to common words. We could color the words differently based on the packages we have already installed on our machines. Try the following code for this:

```
clean_dt$col <- '#b2abd2'
clean_dt$col[clean_dt$word %in% installed.packages()] <- '#e66101'
wordcloud(word = clean_dt$word[1:50], freq = clean_dt$n[1:50],
          random.order = F, rot.per = .35, scale = c(5,.5),
          colors = clean_dt$col[1:50], ordered.colors = T)
```

With this amazing visualization, we close this section and move on the analysis.

Cluster analysis

The idea behind clustering is very simple—group similar things together. Nonetheless, there are many different ways to perform this simple task and none are one-size fits all. It's hard to narrow down the playing field for clustering. There are countless real-world applications and many more to be unveiled.

Scientists Garibaldi and Wang published in 2005 a paper showing how clustering could aid cancer diagnosis. For a long time, the industry has been using it to draw recommendations, segment markets, and detect fraud. Social media can be found in the hall of traditional uses of clustering.

In this section, we are about to check the practical concerns of running a hierarchical clustering with R. Different than k-means clustering, hierarchical clustering is more appropriate to smaller datasets. Hierarchical clustering also does not depend on seemly random processes—the same result will be given no matter how many times in a row it has rolled.

TIP: Package `Ckmeans.1d.dp` is meant to optimize univariate clustering.

To make things easier to understand, let's stick with only the top `25` tweeted packages. Hierarchical clustering can be simply done with the following code:

```
tw_clust <- hclust(dist(clean_dt$n[1:25]))
plot(tw_clust, labels = clean_dt$word[1:25])
```

The first line is inputting `hclut()` with an object obtained through the `dist()` method, and the result is the hierarchical cluster. The results are stored in an object called `tw_clust` (Twitter cluster), which is plotted using `plot()`. This example demonstrates how hard it's to set visualization and analysis apart from each other. Even if the section *Visualizing data* was focused on visualization, it was also drawing an analysis known as **frequency**. This section's analysis could hardly be interpreted without the aid of a dendrogram:

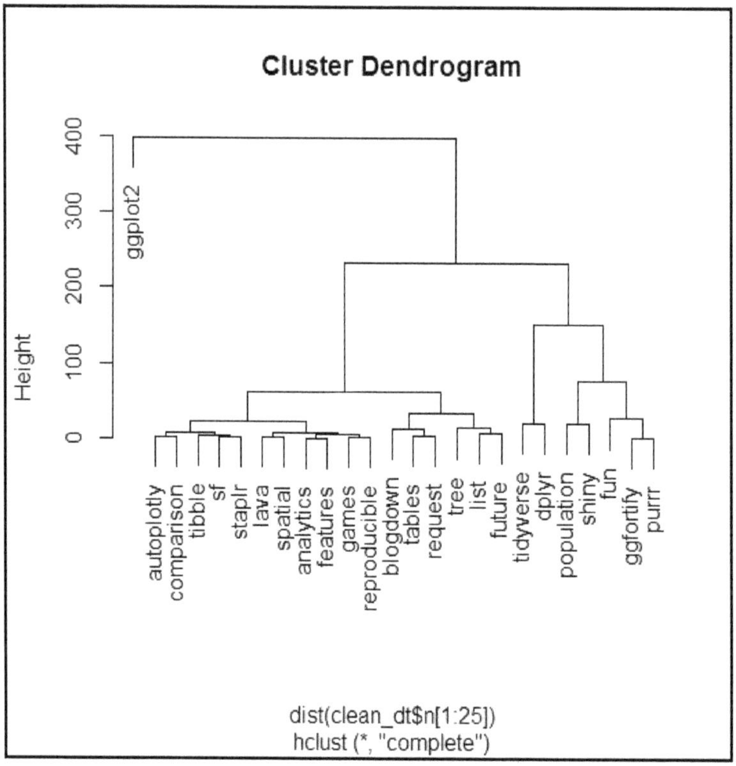

Figure 4.9: Cluster dendrogram

There are two reasons why *Figure 4.8* should not be taken strictly seriously:

- The data might be polluted—many words, such as fun or population, are being accounted for, even if they don't ever make reference to R packages
- There are 25 groups given 25 packages—depending on how a person looks at it, *Figure 4.8* shows any number of clusters between 25 and 1

Both puzzles can be tackled either with simpler techniques or more complex ones. As point number one was already discussed before we are moving on to point number two. The way *Figure 4.8* is designed, the reader can't tell how many clusters (groups) there are. For the analysis to be complete, we need to select how many groups we are accepting.

A very common procedure is to pick how many groups (`k`) are wanted and then slicing tree in the proper height to get that many groups. The `dendextend` library grants useful methods to address this division while also drawing the visualization. Install and load the library:

```
if(!require(dendextend)){ install.packages('dendextend')}
library(dendextend)
```

Once we've properly installed `dendextend`, it's time for us to craft a brand new dendrogram. Try the following code:

```
tw_clust %>% as.dendrogram() %>%
  set('labels', as.character(clean_dt$word[1:25])) %>%
  set('labels_col', k = 3,
      value = c('#e66101','#fdb863','#b2abd2')) %>%
  set('branches_k_color', k = 3,
      value = c('#e66101','#fdb863','#b2abd2')) %>%
  set('labels_cex', 1.1) %>%
  plot()
```

This package practically works by chaining the `set()` command after a dendrogram object—that is why the first chain is converting our `tw_clust` object to a dendrogram. The first `set()` is setting the labels. The next ones are respectively changing the labels' colors, the branches' colors, and the labels' sizes. The following is the result:

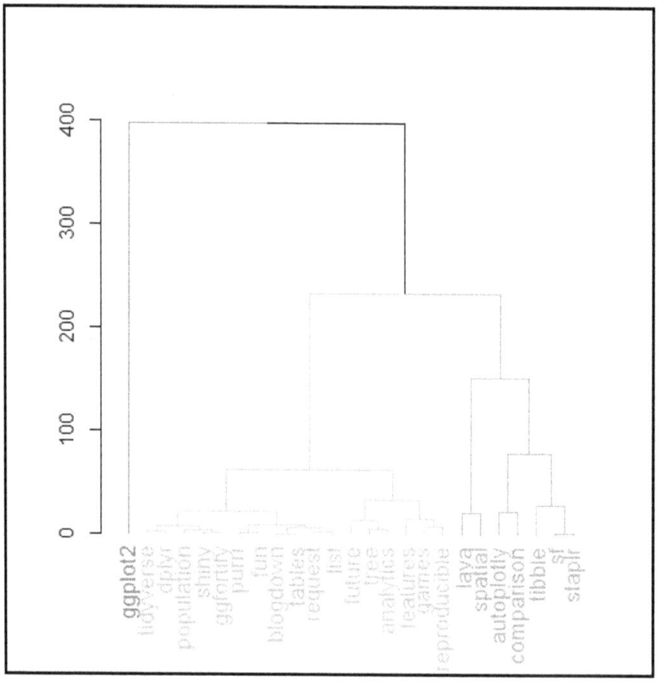

Figure 4.10: Colored dendrogram (k = 3)

A very common rule of thumb tells that `k`—the number of groups—should be equal to `3`. Our dendrogram is relying on this rule but most important is how your cluster performs in the designated task. Assign a test and validation datasets, and test how your model performs there. Use the `cutree()` function to do the separation. The cutting decision could be made either by groups (`k`) or height (`h`):

```
cutree(tw_clust, k = 3)
cutree(tw_clust, h = 250)
```

How would you interpret the results given in *Figure 4.9*? Don't surrender to urge to see it as packages that may come together or something like this. They are not clustered by what they can do either. Packages they are grouped by seemed popular—since the clustering stems from a term frequency analysis.

Summary

In this chapter, you learned what the terms KDD and data mining could mean. You have also learned about diverse ways of retrieving text from the web and even how to get a dwarf name for yourself. Otherwise, you may have learned how to run a term frequency and a clustering analysis. To wrap it up, here are the things that we did with Twitter data:

- Cleaned and transformed data
- Ran a term frequency analysis
- Drew lollipop and word cloud charts to aid interpreting
- Made hierarchical clustering from the term frequency

There is much more we could do with data retrieved from Twitter, such as the following:

- Topic modeling
- Sentiment analysis
- Follower analysis
- Retweet analysis—this might be useful for you to get more retweets
- Favorite analysis

Given that we visited some ways of retrieving and manipulating data from Twitter, I am pretty confident that you can do this by yourself now. Dig in. Write down your research notes. At some point, make a tweet, a blog post, or something like that from what you have learned and found. Publishing your learning process is a very good way to promote yourself.

I hope you liked this chapter as much as I enjoyed writing it. The next chapter is shipping you directly to the analytical land of R. You are about to witness and learn some other practical analysis made real with R, but before you proceed, I expect you to complete the quiz.

Quiz

- **Quiz-tion:** Which of the following packages directly implement functions named after HTTP verbs such as `GET` and `POST` in R?
    1. `ggplot2`
    2. `tidytext`
    3. `dplyr`
    4. `httr`
- **Quiz-tion**: Read the following statements and pick the wrong one:
    1. `rvest` and `httr` can be used to retrieve data from the web
    2. The `gsub()` function is useful to find and replace patterns
    3. Clustering analysis is only useful to the industry and does not have a single application to academic research
    4. The `dendextend` package is able to craft visualizations on the top of clusters
- **Quiz-tion**: Which of the following packages offers an easy interface to the interact with Twitter's API?
    1. `httr`
    2. `rvest`
    3. `rtweet`
    4. `not`

Answers—executing the following code will give you the answers to the quiz questions:

```
set.seed(8080)
round(runif(3,1,4))
```

See you in Antica.

5
Data Analysis with R

"I believe in the power of shared data and technology to help build a better future."

– Paul Allen

Most of this book deals with data analysis with R. This chapter is intended to provide an overview of what data analysis means and what the optimal methods of analysis are. In other words, it provides a holistic overview of how to understand the characteristics of a dataset and how to visualize the information at a glance before pursuing more in-depth analytical methods.

When you first receive a dataset for analysis, it is helpful to get a sense of the high-level characteristics of the data. This generally means performing basic summary operations and thereafter visualizing the information to build an overall notion of important variables, their distribution, cardinality, and various other aspects. While there are tools that claim to automatically provide insight from data, a certain level of domain expertise is needed in order to derive meaningful and useful information from the data.

For instance, time series datasets can be very difficult to analyze in a purely automated manner. The dataset could have missing or incorrect values. There could be embedded characters, for instance, a US Dollar sign in a certain column that does not get interpreted as a numeric column as a result.

In this section, we will explore some of the ways in which we can evaluate the quality and characteristics of various datasets in an effort to find insights from the data:

- Preparing data for analysis
- Data summary and distribution
- Finding relationships in data
- Selecting the right chart types and visualizations
- Saving analysis for future work

Preparing data for analysis

In this section, we will look at some basic characteristics of data and how to read, preprocess, and cleanse datasets. We have seen some of these aspects earlier in `Chapter 3`, *Data Wrangling with R*, and this section is intended to provide a high-level view of the relevant topics.

Data categories

Data can be broadly categorized into two types:

- **Discrete** (or **categorical**): Any value that denotes a category is considered a discrete variable. Examples of discrete variables include most nouns such as fruits, colors, school grades, countries and genders.
- **Continuous** (or **quantitative**): Continuous numbers are numerical quantities on which you can perform arithmetic operations. This includes variables such as weather, temperatures, amounts, and time.

You may also hear of a couple of other variations of data types, which are but sub-categories of either discrete or continuous variables, as follows:

- **Ordinal** (discrete variable): This indicates data that has an order. For example, if we were to rank scores as first, second, and third denoting the top three scores, the numbers one to three are ordinal as they denote an order. They are not considered continuous.
- **Nominal** (discrete variable): This indicates data that does not have any inherent order, that is, which are not ordinal, for example, *Male* = *1* and *Female* = *2*. These are not ordinal since there is no inherent order, but they are nominal in the sense that they denote a naming convention:

Concept	Terminology	Meaning
Type of Variable	Continuous/Quantitative	Numbers on which you can perform arithmetic
	Discrete/Categorical	Qualitative – Alphabetical, or Numeric that simply denotes a 'category'
Variable in an equation	Dependent	The Left-Hand-Side, the y in y = x + 1
	Independent	The Right-Hand-Side, every variable other than the y in y = x + 1 (i.e., x in this case)

Data types in R

As discussed in `Chapter 3`, *Data Wrangling with R*, there are five data types in R:

- **Character**: For string values
- **Numeric**: For numbers with decimal places (for example, 1.2, 3.45, and so on)
- **Integer**: For whole numbers (for example, 1, 2, 3, and so on)
- **Logical**: For Boolean values, `TRUE` and `FALSE`
- **Complex**: For numbers that have an imaginary component (for example, $5 + 3i$)

> Note that, in R, we often use numerical and integer values interchangeably. In fact, an integer value is also a numeric quantity. The main benefit of using numeric instead of integer is that we can represent much larger numbers with the numeric data type.

It is useful to note here that in R, categorical values are generally represented as **factors**. When reading a CSV file using the inbuilt `read.csv` function, R attempts to read all character columns as factors, unless the behavior is suppressed using the command, `options(stringsAsFactors=F)`.

Reading data

R contains inbuilt functions for reading data. The most commonly used format is CSV, that is, CSV files. There are multiple commands to read CSV files. A few are shown as follows. In order to conduct our tests, we will use the `mtcars` dataset in R.

First, we are going to create a copy of the dataset into a new variable called `car_data`:

```
car_data <- mtcars
```

To view the top few rows of the `mtcars` dataset, we can use the `head` command. This is often very useful in getting a quick glimpse of the data we will be working with:

```
head(car_data)
```

The following is the output of the preceding code:

```
> head(car_data)
                   mpg cyl disp  hp drat    wt  qsec vs am gear carb
Mazda RX4         21.0   6  160 110 3.90 2.620 16.46  0  1    4    4
Mazda RX4 Wag     21.0   6  160 110 3.90 2.875 17.02  0  1    4    4
Datsun 710        22.8   4  108  93 3.85 2.320 18.61  1  1    4    1
Hornet 4 Drive    21.4   6  258 110 3.08 3.215 19.44  1  0    3    1
Hornet Sportabout 18.7   8  360 175 3.15 3.440 17.02  0  0    3    2
Valiant           18.1   6  225 105 2.76 3.460 20.22  1  0    3    1
>
```

Create the CSV file:

```
write.csv(car_data,"car_data.csv")
fwrite(car_data, "car_data.csv")
```

We can view the file that was saved in the current directory:

```
list.files(".", pattern = "car_data*")
# [1] "car_data.csv"

# Reading the CSV file
read.csv("car_data.csv") # Base R
read_csv("car_data.csv") # Tidyverse
fread("car_data.csv")   # data.table
```

While these are mostly similar, note that the output is slightly different. The first one, `read.csv`, is from base R (it comes inbuilt in R) and creates `data.frame`. The second, `read_csv`, is from the `tidyverse` package and creates `tibble` as discussed in `Chapter 3`, *Data Wrangling with R*. The third option, `fread`, produces `data.table`, which has different characteristics compared to `data.frame`, but is arguably much faster in reading large amounts of data.

Once you have read the file, the next step is to see what the data contains and the respective data types. This can be done using the `str` command in R. The command, `str` stands for structure and provides a summarized overview of the data types:

```
# To view data type and first few records
str(read.csv("car_data.csv"))     # Base R
glimpse(read_csv("car_data.csv")) # Tidyverse
```

The output of the preceding code is as follows:

```
> glimpse(read_csv("car_data.csv")) # Tidyverse
Parsed with column specification:
cols(
  mpg = col_double(),
  cyl = col_integer(),
  disp = col_double(),
  hp = col_integer(),
  drat = col_double(),
  wt = col_double(),
  qsec = col_double(),
  vs = col_integer(),
  am = col_integer(),
  gear = col_integer(),
  carb = col_integer()
)
Observations: 32
Variables: 11
$ mpg  <dbl> 21.0, 21.0, 22.8, 21.4, 18.7, 18.1, 14.3, 24.4, 22.8, 19.2, 17.8, 16.4, 17.3, 15.2, 10.4, 10.4, 14.7, 32.4,...
$ cyl  <int> 6, 6, 4, 6, 8, 6, 8, 4, 4, 6, 6, 8, 8, 8, 8, 8, 8, 4, 4, 4, 4, 8, 8, 8, 8, 4, 4, 4, 8, 6, 8, 4
$ disp <dbl> 160.0, 160.0, 108.0, 258.0, 360.0, 225.0, 360.0, 146.7, 140.8, 167.6, 167.6, 275.8, 275.8, 275.8, 472.0, 46...
$ hp   <int> 110, 110, 93, 110, 175, 105, 245, 62, 95, 123, 123, 180, 180, 180, 205, 215, 230, 66, 52, 65, 97, 150, 150,...
$ drat <dbl> 3.90, 3.90, 3.85, 3.08, 3.15, 2.76, 3.21, 3.69, 3.92, 3.92, 3.92, 3.07, 3.07, 3.07, 2.93, 3.00, 3.23, 4.08,...
$ wt   <dbl> 2.620, 2.875, 2.320, 3.215, 3.440, 3.460, 3.570, 3.190, 3.150, 3.440, 3.440, 4.070, 3.730, 3.780, 5.250, 5....
$ qsec <dbl> 16.46, 17.02, 18.61, 19.44, 17.02, 20.22, 15.84, 20.00, 22.90, 18.30, 18.90, 17.40, 17.60, 18.00, 17.98, 17...
$ vs   <int> 0, 0, 1, 1, 0, 1, 0, 1, 1, 1, 1, 0, 0, 0, 0, 0, 0, 1, 1, 1, 1, 0, 0, 0, 0, 1, 0, 1, 0, 0, 0, 1
$ am   <int> 1, 1, 1, 0, 0, 0, 0, 0, 0, 0, 0, 0, 0, 0, 0, 0, 0, 1, 1, 1, 0, 0, 0, 0, 0, 1, 1, 1, 1, 1, 1, 1
$ gear <int> 4, 4, 4, 3, 3, 3, 3, 4, 4, 4, 4, 3, 3, 3, 3, 3, 3, 4, 4, 4, 3, 3, 3, 3, 3, 4, 5, 5, 5, 5, 5, 4
$ carb <int> 4, 4, 1, 1, 2, 1, 4, 2, 2, 4, 4, 3, 3, 3, 4, 4, 4, 1, 2, 1, 1, 2, 2, 4, 2, 1, 2, 2, 4, 6, 8, 2
```

Managing data issues

Datasets in the public domain often require a fair amount of cleansing and curation before they can be used. By contrast, the datasets that are used in coursework and tutorials are generally pre-cleaned and presented in a much more organised format than what practitioners may find when working with real-world datasets.

A general list of data challenges that you may encounter are as follows:

Mixed data types

DataFrames in R require a single data type per column of data. The same column may not contain both numeric and character data and when that happens, R coerces the column using the sequence shown as follows:

```
Logical à Integer à Double à Character
```

What this means is that, if say a column contains numeric (integer or double) values and character strings, R will coerce the column to be a `character` column. We can see this by using the `typeof` command:

```
> typeof(c(1,2,"a"))
[1] "character"
```

A dataset containing the symbol `$` in an amount field for instance, would be interpreted as a `character` column even though the column was intended to be numeric. In such cases, it would be essential to leverage string operations in R to cleanse the dataset and prepare it for reading in using the appropriate data types. The string operations have been discussed further as follows.

Missing data

Datasets are also prone to missing information. This is very common in datasets that require user input, for example, in surveys where the user might not have entered all the information in the respective fields. Also, sometimes the data might not even be available or due to restrictions could not be included in the respective dataset.

There are multiple techniques that have been devised to fill in missing values. The methods include simple procedures such as using the mean or median of the columns to more advanced methods in fields such as survey statistics.

A few of the common methods to impute, that is, fill in missing values, have been provided as follows:

- **Imputation using statistical measures of central tendency**: This means using the mean, median, and mode values of the available data in the column to fill in the missing values.
- **Imputation using statistical models**: This means using statistical modelling methods such as regression to create a predictive model with the outcome variable as the column being filled in. We can thereafter use predict to fill in the missing entries.

- **Using data imputation methods such as KNN imputation**: KNN is a clustering technique that attempts to fill in missing data using the points that are closest to it in a multi-dimensional space. In a different sense, it means that KNN attempts to find other rows of data that are similar to the present and fill in the missing value accordingly.
- **Hot deck imputation**: This involves filling in the missing value using a similar record that is randomly selected from the complete dataset. One such method is the *last observation carried forward*, in which case the values are randomized and the value in the record prior to the missing data is used as the new imputed value. In general, hot deck imputation, while used, can be prone to issues such as bias if a large number of missing data is filled in with the same value.

Packages implementing missing data imputation in R include the following:

- *Amelia II: A Program for Missing Data*: `https://gking.harvard.edu/amelia`
- *DMwR: Functions and data for Data Mining with R*: `https://cran.r-project.org/web/packages/DMwR/index.html`
- Packages implementing hot deck:
  - *HotDeckImputation: Hot Deck Imputation Methods for Missing Data*: `https://cran.r-project.org/web/packages/HotDeckImputation/`
  - *hot.deck: Multiple Hot-Deck Imputation*: `https://cran.r-project.org/web/packages/hot.deck/`
- *mice: Multivariate Imputation by Chained Equations*: `https://cran.r-project.org/web/packages/mice/index.html`
- *mi: Missing Data Imputation and Model Checking*: `https://cran.r-project.org/web/packages/mi/index.html`

Handling strings and dates

Managing data containing dates can be challenging because of the various formats in which dates can be represented. Fixing issues in strings is generally less challenging because of the abundance of tools in R to handle and manipulate strings.

Fortunately, there is a very useful package in R called `lubridate` that is invaluable in terms of handling date objects.

There are two main classes of dates/times in R: `POSIXct` and `POSIXlt`. POSIX, which stands for portable operating system interface, defines `POSIXct` as the number of seconds since the Unix epoch, that is, *1970-01-01 00:00.00* UTC, and `POSIXlt` as the string representation of the same in the desired format.

Handling dates using POSIXct or POSIXlt

`POSIXct` converts integers representing the number of seconds since the Unix epoch, that is, January 01, 1970, into corresponding date and time objects in R:

```
unclass(Sys.time())
```

We can derive the date representation using `as.POSIXct` as follows:

```
as.POSIXct(unclass(Sys.time()), origin="1970-01-01")
```

`POSIXlt` is similar to `POSIXct`, but is used for dates represented as characters. As per the R help page, character input is first converted into the `POSIXlt` class by `strptime` numeric input is first converted to `POSIXct`:

```
as.POSIXlt(Sys.time())
```

We can also specify the format in which we'd like to get the output using the appropriate convention, (see `?strptime`).

For example, in order to get the month, day, year format, we can use `%D` shown as follows:

```
format(as.POSIXct(Sys.time()), "%D")
```

Often, your data would contain dates in a given format on which you may need to perform further operations.

If the column has been read in as a string, you'd need to instruct R as to the appropriate format in which the date has been stored in order for R to recognize it as a date, time object. For this, we can use the `strptime` function:

```
strptime("1/1/2000 10:15:45.123", "%d/%m/%Y %H:%M:%OS")
class(strptime("1/1/2000 10:15:45.123", "%d/%m/%Y %H:%M:%OS"))
```

One of the most popular date and time manipulation packages in R is `lubridate`. There are several useful features in `lubridate` and a complete tutorial of the topic is available at CRAN: `https://cran.r-project.org/web/packages/lubridate/vignettes/lubridate.html`:

```
library(lubridate)

mydt <- mdy_hms("1/1/2000 10:15:45.123")
# Same as the prior example, but using the much simpler ymd_hms function in
lubridate
```

A few examples are shown as follows:

```
year(mydt)
month(mydt)
wday(mydt)
```

The main benefit of using such features is the ability to add, subtract, and perform date, time operations on the data, which would otherwise not be possible if the dates were simply treated as strings.

For example, if I had to add `1` day to `2000/01/30`, I can do so after converting the string to be recognized as the appropriate date, time object in R:

```
"2000/01/30" + 1 # This would produce an error message
# Error in "2000/01/30" + 1 : non-numeric argument to binary operator

ymd("2000/01/30") + 1
[1] "2000-01-31"
```

Handling strings in R

R provides a few extremely helpful functionalities for manipulating strings. The following highlights a few of the methods available for performing string operations in R.

Reading data

As discussed before, it is relatively simple to read files in R using the provisions in `read.csv` and other utilities. Subsetting strings can be performed using the standard R indexing methods or by using one of the several string utilities in R such as `substr`, `substring`, `paste`, and `paste0`.

Combining strings

Strings can be combined using `paste`, `paste0`, and other utilities. When using `paste`, the default separator is space:

```
paste("I","think","therefore","I","am")
```

We can use a different separator by using the `sep` flag:

```
paste("I","think","therefore","I","am", sep="-")
```

`paste0` is an extension of `paste` where the separator is null. As a result, all strings are concatenated into a single string unless separators are specified:

```
paste0("I","think","therefore","I","am")
```

In addition to the `sep` flag, there is also a `collapse` flag that can be used to separate the results:

```
paste("grade",c("A","B","C"), sep=" ") # paste with separator space
paste("grade",c("A","B","C"), sep=" ", collapse=",") # paste with separator
space and collapse with "," (comma)
paste0("grade",c("A","B","C"), collapse=",") # paste0 is set to the
separator "" (null)
```

The `stringr` package in R also contains several useful string manipulation functions. One of them, called `str_c` has been shown as follows:

```
library(stringr)
str_c("grade",c("A","B","C",NULL)) # str_c from the stringr package is a
newer (and somewhat simpler) alternative to paste/paste0 in R
```

We can split the string using the following line of code:

```
strsplit("I think, therefore I am",",")
```

Compared to `strsplit`, the `tstrsplit` function performs a transpose operation on the split vector. This is helpful when splitting strings and updating say, a column in a DataFrame:

```
tstrsplit("I think, therefore I am",",")
```

The difference can be easily observed herein:

```
# Create a simple data frame
df <- data.frame(a=c(1,2))

# strsplit creates a vector
```

```
df$s <- strsplit("I think, therefore I am",",")
df

# a                      s
# 1 1 I think,  therefore I am
# 2 2 I think,  therefore I am


# tstrsplit creates a transpose of the vector, t
df$s <- tstrsplit("I think, therefore I am",",")
df

# a               s
# 1 1         I think
# 2 2  therefore I am
```

Simple pattern matching and replacement with R

For pattern matching, `grep` and `grepl` are commonly used. The general syntax is `grep(pattern, text)`:

```
grep("think",c("I think","therefore I am")) # Gives the index of the match
grepl("think",c("I think","therefore I am")) # Gives a logical vector of
the match
```

It is possible to replace only characters that match using `gsub`, `regexpr`, and other pattern matching and replacement functions in R:

```
gsub("th","ab",c("I think","therefore I am")) # To replace all occurrences
of "th" in the text
```

For users who are familiar with regular expressions, R also supports regex patterns (for example, `PCRE`, and so on):

```
gsub("t.","ab",c("I think","therefore I am"), perl=T) # To replace all
occurrences of "th" in the text
```

Printing results

Results can be printed in R using `print`, `cat`, and other commands:

```
# print is often used as a means to document code output as
(function(x){x=10;print ("x is now 10")})()
```

`print` also supports other flags such as digits (number of digits to print), justify (left and right), quote (whether strings should be quoted), for example:

```
print (1.1234567,digits=3)
```

Formatting strings can be done using the format command in R. It is one of the most versatile functions that allows users to present data in a more readable manner. For instance, to add a comma (`,`) separator to numbers, we can use the `big.mark` argument in the format as follows:

```
format(14324234,big.mark=",")
```

Other options as specified in the R help page include the following:

```
# big.mark, big.interval, small.mark, small.interval, decimal.mark,
zero.print, drop0trailing
```

Data visualisation

R has a rich set of inbuilt features to visualize data using a range of chart types. In addition, R also has a range of visualization packages, such as `ggplot2` that produce presentation grade graphics used in publications.

It is a common practice to visualize a dataset to understand the nature of the individual columns of data prior to beginning analysis. Not only does the visualization process shed light on the distribution of the data, but also the contents of the data at a high level.

Having a visual cue also helps in getting insights more rapidly, relative to having to analyze the data manually. Visualizations help to understand the following:

- Distribution of the data
- Presence of outliers
- Cardinality of the data
- Correlated variables
- Multivariate relationships

Types of charts – basic primer

Some of the commonly used chart types are shown as follows using the standard R functions for data visualization.

Histograms

Histograms are used to visualize count data. The chart consists of bars with a *y* axis representing the count and the *x* axis representing the data. The following code demonstrates the use of the `hist` function in R:

```
# Data Visualisation

library(car)
library(RColorBrewer)

data("Salaries")

# Histogram of Salaries of Professors from the Salaries dataset
hist(Salaries$salary/1000, main="Histogram of Salaries", xlab="Salary (in
'000s)", ylab="Count")
```

The output of the preceding code is as follows:

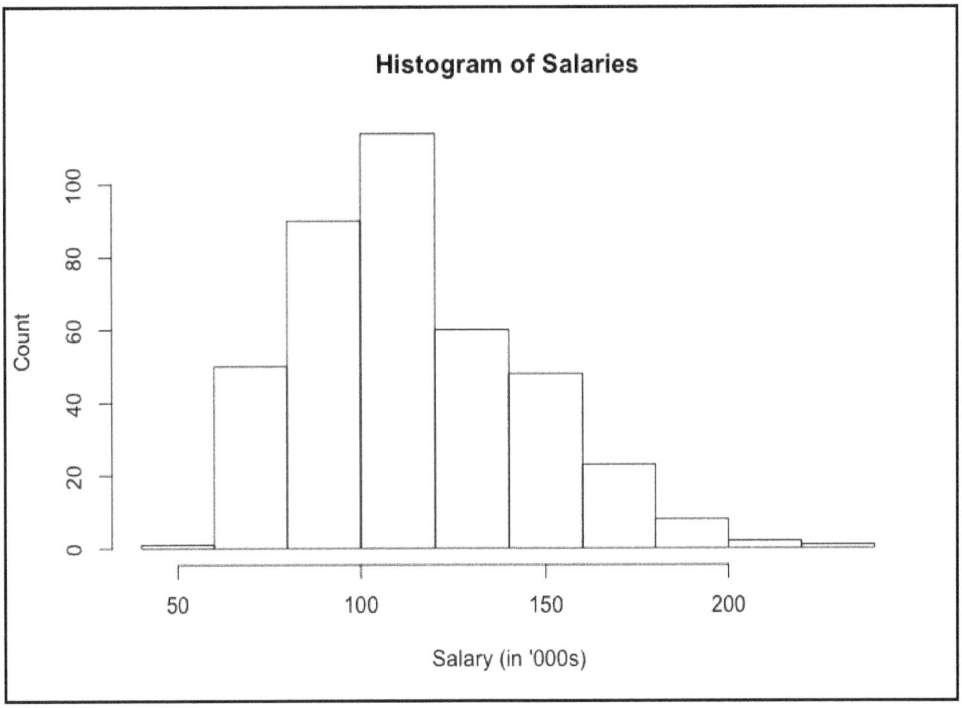

We will be running the same code with a minor change of `col=brewer.pal(8,"Reds")`. This will provide you with the same output as the previous one with the color red:

```
# Same as above with a Brewer Palette
h1 <- hist(Salaries$salary/1000,main="Histogram of Salaries", xlab="Salary
(in '000s)", ylab="Count", col=brewer.pal(8,"Reds"))
```

The output of the preceding code is as follows:

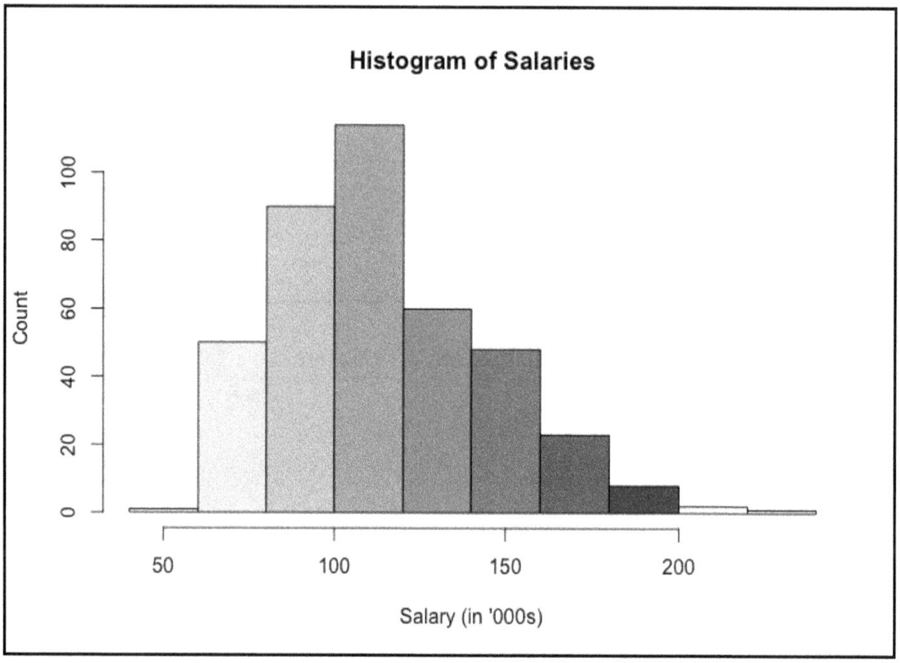

The `hist` function produces several metrics which can be accessed using their respective names (for example, in this case, `h1$breaks`, `h1$counts`, and so on), as shown:

```
names(h1)
# [1] "breaks"    "counts"    "density"   "mids"      "xname"     "equidist"

h1$counts
#  [1]   1  50  90 114  60  48  23   8   2   1

h1$breaks
#  [1]  40  60  80 100 120 140 160 180 200 220 240
```

The pros and cons of using histograms are as follows:

Pros:

Histograms can be used to get a general overview quickly from large datasets.

Cons:

- Can only be used for numeric values
- The bin width can be changed (if equal bin sizes are not used) which might not be able to capture the important aspects of the data

Line plots

Line plots are usually applied using data along a traditional two-dimensional axes. It is perhaps the most common type of chart that we can see in everyday use. In R, plot with `type="l"` will create a line chart as shown here:

```
data("Hartnagel")
?Hartnagel # Canadian Crime-Rates Time Series

plot(Hartnagel$year, Hartnagel$mtheft, type="l", col=brewer.pal(8,"Set1"))
```

The output is as follows:

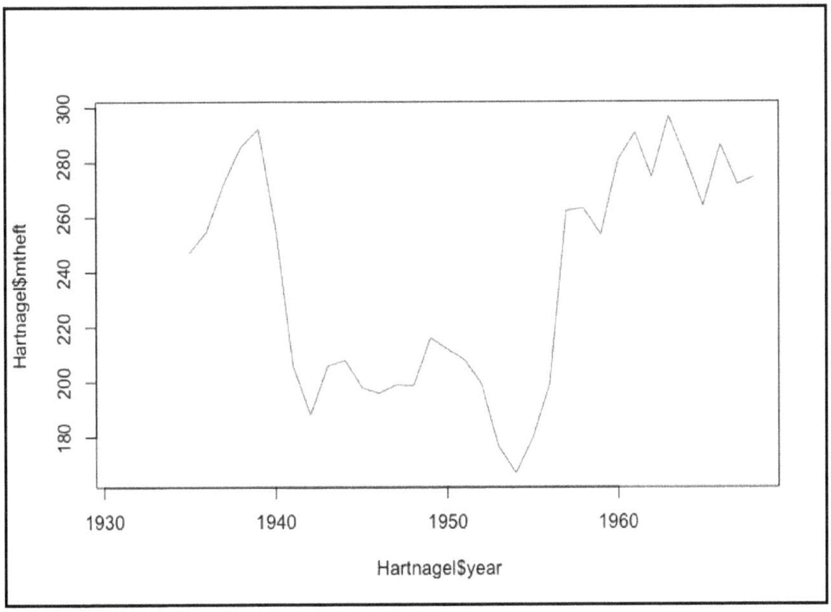

Scatter plots

The following code will be used to create a scatter plot:

```
plot(Hartnagel$year, Hartnagel$mtheft, col=brewer.pal(8,"Set1"))
```

The output is as follows:

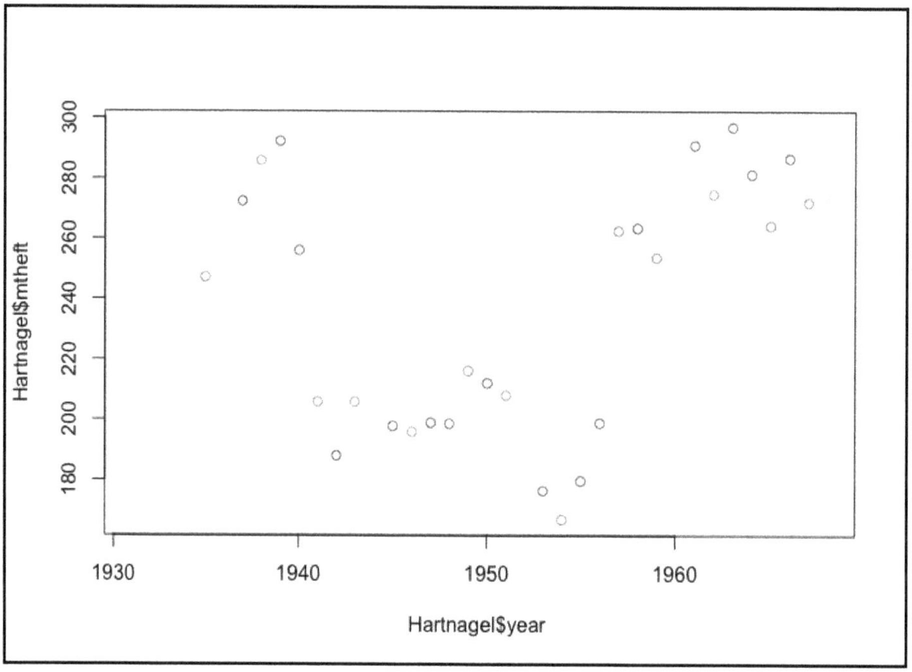

To view the various parameters supported in R graphics:

```
?par
```

Boxplots

Boxplots can be used to get the minimum, median, maximum, and quartiles of the data being plotted. Boxplots also help to identify outliers:

```
b = boxplot(Salaries$salary~Salaries$rank, col=brewer.pal(8,"Set1"))

names(b)
# [1] "stats" "n"     "conf"  "out"   "group" "names"
```

```
b$stats
#          [,1]     [,2]     [,3]
# [1,] 63100.0  62884.0  57800.0
# [2,] 74000.0  82350.0 105890.0
# [3,] 79800.0  95626.5 123321.5
# [4,] 88597.5 104331.5 145098.0
# [5,] 97032.0 126431.0 194800.0
# attr(,"class")
# AsstProf
# "integer"
```

The output is as follows:

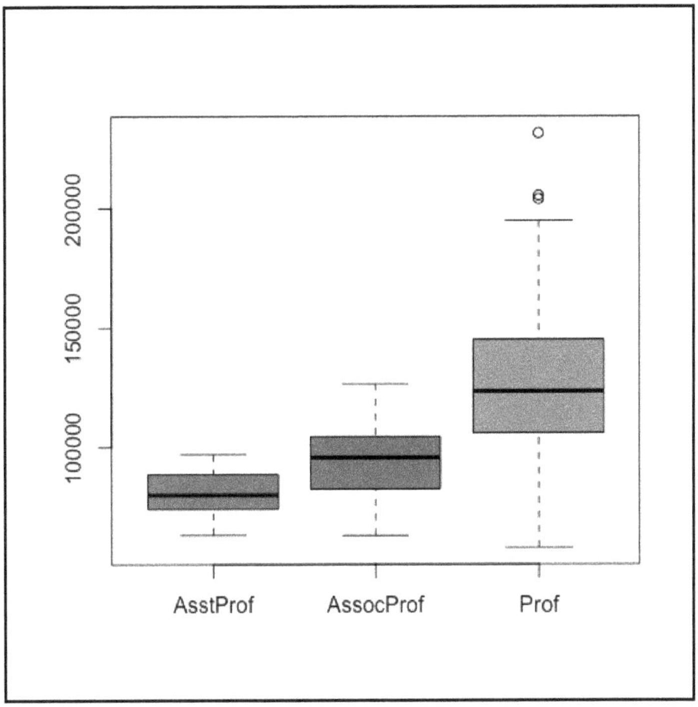

The pros and cons of using boxplots are as follow:

Pros:

Boxplots can be used to get an understanding of the distribution, the outliers, and skewness of the data through an intuitive plot.

Cons:

- Can only be used with numerical variables
- Due to summarization, the original data is not displayed in the charts

Bar charts

Bar charts can be used to compare data across a given *x* axis. Often the *x* axis could represent a temporal value such as time, date, and so on. It is useful as a visualization to see how quantities changed along a certain timeline or with respect to the variable in the *x* axis.

Although they may appear similar to histograms, the main difference in this case is that bar plots can be, and often are, used to represent data beyond simply count information. For instance, if we had to plot the number of convicts per year from the `Hartnagel` dataset, plotting with a histogram on year will simply yield a count of rows by year. Instead, we can use a bar chart as follows.

The example here uses `ggplot2` to display the bar chart:

```
ggplot(Hartnagel, aes(year,mconvict,fill=as.factor
  (year - round(year%%10)))) + geom_bar(stat="identity") +
   scale_fill_discrete(name = "Decade") + xlab("Decade")
   + ylab ("Number of Convicts")
```

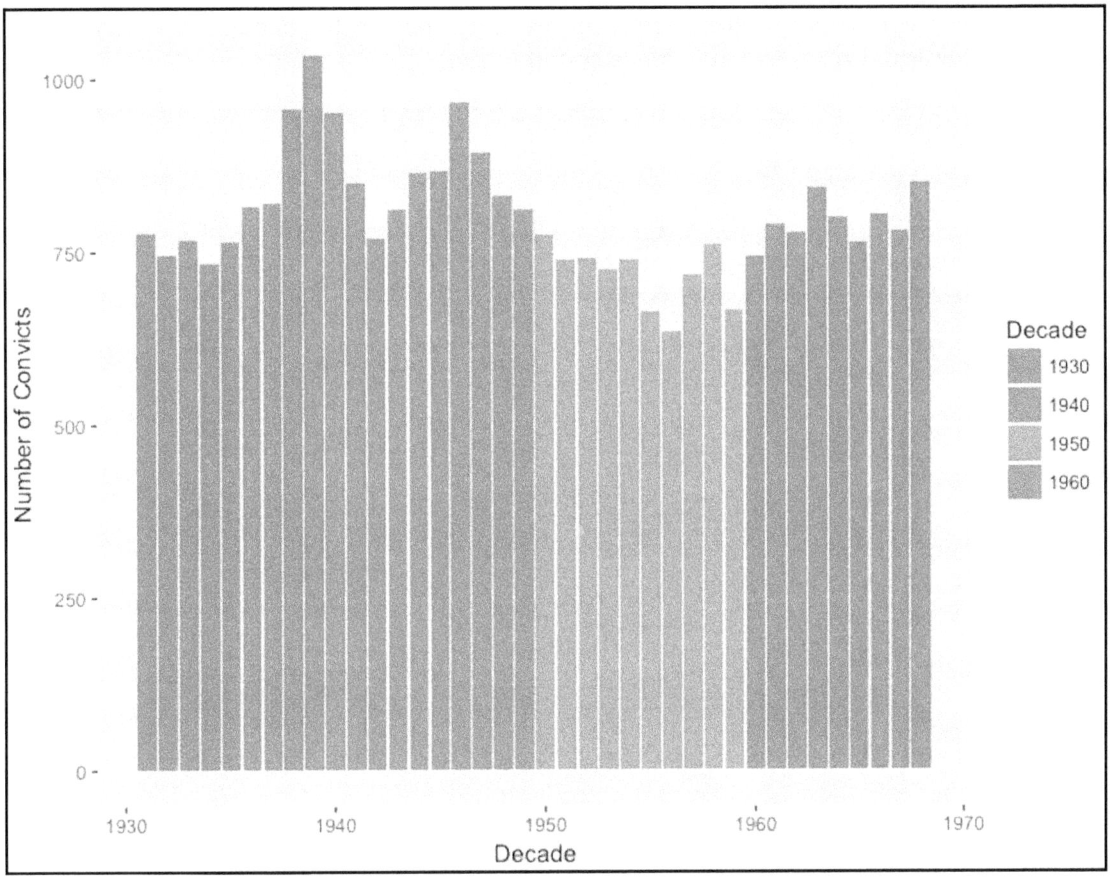

Note that it is fairly simple to draw the same chart with horizontal bars, as follows:

```
ggplot(Hartnagel, aes(year,mconvict,fill=as.factor
  (year - round(year%%10)))) + geom_bar(stat="identity") +
  scale_fill_discrete(name = "Decade") + xlab("Decade") +
  ylab ("Male indictable-offense conviction rate per 100,000") +
  coord_flip()
```

This is especially useful when there are several variable names, the names are long, or the data would be better represented in a horizontal format:

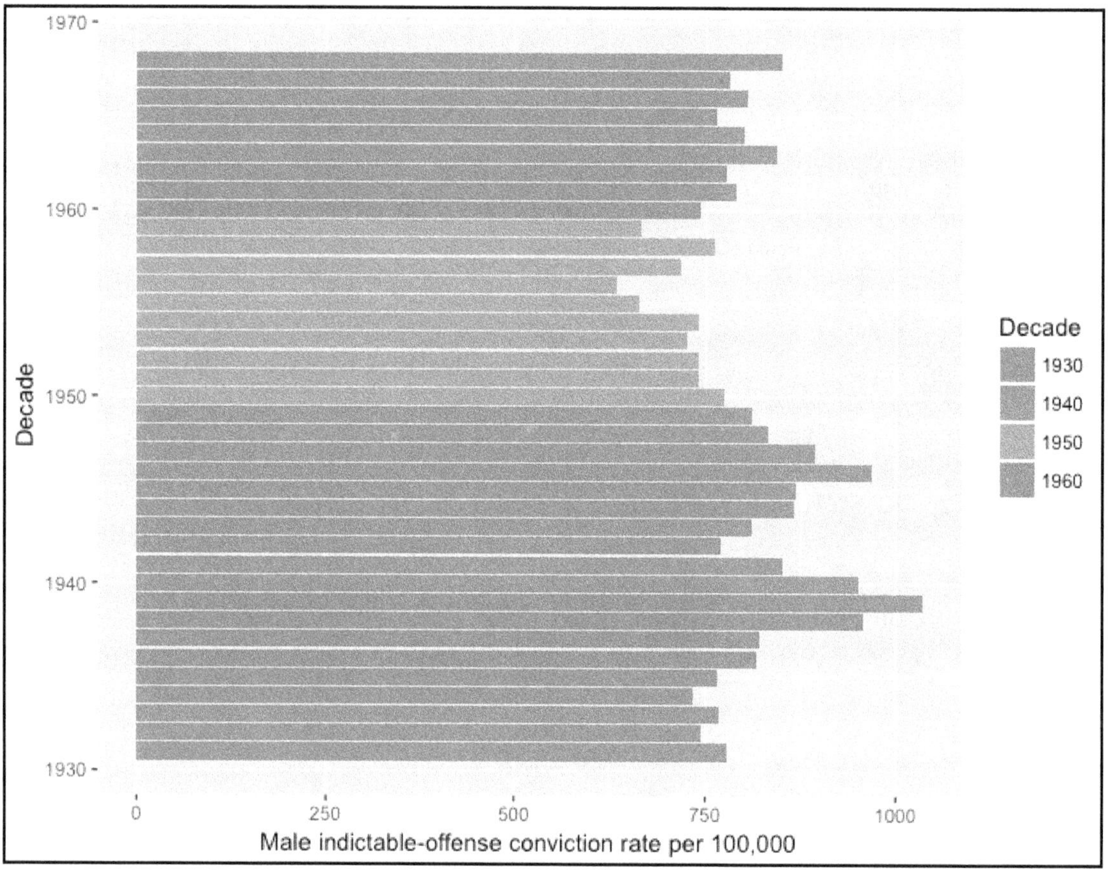

ggplot2 is very sophisticated and hundreds of other chart types can be drawn using basic commands. The following is a stacked bar chart, similar to the ones before, except that the color is based on gender male versus female conviction rate:

```
hm <- melt(Hartnagel, id.vars="year",measure.vars=c("mconvict","fconvict"),
variable.name="gender",value.name="convict")

ggplot(hm, aes(year,convict,fill=as.factor(gender))) +
  geom_bar(stat="identity") + scale_fill_discrete(name = "Gender") +
  xlab("Decade") + ylab ("Number of Convicts")
```

The output is as follows:

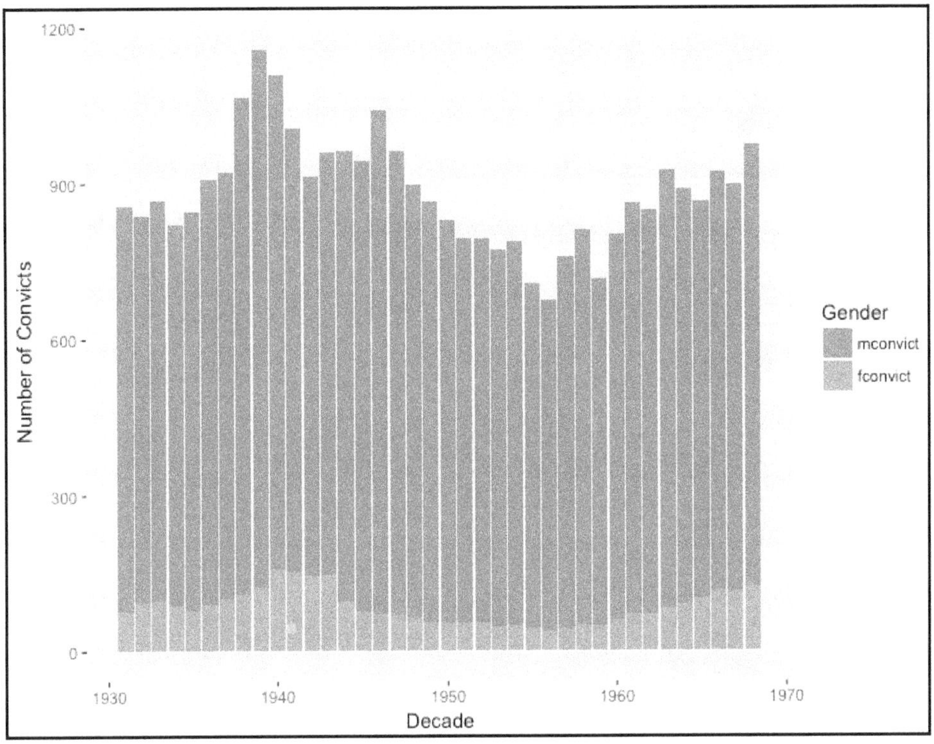

Heatmaps

Heatmaps are a simple but effective way to interpret numeric datasets. They work best when the data to be charted (in a heatmap) has been either aggregated or is of a limited size (rows and columns) so that they can be viewed effectively.

R has a native inbuilt heatmap charting feature. It can be invoked using the R function, `heatmap`.

Alternatively, there are other R packages for creating impressive heatmaps. One such example is shown as follows. The parameters have been referenced from the site package at `https://rlbarter.github.io/superheat/`:

```
devtools::install_github("rlbarter/superheat")

row.names(Hartnagel) <- Hartnagel$year
```

```
superheat(Hartnagel[,-1],heat.pal = c("#b35806", "white",
  "#542788"),heat.na.col = "white", yr = Hartnagel$mconvict,
   yr.axis.name = "Male Conviction Rate",
   bottom.label.text.angle = 90,scale=T,
   left.label.text.size = 3.5,bottom.label.text.size = 4)
```

The output is as follows:

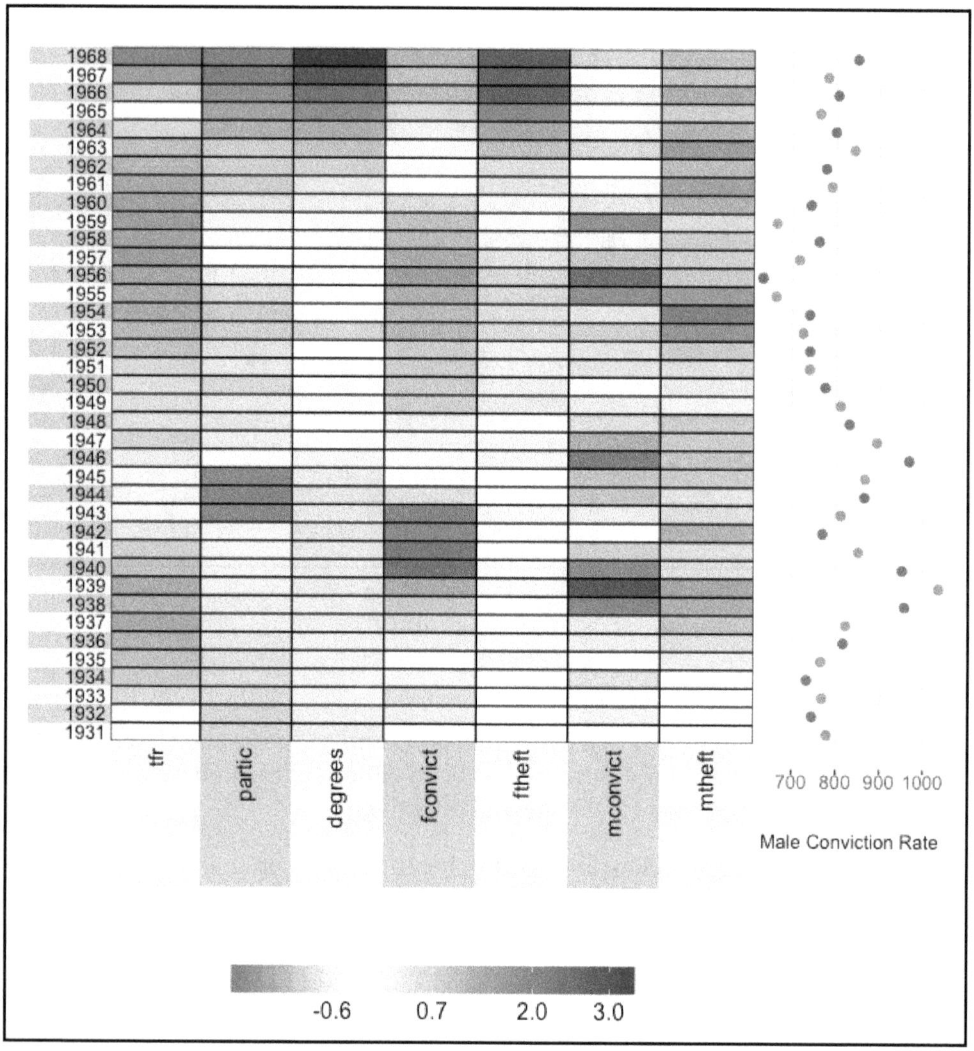

Summarizing data

As noted earlier, there are several facilities in R for summarizing data, both in base R, as well as through multiple R packages.

Using plotting functionalities such as correlograms and trellis plots, users can visualize the data in a holistic or homogeneous view.

For plotting the correlogram, we'll use the R package, ggcorrplot, as follows:

```
install.packages("ggcorrplot")
hcorr <- cor(na.omit(Hartnagel))
ggcorrplot(hcorr,hc.order = T, ggtheme = theme_bw, insig="blank",
  colors = brewer.pal(11,"RdYlGn")[c(1,6,11)])
```

The output is as follows:

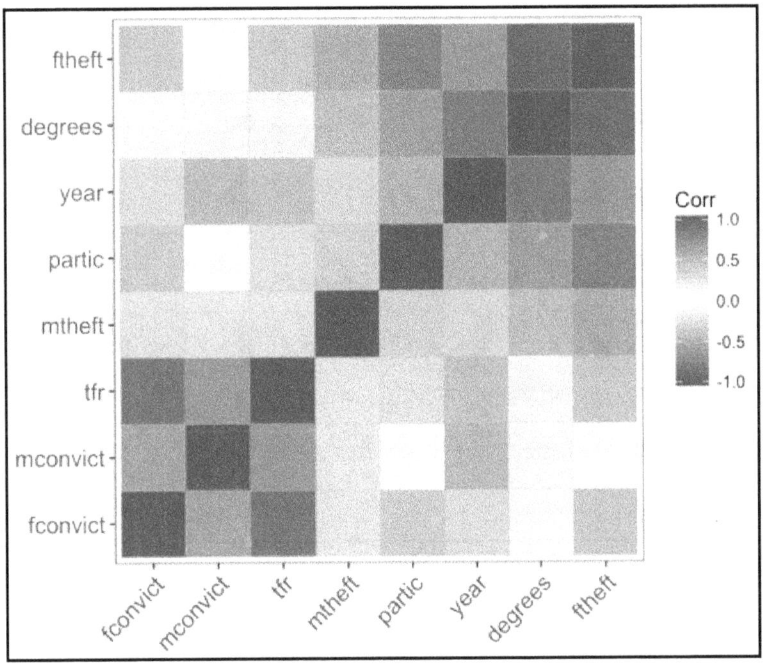

Variables that are more closely correlated are in a darker green shade relative to the ones that are less closely correlated (marked in the reddish-brown color).

Note that simply facilities such as trellis plots also exist in base R and, as demonstrated, simply calling `plot` on the `Hartnagel` dataset will yield the diagram shown as follows:

```
plot(Hartnagel) # Simply calling plot
```

Output is as follows:

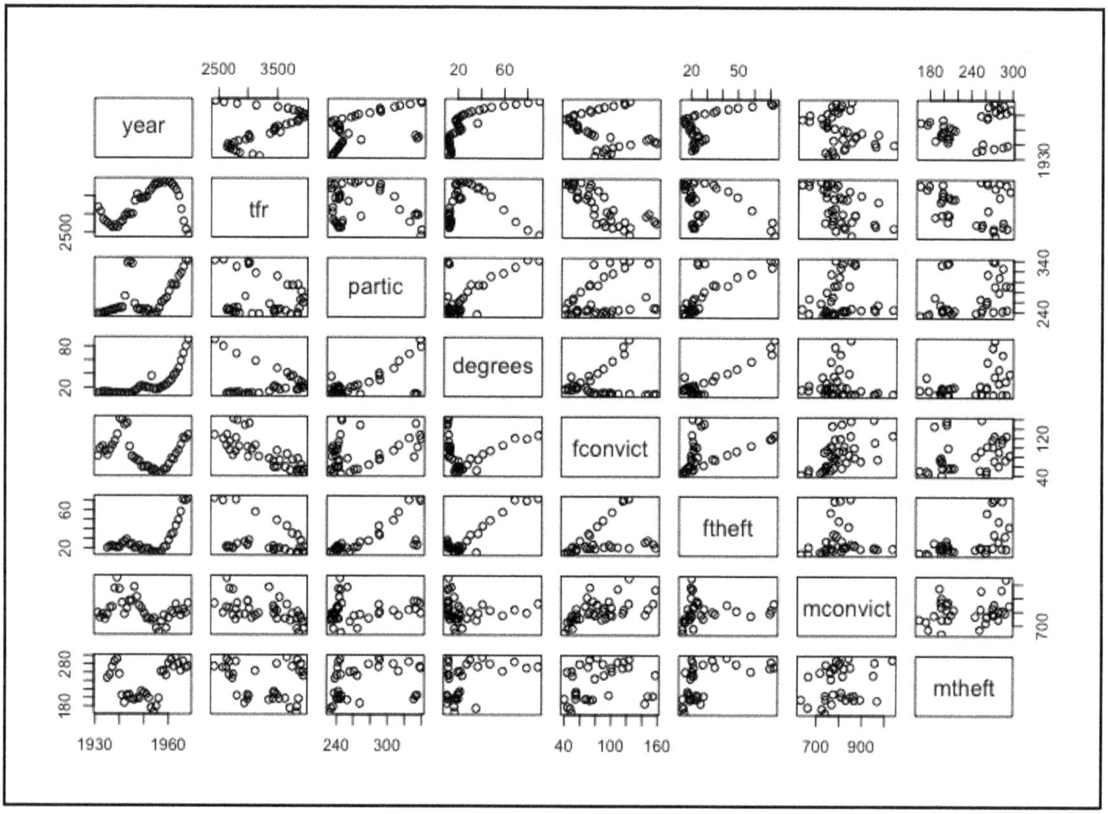

More complex and in-depth visualisations can be leveraged through other R visualization packages. The `tableplot` package allows the programmer to plot both categorical and quantitative data in a single elegant plot (`tableplot`):

```
library(tabplot)
tableplot(Salaries)
```

The output is as follows:

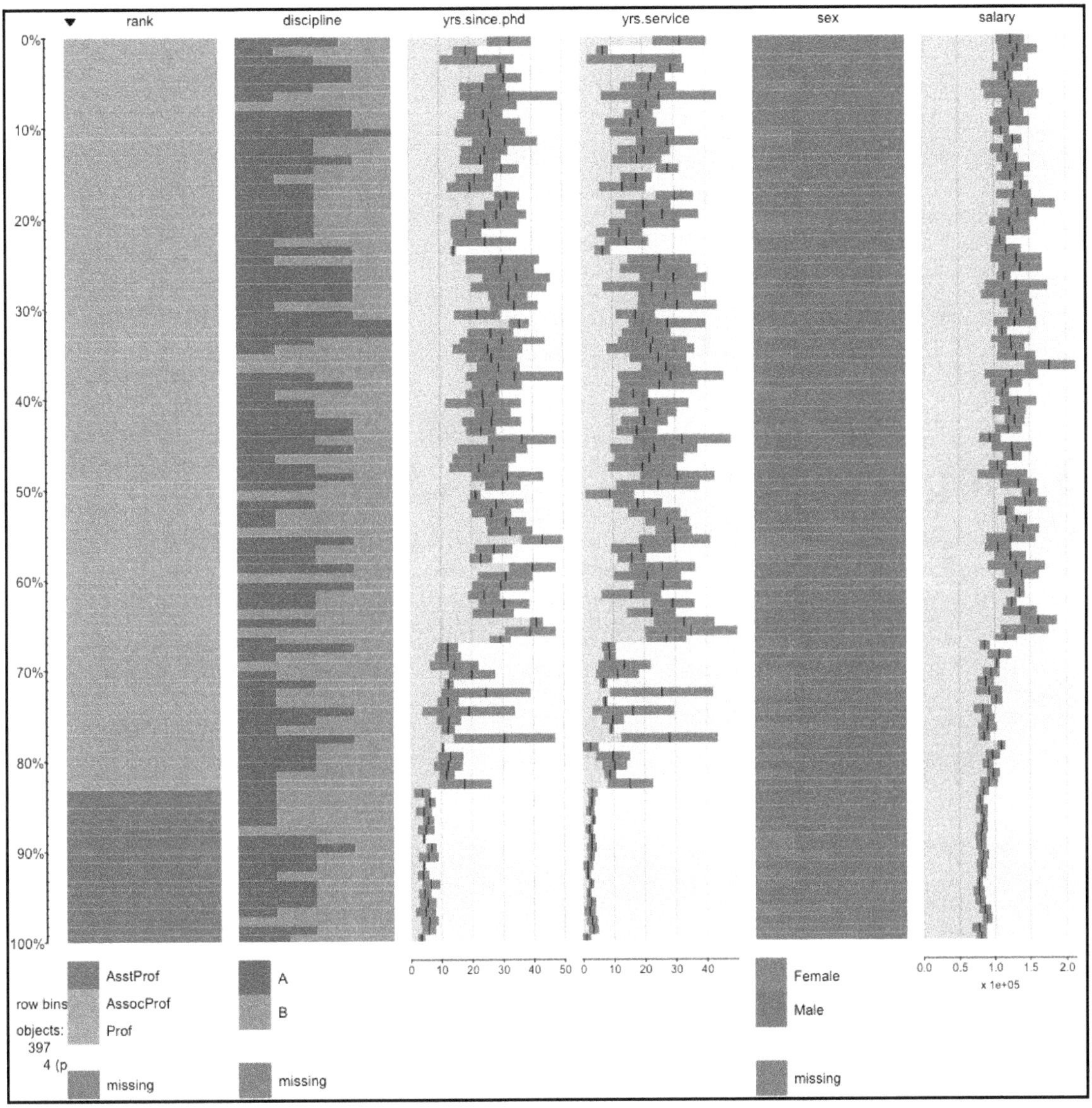

The number of visualization packages in R has grown enormously in recent years. Many of them employ `ggplot` to render images (and often start with the prefix `gg`). A few of the interesting ones are noted as follows:

- `rCharts`: A wrapper for multiple JavaScript libraries such as `polychart`, `nvd3`, and others
- `plotly`: R library for `plotly` with lots of interactive features
- `rBokeh`: A wrapper for the popular Python-based bokey visualization library
- `tmap`: For plotting thematic maps
- `ggnet`: For plotting of network diagrams
- `ggmap`: A library for plotting maps in R
- `gganimate`: To create animated charts in R

Saving analysis for future work

R packages, especially the popular ones, are frequently updated. Although the packages go through a rigorous testing process before being accepted on CRAN, it is sometimes necessary to be able to save your work at a point in time. This comes up often during production development using R packages. Reproducibility of results are also oftentimes needed in regulated environments by regulators such as the FDA.

R provides some unique and mature capabilities to store and persist data at a point in time. To retrieve the results, all the user needs to do is simply revert to a pre-saved version of the work.

The three most popular methods of saving R work in a reproducible framework are:

- **Packrat**
- **Checkpoint**
- **Rocker**

Packrat

Packrat allows users to save the state of a project by creating a local repository where the project dependencies reside. For example, if your code uses certain packages, Packrat, by default, will download those packages into a local repository. In RStudio, users may initialize projects with the packrat option in order to add native support for packrat bundling. Further details on packrat may be found at `https://rstudio.github.io/packrat`.

Checkpoint

Checkpoint is a package from Microsoft (available from the Microsoft R repository). Checkpoint allows users to specify an as-of date to ensure that the packages being used in a project will remain consistent, even if the user installs a newer version. **Microsoft R Archive Network** (**MRAN**) stores daily snapshots of packages and the checkpoint function in essence retrieves the snapshot corresponding to the date specified in the checkpoint function. It is used as follows:

```
library(checkpoint)
checkpoint("yyyy-mm-dd")
```

Further information on checkpoint is available at: `https://mran.microsoft.com/documents/rro/reproducibility`.

Rocker

Rocker, or R on Docker is the most formidable (and stable) form of reproducibility that can be achieved at present, due to the fact that it is not only the packages that are persisted but also the environment in which R has been installed. This is achieved by virtue of the fact that Docker, arguably the most popular platform for containerization, can be used to persist the environment in which the software was developed. Containers share the system kernel, but contain practically everything else such as system libraries, runtime, and other code-related dependencies.

Further information on Rocker is available at `https://github.com/rocker-org/rocker`.

Summary

In this chapter, we learned about some of the basic characteristics of data, common data issues, how to visualize data, and finally how to persist your work for reproducibility. As such, these topics are vast areas in and of themselves and this chapter should hopefully serve as an initial primer in these areas. In the next chapter, we will start exploring the field of machine learning using R. We'll learn about various algorithms in machine learning and the corresponding packages that provide easy access to a vast array of machine learning functionalities through R.

Quiz

1. **Quiz-tion**: Which of the following would usually be a discrete variable in a dataset
    1. The order in which a player elects to bat in a game of cricket
    2. The number of runs scored by a batsman
    3. The time it took to complete a match
2. **Quiz-tion**: What is the package Amelia used for?
    1. To perform chained multi-variate equations in SAS
    2. To load the `Movies` database from IMDB
    3. To address challenges with missing data
3. **Quiz-tion**: There are various packages in R that leverage `ggplot2` such as `ggnet`, `ggmap`, and many others. What does `gg` stand for?
    1. Graphics GUI
    2. Grammar of graphics
    3. GUI generation

Answers:
Q1 - 1, Q2 - 3, Q3 - 2

6

Machine Learning with R

"What we want is a machine that can learn from experience."

– Alan Turing

Machine learning is an interdisciplinary field that involves computer science, neurocomputing, statistics, and more. The idea of machines actually learning can be dated back to Alan Turing and the beginning of **Artificial Intelligence** (**AI**). Although the foundations of machine learning and the vague idea of it could be found earlier in the sayings of the great Turing, it was not until 1959 that the term machine learning, was coined by the computer scientist, Arthur Samuel.

Although such ideas were circulating before 20st century, it only became popular in the first decades of the 21st century; since then, its reputation has skyrocketed. There are many reasons for this having happened—machine learning is extremely useful—but I would mostly point to two different reasons.

First, there is data volume. Huge volumes of data are being produced every day, everywhere. To process all this information, a much more efficient and novel way of doing it was needed. Machine learning methods aimed to solve this problem. Some of their methods are data-hungry and practically each of them is able to handle linear and non-linear relations.

The second reason is feasibility. Algorithms and computing power have improved rapidly; thus, allowing machines to learn from large datasets in a reasonable time. This chapter is designed to introduce readers to the world of machine learning while estabilhing some paralallels with traditional statistics. The chapter also demonstrates how to practially fit several machine learning models through R.

The reader may feel that too much attention is given to unsupervised learning rather than supervised. This approach was purposeful given that later chapters will more cautiously discuss supervised learning methods.

Here is what can be found in this chapter:

- Which big companies are using machine learning
- Linear regression with base R
- Building decision trees with `tree` and `rpart`
- Random forest, bagging, and boosting methods
- Training **support vector machines** (**SVM**) with `caret`
- Building feedforward neural networks using `h2o`

There are several machine learning models already available for R users. In this chapter, quite a few of them will be discussed in a practical manner. But what is machine learning? There are many definitions. The next section is defining machine learning and briefly discussing its use.

What is machine learning?

What do we mean by machine learning? It's an interdisciplinary subject that cares about the development, comprehension, and application of computational methods meant to learn and generalize from datasets; it's usually related but not limited to big data. Machine learning shores up a family of ever-growing methods, suitable for overcoming a wide range of problems.

> I deeply appreciate how it has been used to fight junk email. The way it suggests replies to emails (that hardly are spam) proved to be of enormous aid too.

Such a great ability to solve problems certainly attracted big companies and tech geeks all over the world.

Machine learning everywhere

Netflix is uses machine learning to give you personal recommendations of content to watch; Amazon uses machine learning to recommend products to buy based on what you've already bought. These are the so-called **recommenders**. They are usually (but not only) built using clustering techniques.

Machine learning techniques have been also used to diagnose illnesses. Aside from the application of clustering in cancer diagnosis already mentioned in `Chapter 4`, *KDD, Data Mining, and Text Mining*, neural networks can be trained to read various exams and even predict how likely a patient is to develop certain kinds of diseases—this field is called **predictive medicine** and highly benefits from machine learning advancements.

Saving endangered species is yet another wonderful usage of machine learning. Researchers from the *University of Southern California Center for AI in Society* have trained a neural network to detect illegal hunters that set foot in national parks from Zimbabwe and Malawi. This system is designed to distinguish hunters from animals using heat signatures and was baptized as **Systematic POacher deTector** (**SPOT**).

There are unconventional uses of machine learning models. Some folks are using it to compose songs, poems, and draw figures.

Tech workers, such as Zach Lubarsky and Ethan Phelps-Goodman, are actively engaging in data-driven campaigns to solve social issues. Lubarsky and Phelps-Goodman belong to the Seattle Tech 4 Housing organization, a community dedicated to improving Seattle's residence affordability.

A quick web search will tell you that there are many real-world applications of machine learning as there are stars in the sky. Talking about stars, how do you think that the galactical sized datasets generated by astronomers are being processed? That's right, machine learning.

This collection of methods can be separated into two classes: unsupervised (unlabeled) and supervised (labeled) learning. For the former, there is no target value to fit the models—hierarchical clusters are a good example of those. The objective of unsupervised learning is usually, but not always, to extract features from data rather than actual forecasts.

Next we will be looking at how traditional statistics connect to machine learning. There are many clear connections linking both streams. To mention one, regressions from traditional statistics can also be seen in machine learning applications. Ronald Fisher, a well-renowned statistician, is recognized by some people to be among the first individuals to use machine learning.

Supervised learning models are trained to target one or more variables; hence you need labeled data. **Recurrent neural networks** (**RNNs**) can be cited as a supervised learning technique. Although practical examples for both classes are provided in this chapter, more attention is given to unsupervised learning, since supervised is focused on in further chapters such as `Chapter 8`, *Neural Networks and Deep Learning*.

Although many concepts adopted in machine learning field are essentially the same as the ones that arose from traditional statisticians and forecasters, machine learning has a vocabulary of its own. Differences may have originated due to the main proponents of the field being more related to computing than statistics.

There is no downside to learning this vocabulary. A great way to do so is to relate machine learning terms to statistical ones. Moving on to the next section, we can see how many core ideas from machine learning can be somehow translated into statistical concepts.

Machine learning vocabulary

At the end of the last section, we already hypothesized why machine learning managed to diverge in vocabulary from statistcs. Let me begin this section by discussing why the core ideas converge in essence. Many statistical methods crave to *prae e videre,* that is Latin for *to see something that did not happen yet before it actually does*, or simply, predict.

Prediction tasks, as other pattern recognition duties, often require a very sharp ability to comprehend data and generalize well into yet unseen information. This sort of shared goal drove the distinct efforts from traditional statistics and machine learning to many common places. Also, statistics, virtue to conceive all sorts of events in a probabilistic way makes it very useful to machine learning, which could be another source of shared ground acrross the different fields, not to mention the interdisciplinary nature of machine learning.

No matter the reason for that, machine learning vocabulary can be adapted and understood through statistics. This translation makes it especially easy for lovers of statistics to master machine learning and vice versa. The paper, *Neural Networks and Statistical Models,* written by Warren S. Sarle and published in 1994, showed how machine learning jargon could be related to statistical jargon. Here are some jargons:

Statistical jargon	**Machine learning correspondent**
Model estimation	Model training or learning
Estimation criteria	Cost function
Variables	Features
Independent variables	Inputs
Predicted values	Outputs
Dependent variables	Training or target values

Now that we acknowledge the existence of a link between statistics and machine learning, the time is coming to take a practical tour through the traditional methods of linear regression given by statistics using our beloved R—but not before examining the general tasks that machine learning is up to.

Generic problems solved by machine learning

Whether a problem can be solved through machine learning is only a matter of how much data, creativity, and computational power does one have. Machine learning can be used to aid diagnosis, draw recommendations, classify stellar objects, protect animal life and tackle social issues.

It can likewise be used to detect frauds, such as fraudulent credit card transactions and frauds in spreadsheets. Object , voice and face recognition, outlier detection and **natural language processing** (**NLP**) are few tasks that machine learning is recognized to perform very well already.

Machine learning tasks are frequently classified between regression or classification tasks.

Sharp chatbots, able to pass Turing's test, can be built using machine learning. Brand new content, such as fake news (don't do that), sounds, music, poems, and samples can be all created by those models. You may find that It's very useful to generate samples from noise when you are short on data. These are only some of the numerous tasks that machine learning can smoothly handle.

Linear regression with R

Linear regressions are traditional statistical models. Regressions are meant to understand how two or more variables are related and/or to make predictions. Taking limitations into account, regressions may answer questions such as: *How does the National Product respond to government expenditure in the short run?* or *What should be the expected revenue for next year?*

Of course, there are drawbacks. An obvious one is that linear regression is only meant to grasp linear relations. Plotting variables ahead may give you hints on linearity—sometimes, you can turn things around with data transformation. Note that a relation does not necessarily imply causation.

A strong relation (correlation) could also result from coincidence or spurious relations (also known as third factor or common cause). The latter does not halt your regression as long your intention is to only draw forecasts; nonetheless, true causation is always better.

Imagine that, for some beaches, you can find a strong positive correlation between the number of sodas consumed and drowning. Soda is not causing the drowning but both drowning and sodas are related to the number of swimmers. This is a spurious relation/third factor/common cause. To forbid soda consumption won't stop drowning. Yet, if soda consumption were the only number a policymaker could precisely foresee in a reasonable time horizon, it would be wise to allocate more lifeguards when the soda consumption was about to grow. In the real-world, the calendar (calendar effects) may serve better guidance.

Coincidences are hardly of any use. To check whether you get a coincidence or not, try to predict values from a dataset yet not used to fit the regression. The better results you get from validation and test datasets, the lower chances are to have a coincidence on your hands—(sample) size matters.

In order to imply causation, several precautions must be taken. If you are trusting experimental data, the experiments must be carefully designed. It's much harder to imply causation from observational data but not impossible. For example. causation between cigarretes and cancer were proved using observational data about siblings.

Now, let's get practical. Data will come from the `car` package; hence first things first, let's make sure that `car` is already installed:

```
if(!require(car)){install.packages('car')}
```

The dataset to be used is `car::UN`. In order to get the glimpse of the dataset, try the following code:

```
library(car)
dim(UN)
# [1] 207 7
head(UN)
```

The last command might output a small 6 x 7 table. Row names are named after countries. For the upcoming analysis, only columns 7, infant mortality (per 1,000 live births), and 4, per capita **gross domestic product** (**GDP**) per capita in US Dollars, will be used. As you can see, there are some `NA` (not available) values. It would be better to filter data ahead so we can see the dimension for reliable data alone:

```
dt <- (UN[!is.na(UN[,4])
          & !is.na(UN[,7]), c(7,4)])
#[1] 193  2
```

The filtered dataset is stored in the `dt` object—`!is.na()` was used to search for available values; the `&` operator made sure to filter observations simultaneously available for columns 4 and 7. We ended up with `193` observations from the 207 original ones. It would be reckless to not check whether the relation seems to be linear. A simple plot check is very useful:

```
plot(y = dt[,1],x = dt[,2],
     ylab = 'infant deaths/1,000 live births',
     xlab = 'GDP per caita (U.S. dollars)')
```

As a result, we got the following diagram:

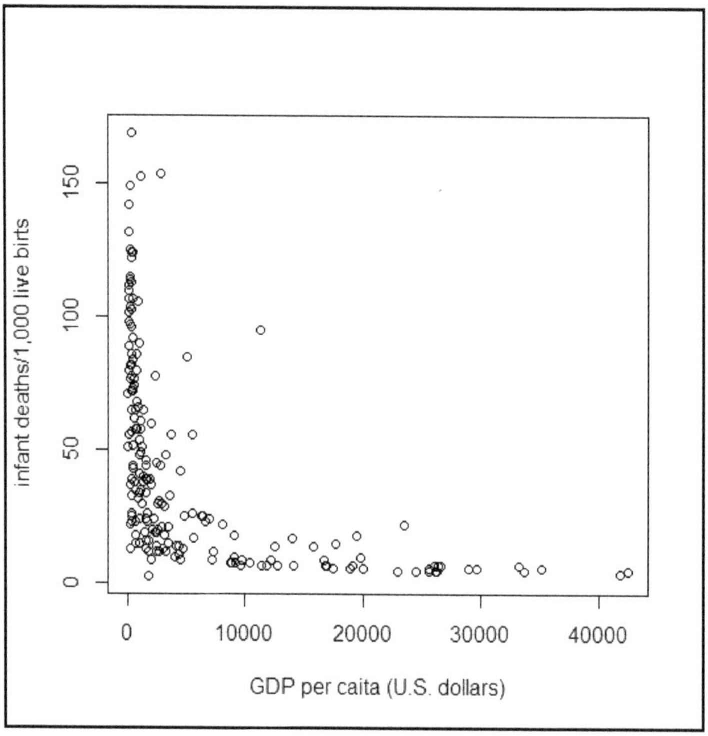

Figure 6.1: UN dataset – several countries infant deaths versus GDP per capita

Using the base plot from R, we crafted a visualization that is good enough for preliminar analysis—not so suitable for publication. Based on *Figure 6.1,* you should never say that the two variables keep a linear relation. As mentioned before, transformations can be useful. The next thing to try is data transformation.

> There are dark deep dungeons where data is tortured to obey someones' filthy interests. Data transformation can be very dangerous if a person doesn't really know what they are doing or has bad intentions. Handle transformations cautiously, otherwise, there is a risk of achieving meaningless insights or wicked results. The transformation we are about to do—the logarithmic transformation—is known for adding a bias, which some software is not prepared to deal with.

Transformations must be meaningful at least. Economists are used to applying the logarithmic transformation to a series of GDPs in order to get growing rates:

```
plot(y = dt[,1], x = log(dt[,2]),
     ylab = 'infant deaths/1,000 live birts',
     xlab = 'GDP growing rate')
```

The result can be seen in the following diagram:

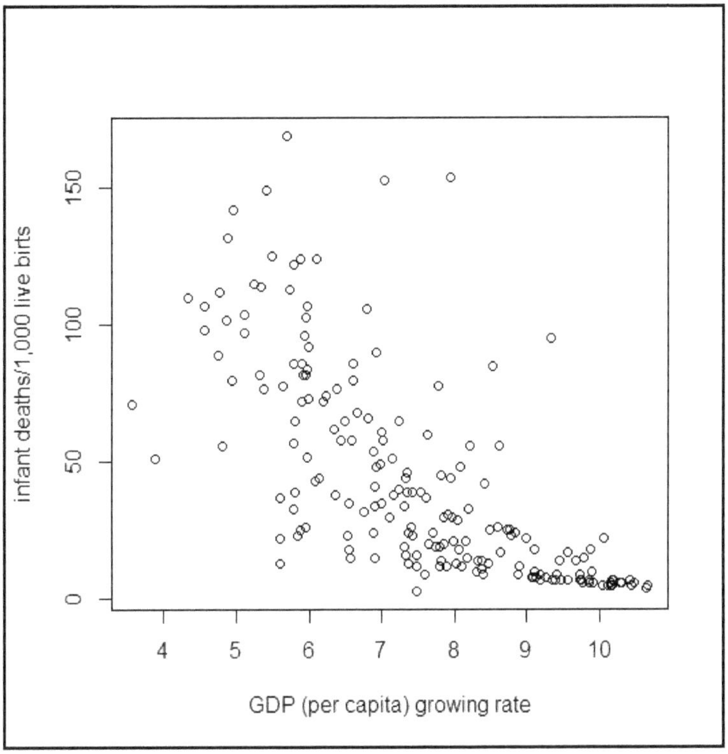

Figure 6.2: UN dataset – several countries infant deaths versus GDP (per capita) growing

The latter diagram carries a much more linear relation in comparison to the former one. To make a point, try to apply the `log()` function four times in a row. I assure you that you are going to end up with a much more linear, and pointless, relation:

```
# here lies the code for 4 logs in a row
plot(y = dt[,1], x = log(log(log(log(dt[,2])))),
     ylab = 'infant deaths/1,000 live birts',
     xlab = 'hardly meaningful variable')
```

The same would apply to differentiation. Since our observations account for single snapshots from several different countries, simply running `diff()` would be meaningless and pointless. After settling for a helpful transformation, let's store the transformed variable before dealing with data partitioning:

```
dt$log_gdp <- log(dt$ppgdp)
```

A new variable called `log_gdp` was created and stored in the `dt` DataFrame. The `sample()` function can be used to split it into estimation and test datasets:

```
# set.seed(5)
n <- sample(dim(dt)[1], size = 40)
dt_est <- dt[-n,]
dt_tst <- dt[n,]
```

Our sampling method is quite simple; it trusted seemingly random numbers to split our original observations across estimation and test datasets. The `sample()` function is sorting `40` numbers from 1 to 193, without replacement. Setting `seed` is necessary if you seek the exact same results from mine. All of the `40` numbers are stored in an object named `n`.

The last couple of commands are asking for every row from the `dt` DataFrame except the ones named by `n`; this leads to our estimation dataset (or `dt_est`). The test data (`dt_tst`) is the one with only the rows named by `n`. We can finally run our regression using `lm()`:

```
reg <- lm(infantMortality ~ log_gdp, data = dt_est)
```

We regressed `infantmortality` (`Y` or dependent variable) against `log_dpg` (`X` or independent variable).

> Regressions in R are made using the `lm()` function. The first argument (formula) must receive an expression—dependent and independent variables are separated by `~`. The subsequent argument is data, bringing the data name for which the expression makes reference to.

It means that we are trying to explain (or forecast) infant mortality using the overall growth rate of GDP per capita. Our equation can be expressed as: $Y = a + bX + e$, where a and b are estimated parameters and e is the error (also referred to as a **residual**). To see the parameters a (intercept) and b, we can simply call `reg` into our console, or we could obtain more detailed information calling `summary(reg)`. The following is what the latter function would output:

```
Call:
lm(formula = infantMortality ~ log_gdp, data = dt_est)

Residuals:
```

```
            Min 1Q Median 3Q Max
-53.7611427921 -17.3120022326 0.0007549473 11.3677416069 118.2849263781

Coefficients:
                    Estimate Std. Error t value Pr(>|t|)
(Intercept) 171.1347249385 10.0014562617 17.11098 < 2.22e-16 ***
log_gdp -17.0245553862 1.2942552335 -13.15394 < 2.22e-16 ***
---
Signif. codes: 0 '***' 0.001 '**' 0.01 '*' 0.05 '.' 0.1 ' ' 1

Residual standard error: 26.348842935 on 151 degrees of freedom
Multiple R-squared: 0.53398820233, Adjusted R-squared: 0.53090203148
F-statistic: 173.02613143 on 1 and 151 DF, p-value: < 2.22044605e-16
```

You can see test values (`p` and `t` values) for individual and grouped parameters estimation; R-squared is another traditional measure. Another very popular and traditional error measure is the **mean squared error** (**MSE**). To calculate it's very simple; actually, in the following, you can find two ways of doing it:

```
mean(residuals(reg)^2)
mean(reg$residuals^2)
# both outputs the same number
# [1] 685.1862
```

Speaking of all of the results we've seen until now, our regression doesn't look good. Single parameters and regression as a whole are statistically significant, that is, hypothesis testing rejects the null hypothesis that single parameters are equal to zero and all parameters are equal to zero altogether (F test) with less than 1% significance level. That was the good part; the bad one is displayed by R-squared, which is very low and a greater one is willed. As for MSE, we always seek lower values.

A parenthesis may be opened here. Good metrics are relative. They really depend on the other available options and goals aswell. R-squared and statistical significance is important if you are after causation. If your goal is mere prediction, you don't intend to address a policy from this; out-of-sample performance may be even more important than statistical significance and/or R-squared. To reach for the out-of-sample MSE using our test data, we can trust the following:

```
out <- predict(reg, newdata = dt_tst)
mean((dt_tst[,1] - out)^2)
# [1] 888.1686
```

The preceding code addressed a prediction using the estimated regression (`reg`) and data not used to calibrate the model (`data_tst`). Next, the actual observed values are subtracted from predicted values, `(dt_tst[,1] - out)`, which leads to a residual. The squared residuals are input as an argument to the `mean()` function, hence giving us the out-of-sample MSE.

As expected, our out-of-sample MSE is bigger than the in-sample MSE. Set a goal to diminish the gap between in and out-of-sample MSE. Always be suspicious if the out-of-sample error shows a better fit. It's possible that you picked a quite small sample for the mission.

We could have done things a little bit differently. We could have skipped some objects. As a result, the code would become a little less readable. On the other hand, we would get ourselves a much smaller code. Additionally, if we had a much bigger dataset, we would also experience non-negligible efficiency gains. The next section will give more details about this.

Tricks for lm

There are couple of ways where you can perform the same task. Sometimes in this book, I may do it more efficiently and sometimes not. There are mainly two reasons that will prevent me from trying a more efficient way:

1. I want to display a more step-wise approach so that newcomers won't feel discouraged
2. I am not that smart

There is always room for improvement. I encourage the reader to look for it every single time. It's okay if you don't succeed or if you find people with more skills than you. Next, you can see the code that I would have pulled if it weren't for reason#1:

```
# set.seed(5)
# n <- sample(dim(dt)[1], size = 40)
reg <- lm(infantMortality ~ log(ppgdp), data = dt[-n,])
out <- predict(reg, newdata = dt[n,])
```

Instead of creating a whole new variable in the dataset, the preceding code will rule the transformation directly into the expression passed to `lm()`. This direct transformation also works with the dependent variable. Another trick is to use brackets to select the calibration and test/validation datasets; this way we won't duplicate the dataset in order to split it.

TIP

You may have noticed already that the `lm()` function will designate an intercept as default. In order to prevent `lm()` from doing this, add a (zero) to the right side of the expression, for example, `lm(infantMortality ~ log(gdp) + 0, data = dt[-n,])` would do it.

Here, we used a single variable to explain infant mortality—we could have used many more if only we had them. This kind of regression that uses two or more independent variables is called **multilinear regression**. Sorry to spoil it for you, but running a multilinear regression with R is extremely easy.

The only thing you need to do is to fill your expression with more variables' names on the right side. Imagine if we have far more variables in our original dataset; these would be something like `life.expectance`, `gov.expe`, `literacy.rate`. We could simply do this:

```
expr <- infantMortality ~ log(gdp) + life.expectance + gov.expe +
literacy.rate
m_res <- lm(expr, data = dt[-n,])
```

Don't try this at your end. We don't actually have these variables so the regression won't work. This rather hypothetical example is designed to exemplify how multilinear regression is done using the `lm()` function. Before closing up this section, I want to show you a couple of functions that are much more useful when it comes to linear regression:

- `glm()`: It's about the same as `lm()` but fits generalized linear models instead. The generalized part is made to deal with heteroscedasticity, a regular problem related to linear regressions.
- `anova()`: This sole function, when input with a fitted linear model (or generalized linear model), will give you the popular analysis of variance, also known as the ANOVA table.

Linear regression is a very wide topic and still, it can be seen as the building block for several other models. The current section gave more attention to how to do it with R. Further studies on the topic could be used both to prevent big flaws in your analysis and to reach for more complex techniques. Sticking with this argument, there is a list of topics I wish the reader to consider:

- **Logistic regressions**: This is a model that can be used to handle classification problems.
- **Experimental statistics**: It all goes down to experimental statistics—how tests are designed and made, what they mean (how to interpret them), and how to collect data.

- **Problems related to linear regression**: There are several problems that could ruin a linear regression. The list goes from heteroscedasticity to misspecification. Some of them are bad for forecasting, other ones could disturb relationship analysis, and a few could hurt both or have no purpose at all. Mostly, be careful about using only a few observations and avoid nonsense relations.
- **ARIMA and GARCH models**: Both are models designed to work around time series. The latter is very useful when it comes to analyzing variance or handling things such as frequency trading.

This section focused on the practical aspects of linear regression using R. It's a rather traditional statistical method used to relate two or more variables than a younger model of machine learning. Yet, it's very useful and its simplicity makes it a feasible option for simpler problems, given that the results can be easily interpreted and don't require much work (or time) to craft them.

While doing data science, stay loyal to the force continuum: bigger guns for big problems, smaller guns for small problems.

Moving forward to the next section, we will be exploring tree-based models, which are a good choice for slightly more complicated problems.

Tree models

Decision trees build tree structures to generate regression or classification models. You can think of it as a collection of chained if, and else if statements that will culminate in predictions. These models are very flexible:

- Categorical and numerical input/output is welcomed
- Classifications and regressions can be made using tree-based models
- Trees can grow very long (and complicated) or small (and simple)

Although it's possible to design very complicated trees, it is not recommended to do so. Over-complicated trees tend to be a great source of overfitting.

Needless to say, it is very easy to implement tree-based models with R. Even more complex algorithms that rely on trees as basic building blocks can be easily implemented with R (more on that in the *Random forests – a collection of trees,*). The current section will make a quick tour through tree-based models using R. Strengths and weakness will be put under the spotlight.

Strengths and weakness

Before getting our hands dirty, we should discuss strengths and weakness related to tree-based models. To begin with strengths, trees are often inexpensive to train and understand (things can get complicated for large trees). Just as training tree models don't usually require much of computational power, understanding how the model is rolling often won't require more than figuring out a simple dendrogram.

As they can be understood with little effort, these models are called **glass-box**. Through a simple visualization, almost anyone can see how such a model is engaging in decisions. Despite their simplicity, tree models are very flexible, meaning they are capable of fitting linear and non-linear relations.

> Glass-box is the opposite of black-box.

This leads us to a downside. Flexibility comes from the ways that a tree can be specified or misspecified. Misspecifying will only cause doom and overfitting. On the other hand, this disadvantage is turned into an advantage when it comes to random forests (more details on those later). If we have no intention of trusting random forests, we can also use some techniques such as bagging, boosting, or pruning.

Tree-based models are a kind of supervised learning and can be used to solve many queries. In order to get practical, we could try ranking bank customers as good and bad payers. Else, we could try to predict prices of commodity prices. Instead, we will be trying to predict voting intentions for the Chilean plebiscite of 1988.

The Chilean plebiscite data

The Chilean plebiscite of 1988 was set to decide whether General Augusto Pinochet—ruler of Chile at the time—should or should not extend his ruling for an additional 8 years. The majority of voters picked *No* (nearly 56%), hence marking the ending the Pinochet's era. Data for voting intentions can be found in the `car` package. The dataset in question is called `Chile`.

Let's start by gathering some knowledge on the dataset. Uncomment and run the first line if you haven't installed `car` yet:

```
# install.packages('car')
library(car)
?Chile
head(Chile)
```

The dataset has eight variables. Four of them are numerical:

- `population`: The size of the respondent's community
- `age`: Measured in years
- `income`: Monthly income (in pesos)
- `statusquo`: Scale of support for the status quo

The remaining four are categorical:

- `region`: A factor with levels for regions—central (`C`), Metropolitan Santiago (`M`), north (`N`), south (`S`) and city of Santiago (`SA`)
- `sex`: This displays `F` for females and `M` for males.
- `education`: A factor with levels for education—primary (`P`), post-secondary (`PS`) and secondary (`S`)
- `vote`: A factor with levels—abstain (`A`), will vote against Pinochet (`N`), will vote in favor of Pinochet (`Y`) and undecided (`U`)

Compared with the dataset just used, `Chile` has a higher dimensionality. Always take care what kind of information you are using. If something could cause a decision tree to lose some of its interpretability, this something is a lot of nodes (input and output). Overcomplicated models usually tend to generalize badly.

Using the Chile dataset, it's time to get practical. Taking advantage of the large number of packages already created for R, let's try a decision tree to predict vote intentions from Chile data. With the following, we see how the strengths and weakness play their roles in a practical example.

Starting with decision trees

Much like when we are learning something new, this will begin with a careless, reckless, flawed (at least on some level) approach. I encourage the reader to seek ways of improving our models and code as we go on. Later, we may end up with very similar or different solutions. If you can't address an alternative at the time or even if your alternative doesn't go well, I guarantee that, by paying that much attention, you will learn more from the reading experience.

A great way to start is by discussing which R packages we could use to make trees, highlighting which features we could expect from each of them. *Table 6.2* introduces briefly some packages used to estimate tree models, as well as popular features for each of them:

Package name	Title	Popular features
tree	Classification and regression tree	Prune can be easily implemented with the tree package
rpart	Recursive partitioning and regression trees	Widely popular package; prune is also implemented by rpart
ipred	Improved predictors	Easily implement bagging for regression, classification, and survival trees
Cubist	Regression modeling using rules with added instance-based corrections.	Train tree-like models that use committees; very similar to boosting techniques
gbm	Generalized boosted regression models	Implement several models using boosting

Table 6.2: Tree-related packages

Bagging, boosting, and committees are more closely related to random forests (**spoiler alert**) as they calibrate several tree models. For this reason, I won't compare ipred, Cubist, and gbm with rpart and tree. Those will only be compared with the randomForest package. In this section, we will be comparing rpart and tree.

Let's get started by splitting the `car::Chile` DataFrame into train, validation, and test sets:

```
dt_Chile <- Chile[complete.cases(Chile),]
set.seed(50)
i_out <- sample(dim(dt_Chile)[1],
                size = round(dim(dt_Chile)[1]*.3))
```

By calling `complete.cases()`, we make sure to eliminate any row that could display `NA`. Although the original dataset had 2,700 observations, only 2,431 of them accounted for complete information for all columns. This complete dataset is now stored by the object called `dt_Chile`.

Fancier techniques for sampling are available, especially for voting intentions. For the time being, this seemingly random approach that uses `sample()` will be enough. Approximately 30% of row indexes from `dt_Chile` were stored into the `i_out` object. There is yet more to do.

Previously in the *Linear regression with R* section, we used a two-part sample approach (train and test). Now we will be using three parts: train, validation, and test. We already ruled what won't be in the estimation dataset (`i_out`); it's time to split it into test and validation sets. Here is a way to do it:

```
val <- i_out[ 1 : (length(i_out) %/% 2)]
test <- i_out[ (length(i_out) %/% 2 + 1) : length(i_out)]
```

The `%/%` operator is simply asking for the quotient given by a division. As the latter code block is designating, the `val` and `test` objects are subsets of `i_out`. Each of these objects is getting around half of its original set, `i_out`. The validation data will be useful later while pruning.

> Do not forget, the `i_out`, `val`, and `test` objects carry indexes related to the real data (`dt_Chile`) and not actual data. Those will be used for subsetting later.

Let's start to grow trees with the `tree` and `rpart` packages.

Growing trees with tree and rpart

There are no big differences between growing trees with `tree` or `rpart`. Both work in similar ways and both depend on the `dtree` package, more or less. As the time-cost of growing trees is often too small, I can't see a reason not to try both, hence explaining how to grow trees using both.

The following shows how to recursively grow a decision-tree model using the `tree` package:

```
if(!require(tree)){install.packages('tree')}
library(tree)
tree_tree <- tree(vote ~ . ,
                  data = dt_Chile[-i_out,],
                  method = 'class',
                  mindev = 0)
```

The very first couple of lines are performing a check-install on the `tree` package and then loading and attaching the whole package. After these two lines, an object called `tree_tree` is being created. The `tree()` function is taking care of creating the decision tree using the `tree` package. Let's get a closer look at its arguments.

It starts with `formula`. By inputting `vote ~ .`, we want the vote variable to be explained for all of the other variables available in the DataFrame. The dot sign (`.`) used like this stands for a quick way to say *all other variables are available*. The package will craft the tree recursively and the order in which we ask for the variables won't change the final result.

Yet, we could name fewer variables. For example, if you only want to build a tree based on regions and income only, naming `vote ~ region + income` would do it. Or naming `vote ~ income + region` would lead to the same results. Notice that the order on the right side of the expression doesn't matter while the variable named on the left side (predicted variable) was not changed.

The next arguments are `data` and `method`. While the latter is input with `'class'`, which is short for classification, the former is input with `dt_Chile[-i_out,]`. Notice how the `i_out` object was used to call only the training set; the minus sign played an essential role here by removing from the set all of the rows that corresponded to the out-sample.

Last but not least, there is the `mindev` argument. The tree is grown recursively, `mindev` sets a criterion on how much a new branch (variable) must contribute in order to get the tree to grow it. By setting it to zero, we allow all variables to participate. Can you figure out how this could go wrong?

> Arguments such as `mindev` are called **control parameters**. In order to meet some other control parameters, try typing `?tree.control` into your R console.

Let's look at what we got so far with the following code:

```
plot(tree_tree)
text(tree_tree, cex = .7)
```

The following shows the mess we got in by setting `mindev = 0` (the default `0.01` would be much better):

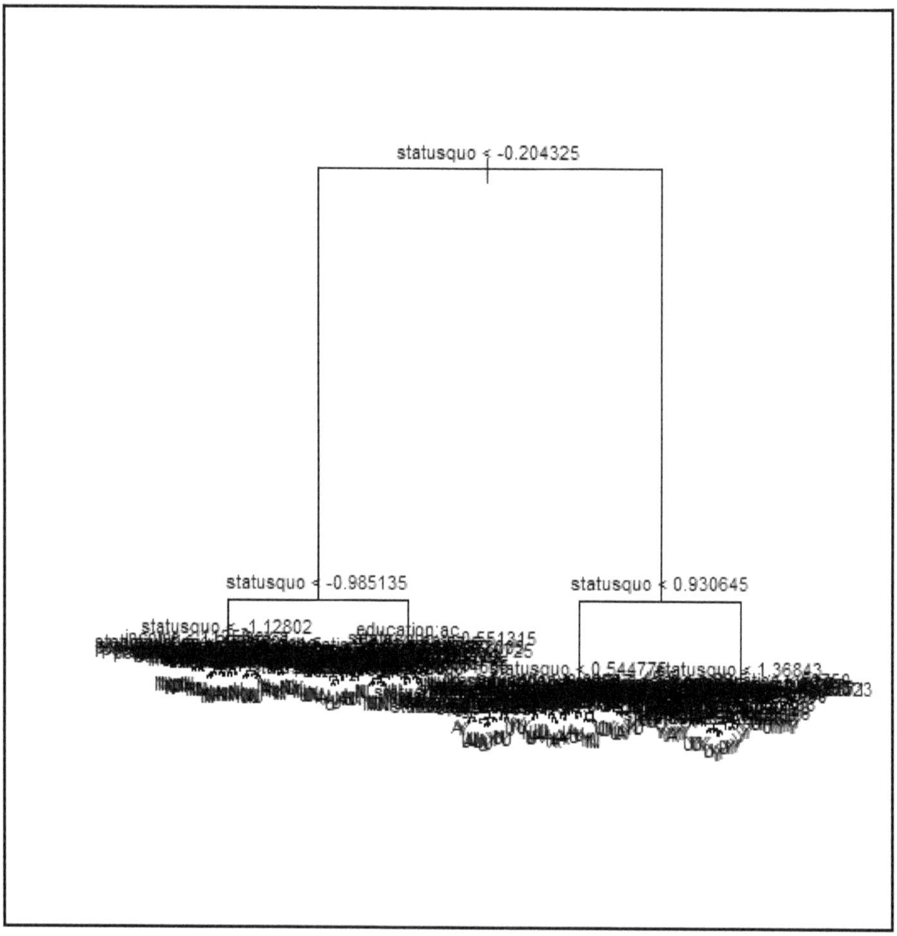

Figure 6.3: First decision tree for vote intentions or, as I like to call it, a mess

Do you recall me saying that a great advantage of decision trees is simplicity? By growing too many nodes, simplicity is likely to vanish.

> A key concept of decision-tree models is nodes. The first (top) node is called **root node**. The last ones (bottom) are called leaf nodes or end nodes. The remaining ones are called chance nodes or intermediary nodes.

In order to print the text that shows how the tree rolls, simply call the object storing it (`tree_tree`). An alternative is to use `summary()`. If inputted with trees created by the `tree` package, `summary()` will only output some brief information about the model; your console won't be flooded with numerous nodes even if you had thousands of them:

```
summary(tree_tree)

# Classification tree:
# tree(formula = vote ~ ., data = dt_Chile[-i_out, ], method = "class",
#     mindev = 0)
# Number of terminal nodes: 220
# Residual mean deviance: 1.05 = 1556 / 1482
# Misclassification error rate: 0.2244 = 382 / 1702
```

The misclassification error rate is an accuracy measure related to classification trees. Trusting the training data, our model missed 22,44% (`382` out of `1702`) of the times. The following code will teach how a very similar tree can be grown using the `rpart` package:

```
if(!require(rpart)){install.packages('rpart')}
library(rpart)
tree_rpart <- rpart(vote ~ .,
                    data = dt_Chile[-i_out,],
                    method = 'class',
                    control=rpart.control(cp = 0))
```

The only thing that's different here is how the control parameter was set. The argument `control` is ruling it. A parameter similar to `mindev` is being named inside the `rpart.control()` function, called `cp`. There are lots of control parameters listed; try calling `?rpart.control()`.

Calling `summary(tree_rpart)` won't give anything similar to `summary(tree_tree)`. We can manually estimate the misclassification error rate with the following code:

```
mean(residuals(tree_rpart))
# [1] 0.2514689
```

The model fitted by `rpart` misclassified around 25,15% of the times. An upside of this package is that it can be combined with `rattle` and `RColorBrewer` in order to create stunning decision-tree visualizations. Check it out:

```
if(!require(rattle)){install.packages('rattle')}
if(!require(RColorBrewer)){install.packages('RColorBrewer')}
library(rattle)
fancyRpartPlot(tree_rpart, sub = '')
```

Figure 6.4 shows the visualization created by the `fancyRpartPlot()` function:

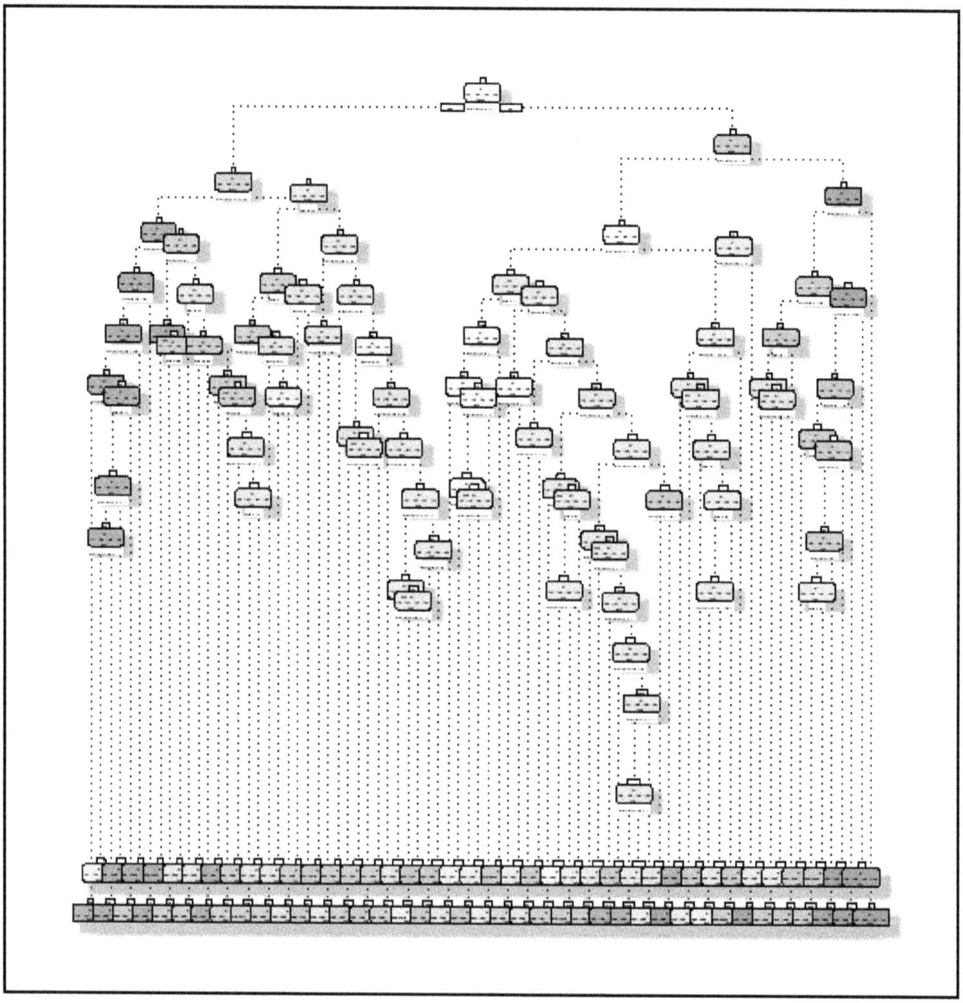

Figure 6.4: Decision-tree visualization created with the rattle package

It is much better than the visualization achieved in *Figure 6.3*—we could use `plot()` and `text()` functions as well—yet it's not thanks to the numerous nodes. As far as we know, only the interpretability may be hurt until now. More often than not, the ability to predict further data is also hurt by having too many nodes but we can't know for sure until we try it on test data.

Let's start by checking `tree_tree` (the decision tree grown with the `tree` package):

```
predict(tree_tree, type = 'class',
        newdata = dt_Chile[test,])

mean(predict(tree_tree, type = 'class',
             newdata = dt_Chile[test,]) == dt_Chile[test, 'vote'])
# [1] 0.569863
```

First, `predict()` was called to ask for a prediction upon the test dataset; a vector of classes is output. Later, `mean()` was combined with `predict()` and a Boolean operator (==) to calculate the hit rate using the test dataset. In order to calculate the misclassification error rate, try replacing == with `!=`.

> Slightly different results may come each time you try to calculate the hit and/or misclassification rate at the test dataset using the `tree_tree` object, unless you set `seed`. This may be due to the `tie` method—it may be random.

About the same could be done to retrieve the predictions and hit rate for the test dataset using `rpart`:

```
predict(tree_rpart, type = 'class',
        newdata = dt_Chile[test,])

mean(predict(tree_rpart, type = 'class',
             newdata = dt_Chile[test,]) == dt_Chile[test, 'vote'])
# [1] 0.6109589
```

The test hit rate for `tree_rpart` was better (61,06%). It does not mean that `rpart` will do better every single time; try both. The trees trained until now are overcomplicated and do not generalize well yet on unseen data. We could squeeze some performance by doing pruning.

To put it simply, pruning will cut off nodes that don't contribute that much to model performance. Too often, this approach leads toward a better out-of-sample performance plus trees that are much easier to understand. The subsequent code block is pruning `tree_tree` while calculating the new hit rate and plotting the pruned tree:

```
p_tree <- prune.misclass(tree_tree,
                         best = 5,
                         newdata = dt_Chile[val,])

mean(predict(p_tree, type = 'class',
             newdata = dt_Chile[test,]) == dt_Chile[test, 'vote'])
# [1] 0.6383562

plot(p_tree);text(p_tree, cex = .7)
```

One way to prune a tree using the `tree` package we used the `prune.misclass()` function. Fill this function with a tree model created by the `tree` package, an integer picking a number of terminal nodes a subtree may have (the `best` argument). This integer pruning parameter, an alternative is the `k` argument, which is a cost-complexity parameter.

TIP

There is no rule for choosing the numbers to input `best` or `k`; try some.

The `prune.missclass()` function should be input at least with `tree` (the `tree` model), `best`, or `k`. There is yet another argument that can improve the pruning, `newdata`. Inputting `newdata` will rule with which data to calculate the pruning parameters; hence, the validation data can help here. The whole pruned tree is stored in an object called `p_tree`.

Using the test dataset, the hit rate for `p_tree` was calculated. The newer rate, 63,83%, shows some improvement in comparison to the one calculated for `tree_tree` (56,98%). Also, the plot feels much more friendly now, as shown here:

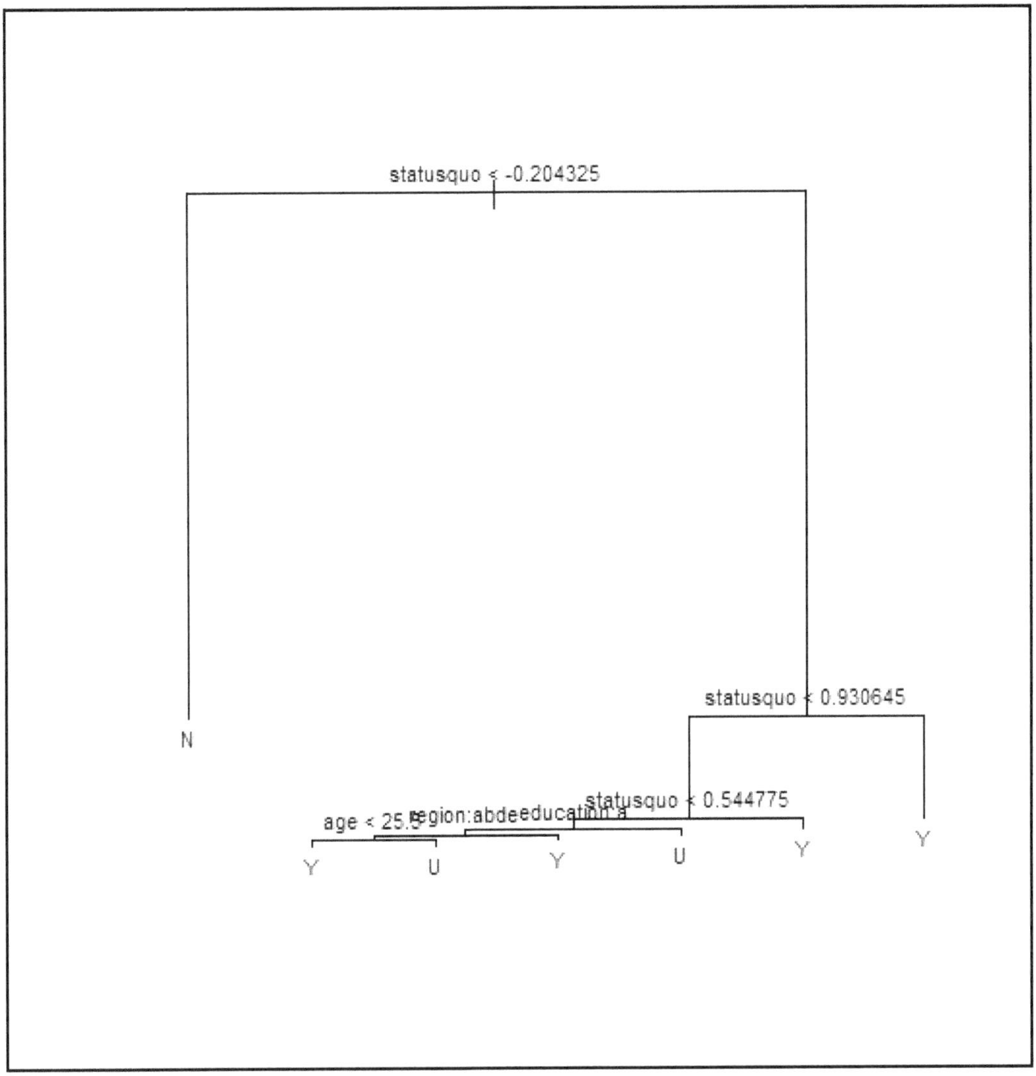

Figure 6.5: Pruned tree (tree package)

We can prune `tree_rpart` using a cost-complexity parameter:

```
p_rpart <- prune(tree_rpart, cp = .01)

mean(predict(p_rpart, type = 'class',
             newdata = dt_Chile[test,]) == dt_Chile[test, 'vote'])
# [1] 0.6356164
```

With rpart, we can call prune() to prune decision trees. The only arguments needed are the tree to be pruned—it must be an rpart object—and the complexity parameter (cp). In comparison to tree_rpart, the pruned tree (p_rpart) gained around 2 p.p. performance in the test dataset.

We can visualize p_rpart using rattle:

```
# library(rattle)
fancyRpartPlot(p_rpart, sub = '')
```

The following diagram shows the results:

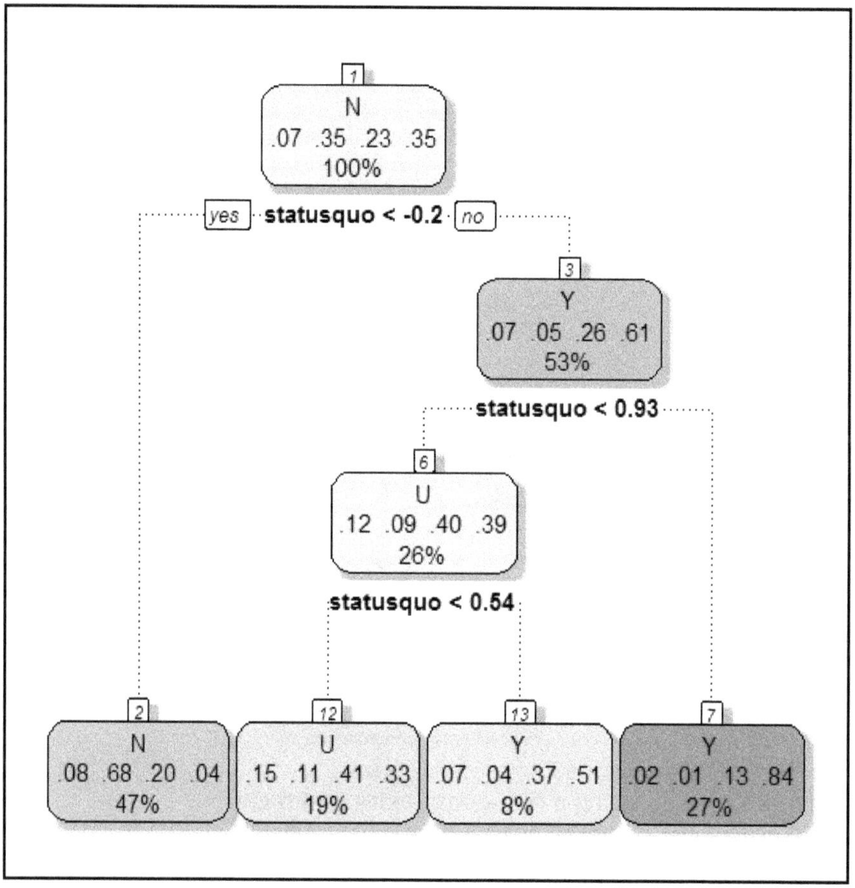

Figure 6.6: Pruned tree (rpart package)

This tree is much easier to understand. The decision made by the node number three is redundant. If node number one was directly connected to node number six, the outcome would be the same. Arguably, the only reason for us to get such complicated trees is that we set off the complexity control parameter in the first place. In the following, I show a code that did not turn off this parameter along with the hit rate for the `test` sample:

```
tree_tree2 <- tree(vote ~ . ,
                   data = dt_Chile[-i_out,],
                   method = 'class',
                   mindev = .01)
mean(predict(tree_tree2, type = 'class',
             newdata = dt_Chile[test,]) == dt_Chile[test, 'vote'])
# [1] 0.6246575

tree_rpart2 <- rpart(vote ~ .,
                     data = dt_Chile[-i_out,],
                     method = 'class',
                     control=rpart.control(cp = .01))
mean(predict(tree_rpart2, type = 'class',
             newdata = dt_Chile[test,]) == dt_Chile[test, 'vote'])
# [1] 0.6356164
```

A point made: less (nodes) is often more (out of sample accuracy) when it comes to decision trees. Decision trees work as foundations for a very famous algorithm called **random forests**. The relation between forests and trees is not a fateful name coincidence. The next section is (not randomly) explores the random forests guided by the awesome R.

Random forests – a collection of trees

It is almost a fact that combined forecasts tend to work better than single forecasts. This phenomenon is called the *Wisdom of the Crowd*. Random forests exploit the *Wisdom of the Crowd* while fitting and combining several trees. Due to this combination task, algorithms such as random forests are also called **ensemble learning**. Random forests are not the only ensemble learning algorithms; bagging, boosting, and committees also fit several models.

In this section, we are not only aiming at random forests but all those other kinds of models and packages that could possibly compete with them. This time we are not benchmarking accuracy only. Time elapsed will be taken into consideration. Note that it is a very simple measure and may widely vary from my end to yours.

The time needed to train a single neural network model is sometimes greater than the time needed to fit hundreds of regressions. Yet, neural networks can represent non-linear relations without the need for express transformation.

Great members of the R community—SiR Andy and SiR Matthew Wiener—ported methods for random forests from Fortran to R. These methods are hanging around the `randomForest` package, just waiting for you to use them. Check if it's already installed to start:

```
if(!requireNamespace('randomForest', quietly = T)){
  install.packages('randomForest')}
```

If your internet connection is locked and loaded, after running the preceding code block, you will make sure to have `randomForest` installed.

Using `requireNamespace()` instead of `require()` to check if a package is already is installed culminates in a small efficiency gain. The former function only attaches the library while the latter attaches and loads it.

Random forests can be used to tackle problems such as classification, survival analysis, and prediction in general. More often than not, random forests can easily outperform single regression and other kinds of single models for both in-sample and out-sample measures. Forests helps to diminish overfitting.

A model overfits when they do very well in the in-sample measures but it derails for out-of-sample ones. If data partitioning is done right, great gaps might indicate that a model is so addicted to the estimation data that it can't generalize well from it. Modelers usually set as a goal to overfit less.

As the package relies on the random `seed` generator, let's start by loading the package and setting `seed`:

```
library(randomForest)
set.seed(1999)
```

Now we can fit a random forest model. `Sys.time()` will be used to calculate elapsed time as follows:

```
time0_rf <- Sys.time()

rf_model <- randomForest(vote ~ . ,
                         data = dt_Chile[-i_out ,],
                         ntree = 450,
                         na.action = na.exclude)

time1_rf <- Sys.time()
```

The preceding chunk starts by creating a variable named `time0_rf` (time zero random forest) and terminates with the creation of `time1_rf` (time one random forest). They respectively account for the system time that immediately precedes and proceeds the random forest model fitting. The difference between them (`time0_rf - time1_rf`) will tell how much time it took to fit our model.

> Many things, apart from how efficient and cost less your model fitting is, will interfere within elapsed time. How good your machine is and programs running in the background are examples of what could affect it as well. Nonetheless, for this context, that time measure will be enough. Other than that, I suggest you try the `tictoc` or `microbenchmark` packages, if you need to benchmark your code.

In between these two variables, the code block is saving a random forest model in a variable named `rf_model`. The function used to calibrate this model carries the same name as the package responsible for it, `randomForest()`. The way we set this is very similar to the way we set single decision-tree models in the section, *Tree models*.

First, we set up a formula (`vote ~ .`). The dot sign is a shortcut for all of the other variables available in the dataset. The argument `data` brings no novelties. It rules the DataFrame used to train the model. The number of trees trained is ruled by `ntree`. Lastly, there is the `na.action` argument. We already know that there is no `NA` at our data (check the *Tree models* section), but if there was, `na.exclude` would make sure to make it vanish from the fitting process:

```
mean(predict(rf_model, type = 'class',
             newdata = dt_Chile[test,]) == dt_Chile[test, 'vote'])
# [1] 0.6547945
time1_rf - time0_rf
# Time difference of 1.061416 secs
```

The best (out-of-sample) hit rate we got until recently for this problem was floating around 63%, 83 %. Using random forests, we could achieve a hit rate near 65%, 48 %. The `print()` and `plot()` methods are also available for `randomForest` objects such as `rf_model`. Try `print(rf_model)` to check a confusion matrix or `plot(rf_model)` to check a graph.

We can try bagging with the `ipred` package. The following code block shows how to make sure it's installed before loading the whole package:

```
if(!require(ipred)){install.packages('ipred')}
library(ipred)
```

With `ipred` installed, we can try bagging the algorithm with the `bagging()` function:

```
time0_bag <- Sys.time()

bag_model <- bagging(vote ~ ., data = dt_Chile[-i_out ,])

time1_bag <- Sys.time()
```

Again, variables were created using `Sys.time()` for benchmarking purposes. Let's check how bagging has rolled:

```
mean(predict(bag_model, type = 'class',
             newdata = dt_Chile[test,]) == dt_Chile[test, 'vote'])
# [1] 0.6356164
time1_bag - time0_bag
# Time difference of 0.350996 secs
```

Bagging did not perform better than random forests but that does not mean that it will go this way every single time. Yet, there is weak evidence about `ipred` being able to beat `randomForest`. There is yet another algorithm that might compete with random forests, which is boosting.

You can fit boosting models with R using the `gbm` package. The reader might face some tricks ahead. Let's start as usual by installing and loading the package we will be using next:

```
if(!require(gbm)){install.packages('gbm')}
library(gbm)
```

Fitting a model with `gbm` is pretty simple. Check it out:

```
time0_gbm <- Sys.time()

gbm_model <- gbm(formula = formula(dt_Chile[,c(8, 1:7)]),
                 data = dt_Chile[-i_out ,],
```

```
                        distribution = 'multinomial',
                        n.trees = 450)

time1_gbm <- Sys.time()
```

The formula input is equivalent to `vote ~ .`. The trick here is to get the DataFrame (`dt_Chile[ , ]`) and tweak the columns order, so the predicted variable will appear in the right-hand side of the expressions after inputting it into `formula()`. With this, I only wanted to introduce an alternative way to set up expressions; `vote ~ .` would work perfectly there.

Next, there is the `data` argument as usual. The news here is coming from the `distribution` argument; as we have multiple categories to classify, `'multinomial'` is the way to go. If we had a binary problem we might like to use `'bernoulli'` instead. If you skip this argument, `gbm::gbm()` will pick it from an educated guess.

> **TIP**
> There are tons of distributions available. Entering `?gbm::gbm()` will help you to find which are available. Deeper knowledge might be needed to optimally pick a distribution.

As `randomForest()` fitted `450` trees, about the same was asked from `gbm()` with `n.trees = 450`. There are many other accessible arguments that can be used to tune your model. They are well described in the documentation; follow them with `?gbm::gbm()`.

> **TIP**
> `summary(gbm_model)` will give a plot displaying the variables contribution to the model. You will notice that, from the seven independent variables, only three contributed and, from those three, `statusquo` alone got more 80% relative influence.

Calculating the hit rate may be a little bit tricker in comparison to what we have seen up to now, but that is not all bad. Predictions are given in a much more detailed (and maybe raw) way. This means that you can aim for higher levels of customization, which is actually an advantage of using R over some black-box statistical software.

We can store the predictions in an object for further examination:

```
pred_gbm <- predict(gbm_model,
                    type = 'response',
                    n.trees = 450,
                    newdata = dt_Chile[test,])
```

Here, we can see how `predict.gbm()` works. The first argument must be a `gbm` class model. The `'class'` argument is not available; the options for this argument are `'link'` or `'response'`. Each of them responds differently depending on the distribution adopted in the fitting phase. Here we asked for the probabilities of each observation being a certain category.

The `n.trees` argument receives how many trees we want the prediction to be built on. This same argument can be also input with a vector; this way you can retrieve predictions for each specific iteration. The last argument, `newdata`, is setting the new dataset used to draft predictions.

The object storing the predictions is a three-dimensional array. The third dimension has a single element. We could access predictions for different iterations if we had input `n.trees` with a vector instead of an integer. That said, this third dimension is not very useful here, so let's transform this object into a two-dimensional DataFrame:

```
pred_gbm <- as.data.frame(pred_gbm[,,1])
```

Notice how the third dimension was subsetted: `pred_gbm[,,1]`. With this, we avoid the column names from being weird. Speaking in terms of forecast, it's much better to have your predictions in terms of probabilities rather than points. You are far more honest saying *There is a 28% chance that Jack will vote yes* than saying *Jack will vote yes*.

If you check `head(pred_gbm)`, you will see that we have interval (probabilities) predictions rather than point predictions (yes, no, and so on). This is actually better in terms of predictions but for the sake of comparability (and simplicity), we have to get point predictions just like the ones we could get for the previous models while setting `prediction.*(type = 'class')`.

However, until this point we have only compared point measures (hit rate), so we have to convert our probabilistic prediction into a point one. We have to check for each row, which is the column holding the greater probability. We can easily work this out with a couple of functions while working with a DataFrame:

```
pred_gbm <- names(pred_gbm)[max.col(pred_gbm, 'first')]
```

Now `pred_gbm` is a vector of characters displaying which vote each person displayed by `test` sample is more likely to choose. With this, we can measure the hit rate:

```
mean(pred_gbm == dt_Chile[test, 'vote'])
# [1] 0.6630137
time1_gbm - time0_gbm
# Time difference of 0.9355559 secs
```

The performance here was enhanced but not for much. It does not necessarily mean that `gbm` ever beats `randomForest`. As a matter of fact, this difference could come from tuning parameters or even the sample picked for test and train. I personally don't have a preference here.

I really appreciate how I can see how each variable has influenced the process using `summary.gbm()` and how I can pick a distribution using `gbm::gbm()`. Yet the results were so close that I am not sure about one performing better than other. The time requested to fit those models are often so small that you might rapidly grow out of excuses for not fitting both at once.

> Even if we had a dataset with high dimensionality, only three variables showed some influence over `gbm` models and probably the same happened to random forest models and simpler decision trees. Luckily for us, the dataset was not so small that it couldn't differ good features from not so good ones. Selecting features from data knowledge is a role of feature engineering.

In this section, we saw how to easily grow random forests and other ensemble learning techniques through R. Let me stress that although random forests can handle classification and regression problems, they are much more likely to deal better with classification problems rather than regression ones.

Another downside is that they are remarked as a black-box type of model in the statistical sense. Next, we are moving forward to SVM models. This is a whole supervised learning technique that can handle regression and classification.

Support vector machines

To put it simply, SVM algorithms search for hyperplanes in order to build classifiers and regressions. The mathematics behind it are nothing but amazing. The core idea behind it is to look for improved perspectives (hyperplanes) in order to separate data points, hence allowing to separate classes that are linearly-inseparable.

In other words, some variables may be linearly-inseparable in the *X*-*Y* dimension but you could apply a transformation (hyperplane transformation) that would give it an extra dimension (*Z*). Looking from this new perspective, you might be able to find a hyperplane that could separate well the distinct classes. In an extreme scenario, this process would burst dimensions right in our faces depending on the problem we were looking at. Lucky for us, there is the kernel trick.

However, there is no need to actually know which transformation to use. All that is asked of you is to pick a kernel function and go with it—the **kernel trick** was truly an ace in the hole for the SVMs. Thanks to convex optimization, SVMs will never be stuck in local optimal but they can suffer from overfitting.

A great way to avoid overfitting is to pick the right kernel and parameters.

I truly recommend the reader study the so-called **kernel trick**. Kernels are very useful because they can replace dot products. As many machine learning algorithms can be entirely expressed in terms of dot products, they can also be expressed (and coded) using kernels instead.

That being said, if you are not a kernel adopter, I encourage you to gather a deeper understanding of kernels; it might help you the next time you are writing down an machine learning algorithm. Which is your favorite kernel? Mine is the radial basis.

Enough with the theory for the moment. Things are going to get practical now. R is ready to deal with SVMs. There is a couple of packages I could name (really a couple): `e1071` and `kernlab`. Where there is smoke, there is fire; and where there are multiple machine learning packages, there is the `caret` package.

The `caret` package gathers many machine learning packages. Training different models with the different packages reunited under the `caret` package is actually very easy. The package is extensively explained here: `http://topepo.github.io/caret/`.

Given that we're exploring SVM now, you may want to take a shortcut and go straight to the following link: `http://topepo.github.io/caret/train-models-by-tag.html#support-vector-machines`.

But you sure will benefit from reading the entire document. Don't worry, you don't need to read it right now. I will quickly introduce you to training an SVM model using a radial basis kernel. The latter link will give you a handful of information about which other alternatives there are for SVMs, while the former will give you a deeper understanding of how to use `caret` and what it's capable of doing.

As `caret` relies on many other packages, we want not only to install it alone but some other package, such as `lubridate`, may be also requested. Let's begin by installing both:

```
if(!require('lubridate')){install.packages('lubridate')}
if(!require('caret')){install.packages('caret')}
```

Even more packages may be requested. How can you know? Call `library(caret)` and pay close attention to warnings; it will tell you if some packages are missing. Install the missing packages if there are any. The next code block shows how to load `caret` and set a `seed` number generator (in some level, SVM depends on a random `seed` generator):

```
library(caret)
set.seed(2018)
```

The random `seed` generator was set so there is a greater chance for you and me to get similar results. A nice feature from `caret` is the tuning grid. Usually, it's possible to name several parameters in order to tune your model. These parameters need to be arranged into a DataFrame. The `exapand.grid()` function can easily create this DataFrame using every possible combination of given values:

```
tune_grid <- expand.grid(sigma = c(.025,.0025,.001), C = c(1,2))
```

After creating `tune_grid`, you can call this object to check how `expand.grid()` has worked things out. Use this tuning grid feature wisely. The more values you set, the more time it will take to train the models, plus you might enhance the risks of overfitting depending on the range used.

There are two parameters you can try while training with the `'svmRadial'` method: `sigma` and `C` (cost). Both have to be given their exact names while stored in the DataFrame that will feed the tuning argument. While `sigma` is a parameter from the radial basis function kernel, the cost is associated with the constraints in the optimization problem.

Now, with the grid in hand, it's time to finally train an SVM model for classification. For the sake of comparability, we will stick with the `dt_Chile` dataset:

```
time0_svm <- Sys.time()

svm_caret <- caret::train(vote ~ . ,
                          data = dt_Chile[-i_out,],
                          tuneGrid = tune_grid,
                          method = 'svmRadial')

time1_svm <- Sys.time()
```

Just as we've done before, the core function used to train the model (its name is actually `train()`) is in between the variables storing the time (`time0_svm` and `time1_svm`). Before bringing in the test-sample results, let's check the training-sample results:

```
mean(predict(svm_caret, newdata = dt_Chile[-i_out,]) == dt_Chile[-i_out,
'vote'])
# [1] 0.6721504
```

A near 67,21% hit rate was the accuracy we got from the in-sample results (`dt_Chile[-i_out,]`). Let's see how it performed in the test sample plus how much time it took to train (keep in mind that it might vary depending on many things):

```
mean(predict(svm_caret, newdata = dt_Chile[test,]) == dt_Chile[test,
'vote'])
# [1] 0.6931507
time1_svm - time0_svm
# Time difference of 1.108781 mins
```

The performance is even better (a 69,31% hit rate), which make me suspicious about it. An even better performance is achieved through validation data, which is also out-of-sample since we did not use it for training. Yet, you should never expect your model to do better in the out-of-sample measures, although it can happen.

The time required to run the model is also considerably higher in comparison with random forests. It went from about one second to about one minute to train the model. That's something to take into account. The `beepr::beep()` trick may be useful here:

```
alert <- function(x, n = 1, s = 8){if(x > 0){cat('Alert #',n,'.\n',sep =
'');beepr::beep(s);Sys.sleep(6);alert(x-1,n+1,s)}}
```

Deciding which kernel function (along with its parameters) to use is a central matter when designing an SVM model. Some algorithms will only allow regressions to be made; others will be suitable for two-classes classification but not for multi-classes classification. Others may be broader and implement regression and multi-class classification.

It's really important to get to know how the algorithm that you are trying really works. Picking the wrong one might be disastrous. This section addressed a brief introduction (theory and practice) about SVMs. For the moment, we've focused on supervised learning methods while mostly dealing classification problems. The next section discusses how these same models we've been using until now can be used to fit regressions, while talking a little bit about error measures. Afterward, we may take a detour around unsupervised learning.

What about regressions?

All of the models we've seen so far could also be set to tackle regression problems and not only classification problems. In order to do so, the only thing that we would need to do is to start the formulas with a continuous variable then. Instead of the regular `vote ~ .`, we would use `<some continuous variable's name> ~ <independent variable #1> + <...> + <independent variable #n>`.

> A misspecified model is either missing important (left out) variables, adding unimportant (irrelevant) variables, or both.

The dot sign shortcut still works for regression problems, but it's probably best to name each variable by name. This way you pay more attention to which variables you are using. Depending on the model you train and sampling size, misspecification will badly injury the out-of-sample performance, in other words, your model won't be fit to make real-world predictions.

> All real-world predictions are out-of-sample.

Feature engineering takes care of creating and selecting features to adjust your models. Some would say that it's more an art than a science and I agree with them. Nonetheless, there are a few tips that could help you to engineer features:

- **Be creative**: Try new things, combine information and always look for alien data. Looking beyond dataset knowledge can really mean a leap forward sometimes.
- **Avoid using highly correlated variables**: Depending on your training algorithm and sample size, correlated variables will cast confusion into models.

- **Trust**: At least on some level trust, in what you learned from living. Search what other people have done while handling the same or similar matters. Go out, observe the world, talk to people about your problem—all this can help in grasping a new perspective that may lead you to the solution.
- **Test**: Think about possible solutions and try them. If your test sample is not too small, the out-of-sample performance may give you hints about whether you are following the right path. But be cautious, even these marks can lead you down the wrong path sometimes—we are dealing with probabilities.

These key steps can help you to engineer features. A new feature might be the watershed that separates you from reaching the high ranks in a Kaggle competition or answering your business question.

All along, we've checked the hit rate, which is also known as probability of detection. Almost exclusively, we have checked the test-sample hit rate. That is because I wanted to keep it simple while focusing on showing how to train a wide variety of models. The hit rate is neither the single nor the best measure available to measure performance over classification models.

TIP

The performance measure for some model you may consider should be at least an approximation of the cost and revenues related to the decisions you may take when relying on this same model. Should false positives be worth as much as false negatives?

That said, the code we've been using to measure performance wouldn't be suitable at first if we tried to address a regression problem. Some adaptions would be required. A more traditional error measure related to regressions is the MSE. In the following, you can see a pseudocode calculating it:

```
mean((predict(<model>, newdata = <data>[<test index>,]) - <data>[<test
index>,<predict variable>])^2)
```

MSE may be the most traditional error measure for a continuous variable but it's not unique. There are far more measures; you may come up with one of your own (hopefully cost-related) and not a single is yet proven to be the best one, no matter what. Moving forward, we will be discussing something we've briefly seem in `Chapter 4`, *KDD, Data Mining, and Text Mining*, and that is be clustering.

Hierarchical and k-means clustering

Cluster analyses are very flexible in terms of tasks they can perform; therefore, it has been proved to be useful in many different situations. To cite some utilities, clusters can be used to build recommenders, extract important features from data that can be used to drive insights, or further feed other models and land predictions.

This section aims to go beyond `Chapter 4`, *KDD, Data Mining, and Text Mining*. The goal here is to deepen the discussion about clusters while trying to retrieve important features from the `car::Chile` dataset using different techniques. Expect to see hierarchical, k-means and fuzzy clusters in this section.

All of the clusters have a huge thing in common; they are all unsupervised learning techniques. Unsupervised means that models won't target a variable during the training; there is no such thing as the dependent variable in clustering. Clusters try to find groups based on how distant/close each observation is from one another.

Primarily, clustering algorithms will differ from each other in what distance measure to use, how to measure the cluster—for instance, I could take one cluster's center as a reference point or alternatively its border—and which steps to follow to find clusters. When it comes to hierarchical clustering, there are top-down (divisive) approaches as well as bottom-up (agglomerative) ones.

Aside from that, some techniques will give you a set of probabilities for a data point to be part of each cluster while others may name a single cluster (probabilityless) for each observation. Although the time complexity of each method is different, I would rather just briefly explain the differences than **de facto** employing a measure this time.

Let's get started with hierarchical clustering. Let's begin with only 10 observations. Clusters essentially are about how close one observation is from another. That said, work with categorical variables may be challenging. Nonetheless, it could be done; we could, for example, coerce a numerical scale. Most often people will rely only on numerical variables instead.

There is an easy way for us to compute the distance for many variables simultaneously: the `dist()` function. Check how we could peek the distance for the first five numerical observations, `dt_Chile[1:5, c(2,4,6,7)]`:

```
dist(dt_Chile[1:5, c(2,4,6,7)])
```

The output text may look like the following table:

	1	2	3	4
1	27500.02366			
2	20000.01823	7500.00583		
3	16.12950	27500.00727	20000.00315	
5	42.05313	27500.00066	20000.00576	26.00010

As you can see, there are distances far too great while others are far too small. That happened due to scales. A quick `summary(dt_Chile[1:5,c(2,4,6,7)])` will give you hints on that matter:

population	age	income	statusquo
Min. :175000	Min. :23.0	Min. : 7500	Min. :-1.2962
1st Qu.:175000	1st Qu.:29.0	1st Qu.:15000	1st Qu.:-1.1050
Median :175000	Median :38.0	Median :35000	Median :-1.0316
Mean :175000	Mean :40.8	Mean :25500	Mean :-0.2388
3rd Qu.:175000	3rd Qu.:49.0	3rd Qu.:35000	3rd Qu.: 1.0082
Max. :175000	Max. :65.0	Max. :35000	Max. : 1.2307

Figure 6.7: Quick summary of five observations, the scales are very different from one another

More often than not, this scale range can negatively affect your cluster. This may be also true for linear regressions, SVMs, and some other models such as neural networks. A usual turnaround to this is data transformation. Yet, there are times when transformation can harass model performance. It could happen due to things such as the following:

- The transformation picked is not suited to the problem
- The problem in question requires data to be untransformed later and this operation can sometimes add unintended biases
- The original bias towards some variable due to its scale was oddly a great hint about how data should be clustered

Mostly used transformations are normalization and standardization. The former will scale your data between the values zero and one while the latter will result in a variable with a mean of zero and a standard deviation of one. Normalization rolls like this:

$$\hat{x}_i = \frac{x_i - min(x)}{max(x) - min(x)}$$

Where $\hat{x}$ is the normalized variable and x is the variable to be normalized. This is also called a max-min transformation. There are other types of max-min transformations. The standardization looks like this:

$$z_i = \frac{x_i - \bar{x}}{S_x},$$

Where z accounts for the standardized variable, $\overline{x}$ is the variable's simple average and S_x is an unbiased estimator for the standard deviation. Which one will we use? None. Let's see how the untouched data does first:

```
h_clust <- hclust(dist(dt_Chile[1:10, c(2,4,6,7)]))
```

Note how the observations used to fit the cluster are nested inside the `dist()` function—`hclust()` has to be fed with a dissimilarity structure. Only 10 observations were used; hence, it's way easier to visualize and understand these models. A wonderful way to visualize clusters is with dendrograms (tree diagrams). The `plot()` method is suited to craft this visualization right away:

```
plot(h_clust)
```

The resulting dendrogram can be seen in *Figure 6.8*:

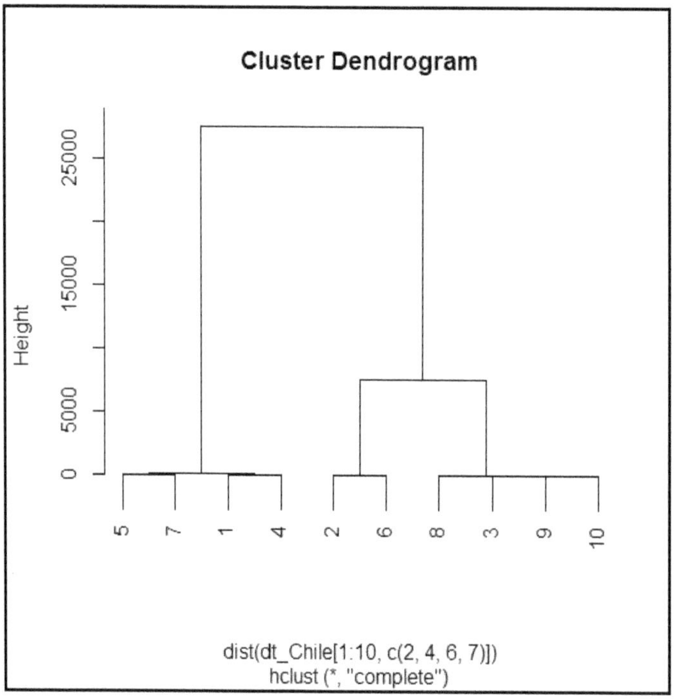

Figure 6.8: Cluster dendrogram with untransformed data

It's not cute, right? Some leaves are flattened. Yet, we can use this cluster to explain some things. Each leaf corresponds to a row index in the dataset. The difference height between a branch and another shows how similar (small heights) or dissimilar (great heights) the observations are from one another.

This matter aside, looking at the dendrogram we can see anything between 10 clusters or 1 huge cluster. One way to decide how many clusters to have is to think about how many groups would look reasonable and then draw a horizontal line splitting the clusters. The following code takes care of the flattened leaves issue while drawing a horizontal line at the height of `5000`:

```
plot(h_clust, hang = .2)
abline(h = 5000, col = 'red', lwd = 2)
```

The `hang` from argument `plot()` is aligning all of the leaves; the `abline()` function is drawing the horizontal line at the height, `h`. The result is displayed in Figure 6.9:

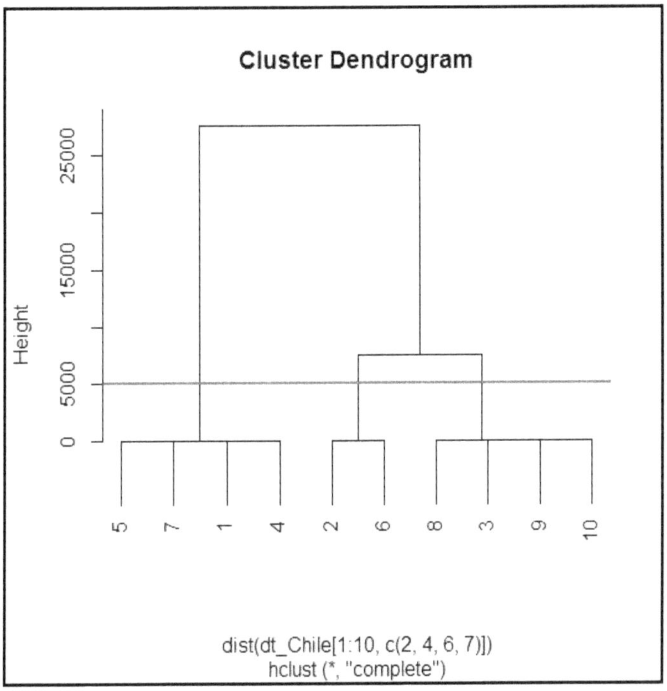

Figure 6.9: Deciding upon how many clusters to use with a straight horizontal line

The red line suggests that observations should be clustered around three different groups. Observations 1, 4, 5, and 7 would form a group; 2 and 6 would go together in another group, while observations 3, 8, 9, and 10 would form the last group altogether. What could these groups possibly be used for?

If each observation accounted for products, you could recommend 6 to whoever bought 2. Or we could create a new variable that would be a factor with three levels. A factor like this could be tried as an independent variable for further models, such as decision trees or random forests (feature engineering with clusters).

Another option is to try some labels in order to see whether clusters could or could not be used directly to predict voters directly. Before we do that, let's also try a hierarchical clustering using transformed data. In order to transform data, an anonymous function will be used:

```
dt_z <- apply(dt_Chile[,c(2,4,6,7)], MARGIN = 2,
              FUN = function(x){ xbar <- mean(x); s <- sd(x); return((x-
xbar)/s)}
              )
```

The `apply()` function was used to apply the anonymous function over each numerical column from the `dt_Chile` DataFrame. The anonymous function is named over the `FUN` argument and was applied to the subsetted columns of the data, given that the margin argument was set to 2 (second dimension means columns, first dimension means rows, and so on).

In R, functions are objects as any others. They can get names to be quickly called later or they can receive no names. The latter type is called an anonymous function.

The following code block will adjust a new cluster using transformed data (only the first 10 observations), plot this new cluster side-by-side with the one that used untransformed data, and give new labels to the leaves; leaves will then account for the voting intentions directly instead of the index:

```
h_clust_z <- hclust(dist(dt_z[1:10,]))

par(mfrow = c(1,2))

plot(h_clust, hang = .3,
     labels = dt_Chile[1:10, 'vote'],
     main = 'Cluster\n(Original data)')

plot(h_clust_z, hang = .3,
     labels = dt_Chile[1:10, 'vote'],
     main = 'Cluster\n(Standartized data)')
```

The result can then be seen in the following diagram:

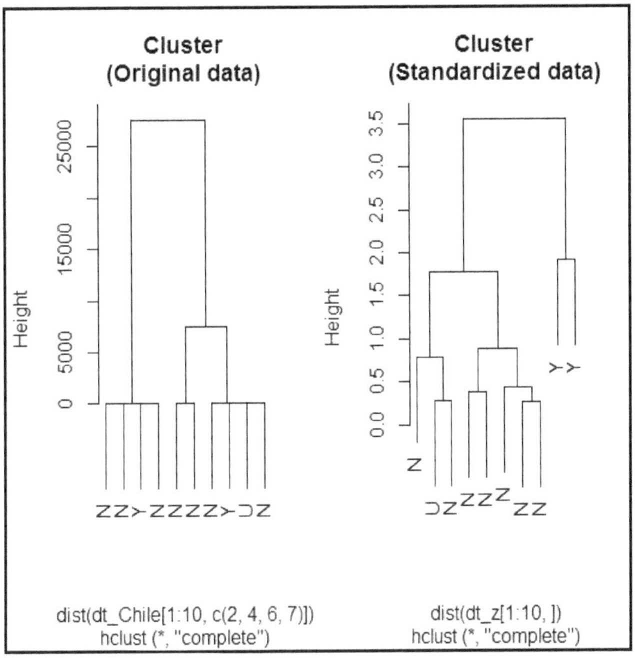

Figure 6.10: Clusters with original and standardized data

Here is how the code worked:

- `hclust()` was called using the standardized data (`dt_z`) to create an object holding the hierarchical cluster with transformed data, which was stored as `h_clust_z`.
- `par()` was called to set `mfrow = c(1,2)`, which split the plot window in a single row with two columns.
- Finally, the `plot()` method was called with different objects (`h_clust` and `h_clust_z`) to plot the dendrograms for the clusters that used respectively the original and standardized data. Notice how the `labels` argument was used to rename the leaves after the voting intentions.

In comparison with the cluster that used original data, the one using standardized data seems to cluster better the groups of `N` (no) and `Y` (yes). Considering the really small sample used, this should not be taken as a consistent result. Let's use the whole sample and see whether we can extract any direct relation between clusters and vote intentions or create important features that will boost performance.

The following code block will not only cluster the 2,431 observations available in `dt_Chile` but also presents a practical way to split data into a given number of clusters:

```
h_clust_z2 <- hclust(dist(dt_z), method = 'ward.D')
cutree(h_clust_z, k = 4)
```

Now the `dt_z` DataFrame, used for clustering, is not limited by its first 10 rows. Also, pay close attention to the `method` argument. It was set to `'ward.D'`, which is a different agglomeration method from the default—type `?hclust` to check all, the available methods.

In the next line, the code block called `cutree()`. This method holds two particularly easy ways to split clusters. Once you input it with a cluster object, you can name `k` and select how many groups you wish to have or you could name `h`, therefore selecting a height to split the three (similar to what we have done graphically).

Notice that it asked `h_clust_z` (only 10 observation) and not `h_clust_z2`. By doing this, we are only preventing the console from being flooded with thousands of entries, but we should use the latter if we aimed at prediction or feature building. Although there are several ways of picking the numbers of groups, researcher's experience, and intuition are usually a better guide.

When done right, there is a non-negligible chance that clustering will give you a hand. Yet, clustering won't extract meaning where there is none. The ultimate test is always real-life applications, but we could start little—that is, checking whether there seems to be a relation among the groups designated and the target variable using `table()`:

```
table(cutree(h_clust_z2, k = 4)[-i_out],
      dt_Chile[-i_out, 'vote'])
```

As we had `4` different categories for the variable, `vote`, I tried to cluster data around four different groups—`cutree( *, k = 4)` is doing it. The brackets are subsetting only the train dataset. As a result, I've got the following table:

	A	N	U	Y
1	13	59	114	194
2	49	300	123	66
3	41	120	116	213
4	24	112	43	115

Figure 6.11: Groups and vote intentions match for the training dataset

At a glance, we see that the four groups originated from the hierarchical clustering are not discriminating very well the vote intentions. Keep in mind that this is an unsupervised learning technique so it's not really aiming to explain voting intentions. Yet, we could put it to test. Guessing from the table, observations that were clustered into the `1`, `3`, and `4` group could be assigned as yes (`Y`) while the remaining ones could be understood as no (`N`).

Combining `mean()`, `sapply()`, an anonymous function, and a Boolean operator, we can retrieve the hit rate for the test sample using this very simple heuristic described by the paragraph behind. The code would look like the following:

```
mean(
  sapply(factor(cutree(h_clust_z2, k = 6))[test],
         FUN = function(x){
           if(x == 1 | x == 3 | x == 4) return('Y')
           else return('N')} )
  == dt_Chile[test, 'vote'])
# [1] 0.5232877
```

As you can see, the hit rate is not far from the chance of guessing a single flip of a coin. The four groups did very poorly in terms of predicting voting intentions directly but it's possible for them to do well as a feature that will aid models to predict the voting intentions correctly. To check that, the following code block is creating a new variable and trying it with a random forest model:

```
dt_Chile$hc_cluster <- factor(cutree(h_clust_z2, k = 4))

#library(randomForest)
set.seed(2010)

rf2 <- randomForest(vote ~ . , dt_Chile[-i_out,])
mean(predict(rf2, type = 'class', newdata = dt_Chile[test,]) ==
dt_Chile[test,'vote'])
# [1] 0.6520548
```

In comparison with the latter random forest model (`rf`), the test sample performance slightly worsened when the groups were included in the model. Some problems are really difficult to tackle given data constraints. I did not know this dataset before I started writing this chapter and its unfortunate ability of misleading models into overfitting has surprised me. Real-life problems are like that sometimes. Some problems are not solved in the blink of an eye.

Data constraints do not only refer to sample size but also to available variables.

Hierarchical clustering results are always reproducible; they don't rely on random seeds. Their time complexity with respect to data size is quadratic. That said, they are not suited to handle big data very efficiently but they are wonderful to handle small datasets given that they can be easily represented in diagrams and you can decide how many groups to have from that.

For the sake of big data, there is k-means clustering; k-means' time complexity is linear with respect to data size. It does mostly well with clusters that are globally allocated. The algorithm starts by seemingly randomly selecting the clusters; therefore, you might get different results each time you run it. To select the number of groups (`k`) beforehand is a requirement.

> On the one hand, `set.seed()` will always be there for you to ensure reproducibility. On the other hand, keep in mind that your results can vary due to the initial `seed`.

Compared to hierarchical clustering, k-means is not that simple. Dendrograms are not as useful as they are for hierarchical clustering. There is a special visualization that will help you to determine the optimal number of clusters when it's unclear how many you should have.

> In our case, the reasonable number of clusters would be four (given the four categories) if we wanted to direct predict the voting intentions; we could have it narrowed down to two if we did not care about undecided and abstains. On the other hand, if we wanted to extract features rather than directly address predictions, the numbers of optimal clusters wouldn't be restricted by the number of categories given by the predicted variable.

This special visualization consists of displaying how the total **within sum of squares** (**WSS**) evolves as the number of predetermined clusters grows. Here is a thing about k-means clusters, given the algorithm's nature, the WSS will always diminish as the number of clusters grows. The trick is to visually find a spot where an additional cluster won't land that much improvement. We can effortlessly craft a visualization like this by turning upon the `factoextra` package:

```
# if(!require(factoextra){install.packages('factoextra')}
library(factoextra)
fviz_nbclust(dt_z, kmeans, method = 'wss')
```

Erase the hashtag and run the first line if you are not sure about having the package already installed. As a result, we get the following:

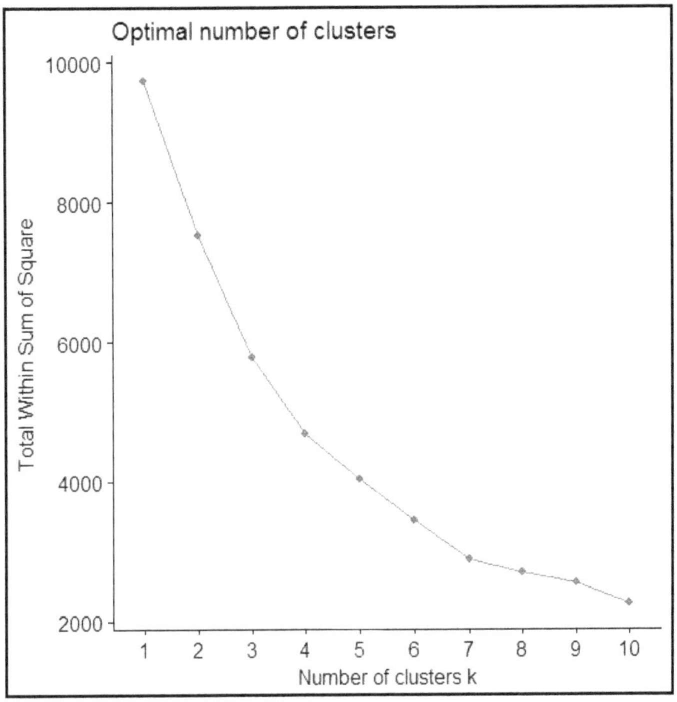

Figure 6.12: Number of clusters (k) and total within sum of square for k-means clustering

Initially, the error rapidly decreases with the increasing number of clustering. We have to spot a number *k* for that one additional group won't contribute that much to decrease the WSS. This is known as the **elbow method** because, at some point, it resembles an elbow.

This method more or less counts on the users' experience and judgment. For example, I clearly spotted an elbow at *k* = 7. Nonetheless, there is a huge cliff before *k* =3. I tested both and three lead me to better results. Here is how to do k-means clustering with three clusters with R:

```
set.seed(10)
k_clust <- kmeans(dt_z, 3)
```

If you call `k_clust` alone, lots of information is displayed, for example, the within cluster sum of squares by cluster. You will also see the cluster characterization that shows the mean of each variable for each cluster. To return this characterization and nothing else, you can append `$centers` to your k-means object (`k_clust$centers`).

Notice that the mean values reported are related to the transformed data (dt_z) and not the original one (dt_Chile). You can retrieve the characterization with respect to the original data with the aggregate() function:

```
aggregate(dt_Chile[, c(2,4,6,7)],
          by = list(clusters = fitted(k_clust, method = 'classes')),
          mean)
```

The first argument is the original dataset (only variables used were subsetted). The second argument, by, is a list giving the groups related to each observation within data. Finally, the last argument is naming the function used to characterize the clusters. We could trust any function, as well. Also, there is no strict rule that will forbid the variables not used to cluster to come along, but make sure to give a function that can handle categorical variables if you are including them.

We could return means for numerical variables and modes for non-numerical ones. Begin by creating a function to find modes (I got it from Chapter 2, *Descriptive and Inferential Statistics*):

```
find_mode <- function(vals) {
  if(max(table(vals)) == min(table(vals)))
    'amodal'
  else
    names(table(vals))[table(vals)==max(table(vals))]
}
```

Now we need a function that checks the variable's class and apply mean() or find_mode() depending on it:

```
mean_or_mode <- function(x){
  if(is.numeric(x)) return(mean(x))
  else return(find_mode(x))
}
```

All it takes to get a characterization like the one just described is to run the following code:

```
aggregate(dt_Chile,
          by = list(clusters = k_clust$cluster),
          mean_or_mode)
```

There are four points I want you to play very close attention to:

1. Data is not subsetted anymore.
2. We used `k_clust$cluster` instead of `fitted(k_clust, method = 'classes')`; both are the same:

```
identical(k_clust$cluster, fitted(k_clust, method = 'classes'))
# [1] TRUE
```

3. We replaced `mean` by `mean_or_mode`, our tailor-made function.
4. None of the data output as a final result (*Figure 6.13*) were directly used to do the clustering. Only `population`, `income`, `age` and `statusquo` were used but not before going through standardization.

The latter `aggregate()` calling will output a table similar to the one displayed in the following diagram:

clusters	region	population	sex	age	education	income	statusquo	vote	hc_cluster
1	SA	189620.23	M	36.19253	S	25402.11	-0.7710496	N	2
2	S	87112.64	F	40.58512	P	22178.90	0.8636202	Y	3
3	SA	226815.07	F	39.79909	PS	135502.28	0.3404584	Y	4

Figure 6.13: Custom cluster characterization

This is how I retrieved a very customized characterization. Do you remember when we assigned the clusters from the hierarchical algorithm to work as a new variable in the dataset? Check how the mode for it matches the group for k-means clustering. This does not mean that they are exactly the same—as a matter of fact, hierarchical set four different clusters while k-means was asked to only assign three.

Here is the code that creates a new variable based on k-means clusters and tests its performance using the random forests model:

```
dt_Chile$k_cluster <- fitted(k_clust, method = 'classes')

set.seed(2010)

rf3 <- randomForest(vote ~ . , dt_Chile[-i_out,-9])
mean(predict(rf3, type = 'class', newdata = dt_Chile[test,]) ==
dt_Chile[test,'vote'])
# [1] 0.660274
```

A bit of improvement is found here but it's unclear whether this is due to the new feature or the random seeds. k-means itself can be highly influenced by the initial random seeds, also random forests. Fuzzy k-means clustering is another option, we can do this with the `fclust` package:

```
if(!require('fclust')){install.packages('fclust')}
```

After making sure `fclust` is installed, we can use `FKM*()` function to do fuzzy clustering:

```
library(fclust)
set.seed(10)
f_clust <- FKM.ent(dt_z, k = 4, conv = 1e-16)
```

As usual, we start by loading the package. Next, we set the random seed generator, given that fuzzy k-means clustering also relies on pseudo-randomness. The `FKM.ent()` function is then used to do fuzzy k-means clustering with entropy regularization. Entropy regularization is a technique that aims to reduce overfitting.

Here is how we can test these clusters with random forests:

```
dt_Chile$f_cluster <- factor(f_clust$clus[,1])
set.seed(2010)
#library(randomForest)
rf4 <- randomForest(vote ~ . , dt_Chile[-i_out,c(-9,-10)])
mean(predict(rf4, type = 'class', newdata = dt_Chile[test,]) ==
dt_Chile[test,'vote'])
# [1] 0.6657534
```

Although the out-of-sample performance is slightly better while adopting the fuzzy k-means clustering, this is not the ultimate proof that it would go that way all the time. In fact, this slightly better improvement can be due to the seeds and not the algorithm itself.

For clustering in general, overleaping data, noise, and outliers can turn out to be quite challenging. As there are several clustering techniques, it is hard to name pros and cons as these might widely vary across different algorithms. The next set of algorithms we're about to see is called neural networks; such a name comes from the biological inspiration that gave birth to it.

Neural networks

These are the models that most fascinate me. From their wide range of applications to their brilliant origin—everything seems marvelous to me. Note that there is no such a thing as an all mighty model and neural nets are not it. They can be distinguished by being very flexible models that can perform both unsupervised and supervised learning.

Even though it's a very powerful method, it's certainly not all powerful. Neural nets are able to capture linear and non-linear relations. Yet, everything will depend on how you design the networks (researcher's ability and experience), how complex is the problem at hand, and how many observations do you have.

Computational constraints can also be a bottleneck. As powerful as they are known to be, neural networks are not remembered as computationally inexpensive methods. It's not hard to find problems that can't be efficiently handled by consumer grade computers. Cloud computing is usually the best and cheaper way out of this problem. Nonetheless, if you are dealing with sensible data, you might consider transforming it to ensure anonymity first, or not working with clouds at all.

This section will only briefly discuss the nuts and bolts of neural networks. More details on that are about to be delivered in `Chapter 8`, *Neural Networks and Deep Learning*. There you might find a practical guide to the `keras` package, which enables us to use TensorFlow directly from R. Here you may find a very condensed practical guide to `h2o`.

The very first time I ever saw a neural network working was when I was learning how to play Super Mario Bros. Surprisingly enough, the AI got to know shortcuts that someone hardly noticed before. The second time I saw it, an artist was using neural networks to craft figures.

Neural networks are a universe within themselves. There is much to talk about but let's stick with this: with some degree of simplicity, neural nets imitate how neurons transmit/interpret information by arranging nodes into three kinds of layers (input, hidden, and output layers).

There are many hyperparameters to take into consideration when you are about to train a neural net. If you are new to neural networks, you may only learn quite a few things from this section but don't worry, you will see a lot more of it in `Chapter 8`, *Neural Networks and Deep Learning*.

By chaining enough hidden layers with a sufficient number of hidden nodes, neural nets can (slowly) approximate any sort of linear and nonlinear functions. Here is a representation of a neural network that I have designed to predict Brazilian live cattle prices for a forecast horizon of 60 business days:

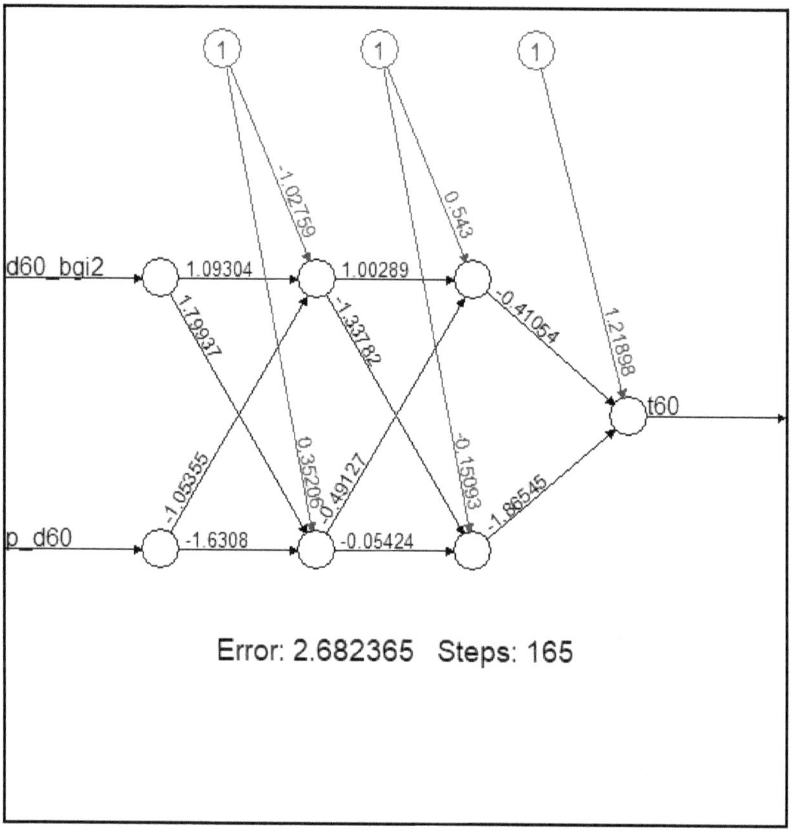

Figure 6.14: Neural network designed to predict Brazilian live cattle prices within 60 business days

The preceding diagram displays a fully connected feedforward network—there are various sorts of network architectures available—trained with the `neuralnet` package. The blue circles represent bias nodes. In the left, you can see a couple of black circles stacked. These are the input nodes, information flows from them to the rest of the network. Information flow is marked by the arrows.

> Bias nodes will always output the name number that will be multiplied by a weight. The number is usually one and the weights are hyperparameters subject to training.

Nodes are providing the next ones with numeric information that is multiplied by a number. These multipliers are called **weights** and are shown by *Figure 6.14* right above the arrow connecting a node to some other. Weights are hyperparameters that learning algorithms such as the Adam optimization and backpropagation will seek to improve.

Once a node gets all of the balanced numeric information coming from other nodes (and sometimes itself), it will sum all of them and apply a given function (activation function—another important decision to make). This functions' results will land on another node that will repeat the process until the output node, the lone single node displayed in the extreme right of *Figure 6.14*. Output nodes are the ones giving the output.

> Input nodes don't have activation functions. They simply send over whatever they are input with. Notice that they still count on weights to balance their output to each node they are connected with.

There is still much to talk about with the nuts and bolts of neural nets in general, but for the time being, I will keep such details for `Chapter 8`, *Neural Networks and Deep Learning*. Let's see how the `h2o` package can be used to train neural network models.

Introduction to feedforward neural networks with R

The package `h2o` comes from the H2O.ai company. With it, you can train several machine learning models, including feedforward neural networks. Although the commands will be passed through the R console, the heavy lift will be done using Java— the `h2o` package for R is actually an interface.

That said, having Java installed is a requirement. If you are sure about having Java installed, make sure the `h2o` package is installed too:

```
install.packages('h2o')
```

Now we need to load the `h2o` library and initiate the package:

```
library(h20)
h2o.init(nthreads=-1, max_mem_size='2G')
```

The `h2o.init()` function will initialize and connect to h2O. The `nthreads=-1` argument will demand all available CPUs' cores to be used, this makes the training much faster. With max_mem_size, we set the maximum amount of RAM memory that h2O will be allowed to use, the recommendations stand for four times the dataset size—rest assured that 2 GB will be more than enough.

> Although different people may define it differently, usually neural networks with more than two hidden layers (the layers between input and output nodes) are called deep learning models.

To train our neural network model, we use the `h2o.deeplearning()` function. Datasets can be manipulated by `h2o` or R; nonetheless, they have to be loaded in `h2o` in order to be used both for training and prediction purposes. The function `as.h2o()` is able to deal with it:

```
time0_nn <- Sys.time()

nn <- h2o.deeplearning(x = 1:7,
                       y = 8,
                       training_frame = as.h2o(dt_Chile[-i_out,1:8]),
                       validation_frame = as.h2o(dt_Chile[val,1:8]),
                       hidden = c(6,6),
                       standardize = T,
                       activation = 'Tanh',
                       l2 = .0025, epochs = 50,
                       reproducible = T,
                       seed = 10)

time1_nn <- Sys.time()
```

There are many parameters to talk about:

- `x`: Gives the indexes for the columns that will be used as input
- `y`: The index for the column to be used as output (target variable)
- `training_frame`: The dataset used to train the model (notice how `as.h2o()` was called)
- `validation_frame`: The dataset used to validate the model (`as.h2o()` again)
- `hidden`: A vector dictating the number of nodes to be used in each hidden layer (the number of hidden layers is given by its length)
- `standardize`: This is a Boolean saying whether to standardize data or not
- `activation`: This is a string making reference to the activation function to be used (`'Tanh'` goes for tangent hyperbolic)

- `l2`: L2 regularization parameter, this is a technique used to avoid overfitting
- `epochs`: This sets the epoch parameter for the backpropagation algorithm
- `reproducible`: This is a Boolean that will demand the process to be reproducible or not
- `seed`: An integer, it must always be set if `reproducible = TRUE`

There are many hyperparameters to think about when designing neural nets; we will discuss more in `Chapter 8`, *Neural Networks and Deep Learning*. For the moment, let's see how the training has gone. Simply call `plot(nn)` to get the following diagram:

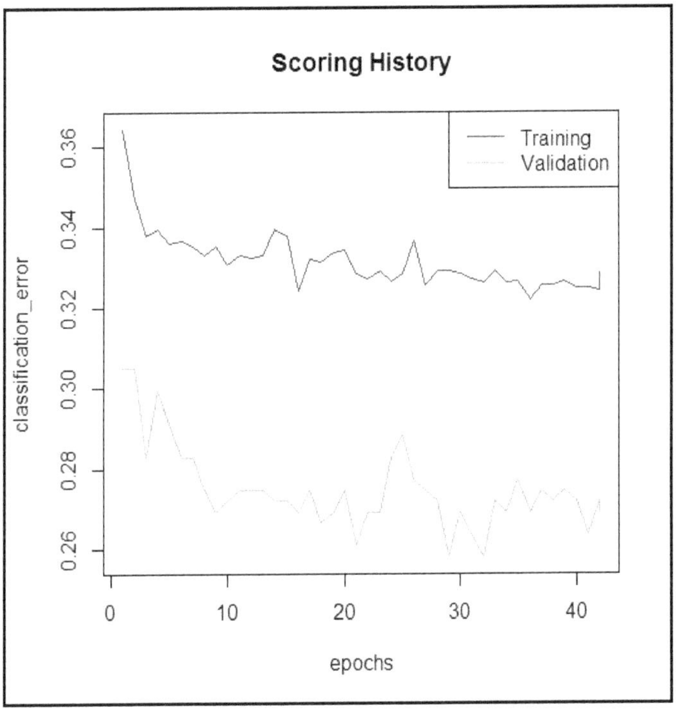

Figure 6.15: Training scoring history

Here we see how the scoring has gone through the training. Thanks to the `validation_frame` argument, we had a validation line to compare with the training one. If the validation line went up while the training one was going down, this would be a mark of overfitting.

To evaluate the test sample hit rate as we've done before, we need to extract predictions using the test sample and convert the results into an R object (such as a matrix) to only then compare the results:

```
nn_pred <- h2o.predict(nn, newdata = as.h2o(dt_Chile[test,1:8]))
nn_pred <- as.matrix(nn_pred)
mean(nn_pred[,1] == dt_Chile[test,'vote'])
# [1] 0.6849315
time1_nn - time0_nn
# Time difference of 2.173553 secs
```

The `h2o.predict()` function is used to gather the predictions. Again, `as.h2o()` had to be called with a DataFrame. The first line creates the object holding the predictions, by this point `nn_pred` will be an `H2Oframe` type of object. Nesting it into `as.matrix()` will turn it back into a more R natural object. The first column of `nn_pred` shows a class type prediction while the other ones are probabilistic.

The performance achieved in the test sample (68,49%) was very close to the one displayed by SVMs (69,31%) using far less time; less than 3 seconds compared to a little more than 1 minute used to train the SVM model. Multiple threading might have something to do with the time it took (for me) to train both models.

TIP

To build functions from scratch aimed at training/fitting a certain model is a great way to master that model. You are not likely to program in a optimal way at first but if you do, consider sharing with the community.

Yet, there is no way to say that SVMs are absolutely better than neural nets nor that neural nets overplay SVMs. Both are cutting edge models that are likely to overcome difficult problems if you have enough data. With this, we wrap up this chapter about machine learning. In the next chapter, we will talk about predictive analytics.

Summary

In this chapter, we discussed machine learning and why it is everywhere. We also looked at supervised and unsupervised machine learning. We discussed the reason that machine learning creates its own vocabulary and how it relates to the statistical vocabulary.

Many other methods were discussed:

- tree models, their strengths and weakness
- essemble methods such as random forests
- hierarchical and k-means clustering

Finally, the chapter introduced feedforward neural networks with R using the `h2o` package. In the next chapter, we will cover ways in which we can evaluate the quality and characteristics of various datasets in an effort to find insights from the data.

Quiz

1. **Quiz-tion 1**: Which statement about machine learning is NOT CORRECT?
    1. Machine learning is interdisciplinary
    2. It is only used by the finance industry
    3. Non-profit organizations are using it to solve ambiental and social issues
    4. Machine learning techniques can be used to build recommenders
2. **Quiz-tion 2**: About machine learning algorithms—it would be wrong to say that:
    1. Hierarchical clustering and k-means clustering are unsupervised learning techniques
    2. Random forests can be characterized as ensemble learning
    3. Neural networks can't deal with classification problems
    4. Transformations can sometimes improve clustering

3. **Quiz-tion 3**: Which of the following tricks are said to be related to SVM models?
    1. The hat trick
    2. The kernel trick
    3. The mirror trick
    4. The dragon-slayer trick

Answers

```
set.seed(2000)
round(runif(3,1,4))
```

7
Forecasting and ML App with R

> *"The key to making a good forecast is not in limiting yourself to quantitative information."*
> – *Nate Silver*

In this section, we will develop a forecasting and machine learning application using R Shiny. As programmers, we tend to be more intent on developing code than necessarily getting involved in developing web-based frontends and dashboards. The latter is best developed using JavaScript, Node.js, and HTML/CSS.

> Note that this chapter contains an advanced application developed in R Shiny. For those new to Shiny, it would be helpful to review `Chapter 11`, *Going to Production with R*) prior to attempting the ML R Shiny application provided herein

Most languages provide a means to expose the functionality of the underlying code to the end user through GUI-based tools. Frameworks such as Qt can be leveraged using C++, Python, and other languages to build robust frontend interfaces. And today, iOS and Android are two of the most commonly used platforms for mobile UI and app development.

The equivalent to such technologies that allow users to expose the functionality of their backend code through web-based or desktop interactive components in R is Shiny. The platform provides a rich, mature, and user friendly interface through which developers can create complex interactive web pages fully integrated with the R ecosystem.

In addition, there are several other packages that have been developed by R users across the world that extend the functionality of Shiny and provide new features that allow users to create advanced visual effects. Such packages have permitted R users to forego learning JavaScript as they have made it incredibly easy to create and launch web applications, all from within the familiar RStudio ecosystem.

In this chapter, we will look at the basics of developing R Shiny applications and also create a fully-featured web-based R a priori application. RStudio has a very close integration with the R Shiny framework and users can develop the apps directly from RStudio. In this chapter, the following topics will be discussed:

- Getting started with R Shiny applications
- Developing an R Shiny application for forecasting

The UI and server

Each R Shiny application consists of two primary sections, which are the UI section and the server section. The UI, as the name suggests, is used to define the user interface, whereas the server section is used for executing the underlying R server side code. The `shinyApp` function is used in order to launch the application using the `ui` and `server` definitions.

The UI object holds the R Shiny widgets used to prepare the frontend components that the user will interact with while using the application.

A few toy examples have already been included as part of the RStudio programming environment. In order to launch an R Shiny application, run the following code in RStudio:

```
library(shiny)
runExample("01_hello")
```

This will launch a basic R Shiny app, shown as follows:

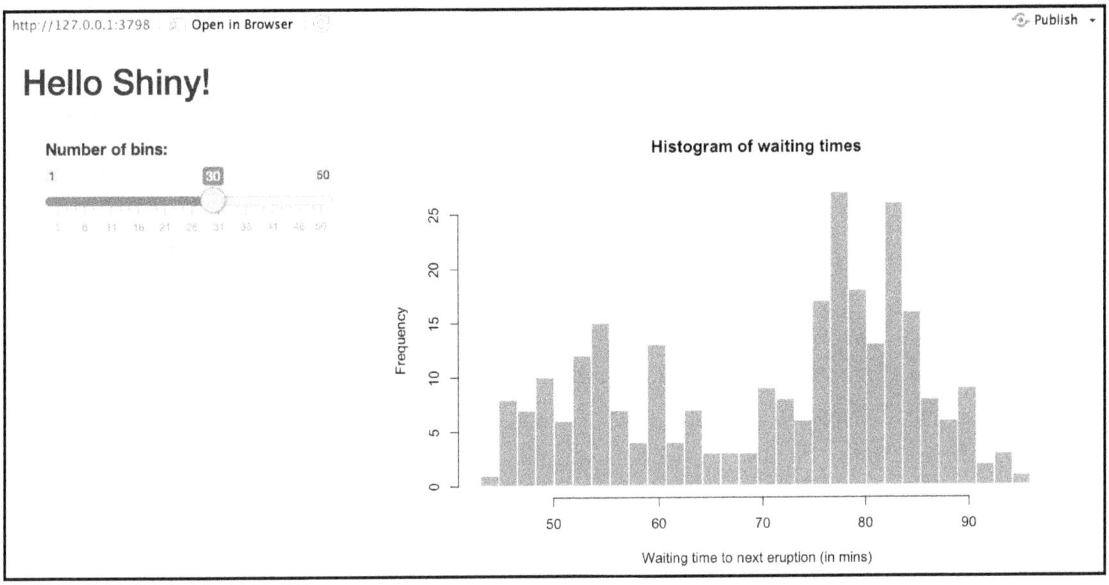

You can view the other applications available as examples by simply executing the following command:

```
runExample()
Valid examples are "01_hello", "02_text", "03_reactivity", "04_mpg",
"05_sliders", "06_tabsets", "07_widgets", "08_html", "09_upload",
"10_download", "11_timer"
```

The actual code of the first application (shown previously) is given as follows. Note that `ui.R` consists of several building blocks such as `pageWithSidebar`, `headerPanel`, `sidebarPanel`, and `mainPanel`. These are standard components that form the page layout and add structure to the overall application:

```
# ui.R
library(shiny)

# Define UI for application that plots random distributions
shinyUI(pageWithSidebar(

  # Application title
  headerPanel("Hello Shiny!"),

  # Sidebar with a slider input for number of observations
  sidebarPanel(
    sliderInput("obs",
                "Number of observations:",
```

```
                    min = 1,
                    max = 1000,
                    value = 500)
    ),

    # Show a plot of the generated distribution
    mainPanel(
      plotOutput("distPlot")
    )
  ))
```

R Shiny also provides a number of inputs, for example, `sliderInput`, `textInput`, `selectInput`, and so on. These are used for making selections such as with drop-down menus and other methods:

```
# server.R
library(shiny)

# Define server logic required to generate and plot a random distribution
shinyServer(function(input, output) {

  # Expression that generates a plot of the distribution. The expression
  # is wrapped in a call to renderPlot to indicate that:
  #
  #  1) It is "reactive" and therefore should be automatically
  #     re-executed when inputs change
  #  2) Its output type is a plot
  #
  output$distPlot <- renderPlot({

    # generate an rnorm distribution and plot it
    dist <- rnorm(input$obs)
    hist(dist)
  })
})
```

The preceding showcased a basic R Shiny application that allows R developers to expose the results of their work via a user friendly web interface.

Forecasting machine learning application

The following section shows how to create an R application to perform forecasting on pharmaceutical medicine sales data using information obtained from NHS (UK) **General Practitioner** (**GP**) datasets, available at `https://bit.ly/2Fxw9x4`.

The dataset contains GP prescription data, which lists the medications that were prescribed by physicians to patients in the UK. Using the historical data for sales, we will attempt to predict future sales, both by quantity and revenue:

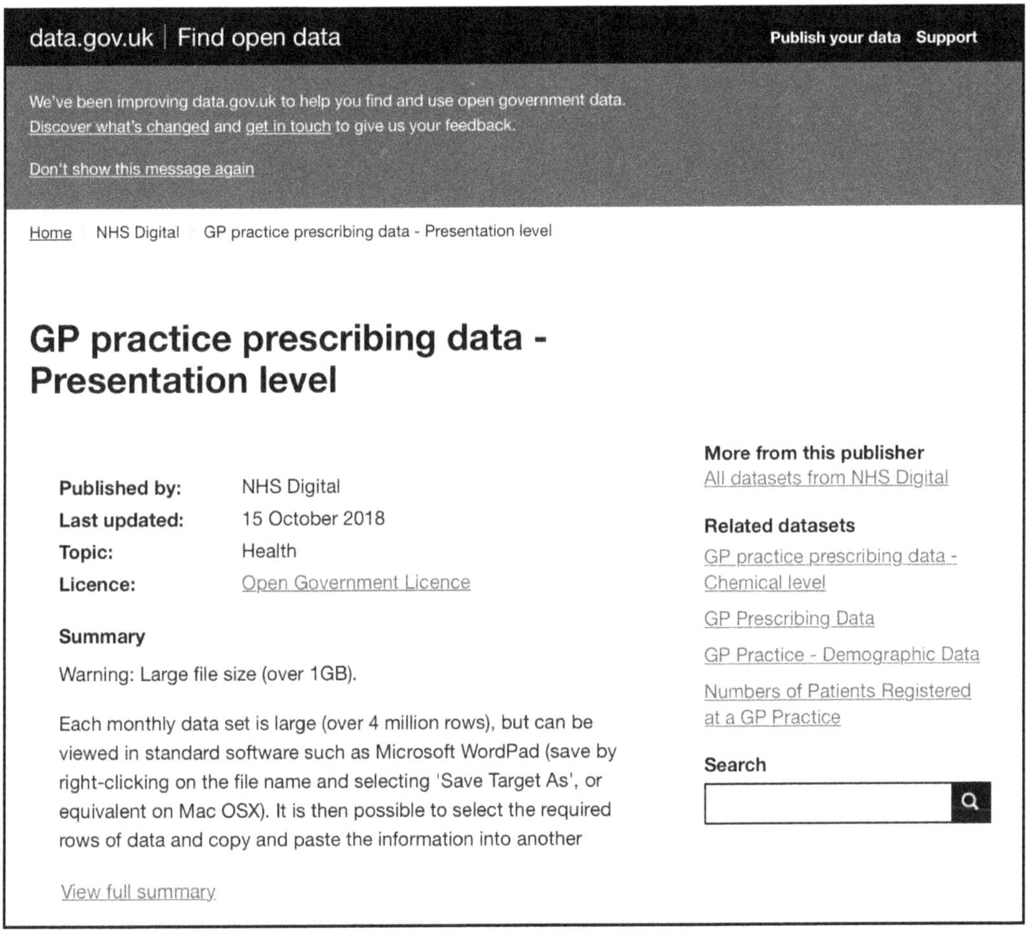

For the benefit of the readers, we have already provided a smaller version of the data in our code repository. Note that the application uses sophisticated and elegant customisations. This has been achieved using custom CSS styles and different API libraries. The user may want to ensure that all the libraries are installed prior to executing the code. For the benefit of the user, we have also added commands in the code to automatically install the requisite libraries where needed. The code for the application is as follows, where we first start by importing libraries:

```
# R Shiny Forecasting Application

# Load all libraries

if(!require("devtools")) devtools::install_github("devtools")
if(!require("shinyWidgets"))
devtools::install_github("dreamRs/shinyWidgets")
if(!require("data.table")) install.packages("data.table")
if(!require("DT")) install.packages("DT")
if(!require("forecast")) install.packages("forecast")
if(!require("ggplot2")) install.packages("ggplot2")
if(!require("shinyjs")) install.packages("shinyjs")
if(!require("plotly")) install.packages("plotly")
if(!require("xts")) install.packages("xts")
if(!require("prophet")) install.packages("prophet")
if(!require("tidyverse")) install.packages("tidyverse")

library(shiny)
library(shinydashboard)
library(data.table)
library(DT)
library(forecast)
library(ggplot2)
library(shinyjs)
library(shinyWidgets)
library(plotly)
library(xts)
library(prophet)
library(tidyverse)
teger(substring(x,1,4)), as.integer(substring(x,6,8)))}
```

In case any package used from GitHub has an error, try installing the package as-is with `install.packages("name of package")`. Now, let's load the forecasting data using the following code block:

```
colorp <- c("#00526d","#de6e6e","#006d00","#6d4736","#8f29a6")

# Helper Functions
```

```
fm <- function(x){c(as.integer(substring(x,1,4)),
  as.integer(substring(x,6,8)))}


##### Forecasting Data

productdb <- readRDS("productdb.rds") # Loads the NHS Prescription data
products <- (unique(productdb$BNFNAME))
productslower <- tolower(products)

productdb2 <- productdb[,.(SUMQ=sum(QUANTITY)),
by=c("BNFNAME","CHEMSUB")][order(-SUMQ)]
setkey(productdb2,CHEMSUB)


getTop5 <- function(x){
  CHEM <- productdb2[BNFNAME==x]$CHEMSUB[1]
  productdb2[CHEMSUB==CHEM]$BNFNAME[1:5]
}
```

The UI section is one of the two primary sections in R Shiny packages (the other being the server section). The UI section is used to create the frontend for the application:

```
# The UI Section

ui <- dashboardPage (skin="green",
                     dashboardHeader(title = "Forecaster"),
                     dashboardSidebar(
                       useShinyjs(),
                       uiOutput("selectedapp"),
conditionalPanel(condition="input.selectedapp=='forecast'",sidebarMenu
(uiOutput("products"),
uiOutput("forecastmodel"),
uiOutput("forecastmetric"),
uiOutput("decompose")
                       ))),
dashboardBody(
tags$head(
tags$link(rel = "stylesheet", type = "text/css", href = "packt.css"),
tags$link(rel = "stylesheet", type = "text/css", href =
"//fonts.googleapis.com/css?family=Fanwood+Text"),
tags$link(rel = "stylesheet", type = "text/css", href =
"//fonts.googleapis.com/css?family=Varela"),
tags$link(rel = "stylesheet", type = "text/css", href = "fonts.css")),

fluidRow(
tabsetPanel(id="inTabSet",
tabPanel(title = "Placeholder", value="miscTab"),
```

```
tabPanel(title = "Forecasting",
value="forecastTab",fluidRow(plotlyOutput("top5plot")),hr(),
fluidRow(column(5,fluidRow(plotOutput("autoplotforecast",
height="325px")),fluidRow(plotOutput("autoplot", height="325px"))),
column(7,dataTableOutput("forecastdata"))),hr(),fluidRow(dataTableOutput("p
roductdata")))))),
                      title = "Predictive Analytics"
)
```

We'll now define the section for server—this is where the backend code of the R Shiny application is entered:

```
server <- function(input, output, session) {
  observeEvent(input$selectedapp, {
    if(input$selectedapp=="forecast") {
      updateTabsetPanel(session = session, "inTabSet", selected =
"forecastTab")
    }
  })
  output$selectedapp <- renderUI({
    selectizeInput("selectedapp", "App Selection", choices =
c("Forecasting"="forecast"), selected="forecast")
  })
```

We'll use several models for forecasting. Most of them are available in the `forecast` package by Rob Hyndman. It is one of the staple packages in R for all forecasting tasks. In addition, we have also used MCMC, using the respective functionality from the `prophet` package released by Facebook:

```
 ######## Forecasting Code ##############

  # Selection of product that will be used for forecasting

  output$products <- renderUI({
    selectizeInput("products", "Product Name", choices = NULL, multiple =
FALSE)
  })
  updateSelectizeInput(session, 'products', choices = products, server =
TRUE, selected = products[1])

  # Selection of forecasting model

  output$forecastmodel <- renderUI({
    selectizeInput("forecastmodel", "Forecasting Model", choices =
c("Auto"="auto","Holt-Winters"="hw","TBATS"="tbats","Auto
ARIMA"="autoarima","Markov Chain Monte-Carlo"="mcmc"), multiple = FALSE,
selected="auto")
```

```
  })
  # Selection of forecasting metric of interest (Sales / Quantity)

  output$forecastmetric <- renderUI({
    selectizeInput("forecastmetric", "Forecasting Metric",
      choices = c("Sales Revenue"="rev","Quantity"="trx"),
      multiple = FALSE, selected="rev")
  })
  # Should we decompose Error-Trend-Seasonality in the data?
  output$decompose <- renderUI(
    prettyCheckbox(inputId = "decompose",
label = "Decompose ETS", value = TRUE,
icon = icon("check"), status = "success",
animation = "rotate")
  )
```

Reactive functions in R Shiny get executed when a certain trigger or action takes place. In this case, whenever the use changes any product or forecast metric, the code is rerun and the forecasts are also re-computed:

```
# R Shiny Reactive Function

  getProdData <- eventReactive(c(input$products,input$forecastmetric), {
    dt1 <- productdb[BNFNAME==input$products]
    if(input$forecastmetric=="trx") {
      dt1$Metric <- dt1$QUANTITY
    } else if(input$forecastmetric=="rev") {
      dt1$Metric <- dt1$ACTCOST
    }
    dt1
  })


  output$productdata <- renderDataTable({
    dt1 <- getProdData()
    datatable(dt1, width="500px", options = list(pageLength=30,dom =
't',columnDefs = list(list(className = 'dt-left', targets =
"_all"))),rownames = FALSE,caption = htmltools::tags$caption(style =
'caption-side: top; text-align: left; color:#de6e6e;','Table 2: ',
htmltools::h5('Sales Data from NHS Records'))
    )
  })
  # Create a ts (time-series) object
  createTS <- eventReactive(c(input$products,input$forecastmetric), {
    dt1 <- getProdData()
    tsd <- ts(dt1$Metric, start=fm(dt1$month[1]),
end=fm(dt1$month[length(dt1$month)]), frequency=12)
```

```
    list(tsd=tsd,data=dt1)
  })
  # Read Sales Data and find top 5 products in the same category

  getSalesData <- eventReactive(c(input$products,input$forecastmetric),{
    top5 <- getTop5(input$products)
    if(input$forecastmetric=="trx") {
      res <- data.frame(productdb[BNFNAME %in%
top5][,.(month,BNFNAME,QUANTITY)])
      setnames(res, c("Month","Product","Metric"))
    } else if(input$forecastmetric=="rev") {
      res <- data.frame(productdb[BNFNAME %in%
top5][,.(month,BNFNAME,ACTCOST)])
      setnames(res, c("Month","Product","Metric"))
    }
  })
```

IMPORTANT: do not change the name `productdata`; it is linked to a CSS property.

The `getforecast` function is the main section where the logic of the code is executed. Note that we are using a time-series data structure. Time-series data structures are extremely useful for expressing temporal data and performing temporal operations, such as calculating moving averages:

```
  # Run the forecasting model

  getforecast <-
eventReactive(c(input$forecastmodel,input$forecastmetric),{
    m <- input$forecastmodel
    tsdata <- createTS()
    tsd <- tsdata$tsd
    data <- tsdata$data
    extra=""
    # "Auto","Holt-Winters","TBATS","Auto ARIMA"
    if (m=="hw"){
      res <- forecast(HoltWinters(tsd))
    } else if (m=="autoarima"){
      res <- forecast(auto.arima(tsd))
    } else if (m=="tbats"){
      res <- forecast(tbats(tsd))
    } else if (m=="auto"){
      res <- forecast(tsd)
    } else if (m=="mcmc"){
      dtx <- tsdata$data[,.(ds=as.Date(paste0(month,"-01"),format="%Y-%m-
```

```
%d"),y=Metric)]
      m <- prophet(dtx)
      nperiods <- 22
      future <- make_future_dataframe(m, periods = nperiods, freq =
'month')
      origres <- predict(m, future, mcmc.samples = 1000)
      res <- data.frame(origres %>% rename (month=ds) %>% slice((n()-
nperiods):n()))
      row.names(res) <- substr(res$month,1,7)
      res$month <- NULL
      res <- res[,c(sort(names(res)[names(res) %like%
"yhat*"]),names(res)[!names(res) %like% "yhat*"])]
      setnames(res,gsub("yhat","fcst",names(res)))
      extra = list(m=m,origres=origres)
    }
    list(res=res,extra=extra)
  })
```

`Autoplot` functionalities automate the logic of selecting the appropriate parameters for plotting charts. While this can be useful, the reader may want to further customize and use more specific plot functions when needed. It is being used here to lessen the chances of errors as the code will be used across various environments:

```
 # Plotting the data I

  output$autoplot <- renderPlot({
    tsdata <- createTS()
    tsd1 <- tsdata$tsd
    pl1 <- autoplot(tsd1)
    pl1 + theme(legend.position = "bottom") +
      ggtitle(paste0("Chart 2: Time-Series Data (Actuals)",
pl1$labels$title)) +
      theme(plot.title = element_text(color="#de6e6e", size=12, face =
"bold")) + ylab("Quantity")
  })
  # Plotting the data II

  output$autoplotforecast <- renderPlot({
    tsd1 <- getforecast()
    tsdres <- tsd1$res
    tsdextra <- tsd1$extra
    if(input$forecastmodel=="mcmc"){
      plot(tsdextra$m, tsdextra$origres ) + theme_linedraw()
    } else {
      pl <- autoplot(tsdres)
      pl + theme(legend.position = "bottom") +
        ggtitle(paste0("Chart 1: ", pl$labels$title)) +
        theme(plot.title = element_text(color="#de6e6e", size=12, face =
```

```
"bold")) + ylab(input$forecastmetric)}
  })
```

Plotly has become one of the fastest growing and popular platforms for charting in R. Other APIs, such as Python, are also available. For more information, visit `https://plot.ly`. The following code shows plotting the data using the Plotly API:

```
output$top5plot <- renderPlotly({
    data=getSalesData()
    dc <- dcast(data, Month ~ Product)
    dc$Month <- factor(dc$Month, levels = dc$Month)
    dc$Month <- as.yearmon(dc$Month)
    Quantity <- dc[,2]
    hovertext0 <- paste0(dc$Month,":<b> ",((names(dc))[2])," ",Quantity)
    pplot <- plot_ly(data = dc, x = ~Month, y=~Quantity, type="scatter",
mode="lines", name=((names(dc))[2]), line = list(color = colorp[1],
width=2.5), hoverinfo = "text", text = hovertext0)
    pplot <- pplot %>%
layout(legend = list(x = 0.1, y = 1.2, orientation = 'h'),
plot_bgcolor='rgb(254, 247, 234)',paper_bgcolor='rgb(254, 247,
234)',hovermode = 'compare',annotations = list(
list(xref = "paper", yref = "paper", xanchor = "left", yanchor = "right",x
= 0.01, y = 1.05, showarrow = F,
text = "<b>Top 5 Products in the same category</b>",
font = list(size = 14))
))
    colorp <- c("#00526d","#de6e6e","#006d00","#6d4736","#8f29a6")
    for (i in c(3:ncol(dc))){
      # print (i)
      yval <- dc[,i]
      nameval <- names(dc)[i]
      hovertext <- paste0(dc$Month,":<b> ",nameval," ",yval)
      pplot = pplot %>% add_trace(y = yval, name=nameval, line = list(color
= colorp[i-1], width=2.5), hoverinfo = "text", text = hovertext)
    }
    pplot
  }
  )
```

We use `datatable` in the following code to create nicely formatted HTML tables. The default tables are also quite elegant, but for the purposes of this exercise, we have leveraged CSS and data tables to add custom styles to the code. The following code shows the result in table format:

```
    output$forecastdata <- renderDataTable({
     currency=''
     tsd2 <- getforecast()
     result <- data.frame(tsd2$res)
     result <- data.table(Period=rownames(result),round(result,2))
     if(input$forecastmodel=="mcmc") {
       dtr <- data.table(result)
       result <- dtr
     }
     if(input$forecastmetric=="rev") {
       result <-
cbind(Period=result$Period,result[,.SD*1.4,.SDcols=names(result)[!names(res
ult) %like% "Period"]])
       if (!input$forecastmodel=="mcmc") currency='$ ' # Suppressing $ sign
for mcmc revenue forecasts due to rendering issue
     }
     datatable(result, options = list(pageLength=30, scrollX = TRUE, dom =
't',columnDefs = list(list(className = 'dt-right', targets =
"_all"))),rownames = FALSE,
caption = htmltools::tags$caption(
style = 'caption-side: top; text-align: left; color:#de6e6e',
'Table 1: ', htmltools::h5('Forecast Values with 80/95 % Confidence
Intervals'))
     ) %>% formatCurrency(2:ncol(result),currency)
   })
}


# Run the application
shinyApp(ui = ui, server = server)
```

The resulting application will appear as follows:

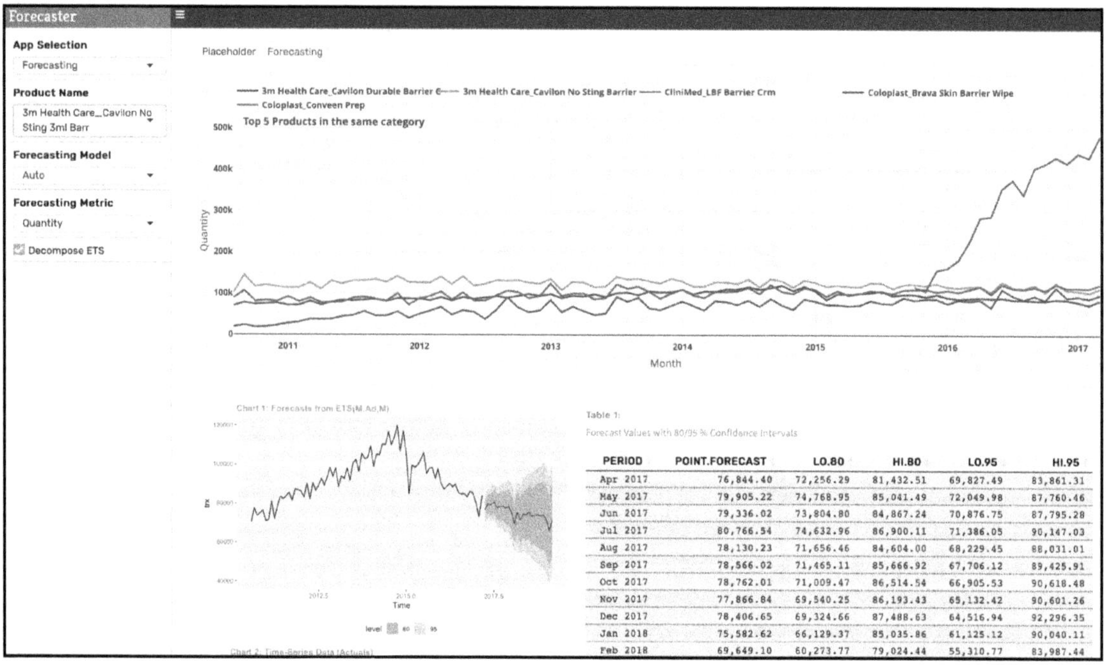

Application details

There are three main sections of the application. The left-hand bar allows users to select the product of interest, the forecasting model to be used, and finally, the metric to forecast on (quantity and revenue):

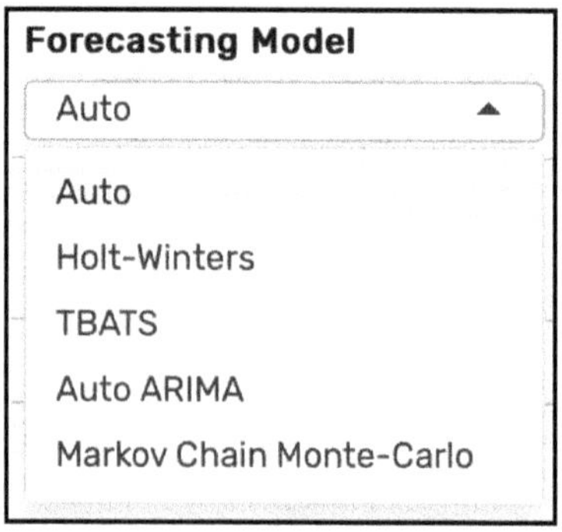

The preceding forecasting models are supported (**Auto**, **Holt—Winters**, **TBATS**, **Auto ARIMA**, and **Markov Chain Monte-Carlo**). The forecasting metrics are as follows:

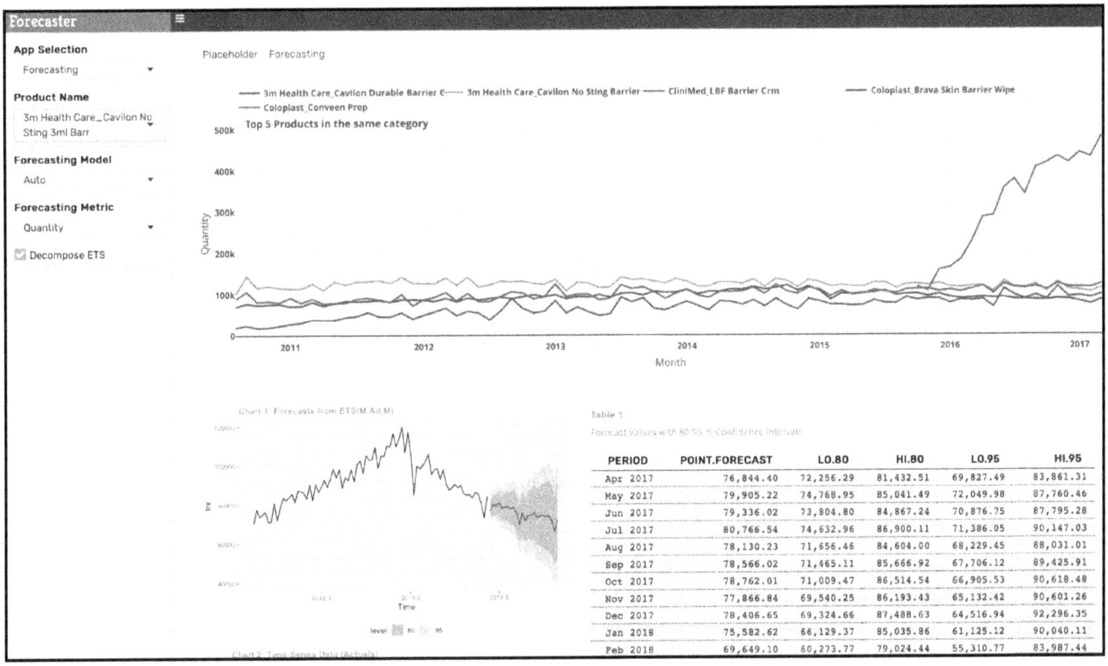

The main screen shows a chart that compares the metric of interest across the top five products in the same category as the product selected in the left-hand menu. The chart has been plotted using the Plotly API available from: `https://plot.ly/r/`:

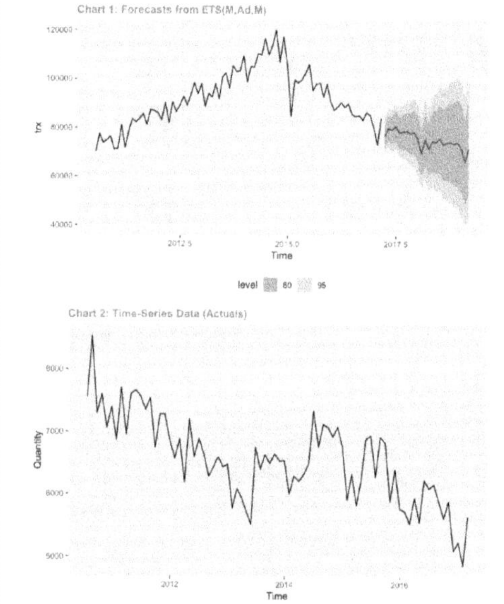

Table 1:

Forecast Values with 80/95 % Confidence Intervals

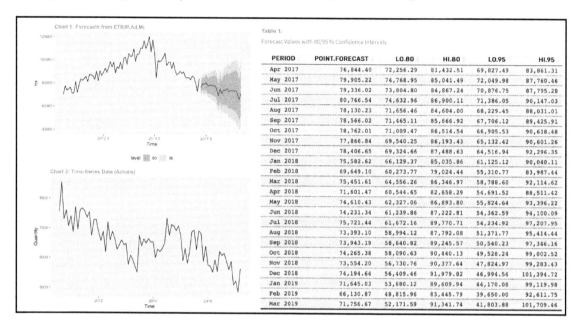

PERIOD	POINT.FORECAST	LO.80	HI.80	LO.95	HI.95
Apr 2017	76,844.40	72,256.29	81,432.51	69,827.49	83,861.31
May 2017	79,905.22	74,768.95	85,041.49	72,049.98	87,760.46
Jun 2017	79,336.02	73,804.80	84,867.24	70,876.75	87,795.28
Jul 2017	80,766.54	74,632.96	86,900.11	71,386.05	90,147.03
Aug 2017	78,130.23	71,656.46	84,604.00	68,229.45	88,031.01
Sep 2017	78,566.02	71,465.11	85,666.92	67,706.12	89,425.91
Oct 2017	78,762.01	71,009.47	86,514.54	66,905.53	90,618.48
Nov 2017	77,866.84	69,540.25	86,193.43	65,132.42	90,601.26
Dec 2017	78,406.65	69,324.66	87,488.63	64,516.94	92,296.35
Jan 2018	75,582.62	66,129.37	85,035.86	61,125.12	90,040.11
Feb 2018	69,649.10	60,273.77	79,024.44	55,310.77	83,987.44
Mar 2018	75,451.61	64,556.26	86,346.97	58,788.60	92,114.62
Apr 2018	71,601.47	60,544.65	82,658.29	54,691.52	88,511.42
May 2018	74,610.43	62,327.06	86,893.80	55,824.64	93,396.22
Jun 2018	74,231.34	61,239.86	87,222.81	54,362.59	94,100.09
Jul 2018	75,721.44	61,672.16	89,770.71	54,234.92	97,207.95
Aug 2018	73,393.10	58,994.12	87,792.08	51,371.77	95,414.44
Sep 2018	73,943.19	58,640.82	89,245.57	50,540.23	97,346.16
Oct 2018	74,265.38	58,090.63	90,440.13	49,528.24	99,002.52
Nov 2018	73,554.20	56,730.76	90,377.64	47,824.97	99,283.43
Dec 2018	74,194.64	56,409.46	91,979.82	46,994.56	101,394.72
Jan 2019	71,645.03	53,680.12	89,609.94	44,170.08	99,119.98
Feb 2019	66,130.87	48,815.96	83,445.79	39,650.00	92,611.75
Mar 2019	71,756.67	52,171.59	91,341.74	41,803.88	101,709.46

The second half of the screen shows the plots of the actual data versus the predicted value, with the respective confidence intervals shown in the shaded areas in the first plot image.

The right side of the section lists the forecasted values, along with the 80% and 95% confidence intervals:

Table 2:
Sales Data from NHS Records

MONTH	BNFNAME	ACTCOST	QUANTITY	CHEMSUB	METRIC
2010-08	3m Health Care_Cavilon No Sting 3ml Barr	54518.58	7559	Skin Fillers And Protectives	7559
2010-09	3m Health Care_Cavilon No Sting 3ml Barr	61434.85	8527	Skin Fillers And Protectives	8527
2010-10	3m Health Care_Cavilon No Sting 3ml Barr	52582.01	7292	Skin Fillers And Protectives	7292
2010-11	3m Health Care_Cavilon No Sting 3ml Barr	54820.75	7599	Skin Fillers And Protectives	7599
2010-12	3m Health Care_Cavilon No Sting 3ml Barr	50962.04	7061	Skin Fillers And Protectives	7061
2011-01	3m Health Care_Cavilon No Sting 3ml Barr	53345.9	7394	Skin Fillers And Protectives	7394
2011-02	3m Health Care_Cavilon No Sting 3ml Barr	49534.52	6858	Skin Fillers And Protectives	6858
2011-03	3m Health Care_Cavilon No Sting 3ml Barr	55615.69	7700	Skin Fillers And Protectives	7700
2011-04	3m Health Care_Cavilon No Sting 3ml Barr	49971.22	6947	Skin Fillers And Protectives	6947
2011-05	3m Health Care_Cavilon No Sting 3ml Barr	54943.66	7604	Skin Fillers And Protectives	7604
2011-06	3m Health Care_Cavilon No Sting 3ml Barr	55323.1	7661	Skin Fillers And Protectives	7661
2011-07	3m Health Care_Cavilon No Sting 3ml Barr	54619.06	7565	Skin Fillers And Protectives	7565
2011-08	3m Health Care_Cavilon No Sting 3ml Barr	53093.28	7352	Skin Fillers And Protectives	7352
2011-09	3m Health Care_Cavilon No Sting 3ml Barr	54413.82	7535	Skin Fillers And Protectives	7535
2011-10	3m Health Care_Cavilon No Sting 3ml Barr	48704.49	6746	Skin Fillers And Protectives	6746
2011-11	3m Health Care_Cavilon No Sting 3ml Barr	52585.04	7281	Skin Fillers And Protectives	7281
2011-12	3m Health Care_Cavilon No Sting 3ml Barr	52632.39	7276	Skin Fillers And Protectives	7276
2012-01	3m Health Care_Cavilon No Sting 3ml Barr	49459.28	6861	Skin Fillers And Protectives	6861
2012-02	3m Health Care_Cavilon No Sting 3ml Barr	47578.07	6576	Skin Fillers And Protectives	6576
2012-03	3m Health Care_Cavilon No Sting 3ml Barr	49792.63	6881	Skin Fillers And Protectives	6881
2012-04	3m Health Care_Cavilon No Sting 3ml Barr	44710.94	6191	Skin Fillers And Protectives	6191
2012-05	3m Health Care_Cavilon No Sting 3ml Barr	52084.8	7199	Skin Fillers And Protectives	7199
2012-06	3m Health Care_Cavilon No Sting 3ml Barr	47665.67	6602	Skin Fillers And Protectives	6602
2012-07	3m Health Care_Cavilon No Sting 3ml Barr	49825.06	6890	Skin Fillers And Protectives	6890
2012-08	3m Health Care_Cavilon No Sting 3ml Barr	48028.42	6642	Skin Fillers And Protectives	6642
2012-09	3m Health Care_Cavilon No Sting 3ml Barr	45282.66	6273	Skin Fillers And Protectives	6273
2012-10	3m Health Care_Cavilon No Sting 3ml Barr	46453.93	6431	Skin Fillers And Protectives	6431
2012-11	3m Health Care_Cavilon No Sting 3ml Barr	47591.56	6593	Skin Fillers And Protectives	6593
2012-12	3m Health Care_Cavilon No Sting 3ml Barr	46444.13	6431	Skin Fillers And Protectives	6431
2013-01	3m Health Care_Cavilon No Sting 3ml Barr	46817.73	6473	Skin Fillers And Protectives	6473

The third and final section shows the actual data in tabular format. Note that the data is aggregated by month and the columns show the actual cost, the quantity, and other related information:

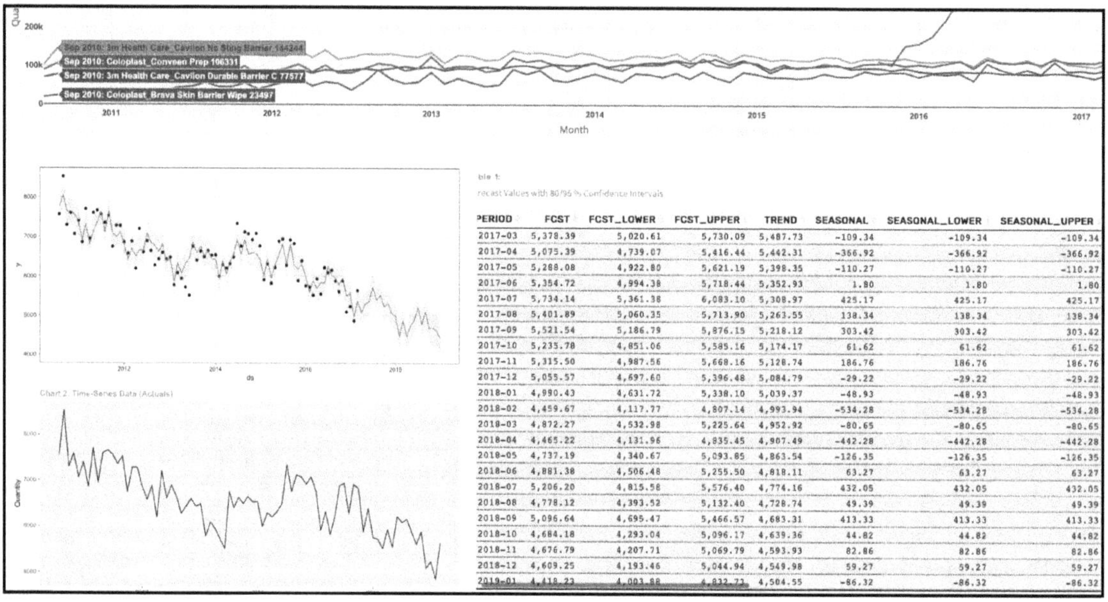

PERIOD	FCST	FCST_LOWER	FCST_UPPER	TREND	SEASONAL	SEASONAL_LOWER	SEASONAL_UPPER
2017-03	5,378.39	5,020.61	5,730.09	5,487.73	-109.34	-109.34	-109.34
2017-04	5,075.39	4,739.07	5,416.44	5,442.31	-366.92	-366.92	-366.92
2017-05	5,288.08	4,922.80	5,621.19	5,398.35	-110.27	-110.27	-110.27
2017-06	5,354.72	4,994.38	5,718.44	5,352.93	1.80	1.80	1.80
2017-07	5,734.14	5,361.38	6,083.10	5,308.97	425.17	425.17	425.17
2017-08	5,401.89	5,060.35	5,713.90	5,263.55	138.34	138.34	138.34
2017-09	5,521.54	5,186.79	5,876.15	5,218.12	303.42	303.42	303.42
2017-10	5,235.78	4,851.06	5,585.16	5,174.17	61.62	61.62	61.62
2017-11	5,315.50	4,987.56	5,668.16	5,128.74	186.76	186.76	186.76
2017-12	5,055.57	4,697.60	5,396.48	5,084.79	-29.22	-29.22	-29.22
2018-01	4,990.43	4,631.72	5,338.10	5,039.37	-48.93	-48.93	-48.93
2018-02	4,459.67	4,117.77	4,807.14	4,993.94	-534.28	-534.28	-534.28
2018-03	4,872.27	4,532.98	5,225.64	4,952.92	-80.65	-80.65	-80.65
2018-04	4,465.22	4,131.96	4,835.45	4,907.49	-442.28	-442.28	-442.28
2018-05	4,737.19	4,340.67	5,093.85	4,863.54	-126.35	-126.35	-126.35
2018-06	4,881.38	4,506.48	5,255.50	4,818.11	63.27	63.27	63.27
2018-07	5,206.20	4,815.58	5,576.40	4,774.16	432.05	432.05	432.05
2018-08	4,778.12	4,393.52	5,132.40	4,728.74	49.39	49.39	49.39
2018-09	5,096.64	4,695.47	5,466.57	4,683.31	413.33	413.33	413.33
2018-10	4,684.18	4,293.04	5,096.17	4,639.36	44.82	44.82	44.82
2018-11	4,676.79	4,207.71	5,069.79	4,593.93	82.86	82.86	82.86
2018-12	4,609.25	4,193.46	5,044.94	4,549.98	59.27	59.27	59.27
2019-01	4,418.23	4,003.88	4,832.73	4,504.55	-86.32	-86.32	-86.32

One of the options in the forecasting model menu includes MCMC, which is a more sophisticated forecasting method available via the `prophet` package in R. It was released by Facebook and contains advanced forecasting capabilities. That said, practitioners tend to rely more heavily on time-tested techniques such as **Holt—Winters** and **ARIMA**, both of which have also been included as options in the drop-down menus.

Summary

In this chapter, we saw an example of a forecasting and machine learning application built using R Shiny, and a number of supporting packages. In the next chapter, we will delve deeper into machine learning and work with neural networks, which have become one of the most prominent algorithms currently used across the world for advanced and sophisticated machine learning applications.

Quiz

1. **Quiz-tion**: What are the two basic components of all Shiny applications?
    1. UI and server
    2. Frontend and backend
    3. RStudio and Shiny
2. **Quiz-tion**: What is the R package for Shiny applications?
    1. RStudio
    2. Shiny
    3. ShinyR
3. **Quiz-tion**: What is the `prophet` package?
    1. A forecasting package developed by Facebook
    2. A machine learning library
    3. An extension to the forecast package in R

Answers:

Q1-1, Q2-2, Q3-1

8
Neural Networks and Deep Learning

"Some people worry that artificial intelligence will make us feel inferior, but then, anybody in his right mind should have an inferiority complex every time he looks at a flower."
– Alan Kay

There is a new gold rush going on, but this time *gold* means deep learning. Brand-new start-ups and traditional enterprises are looking toward **Neural Networks** (**NN**) and deep learning. As one of the most powerful programming languages for data scientists, R is sailing on this tide.

One of the most promising backend deep learning engines is TensorFlow from Google. Keras permits the user to work with TensorFlow and some other great engines, allowing fast experimentation. Simple codes and a wide variety of modern neural architectures are some of the strengths featured by Keras, compared to competing frameworks.

This chapter will demonstrate how to design and train deep learning models using the R interface for Keras, but not before going through several core concepts of deep learning and NN. These concepts are not only meant to help with models' understanding the models, but also to point out what should and shouldn't be done with them.

Here is what readers can expect from this chapter:

- Learn how NNs are used in our daily lives
- Get to know the biological inspiration for **Artificial Neural Networks** (**ANNs**)
- Get an introduced to the model's pieces: nodes, activations function, and layers
- Learn the most popular learning algorithms
- Meet TensorFlow and Keras
- Fit a deep learning classification model from scratch using Keras

Daily neural nets

Deep learning models are the typical models of this big data era. They are data hungry; nowadays, there is tons of data to be processed. Also, they are computational requesting compared to the traditional linear regression models; older computers were not able to train useful networks. They only turned out to be feasible after the development of the first backpropagation algorithms, along with some computational advancements.

One of the first NN breakthroughs that earned great respect in the community was the outstanding performance achieved by a **Deep Convolutional Neural Network** during the LSVRC-2010 contest. Such a contest aimed to classify 1.2 million high-resolution images into 1,000 different classes.

After the 2010 breakthrough, NNs became one of the most popular models in the **Artificial Intelligence** (**AI**) field.

Back in those days, such a model took around a week to be trained. With the advent of cloud computing, along with hardware, algorithms, and software improvements, in the early days of 2018, the same model could be trained through an inexpensive cloud service within a couple of hours. Industries and universities started to trust these models a lot more. A hype arose around AI. Deep learning became a buzzword.

PwC consulting estimates show that up to 2030, AI will contribute up to 13 trillion dollars to the world's economy by augmenting production and consumption. As a cutting-edge technique, NNs and their deep learning models are among the core gears that enable this whole movement.

AI has worked as the theme for many Hollywood plots over the years. *The Terminator* (1984) and *Matrix* (1999) are examples of plots where evil AIs are taking control of the world. In *Avengers: Age of Ultron* (2015), AIs are both the problem and the solution: a bad-intentioned AI (Ultron) becomes the core villain and a well-intentioned one (Vision) helps the good guys to defeat the bad one.

NNs are likely to greatly impact the way that we produce, build, and consume. Social relations might also be affected by NNs. Universities and non-profit organizations are using it to protect the environment and demand better policies. Indeed, to volunteer for a non-profit organization is a great way to give your data science career a boost. Even better would be to proactively found an organization of your own.

Here are some general characteristics of NNs:

- Unsupervised or supervised learning techniques are available
- Regression and classification tasks can be performed with them
- By employing enough hidden layers and nodes, it's possible for the NNs to approximate any sort of function (linear or non-linear); neural nets are known as universal approximators
- General tasks that they are known to perform well include fraud detection, natural language processing, and face and voice recognition

To mention practical enterprises, TensorFlow, which is Google's open source project for deep learning and one of the engines featured by Keras, has a lot of successful history built on top of it. It has been used to diagnosis diabetical retinopathy, monitor maritime life, and is behind the smart reply laid out by Gmail.

Ironman's J.A.R.V.I.S. was originally a natural language processing application designed by Tony Stark.

NNs are truly unique and marvelous. Nowadays, these models stand somewhere between science and magic. Sure, there are downsides (more about them later), but given their capabilities and brilliance, it does not sound like a surprise to me that neural nets and deep learning already participate so much in our daily lives.

By the time I have finished writing this book, some deep learning applications are hard to distinguish. A bunch of well-designed chatbots can be easily mistaken for real people. On the other hand, some clickbait headlines and fake news are pretty easy to tell apart.

This brief section's intention was to reinforce the influence and capability that NNs have. In the next one, you will see why every deep learning model is an NN, but not every NN is a deep learning model. Understanding NNs in more detail might be helpful to learn the dos and don'ts of these models; that is what the next section is aimed at.

Overview – NNs and deep learning

This section is designed to introduce the core components of NNs and deep learning. For those who already are familiar with NNs, it may feel like a condensed overview of the topic, but feel free to jump to the next section if you are here only for the practical tips about Keras.

An NN, or ANN to avoid any confusion, is a powerful method that can approximate any sort of function, linear or not. If you don't know anything about ANNs, here you will get the basics: the main components, and how the training takes place. You might learn which are the hyperparameters and algorithms to choose while building a network. We will discuss matters such as the following ones:

- How many nodes should I use in each layer?
- Which activation functions should I use?
- How is data transformation likely to alter the results?
- Which error measure should I adopt?
- Which training algorithm (training strategy) should I pick?
- What kind of network should I have?

Deciding upon a network and its architecture is usually a serious consideration, as the preceding list may have demonstrated, and requires many decisions to be made. Moreover, as generic modeling tasks are frequently tagged as artistic quests, due to how much creativity they demand, so also is NN modeling.

Creativity is certainly related to the creation and development of NNs. The idea that inspired NNs has been floating around for quite a long time. As the name suggests, it came from neuroscience and was based on a basic understanding of how neurons work.

Neuroscience inspiration

Neurons are complex cells that can deal with several different operations. One of their functions is to handle stimuli; they are responsible for making us see, feel, and think. They work through chemical and electrical stimulus usually passed from a neuron to the next one in the network.

Machine learning ANNs were greatly inspired by how the real biological NNs work, and how they balance stimuli and pass them through other neurons. In the following diagram, you will find a detailed model of a single neuron:

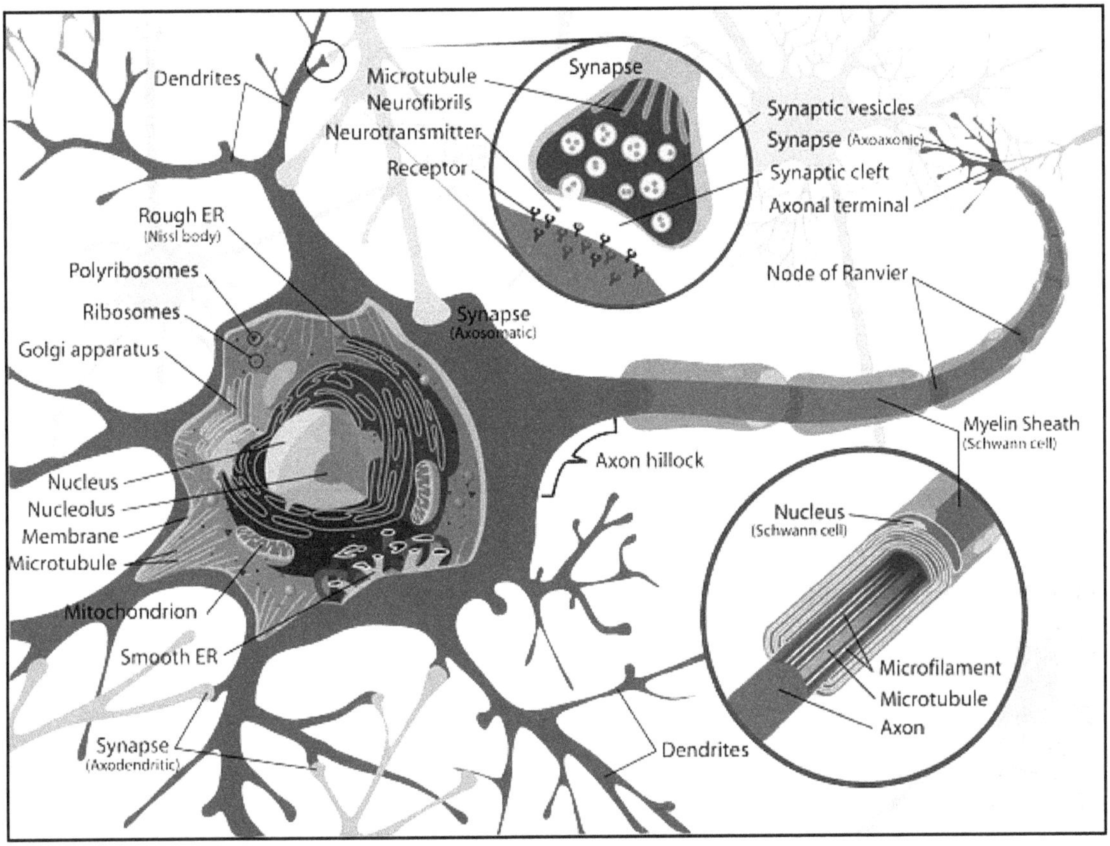

Figure 8.1: Neuron representation source: pixabay

There are several types of neurons; the one displayed in the preceding diagram resembles a motor neuron. Extreme left, the reader can see several ramifications. These are the dendrite trees, which receive stimulus. Extreme left, the ramifications are the synapsis, which transmits stimulus.

ANN nodes

ANN nodes are simplified (mathematical) versions of what is displayed in *Figure 8.1*. They gather numerical inputs that are balanced through weights, summed together (frequently along with a constant, or bias if you will), applied to a given function, and then output as a result. Such a result could be a final result given by an output node, or handled over to another node (and sometimes also to the exact same node if we have a recurrent setting). The following diagram illustrates the functioning of an ANN node:

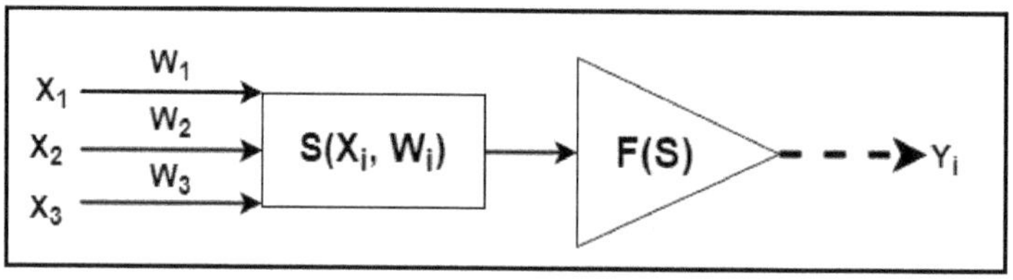

Figure 8.2: ANN node

In the preceding diagram, the node is receiving three different inputs (**X_1**, **X_2**, and **X_3**). All of them are balanced by weights (**W_1**, **W_2**, and **W_3**) and summed. The **$S(X_i,W_i)$** is taking care of the sum, and such a function can be expressed as follows:

$$S(X_i, W_i) = (\sum_{i=1}^{n} X_i W_i) + b$$

The letter *b* represents a bias, and few architectures won't have this. After everything is summed, they go through an **activation function**, which the diagrams represent as the *F(S)* function inside the triangle. The result of such a function is output as Y_i, which can be handed to another node or work as the final output.

Input nodes are the inputs of your model. They are generally preprocessed data and hold neither summation nor activation functions.

Activation functions play a very special role in the NN design.

Activation functions

Picking good activation functions makes training much easier. Also, the activation function choice may entail at least two shoulds: the way you should transform data and the way binaries (if there are any) should be formatted. There is an infinity of activation functions available; actually, it could be any continuous function—you can make one of your own.

> The only requirement for a function to be eligible as an activation function is to be derivable, or at least that you can assume a reasonable proxy for the points you can't derive.

Here is are a list of popular activation functions:

- **Rectified Linear Unit (ReLU)**:

$$F(S) = max(S, 0)$$

- **Leaky Rectified Linear Unit (Leaky ReLU)**:

$$F(S) = max(S, \alpha S)$$

- **Hyperbolic Tangent (Tanh)**:

$$F(S) = \frac{2}{1 + e^{-2S}} - 1$$

- **Sigmoid**:

$$F(S) = \frac{1}{1 + e^{-S}}$$

People that are used to time-series modeling are usually into things such as modeling the series in the differences, instead of in a level. That's because they frequently rely upon linear methods that demand stationarity, and if series is not stationary in level, it might be in the first difference.

Transformations such as difference could help in specific cases but are not what is generally looked for before the ANN training starts (preprocessing stage). To understand why it's good to look at the activation function form, the following shows the **ReLU**, **Tanh**, and **Sigmoid** response to inputs between the **-3** and **3** range:

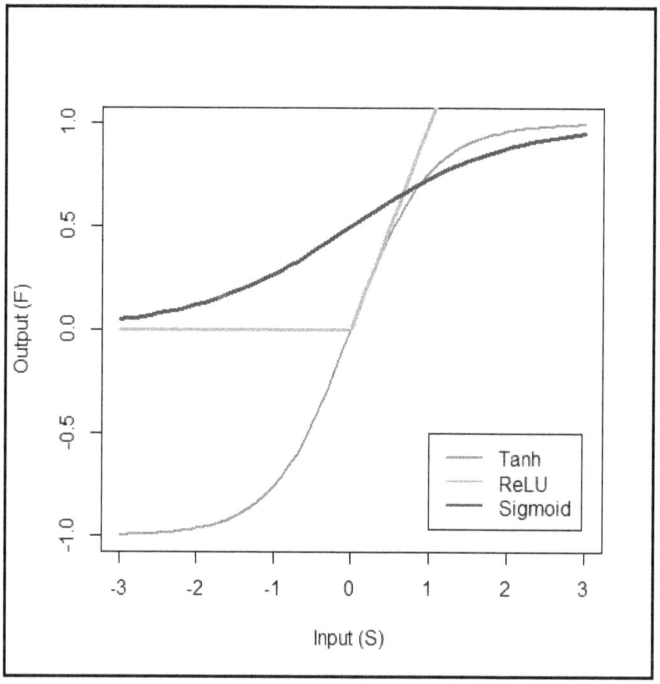

Figure 8.3: Popular activation functions behavior

The limits for the **ReLU** function are between zero and infinite. Tanh goes from **-1.0** to **1.0**, while **Sigmoid** goes from zero to one. In a perfect world, the range of your inputs wouldn't matter, and the weights would do a wonderful job by rescaling your variables if required. In the real world, if your input range doesn't match the activation functions that well, you might get stuck in a local optimal during the training.

TIP

If you're using **Tanh** as an activation function, try to use **-1.0** and **1.0** as binaries instead of one and zero.

Generally, standardization will help a lot, but there are most certainly alternatives. The activation function that I mostly used when I got started was Tanh, and due to this, the transformation that I am most used to is a max–min type of transformation that coerces my data into a range between *-1* and *1*, and it makes training a lot smoother. It goes like this:

$$\hat{x} = \frac{2x - 2min(x)}{max(x) - min(x)} - 1$$

There are lots of transformations and lots of other kinds of max–min transformations. The most common one will scale data into a range of zero to one.

$\hat{x}$ stands for the transformed variable. It's also good to transform the output if you are dealing with a regression problem. Just don't forget that you might have to redo and undo the transformation later. Store the key numbers (max and min) for each variable someplace; this way, you can freely redo or undo the transformation as it pleases you.

Sigmoid and Tanh were the first ones (in this order) to become popular. Tanh solves some of the problems carried by sigmoid. Yet, ReLU seems to stand out as an activation function, meaning that it should be a safe choice. ReLU is not all perfect; Leaky ReLU solves some problems with regular ReLU.

Maxout is yet another alternative activation function, but it greatly increases the number of parameters, so there is a trade-off. Output nodes usually demand different types of activation functions. Linear activation functions are usually the best choice for regression problems, while `softmax` tends to outperform classification problems.

A single node with a proper activation function does not make a network. To have an ANN, you must have many nodes arranged in layers.

Layers

There are three basic types of layers: **input layers**, **hidden layers**, and **output layers**. They respectively contain the input, hidden, and output nodes. Generally, you might have only a single input layer and a single output layer—each can contain one or more nodes—but you can have as many hidden layers as you want.

The number of input nodes is equal to number of input variables. The number of output nodes must be equal to the number of variables or categories predicted.

The following diagram shows a hypothetical arrangement for a feedforward NN:

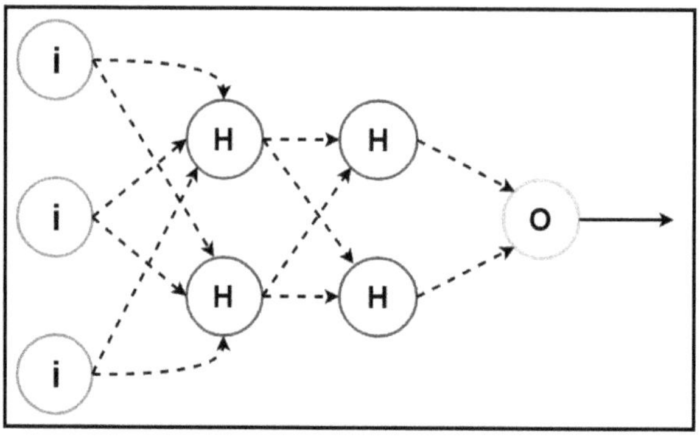

Figure 8.4: Feedforward NN representation

Each circle represents a node, and the dashed arrows represent the connection between them. The inscriptions inside a node show which basic type it is: **i** means input, **H** for hidden and **O** for output. Such a network has one input layer with three input nodes, two hidden layers with two hidden nodes each, and one output layer with one output node.

> Cutting unnecessary inputs, which can be a tricky task, can spare you training time and bump upaccuracy. Don't look for correlation and partial correlation because that only matters for linear relations, and ANNs will look at both linear and non-linear relations at the same time (if you have enough data). Genetic algorithms are usually helpful, but they also take time to run.

Each additional hidden layer looks into more complex features within data. For example, an NN trained to recognize faces may only recognize silhouettes in the first hidden layer; a second hidden layer may recognize shapes, while a third one is able to recognize noses, eyes, and mouths.

As you go deeper into hidden layers, more complex features are being explored, meaning that you might need more layers for more complex tasks, while easy ones can be dealt with by only a couple of hidden layers. Deep learning involves ANN models with more than a single hidden layer; this is, the reason every deep learning model is an ANN but not every ANN is considered deep learning.

Even if the problem at hand is so simple that only requires a single hidden layer, more often than not, arranging hidden nodes into two consecutive hidden layers will most probably lead to less time required to train the network and more accuracy. One must agree that if the problem at hand is simple enough, ANNs wouldn't be required at all.

The design of layers and nodes through an ANN is called an **architecture**.

The architecture that it made the breakthrough during the LSVRC-2010 contest had seven hidden layers. There is no magic rule that will give you the best architecture for the problem at hand. Usually, the best place to start is searching for what has worked for other people with similar problems. From there, you can work your mojo by exploring alternative solutions.

There are techniques that can help you through exploration, such as grid search, random grid search, and genetic algorithms.

Besides their basic denomination—input, hidden, and output—layers can also be called by how they work. For example, the ones displayed in *Figure 8.4* would be called dense layers (or fully connected) because they are fully connected to the next layers.

The most common layers are these:

- **Dense** (fully connected): Nodes are fully connected to the layer behind it. Each connection is weighted by a trainable parameter called a weight. This means that no information is spared and there are lots of parameters to balance during the training, which makes this layer costly.
- **Normalization**: Normalizes the activations from the previous layer at each batch. Batches are small samples of fixed sizes; one batch at a time is used to update the trainable parameters.
- **Convolutional**: Layers that slide (convolve) over the whole input, looking to it over fixed-size windows. They are well known for their good performance in computer vision problems.
- **Max pooling**: Reduces the dimensionality of the output, making it a great companion to the convolutional layer, which often increases the dimensionality.
- **Recurrent**: Recurrent layers enable the output to affect the same node it came from. They are frequently used in time-related problems, such as stock price prediction.

Each of these specialized layers works in a specific way; in other words, they are better suited for doing different things. Convolutional layers are pretty common for networks dealing with classification through images. Recurrent layers are frequent in architectures designed to handle time-series regression problems. Dense is common to all sorts of networks.

> It's common to have more than one type of specialized layer in the same network.

Once the architecture is locked, it is finally time to train the network. Training will require a specific algorithm (training strategy) to do it. It's usually not that hard to pick one, given that there are plenty that will effectively handle the training task. The backpropagation algorithm was the one that first stood, as feasible, improved versions, such as Adams, were developed later.

Training algorithms

Until now, we've seen that nodes act like functions, and they are chained together in a network. Another way to think about NNs is that they are nested functions—they really are. Through settling on the best weights, they can approximate almost any function and properly handle the given task; thus, this is why they are called **universal function approximators**.

Finding the best weights is essentially an optimization task. Nesting and the usual huge amount of parameters make this particular task a little bit challenging. Neural nets only became feasible after the first efficient algorithms came out. Backpropagation was the method that first stood up for the assignment.

> Several variations of backpropagation were developed over the years, and if I had to bet, I would say that many more might come out in the near future. These variations are very competitive. Personally, one that I like very much is Adams.

Backpropagation applies gradient descent to the network in a layered manner. Instead of sticking with notations, I may here only give an intuition about how gradient descent and the backpropagation works. Looking into further details surely is worthwhile, especially if you wish to do some research on the subject.

The idea of gradient descent is pretty straightforward. Imagine that you are walking on a function. If you care to know the slope at the point you currently are, you would know which direction to walk to reach greater or lower highs. Walking in the opposite direction of the slope will eventually lead to one of the following outcomes:

- You will get very close to a local minimum, which could be a global minimum (or not)
- You may walk miles and miles until you get tired and give up

Walking down a function is kind of what gradient descendent does. It will look at the slope at a given point by looking at the derivative of the function in question while walking in the opposite direction. With this approach, gradient descent is likely to arrive at a local minimum, which may or may not be a global minimum, or walk in the same direction for ages until it chooses to terminate, after walking a very long path.

The step size is also something to decide upon. Gradient descent depends on a cost function to work its magic. The quadratic cost is the traditional one, but there is also cross-entropy, categorical cross-entropy, exponential, **Itakura-Saito** distance, and many others.

This explains why we look for activation functions that can be easily derived and also relates to why the algorithm is likely to get stuck in local optimals if data is not properly scaled. Assuming that there is a global minimum, gradient descendent is not sure to get to it, but as long it gets close enough, the ANN will be fine.

Gradient descendent is the pillar that supports the algorithms used to train NNs. On top of it, all the differences between them are either a requirement to translate such optimization into computational and network contexts or strategies designed to deliver more efficiency by demanding fewer steps to converge, or converging with more accuracy.

Additionally, it's important to state that training algorithms for ANN usually come with their own share of parameters that are very likely to interfere with the training, so it's another thing to keep an eye on.

NNs are a bunch of nested functions. An application of gradient descendent to the neural nets would require that all the partial derivatives with respect to the error for every single weight be computed; that is what backpropagation does, which allows the proper training of NNs.

To compute such partials, backpropagation highly relies on a very popular derivative rule, the chain rule.

Although there are many learning algorithms, backpropagation and some related concepts are common to many of them. The following is a list with a brief explanation of the most popular ones:

- **Batch**: To update the weights using the whole dataset at one time would be computationally impracticable for the majority of networks. What is done instead is the weights are updated by random subsets called **mini-batches**. Batch-size is usually an accessible hyperparameter in training algorithms.
- **Epoch**: One complete data pass through the network. Many might be required during the training, but too many will cause the network to generalize badly, resulting in overfitting. Setting a validation dataset usually helps to pick the right number of epochs.
- **Learning rate**: It reduces the possibility of overshooting by allowing that only a fraction of the gradient is to be used to update the weights. It's a frequent hyperparameter, and although it requires some testing, common values range from *0.01* to *0.001*.

To choose hyperparameters such as batch-size, epochs, and learning rate might be difficult and require some testing and time, but choosing the proper training algorithm may not be that difficult. Adam (**Adaptative Moment Estimation**) frequently outperforms resilient backpropagation, momentum, **Stochastic Gradient Descent** (**SGD**), and **Nesterov**.

Judging by how fast-paced this research field has proved to be, I bet that Adam will become obsolete someday in the future. A good way to be warned is to frequently read research and stay tuned for updates to your favorite deep learning framework, since really good algorithms are more likely to make their way into it.

Don't ever fear to experience new approaches or try new solutions.

NNs are relatively young and have imposed a pretty fast pace of evolution. Lots of opportunities both from a business and a research perspective are available. At this point, this chapter displays a lengthy list of hyperparameters to look after while designing a NN. To put it on a short list, some decisions that are relatively easy to make prior to training are these:

- How many input and output nodes to have
- Which activation functions to use
- Which training algorithm (strategy) to use

Some others choices may require a little more testing:

- How many hidden layers to have
- How many hidden nodes to have in each layer
- Which types of hidden layers to have
- How to select batch-size, epochs, and learning rate

To find fine hyperparameters in the latter list might require some testing, since they highly depend on the specific problem to be solved and the computational power available. The task is not to find the best ever configuration but to find one that will solve your problem in the feasible time.

If you are worried about the large number of decisions you might have to make, don't worry. Experience is a great teacher, and there is much you might learn from experimentation. Before you realize it, you will be cleaning data for eternity, while designing very good networks in the blink of an eye.

While this section was theoretical, the next one will come with a more practical approach. We will see how Keras can be used to build NNs from scratch.

NNs with Keras

Knowing, at least intuitively, the components of a deep learning model and how they interact is a must before going any further into practical details. The practical details might change with respect to which deep learning framework and API to be used; this chapter uses Keras. It will give access to Google's TensorFlow and some other frameworks.

Keras is the ancient Greek word for horn, which makes reference to *Odyssey*, written by Homer. In his narrative, the spirits that came from a gate made of polished horn had fulfilling visions and accurate predictions.

Building cutting-edge models using Keras is easy. The workflow usually goes as follows: once you are done with data preprocessing, you design the network's architecture and choose a learning strategy, a cost function, and measures to track. The next steps are training and testing.

The process of designing a new network is rarely linear such as the one just described. Going back and forth is almost inevitable if you want to improve a network.

Four words could be used to summarize (usual) workflow: **design**, **compile**, **train**, and **test**. Although the ANN models are usually very complex, to build a very good one from scratch using Keras is very simple; it skips a bunch of human steps without losing flexibility. First things first, the environment must be properly setup.

Getting things ready for Keras

To use Keras properly, many other packages and programs must be installed. The way any of these programs are installed might vary according to the **Operational System** (**OS**) you are using, and I shall point to the websites where you can find download links and instructions.

Some cloud servers can be easily prepared for the use of R and Keras, while others will require more work to be done. Selecting the appropriate server and developing a routine to make these environments ready, as well as computing the time you will need to get it done, is very important.

Both the Keras library and TensorFlow are written in Python, so it makes sense to get it installed first. Get version 3.x through the official website: `https://python.org`.

You can install it through Anaconda if you prefer (`https://www.anaconda.com/download`). Now, let's install the following Python modules (or libraries if you will):

- `numpy`
- `scipy`
- `gaphviz`
- `keras`
- `tensorflow`

- `matplotlib`
- `pydot-ng`
- `h5py`

TIP: You can find the `gaphviz` library `https://graphviz.gitlab.io/download/`.

We can install Python modules using the `reticulate` package but only if you installed Anaconda and marked the `PATH` option. If you want to install them using `reticulate`, install the package first:

```
if(!require('reticulate')){install.packages('reticulate')}
library(reticulate)
```

The next step is to use `py_install` to install all the packages, and this step can take several minutes:

```
py_install('numpy')
py_install('scipy')
py_install('graphviz')
py_install('keras')
py_install('tensorflow')
py_install('matplotlib')
py_install('pydot-ng')
py_install('h5py')
```

If the `pip` command is available in your system, there is a way to install them through the R console:

```
modules <- c('numpy','scipy','graphviz',
             'keras', 'tensorflow',
             'matplotlib','pydot-ng','h5py')
for(i in modules){
  system(paste('python -m pip install --upgrade', i, sep = ' '))
  }
```

It is also recommended to install a **Basic Linear Algebra Subprogram** (**BLAS**) to optimize some operations that may take place on your machine. **OpenBLAS** might optimize tensor operations running on your CPU. The following website has download links, installation instructions, and a manual: `https://www.openblas.net/`.

Training your networks using GPU is usually faster than training them in a CPU. If you have an NVIDIA graphic card, it might be possible for Keras to train your networks with it. Make sure your card is compatible with CUDA. If it is, follow the next steps:

1. Update your driver (`http://www.nvidia.com/Download/index.aspx?`)
2. Download and install CUDA (`https://developer.nvidia.com/cuda-zone`)
3. Download and install cuDNN (`https://developer.nvidia.com/cudnn`)

It's time to turn back to R's console again. It's better to have a recent version of the `reticulate` package installed; make sure to have `devtools` installed, and run the following:

```
devtools::install_github('rstudio/reticulate')
```

Package `reticulate` is meant to run Python through R. Having this version from RStudio's GitHub might prevent some annoying bugs coming up while running Keras with R. If you're missing `devtools`, run `install_packages('devtools')` before running the latter code.
Another thing to do in your R console is to install the `keras` package and Keras itself:

```
install.packages('keras')
library(keras)
install_keras()
```

Notice that the `keras` package was not only installed but it was installed, loaded, and had a function called (`install_keras()`). Having the environment properly set is really important. Although this section covers lots of requirements, the real extent of need may vary from context to context. Keep an eye open for any warning sign that may arise.

The preparations have been made, so it's finally time to get practical with Keras. The next topic will discuss data gathering, preprocessing, network design, training, and evaluation.

Getting practical with Keras

With all the things in place, it's time to look at practical examples. Under this topic, we will build and store a deep learning model from scratch using Keras. To get started, we need a dataset. You might be thinking *here comes MNIST data again.* but not this time. We will look for data in the **University of California, Irvine** (**UCI**) Machine Learning Repository.

> The UCI Machine Learning Repository has lots of datasets you can play with. Kaggle is another interesting source. Ask redditors for data at `https://reddit.com/r/data`

You can check all the UCI's datasets in the following link: `https://archive.ics.uci.edu/ml/datasets.html`

The dataset used is about credit card default. It can be found here: `https://archive.ics.uci.edu/ml/datasets/default+of+credit+card+clients`.

This data has 30,000 observations about credit card owners. The available variables go from credit card limits to payment history details, all the way to default status. We can download the data directly from the R console. The following code block creates a temporary file, stores the download URL in a string, and downloads the data:

```
tmp <- tempfile(fileext = '.xls')
url <-
'https://archive.ics.uci.edu/ml/machine-learning-databases/00350/default%20
of%20credit%20card%20clients.xls'
download.file(url, destfile = tmp, method = 'curl')
```

Note how the temporary file was given an `.xls` extension using the `fileext` argument. Next, we will read such a file using the `readxl` package; make sure to have it installed:

```
if(!require(readxl)){ install.packages('readxl')}
```

Once we're sure that `readxl` is installed, it is time to move on and read the data. Load the package and call the `read_xls` function to read the data downloaded into the temporary file (`tmp`):

```
library(readxl)
dt <- read_xls(tmp, skip = 1)
# unlink(tmp)
```

Spot the `skip = 1` argument inside `read_xls()`; it's skipping the first row of the data file. This row contained alternative names for the variables. The latter code block sticks with the more intuitive names given by the second row. Observations begin after the third row. There are 30,000 observations from 25 variables. Here is what we can do to peek inside:

```
summary(dt)
head(dt)
```

Due to the large number of variables, I won't reproduce the results given by the previous code block, but you can check it at your end. Here is a description of the variables:

- `ID` (first column): Integers related to the credit card owners.
- `SEX` (column 2): A categorical variable with two levels (expressed numerically).
- `EDUCATION` (column 3): A categorical variable expressed numerically, ranging from zero to six.
- `MARRIAGE` (column 4): A categorical variable where *one* stands for married, two for single and three for other.
- `AGE` (column 5): An integer representing how many years old the credit card owner was.
- `PAY_*` (columns 6 to 11): A discrete variable displaying duly payment (*-1*) or the number of months the payment has been delayed. Each column represents a distinct measure in time.
- `BILL_AMT*` (columns 12 to 17): Bill statement for distinct months.
- `PAY_AMT*` (columns 18 to 23): The amount of previous payments for distinct points in time.
- `default payment next month` (column 24): A binary (*0-1*) indicating whether the payer defaulted in May 2005.

With a dataset such as this, we ought to train a deep learning model to predict credit card defaults. From the untouched data to a completely trained deep learning model, we have a long way to go. It's usually helpful to transform your data in some way. To fit it into the range of zero and one, there is a particularly convenient max-min transformation. It goes like this:

$$\hat{x}_i = \frac{x_i - min(x)}{max(x) - min(x)}$$

This function will map any variable into a range from zero to one if `max(x)` differs from `min(x)`. An R version of such a function would go like the following:

```
max_min <- function(x){
  return((x - min(x))/(max(x)-min(x)))
}
```

Trust the following code to apply such a transformation to all non-categorical variables:

```
dt[,c(2,6:24)] <- apply(dt[,c(2,6:24)], 2, max_min)
```

Notice how subset indexes were called to `apply` the transformation only to non-categorical variables. Such a transformation does mostly good to non-categorical variables. Although there is a slight possibility of doing well with categorical ones, if that happened, I would leave it to chance.

Yet, the categorical variables should not be left out in the cold. They should be transformed as well, but this calls for a different kind of transformation. One that is frequently used is called **one hot encode**. Imagine that you have a categorical variable with two levels; one hot encode would create binary variables for each of those levels.

So, a single categorical variable with two levels would become two binary variables. A variable with three levels would become three binary variables and so on. One hot encode is also known as **dummy coding**. There are other options available, but apart from how one hot encode increases the dimensionality, it's usually the best option for deep learning models.

To encode our data using one hot encode is very easy; Keras has a method called `to_categorical()`, which makes this conversion. The following code block demonstrates this:

```
library(keras)
dt[,c(3:5,25)] <- apply(dt[,c(3:5,25)], 2, to_categorical)
```

As you might suspect, there will be dimensionality incompatibility, since the one hot encode increases dimensionality and the encoded variables are being stored in the same columns they came from. Examining the DataFrame (`dt`) afterward, you will see that the original columns now have higher dimensions. To fix that, we coerce `dt` into a `matrix` type of object:

```
dt <- as.matrix(dt)
```

Oddly, three categories for sex have been created. Errors such as these can happen. The way out of it is to develop routines that prevent these failures from staying hidden. Given the transformation, no category should amount to zero, but non-existent ones will. A quick check would go as follows:

```
apply(dt, 2, sum) != 0
```

After running this block, we shall return either `FALSE` or `TRUE` for each column. The ones displaying `FALSE` might be problematic, and they are summing zero. The variable `SEX.1` sums zero. Such a variable won't make any difference to our model. Also, does `ID`, given the unique identification should not be of any help to the model.

> The `sum != 0` trick only works because we have only dummies and variables ranging from zero to one. Otherwise, the sum zero would not guarantee that all the values were zero.

To eliminate these variables, run the following code:

```
dt <- dt[,-1]
dt <- dt[,apply(dt, 2, sum) != 0]
```

While the first line eliminates the `ID` variable, the second one eliminates any row that sums zero. We still have to split our data into validation and training samples. Let's start by sorting the row indexes:

```
set.seed(50)
n <- sample(x = 30000, size = 5000)
```

Then variable `n` is now storing `5000` numbers ranging from `1` to `30000`. These are the indexes that are ruling the validation dataset. These account for a little more than 16% of the complete dataset. There is no magic ratio, but researchers usually use something around 15% to 30% percent of the whole sample as validation and test sets.

To keep it organized, we can split the original array into separated objects:

```
train_dt <- dt[-n,1:33]
train_target <- dt[-n,34:35]
```

The objects `train_dt` and `train_target` are respectively holding the inputs and outputs designated to train the upcoming model. Notice how we're not selecting the rows given by the indexes stored in `n`. To designate the validation sets, we only select those rows:

```
val_dt <- dt[n,1:33]
val_target <- dt[n,34:35]
```

Validation inputs and outputs are respectively stored by `val_dt` and `val_target`. We can finally remove `dt` from the environment. This will clear some room in the memory:

```
rm(dt)
```

I told you that it was a long run. You did it. You managed to handle data well. It's training time. Load `keras` again, just to be sure:

```
library(keras)
```

The most common deep learning models are sequential. That is, layers are stacked (connected) in a linear fashion; they are designed in sequence, only sending information to the layer coming immediately next, and only receiving information from the one immediately before it. These models can be designed using `keras_model_sequential()`:

```
heracles_1 <- keras_model_sequential() %>%
  layer_dense(units = 25, activation = 'relu', input_shape = 33) %>%
  layer_dense(units = 15, activation = 'relu') %>%
  layer_dense(units = 6, activation = 'relu') %>%
  layer_dense(units = 2, activation = 'softmax')
```

This first model was called `heracles_1` after the ancient Greek demigod Heracles. During the design phase, the layers are stacked using pipes (`%>%`). The preceding code block stacks four dense layers one after another; all but the last are using `relu` activation functions. The last one (output layer) is using `softmax`.

Whenever you are working with `keras_model_sequential()`, except for the first layer, you don't need to specify how the inputs for each layer will look. Keras get that from the format of the last layer.

After calling `keras_model_sequential()`, the layers were designated using the `layer_dense()` function. Such a function adds a fully connected (dense) layer. Other specialized types of layers are available as well. The first layer is the only one that needs the `input_shape` argument, which dictates how many inputs there will be.

Variables encoded with one hot encode shall count as more than one variable.

The `units` and `activation` arguments are both common to every layer added. While the latter rules the activation function to be used, the former command uses the number of nodes in each layer. With this, we ended with an NN with one input layer with 33 nodes, and three hidden layers using ReLU as activation functions with respectively `25`, `15`, and `6` hidden nodes. The last layer is an output layer with two nodes that uses a `softmax` function for activation.

Given that we encoded the predicted variable using one hot encode, the single categorical variable was turned into two dummies.

To visualize the design of `heracles_1`, try it with `summary()`:

```
summary(heracles_1)
```

The result can be seen in the following screenshot:

```
Layer (type)                 Output Shape                 Param #
=================================================================
dense_1 (Dense)              (None, 25)                   850
_________________________________________________________________
dense_2 (Dense)              (None, 15)                   390
_________________________________________________________________
dense_3 (Dense)              (None, 6)                    96
_________________________________________________________________
dense_4 (Dense)              (None, 2)                    14
=================================================================
Total params: 1,350
Trainable params: 1,350
Non-trainable params: 0
_________________________________________________________________
```

Figure 8.5: Summary for heracles_1

It's not that hard to find out there are very complicated deep learning models with tens or hundreds of hidden layers. Even for such a simple model with only three hidden layers as `heracles_1`, there are `1,350` parameters to train. That's how computationally costly neural nets are.

Once the design phase is terminated, it's time to start the compile one. Simply pipe our model to `compile()`. With it, the user chooses the optimizer (or training strategy), the `loss` function and the accuracy metrics to follow. Other aspects such as the learning rate and other hyperparameters associated with the optimizer are also designated here.

Different than what is usual in R, `compile()` will modify the existing network. Given that, there is no need to save it in an object, as the existing object will already be updated if you roll something like the following:

```
heracles_1 %>% compile(
  optimizer = optimizer_adam(lr = .001),
  loss = 'categorical_crossentropy',
  metrics = c('accuracy')
)
```

The `heracles_1` network will be compiled using Adam's optimizer. The learning rate (`lr`) was set to `.001`, which is the default—I only meant to show how to access it. The `loss` function will be `categorical_crossentropy`, very adequate for classification problems where there are two or more classes given by distinct output nodes. Accuracy was chosen as the fitness metric. It's possible to pick more than one.

Although after the design, I mentioned how expensive these models are, it is not until the training phase that this characteristic becomes evident. It's important to notice that even if there are `1,350` trainable parameters, this model is still pretty lean compared to other models used for image, video, and text classification (for example):

> Thanks to computational advancements and code improvements, training a network such as `heracles_1` is relatively fast. It took me less than a minute. When I first started to use these models, an even simpler network would take me at least five minutes to train.

The heavy lifting is only done during the training process, which is very cool. During the training, you got to check the progress as a verbose displayed in the console, and in a graph shown in the **Viewer** tab (RStudio users only). It's even cooler if you designated validation samples. This way, you can check the `loss` function and fitness metrics for the training and test samples.

To train a compiled network using Keras, you have to pipe the `fit()` method. Similar to what is done with `compile()`, there is no need to save the result into a new object:

```
heracles_1 %>% fit(x = train_dt,y = train_target,
                   epochs = 10, batch_size = 150,
                   validation_data = list(val_dt, val_target))
```

Here, we set the training input (`x`) and the training output (`y`). Size matters. Besides being of the same length, `x` must have a number of variables equal to the input shape, while `y` must have the same number of variables as the units in the last layer (output layer).

Inside `fit()`, you may also designate the validation sets (`validation_data`) as a list or pick a ratio (`validation_split`) and `fit` will split the samples. Some other hyperparameters such as `epochs` and batch-size (`batch_size`) are chosen in this step.

During the training, a graph showing how the training is going will be displayed, just like in the following diagram:

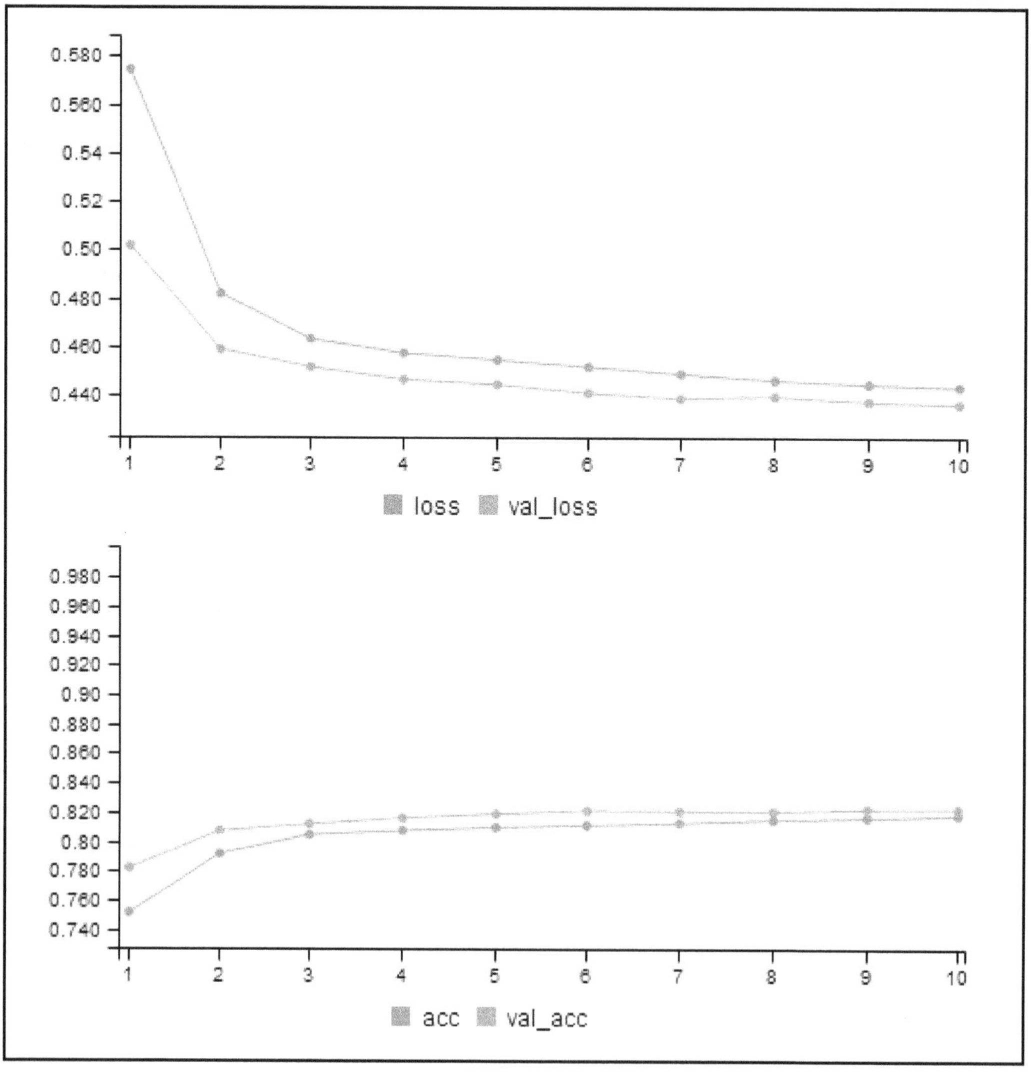

Figure 8.6: Training graph

If a split ratio or validation set was assigned, `loss` and the fitness metrics will not only be displayed for the training (blue line) set but also for the validation set (green line). A graph like this is very useful to identify problems that may occur during training. If the model gets stuck someplace or becomes overtrained, this graph will tell you.

As *Figure 8.6* suggests, training has gone smoothly. Training and validation metrics are pretty close together. If the training `loss` was going down while the validation `loss` was going up, that would be a sign of overtraining. The model would be so addicted to the training set that it would fail to generalize well into as-yet-unseen data.

Luckily, that was not what happened. If that was the case, there would be things to do: lowering the learning ratio, using fewer epochs, using dropout or other regularization techniques. More on that later, but for the time being, let's move to the evaluation phase. To evaluate a model, we pipe the `evaluate()` method to the network:

```
heracles_1 %>% evaluate(train_dt, train_target)
# 25000/25000 ...
# $loss
# [1] 0.4409437
#
# $acc
# [1] 0.817
```

A progression bar will be outputted with it. Inside the `evaluate()` method, input the model's input and output. Using the training data, the model showed 81.7% accuracy:

```
heracles_1 %>% evaluate(val_dt, val_target)
# 5000/5000 ...
# $loss
# [1] 0.4362364
#
# $acc
# [1] 0.8224
```

The model performed slightly better with the validation data. Accuracy reached 82,24%. Is that a good mark? To answer such a question, benchmarks must be established. Since credit card defaults aren't supposed to be that common, we could compare the accuracy with the proportion of non-defaults.

This way, we make sure that our model is not guessing no default every time. Given that default was encoded using one hot, we can use `mean()` to compute the proportion of non-default:

```
mean(train_target[,1])
# [1] 0.77812
mean(val_target[,1])
# [1] 0.7822
```

The network did better than simply guessing no default all the time. Another thing we can see from that is how unbalanced the dataset is. Although this data was pretty unbalanced, it did not negatively affect the network. If it does, there is a pretty cool way to solve that. It consists of changing the weight of the class that shows up the least so that missing that class will cost more.

I would say that `heracles_1` did a very good job, and it's worth saving. There is a specific function to save Keras's models:

```
save_model_hdf5(heracles_1, filepath = 'heracles_1.hdf5',
                overwrite = T, include_optimizer = T)
```

We could make `heracles_1` vanish:

```
rm(heracles_1)
```

And we could load it again using `load_model_hdf5()`:

```
heracles_1 <- load_model_hdf5(filepath = 'heracles_1.hdf5')
```

But what if `heracles_1` had overfitted a lot? I would try to use `dropout`. What if it had struggled a lot to learn? I would try Leaky ReLU. The next code block shows how to use dropout and to use Leaky ReLU rather than the regular ReLU:

```
heracles_2 <- keras_model_sequential() %>%
  layer_dense(units = 25, input_shape = 33) %>%
  layer_activation_leaky_relu(alpha = .3) %>%
  layer_dropout(rate = .2) %>%
  layer_dense(units = 15) %>%
  layer_activation_leaky_relu(alpha = .3) %>%
  layer_dropout(rate = .1) %>%
  layer_dense(units = 6) %>%
  layer_activation_leaky_relu(alpha = .3) %>%
  layer_dropout(rate = .05) %>%
  layer_dense(units = 2, activation = 'softmax')
```

To adopt Leaky ReLU, we suppressed the `activation` argument inside `layer_dense()` and piped `layer_activation_leaky_relu()` right next to `layer_dense()`. Notice the argument `alpha`. It's a very important parameter for `Leaky ReLU`—regular ReLU can be seen as a Leaky ReLU with `alpha` set to zero.

To use dropout in a layer, we simply have to pipe `layer_dropout()`. Do not forget to assign the `rate` argument inside it. It must range between zero and one. Layers with more units can afford a greater dropout ratio, while layers with fewer units should have it closer to zero. This discussed how to design, train, evaluate, save, and load a model using Keras.

Further tips

It will be handy to have a few tips that might be helpful while solving other problems, and also mention some topics that might help those who want to go further into deep learning. The first tip I am going to give you is about reshaping arrays. It is very common for R users to reshape arrays this way:

```
dim(<array object>) <- c(<new dimensions>)
```

Unfortunately, this might not work every single time because while R uses a column-major order, `numpy` and other libraries called by `keras` use a row-major order as default. For this, we can use something like the following pseudo code:

```
<array object> <- array_reshape(<array object>, c(<new dimensions>))
```

This is a really good trick, and I hope you don't get caught by it. If you are interested in learning more about column-major and row-major, you can find rich information in the following vignette: `https://cran.r-project.org/web/packages/reticulate/vignettes/arrays.html`

Although this chapter did not tackle a computer vision problem, Keras definitely has the power to do so. These problems are frequently solved with a combination of convolutional and max pooling layers. Both have 2D and 1D versions; here is how to call them:

- `layer_conv_2d()`
- `layer_conv_1d()`
- `layer_max_pooling_2d()`
- `layer_max_pooling_1d()`

Usually, when dealing with 2D layers you will need to flatten the output. This is done with `layer_flatten()`. Preprocessing words, phrases, and documents comes with its own nuts and bolts. Here is a list of useful functions to preprocess text data:

- `pad_sequences()`
- `skipgrams()`
- `text_hashing_trick()`
- `text_one_hot()`
- `text_to_word_sequence()`

Without going into detail, the reader will find a list of wonderful topics to study under the label of NNs and deep learning:

- **Adaptive learning**: Some people tend to characterize deep learning as the third generation of AI and adaptive learning as the fourth generation.
- **Data augmentation**: Have you ever felt as if you haven't enough data to work on your problem? Data augmentation may help. It's very easy to implement with Keras, especially for computer vision problems.
- **Reinforcement learning**: Do you wish to train a network to play a game or chat with humans? Reinforcement learning is the way to go.
- **Generative Adversarial Networks** (**GANs**): Deep convolutional GANs can mimic real datasets.

We barely scratched the surface of neural nets, and there is much more to learn. If you are willing to use Python directly to call Keras, rather than using R as a middleman, I do recommend Mike Bernico's *Deep Learning Quick Reference*.

NNs are a whole universe in terms of how much there is to master and discover. Although they're very flexible and can tackle a whole bunch of different tasks, don't forget they're a black-box type of model. Nonetheless, they are amazing and worth the time required to master them.

Summary

In this chapter, we saw what is NNs, how it is present in our daily life, and how it was inspired by neuroscience. It also covered deep learning. The following list briefs the deep learning concepts explored in the present chapter:

- Neurons (or nodes)
- Activation functions
- Layers (input, output, and hidden)

In practice, it introduced how to design and train deep learn models through Keras while exploring UCI credit card data. Techniques meant to fight overfitting were also demonstrated during the objective example. Over the next chapter, readers will learn about Hidden Markov models.

Quiz

1. **Quiz-tion**: Network layers can be characterized by the position they have in the architecture, as well as from the specialized task they perform. Which three names could we give them?
    1. Converging, cognitive, and core layer
    2. Input, hidden, and output layer
    3. Dense, fully connected, and power layer
    4. Blue, red, and green layer
2. **Quiz-tion**: Which of the following names is not directly related to activation functions?
    1. ReLU
    2. Convolutional
    3. Tanh
    4. Sigmoid
3. **Quiz-tion**: Which of the following statements is false?
    1. **Artificial Neural Networks** (**ANN**) were inspired by neuroscience
    2. Adams is a very popular training algorithm (strategy)
    3. ANN can be only used for fraud detection
    4. Epochs, learning rate, and batch-size are hyperparameters

Answers—executing the following code will give you the answers to the quiz questions:

```
set.seed(8)
round(runif(3,1,4))
```

9
Markovian in R

"Statistics is the grammar of science."

– Karl Pearson

Markovian-type models are yet another option to exercise pattern discovery. The idea behind **Hidden Markovian Models** (**HMMs**) is both clever and very useful. Although some people would only recognize them for their ability to model time series, HMMs are also suitable for things such as speech recognition and computer vision.

In this chapter, readers will find a brief review of Markovian models and the HMM, a discussion about where HMMs can be applied, and of course, a practical guide, teaching the nuts and bolts of deploying HMMs through R.

In this chapter, we will cover the following topics:

- Markovian models basics
- **Hidden Markovian Models** (**HMMs**) basics
- Incorporate information about the past x prediction about the future
- Time series

Markovian-type models

The title of Markovian-type model may be applied to any model that strongly relies on the theoretical foundations drawn by the mathematician Andrey Markov (1856-1922), who describes a system with a set of states and transitional probabilities. The idea behind it is as straightforward as it is aged: Markovian models are sustained by Bayes' theorem.

You may ask—why trust such a model rather than younger ones such as neural networks? Even though neural nets are very powerful indeed, they may be too general given some tasks. Moreover, combining models usually enhances the final result. That said, consider adjusting a Markovian model only for the sake of combining it with other models you may already have.

This section will briefly introduce the fundamentals of Markovian models and HMMs, but not before listing the real-world application of Markovian models.

Markovian models – real-world applications

This book is being written in the year 2018, and Markovian models seem a little bit overlooked by the general public. There is a great hype around deep and adaptive learning, which tends to divert the attention from more traditional models such as the ones that belong to the Markovian family.

Although Markovian models do very well on chronological data, which explains how well they are doing in the finances field, these models are suitable for exploring any relation that can be conveyed in a set of interconnected states of a system. The list of real-world applications can grow very big but, for simplicity's sake, we will quote only a few, as follows:

- **Typing word prediction**: To predict the word we will type based on the latter word or the letters inserted which is a task that can be done using Markovian models.
- **Chatbots**: Applications that recognize speech and talk back to humans can be developed using Markov's theory.
- **Page rank**: Given these models' properties (more on that later), no matter in what web page a person started, if the surfing goes on for long enough, the probability of landing in a specific page is fixed. Some would say that Google's page rank algorithm is an improved version of Markov's theoretical development.
- **Finances**: Economists are used to thinking about events as stochastic processes; Markovian models are an excellent way to model those events. Markovian models are also described as state space models, which are broadly used in the industry to bear predictions and design scenarios.

As you may wonder, all of these tasks can also be performed using rival models. For example, deep learning could likewise handle any of that. Even though different contests had established benchmarks favoring markovian or deep learning models, generally speaking, the evidence suggests that not a single broader class of model is yet to outperform all the rivals disregarding specific problems and scoring measures.

More complicated models won't necessarily outperform simpler ones.

There are at least two reasons that would reasonably prevent you from deploying solutions generated over a complex model. Understandability is a reason. Some problems may require the solution to be easy to understand and interpret. Those hardly come along with complex models, which are usually tagged as black-box models in contrast to simpler ones, called **glass-box**.

Whether a model can be called a glass-box or black-box is not a matter of built-in complexity. These terms are related to whether it's easy (glass-box) or hard (black-box) to understand how a model is making the decisions, in other words, the inner workings, and what is happening inside.

Another reason would be that a problem simply doesn't work well with complicated solutions. The problem being too simple or data being too scarce are very common issues. But there is another, greater reason that would prevent any promising forecaster from ignoring a simpler model.

Collectives beat individuals; frequently, combined models perform better than individual ones. In fact, there is a whole field that studies how to merge models. Even though a chatbot developed using deep learning might outperform another one made through HMMs, the deep learning model could be improved if it received the HMMs' result as an input. Moving on, the following paragraphs look at the foundations of the Markov model.

The Markov chain

What do all the Markov-type models have in common? All of them are essentially based on the same stochastic process, which is better known as the **Markov chain**. Under this section, you will find a brief review of the fundamental ideas and properties that follow the Markov chain.

Even though this section relies on some statistical terms and matrixial notations, it is designed to be accessible, regardless of that.

Stochastic processes are frequently assumed to be **independent and identically distributed (i.i.d.)**. Borrowing the dice analogy, this assumption rules that no matter what the past rolls were, they won't affect the likelihood (probability) of the next roll. The Markov chain won't assume i.i.d.; instead, it will define a set of systems' transitional probabilities, meaning that the likelihood of the next state (outcome) will be a function of the current state.

Using a matrixial notation, a system S with three states could be described as follows:

$$S = \begin{bmatrix} S_1 \\ S_2 \\ S_3 \end{bmatrix}$$

Where S_1, S_2, and S_3 represent different states of a system. States could be (almost) anything. They could tell whether the weather is sunny, rainy, or snowy, or whether an internet user is currently navigating through website *A*, *B*, or *C*. Given each state, Markov defines transitional probabilities, which lists the chances for the system's state in the next time step.

> For the sake of simplicity, this chapter refers to the Markov chain as a time discrete process. The Markov chain can also be designed where time is taken as being continuous—a more realistic assumption.

A transitional probability can be expressed as a conditional chance:

$$P(X_{t+1} = S_i | X_t = S_j) = p_{ji}$$

Generically, the transitional probability p_{ji} describes the probability for the system to assume the state S_i during the time step *t+1*, given the state S_j during time step *t*. This elegant device, transitional probability, drops the independence assumption from the stochastic process, adding it to an extra layer of complexity.

Transitional probabilities are directly related to one of the most commented properties of the Markov chain. It asserts that the system's chance of getting in a certain state next time only depends on which state it is currently in. Thus, all of the past distance doesn't matter if you're willing to make inferences about the future.

> Markov chains can also be designed to look into further time steps in the past.

For a system with n states, there will be n^2 transitional probabilities. These are frequently expressed as a matrix. Departing from the set of states S described previously, the transitional matrix (T) would look like the following:

$$T = \begin{bmatrix} p_{11} & p_{12} & p_{13} \\ p_{21} & p_{22} & p_{23} \\ p_{31} & p_{32} & p_{33} \end{bmatrix}$$

Where p_{12} is the probability for the system to jump into state two (S_2), given it was in the state 1 (S_1) before; p_{32} would be the probability of jumping into state two (S_2), given it was in state three (S_3) before. No element should be negative and each row should sum one.

The transitional matrix could also be represented in an alternative way so that the columns will sum one. A matrix where no element is less than zero and each row (or column) sum one is called a **Markov matrix**.

Representing the transitional probabilities through the transition matrix is useful for computational purposes. On the other hand, there could be a history, which can be represented through the following diagram so that things would be much easier to understand. It might look a little bit silly but it's for a very good reason.

The tale goes like this: there was a little polygon called **Circled Squared Triangle** (**CST**). The little CST was cursed by a witch, she said, *every morning you may or may not turn yourself into a different shape and the odds will only be related to your current shape*:

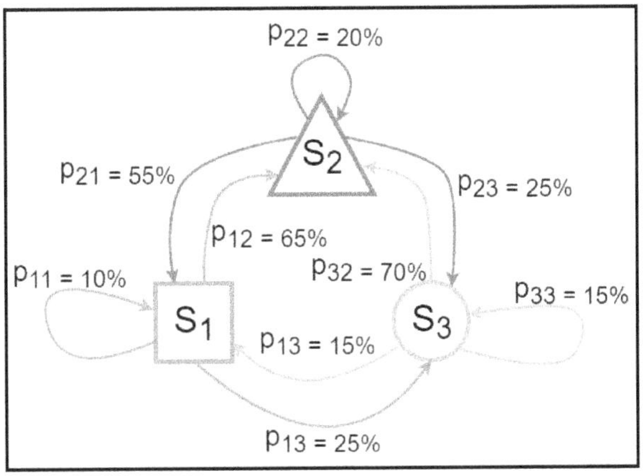

Figure 9.1: CST diagram representation

The preceding diagram illustrates both how the Markov chain works and the tale about CST. Keeping in mind that this is a time-ordered process, the diagram displays all the basic elements from a Markov process. There is a set of states—square (S_1), triangle (S_2), and circle (S_3)—to iterate from, and a set of ruling probabilities.

> Markov chains frequently come along with a vector of initial probabilities (π).

Although the diagram is a great way of explaining how the whole process goes on, the matrix is the usual way to represent it. The matrix form is also useful to do computations. To draw the transitional matrix, the rows have to sum one. The current example's transitional matrix would look like the following:

$$T = \begin{bmatrix} 0.10 & 0.65 & 0.25 \\ 0.55 & 0.20 & 0.25 \\ 0.15 & 0.70 & 0.15 \end{bmatrix}$$

A matrix for which all the rows individually total one is called a **Markovian matrix**. The element a_{12} (first row, second column) shows that if the system is at state one (row one), there is a 65% chance that it will turn into state two (column two) during the next time step. The whole idea is pretty straightforward, but what is it used for?

> In a Markov process, it's possible for a state to culminate in that very same state in the next step. This is called a **self-transition**. Probabilities for self-transitions are displayed at the main diagonal from the transitional matrix.

To begin with, you can use it to answer questions such as, *How likely is it to get the sequence 1, 1, 2, 3, 1*? Analytically-wise, the Markov chain is able to give you the chance of a particular sequence of states to happen. You can either assume a transitional matrix to do so or easily estimate one. But there is far more to it than that.

Generally speaking, Markov models can aid in almost any kind of time-related pattern discovery process: this can be guessed from the previous explanation. So, what would be the next letter that would be typed next, based on the letter that would be entered now? What would be the video that would be watched next based on the current one? All of these are questions that could be answered through Markov models.

The real question is: does a sequence of events produce a pattern that can be modeled and exploited?

Basically, if you can model the subject as a sequence of events, there is a great chance to uncover a pattern using Markov, if there is a relevant pattern to be discovered. This explains why this kind of model has been used for such wide fields of research, from French poetry all the way to finance. There are some really cool applications of Markov in finance, which we will approach later in this chapter.

Before we dive into the practical example, there is another Markov type-model worthy of a mention: the HMM. While regular Markov models assume that the real system's state is directly observable, HMMs go the other way. For the latter, the actual system's states are not directly observable, instead, you can only look at a variable that will be probabilistically related to the system's states.

Think of it in this way. In regular Markov, the states of a system could be the weather—sunny, cloudy, or rainy—and such information would be available steadily, you can peak at the weather. For hidden Markov, the states of a system would be the weather and you could only look at your neighbors' outfit to infer whether the weather is sunny, cloudy, or rainy.

In the HMM, the states are invisible (hidden), but they generate a set of observations that are probabilistically related to the invisible (hidden) states. These observations are called **visible states** or simply observations.

The name hidden Markov is very self-explanatory when looking from this prism. HMMs are regular Markov with an extra layer of complexity. Besides the transition probabilities (T) and the vector of initial probabilities (π), the HMM also requires a matrix of observation probabilities (B), which dictates the probabilities of each invisible state S_i generating each visible state M_j.

HMM models can be expressed as a function of T, π, and B.

Essentially, Markov models, both hidden and regular, are used to solve two kinds of problems:

- **Evaluation problem**: Consists of estimating the probability for a model *M* generating a given sequence of states. The HMM will evaluate the probability given a visible sequence instead.
- **Learning problem**: It is a problem where the parameters of a Markov model (transitional matrix, initial probabilities, observation probabilities) have to be learned/estimated from a training sample.

Additionally, there is an extra kind of problem being solved exclusively through the HMM. It's called a decoding problem, which consists of inferring the most likely sequence of hidden states based on an observed sequence of visible states (observations).

Think about a word recognition problem. One way of tackling it is by building a single HMM for all the words. The hidden states would be all the characters in the alphabet. Transition and initial probabilities would be calculated from a language model, while observations would be made of typed characters segmented from images.

Now, all that is left is to determine the best sequence of hidden states produced by an image; that is, word recognition. The solution just described looks at the word recognition problem as a decoding problem. The proposed model is only one out of several ways of solving it using the HMM.

How to solve problems like the ones discussed before? Brute force might get things done for when there are only a few possibilities to explore. On the other hand, if the possibilities are plentiful, there are more clever and efficient ways of doing it:

- Evaluation problems can be solved through forward-backward HMM algorithms
- Decoding problems are most easily solved by **Viterbi** algorithms
- Learning problems can be solved through the **Baum—Welch** algorithm

Although the HMM is actually applied to as many fields as there are, it is heavily used in finance. The next section shows how you can build and analyze the HMM through finance data using R. Keep in mind that you shouldn't invest your money based on that alone. Investing is always risky and you need to study a lot before trusting any protocol—there are no shortcuts.

Programming an HMM with R

The HMM can be used in the finance field for a great number of things. Features such as regime identification, volatility clustering, and anti-correlation (return and volatility) can all be extracted from financial data through using the HMM. R has several great packages to deal with the HMM. This chapter uses one called `ldhmm`, which implements the homogeneous first-order HMM.

This link will guide you through the package documentation: `https://cran.r-project.org/web/packages/ldhmm/ldhmm.pdf`. The word first-order means that the state in time *t* is only influenced by the state in time *t-1*. Make sure that you have `ldhmm` installed by using the following code:

```
if(!require('ldhmm')){install.packages('ldhmm')}
```

Let's begin with data. The `ldhmm` package comes with daily data from the **Standard & Poor 500 Index** (**SPX**). Run the following code to load and store the dates, closing prices, and log returns from January 01, 1950 to December 31, 2015:

```
library(ldhmm)

dt <- ldhmm.ts_log_rtn(symbol = 'spx',
                        on = 'days')
```

Notice the `symbol` argument inputted with the `'spx'` string. It points toward the index to be returned, in this case, the SPX. An alternative to it could be the CBOE **Volatility Index** (**VIX**), which could be returned by using the `'vix'` string instead. The `on` argument dictates the data frequency.

The standard value for the `symbol` variable is actually `'spx'`, but the standard frequency is weekly (`on = 'weeks'`).

After running the last code block, the data will be stored in a list called `dt`. Recover vectors for the date, closing prices, and log returns by calling `dt$d`, `dt$p`, and `dt$x`, respectively. You can visualize the closing prices evolution in the long term by running the following code block:

```
plot(y = dt$d, x= dt$p, type = 'l',
     ylab = 'SPX closing prices',
     xlab = 'time')
```

It is a good idea to combine `ggplot2` with `ggthemes` draw an improved plot:

```
library(ggplot2)
library(ggthemes)
ggplot(data = data.frame(x = dt$d, y = dt$p)) +
  geom_line(aes(x = x, y = y), size = 1.5) +
  ylab('SPX closing prices') +
  xlab('time') +
  theme_pander(base_size = 16)
```

The result is displayed in the following diagram:

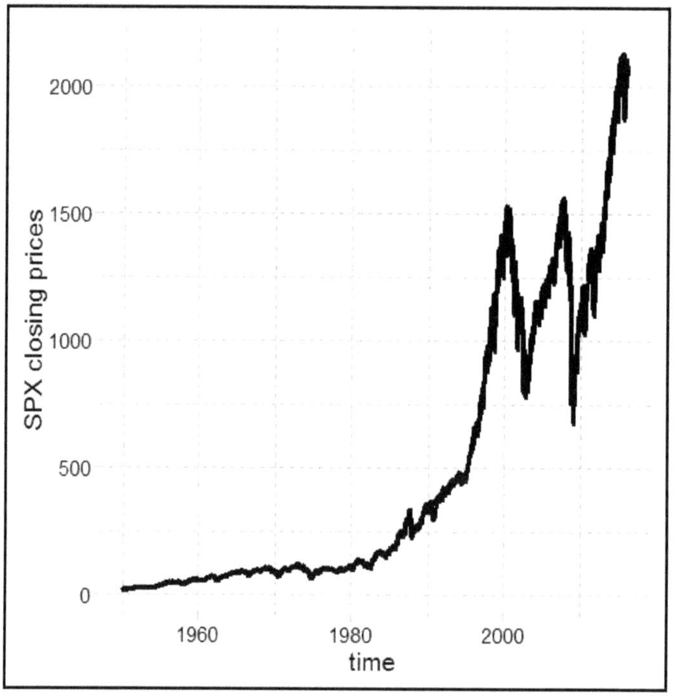

Figure 9.2: The long-term evolution of closing prices for the SPX

Alternatively, you can visualize the long-term evolution of the log return for the SPX:

```
plot(x = dt$d, y= dt$x, type = 'l',
     ylab = 'SPX log return',
     xlab = 'time')
```

Drawing it with `ggplot2` and `ggthemes` is also possible, as follows:

```
ggplot(data = data.frame(x = dt$d, y = dt$x)) +
  geom_line(aes(x = x, y = y), size = 1.1) +
  ylab('SPX log return') +
  xlab('time') +
  theme_pander(base_size = 16)
```

The result can be seen in the following diagram:

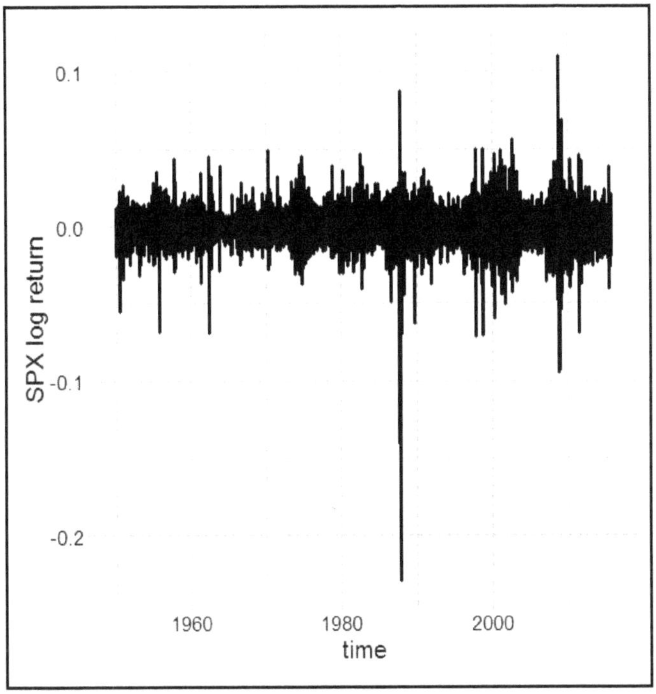

Figure 9.3: The long-term evolution of log returns for the SPX

Even though there are some serious outliers that most possibly will make modeling difficult, removing them is not always advised. Removing observations should always be a well-thought out decision, widely documented, and very well justified; otherwise, any conclusions drafted by such a model might be doubtful.

The most intuitive way of looking at the stock market is as if it has only two regimes: normal and crash. Normal is also known as the bull market. A bull market usually drives both prices and returns up; things are going very well and you should buy and hold stocks. These are some of the characteristics of a regular regime, but what about crash regimes?

Crash regimes are also known as the **bear market**. A market like this is panicking. Prices are mostly falling, volatility is rising beyond regular levels, and returns tend to be negative. This dualism between bear and bull markets facilitates the understanding because this is the way we are used to seeing things.

Bear and bull will be the hidden states within our HMM. We could go way farther and define 5, 10 hidden states—that is an advantage of using the HMM, you can get a broader spectrum of regimes instead of the two usual ones. Nonetheless, for this example, we will stick with the two states paradigm.

Let's store the number of states in a variable called `states`:

```
states <- 2
```

The `ldhmm` package defines a parameter space for the HMM within univariate mixing distributions, a transition probability matrix, and an initial state probability vector.

> The mixing distribution is the single distribution that's made out from the combination of individual distributions for each *n* hidden state.

For each state, we need to guess an initial mean and standard deviation in order to start looking for actual values. The better your guess, the easier to the convergence will be. Usually, the initial guess would be done using the actual `ldhmm`, but we will rather take a shortcut and use k-means clustering instead. To use the k-means cluster, fit and store the clusters in a brand new variable:

```
set.seed(9)
k_2 <- kmeans(dt$x, 2)
```

The `kmeans()` function takes care of fitting the k-means clustering with two clusters ($k = 2$) on the log of returns. Take note that the random seed generator is being selected, given that k-means relies on pseudo-randomness. The `k_2` variable is a list with information about the two clusters. A vector naming each cluster membership can be accessed by entering `k_2$cluster`.

You can use `ggplot2` to visualize the result:

```
library(ggplot2)
ggplot(data = data.frame(x = dt$d, y = dt$x, k = factor(k_2$cluster))) +
geom_point(aes(x = x, y = y, color = k), alpha = .4)
```

The outcome is displayed in the following diagram:

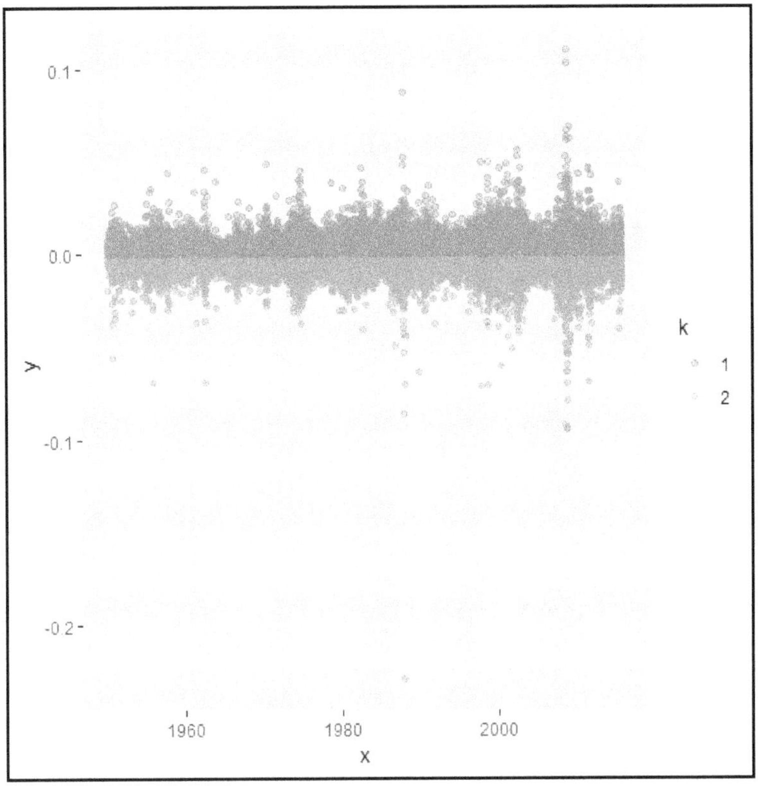

Figure 9.4: Distinction between the two clusters defined with k-means

Keep in mind that we do not intend to draft great insights from this simple trick. The sole intention is to (maybe) take a shortcut and define good initial guesses for the parameters from the mixing distribution. The parameters required are the mean, standard deviation, and lambda for each of the states.

> `ldhmm` is based on lambda distributions, which means that the lambda is also a parameter to be set and uncovered.

The following code block is estimating the initial mean based on the two clusters:

```
mean_1 <- mean(dt$x[k_2$cluster == 1])
mean_1
# [1] 0.005838372
```

```
mean_2 <- mean(dt$x[k_2$cluster == 2])
mean_2
# [1] -0.007473948
```

The means for the groups are being stored by the variables `mean_1` and `mean_2`. From these values, you can guess that cluster one (positive returns) means bull market while cluster two (negative returns) means bear market. Take note of these values because they will change as we learn the parameters for the HMM.

The following code block is estimating the standard deviations based on the clusters:

```
sd_1 <- sd(dt$x[k_2$cluster == 1])
sd_1
# [1] 0.006667836
sd_2 <- sd(dt$x[k_2$cluster == 2])
sd_2
# [1] 0.007827308
```

Assuming that clusters one and two, respectively, mean bear and bull market, you can guess that the bull regime is slightly more volatile than the bear. Nevertheless, the clusters are only a starting point. The task of characterizing the regimes will be dealt with by the HMM.

One last parameter to define for each state is the lambda. Distributions for each state are parameterized by a mean, a standard deviation, and a lambda—those are called **univariate lambda** functions. The lambda may be harder to guess; luckily, `ldhmm` is very efficient in converging to the right value. In the following code block, set the initial value of lambda at `1.3`:

```
param <- matrix(c(
  mean_1, sd_1, 1.3,
  mean_2, sd_2, 1.3),
  states, 3, byrow = T)
```

Initiate the transition matrix for the two `states` with the following code:

```
t <- ldhmm.gamma_init(states)
```

Start the HMM model using both the transition matrix `t` and the parameters defined before in `param`:

```
hmm <- ldhmm(states, param, t, stationary = T)
```

Finally, it's time to optimize the HMM using **maximum likelihood** (**MLE**). It can take a while:

```
hmm_mle <- ldhmm.mle(hmm, dt$x, decode = T, print.level = states)
```

Additionally, the algorithm may fail to converge sometimes—try different parameters (`param`) and run the last two code blocks again. It may be that you succeed at the first attempt. An object called `hmm_mle` is created.

A great way to visualize the results is by drawing an awesome plot. The `ldhmm` package comes with an easy way to draw such a plot; try the `ldhmm.oxford_man_plot_obs()` function with the recently fitted HMM object (`hmm_mle`). Make sure you have access to the internet:

```
ldhmm.oxford_man_plot_obs(hmm_mle)
```

The result is displayed in the following diagram:

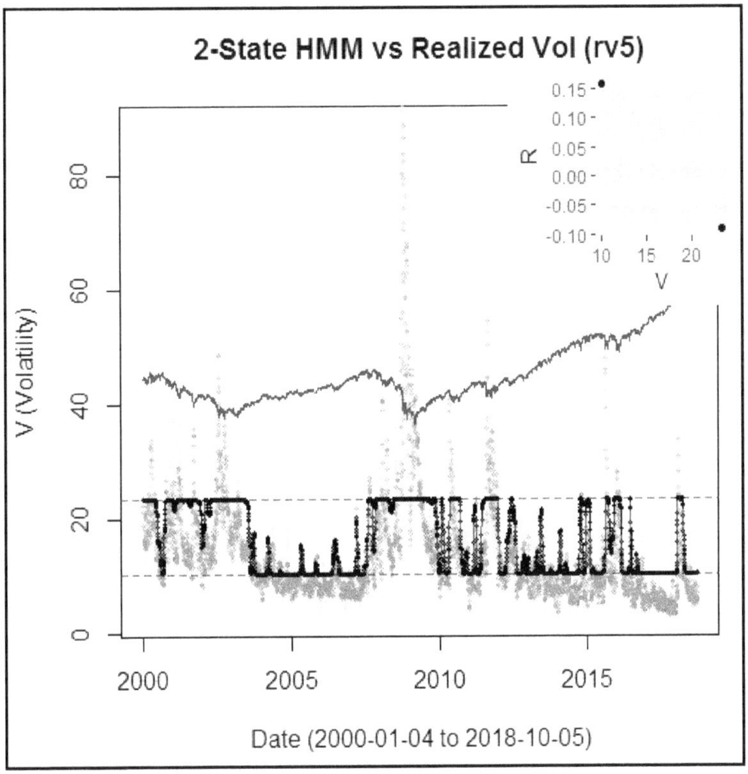

Figure 9.5: Two-states HMM vs realized volatility (Oxford-man data)

Spot the blue lines. The solid blue line is the SPX price index (rescaled), while the dashed ones show the volatilities from the HMM states. The red lines are the daily volatility, while the red dots are a five-day moving average volatility. The black dots are the expected volatility given by the HMM.

We can easily return the parameters from the mixing distributions using the following code:

```
hmm_mle@param
#                 mu sigma lambda
#[1,] 0.0006179082 0.006958493 1.418622
#[2,] -0.0003603437 0.013167661 1.710069
```

Type `hmm_mle@param` to return the mean, the standard deviation, and the lambda for each state. We get one parameterized distribution for each state—together they make the mixing distribution.

You can compare the mean and standard deviation with the very first ones we guessed using k-means clustering. Our initial guesses for the means were actually very close (but do not expect this trick to work this well every situation). The distribution with the positive mean can be associated with the bull market (regular regime) while the one with negative value represents the bear market (crash regime).

If we had discrete observations we would have observations probabilities (B) instead of the mixing distribution. Given that our observations and the log return are continuous, we get the mixing distribution. You can easily return the transitional matrix by looking at `@gamma`:

```
hmm_mle@gamma
#           [,1] [,2]
#[1,] 0.99339020 0.006609796
#[2,] 0.01631626 0.983683738
```

After typing `hmm_mle@gamma`, the console will output the transitional matrix for our recently fitted HMM model (`hmm_mle`). Notice that the column's sum is always one. There is another feature, called `@delta`, which shows how much time the system was in each state:

```
hmm_mle@delta
#[1] 0.7116907 0.2883093
```

The system was in regular regime 71.16% of the time. The local statistics for each state can be returned using `@states.local.stats`:

```
hmm_mle@states.local.stats
#              mean sd kurtosis skewness length
#[1,] 0.0005747770 0.006296764 3.821433 -0.05581264 11977
#[2,] -0.0004506958 0.015358800 17.010688 -0.79468256 4628
```

The columns display the `mean`, `sd`, `kurtosis`, `skewness`, and `length` for the two hidden states. These values were empirically obtained through data. The theoretical statistics can be accessed through the `ldhmm.ld_stats()` function:

```
ldhmm.ld_stats(hmm_mle)
#              mean sd kurtosis
#[1,] 0.0006179082 0.006326602 3.990262
#[2,] -0.0003603437 0.014766342 4.890151
```

The result from the last two code blocks can be compared to check whether the theoretical values closely follow the ones empirically obtained. For most of them, the answer is *yes, they do follow each other very closely*, but not for `kurtosis`, given by the second state.

Summary

This chapter's brief example was meant to introduce the reader to the matter of the Markovian models, especially the HMMs. Keep in mind that this broader class of models has applications in several distinct fields, from traditional ones to the newest.

A single chapter dedicated to the HMM might be too small to contain the vast world within Markov and the reader may feel as if it has gone too fast. Nonetheless, I encourage you to keep studying this subject because such models encounter great acceptance, both among scholars and businessmen.

Over the next chapter, we will be learning about data visualization and ways to improve plots, retrieve data, and prepare data. Go through the quiz before advancing into the chapter ahead.

Quiz

1. **Quiz-tion**: Pick the phrase that's giving incorrect information about Markov models:
    1. Markov models are used in finance
    2. They were never used to study French poetry
    3. They are named after the mathematician Andrey Markov
    4. There are many different applications of the Markov models
2. **Quiz-tion**: About the HMM, it's wrong to say that:
    1. The so-called hidden states are always known
    2. The parameter space of an HMM also comprehends the transitional matrix
    3. They found application in finance
    4. The hidden states are related to the observations which are sometimes called visible states

Answers—executing the following code will give you the answers to the quiz questions:

```
set.seed(9)
round(runif(2,1,4))
```

10
Visualizing Data

> *"Any authentic work of art must start an argument between the artist and his audience."*
> *– Rebecca West*

"*Did you understand, or would you like me to draw it?*" You might offend someone asking this way, but I would prefer if you drew it. Understanding information displayed in well-designed plots is much easier/faster. Plots are an amazing way to display information and an important skill to master.

This chapter's primary goal is to draw similar plots using different packages. While giving a brief overview of the different drawing packages, this chapter will also give tips about the ways to retrieve data, process it, and improve your plot.

In this chapter, the following topics will be covered:

- Retrieving data from the World Bank Data API
- Preparing the data to plot
- Drawing bubble plots with `ggplot2`
- Building interactive plots with `ggvis`, `plotly`, and `rCharts`
- Using Google Charts through R
- Building interactive choropleths (maps) with `googleVis`

Retrieving and cleaning data

First things first, we must get data. We also need to clean it before doing any drawing. The `wbstats` package will be used to get data. It retrieves data from the World Bank Data API. This section will demonstrate how to use `wbstats`. Data obtained and cleaned through this section are going to be later used to make plots.

Worldwide data about inequality, education, and population will be searched. All of these can be retrieved from the World Bank Database. Start by downloading `wbstats` if don't have it yet. If you are not sure whether you have it, simply run the following code:

```
if(!require('wbstats')){install.packages('wbstats')}
```

Load the `wbstats` library and enter `wbcache()` to download an updated list of available countries, indicators, and source information:

```
library(wbstats)
update_cache <- wbcache()
```

One can investigate the available information by entering `str(update_cache)` in the console.

During this chapter, worldwide information about income inequality (as `GINI Index`), education (as mean years of schooling), and population are going to be used. Let's begin with `GINI Index`. Try `wbsearch(pattern = 'gini')` and assign it to an object for further investigation, just like in the next code block:

```
gini_vars <- wbsearch(pattern = 'gini')
```

The `gini_vars` object is a DataFrame containing 178 rows and 2 columns: `indicatorID` and `indicator`. Such a DataFrame shows all of the available topics related to the `pattern`: `gini`. Inputting the topic you're interested in into the `wbsearch()` function is essential.

I encourage the reader to try `head(gini_vars)` at this point. Notice the `indicator` column. It briefly describes each of the available topics; `indicatorID` shows the correspondent ID for that information. After investigating `gini_vars` a little bit, I found the information I was looking for; it was described under the `indicatorID 3.0.Gini`:

```
gini_vars[gini_vars$indicatorID == '3.0.Gini',]
#    indicatorID        indicator
# 10784 3.0.Gini Gini Coefficient
```

Inputting `wb()` with the desired `indicator` will return the complete DataFrame regarding such a topic:

```
dt_gini <- wb(indicator = '3.0.Gini')
```

The last code block is looking for the `3.0.Gini` indicator and storing it in `dt_gini`. By the time I got it, the DataFrame contained 232 observations of seven variables. It may be different for you. The names for the variables returned are given by default.

Only three variables will be required by this chapter: `value`, `date`, and `country`. The first one, `value`, holds the value for the queried indicator; the last two are pretty much self-explanatory. The next code block is getting data about education:

```
edu_vars <- wbsearch(pattern = 'years of schooling')
edu_vars[edu_vars$indicatorID == 'UIS.EA.MEAN.1T6.AG25T99',]
#                   indicatorID
indicator
#499 UIS.EA.MEAN.1T6.AG25T99 UIS: Mean years of schooling of the population
age 25+. Total
dt_edu <- wb(indicator = 'SE.SCH.LIFE')
```

The mean `years of schooling` of the population aged above `25` years old was the variable selected to represent education. The next code block retrieves data about population:

```
pop_vars <- wbsearch(pattern = 'total population')
pop_vars[pop_vars$indicatorID == 'SP.POP.TOTL',]
dt_pop <-wb(indicator = 'SP.POP.TOTL')
```

At this point, all of the data that we need is split into different datasets. Having your data stored in a minimal DataFrame is a good practice, so that is something to work on. Each DataFrame has seven variables, but I am only interested in three of them for each frame. Let's reduce `dt_gini`:

```
dt_gini <- dt_gini[, c('date', 'value', 'country')]
```

Except for the variables named inside the brackets, all of the other variables were dropped. We can check the remaining ones using `names()`:

```
names(dt_gini)
#[1] "date"    "value"   "country"
```

As a default, the queried indicator is always named `value`. This may cause confusion when the time comes to merge the different DataFrames. We can rename this variable using `names()`:

```
names(dt_gini)[2] <- 'gini'
```

Notice how a single index was called inside the bracket. This way, we could change the name of the value variable alone. The next code block is doing the same for the DataFrames, dt_edu and dt_pop:

```
dt_edu <- dt_edu[, c('date', 'value', 'country')]
names(dt_edu)[2] <- 'mean_yrs_schooling'
dt_pop <- dt_pop[, c('date', 'value', 'country')]
names(dt_pop)[2] <- 'population'
```

The next thing to do is to merge the datasets. To do so, we must have a single matching ID for each DataFrame—neither date nor country alone could do it. The solution is to create a new variable combining both. The following code block uses paste() to do so:

```
dt_gini$merge_key <- paste(dt_gini$date, dt_gini$country,
                           sep = '_')
dt_edu$merge_key <- paste(dt_edu$date, dt_edu$country,
                          sep = '_')
dt_pop$merge_key <- paste(dt_pop$date, dt_pop$country,
                          sep = '_')
```

Once we created matching unique IDs for rows in all DataFrames, merging the different DataFrames is actually pretty easy. For the sake of organization, the merged DataFrame will be stored in a new variable, dt. Merge dt_edu with dt_gini:

```
dt <- merge(dt_edu, dt_gini, by = 'merge_key', all = F)
```

The merge() function is doing the heavy lift. The first two arguments are the DataFrames to be merged. Later, we have the by argument, which carries the variable used to merge both datasets. Setting all to FALSE (F) prevents the new data set from containing any observation that is not present in both DataFrames at the same time. Merge dt with dt_pop:

```
dt <- merge(dt, dt_pop, by = 'merge_key', all = F)
```

Data is now reunited in a single DataFrame. Nonetheless, it has far more variables than we need. In pursuance of a minimal DataFrame, the code block ahead is keeping only the variables that are going to be used later:

```
dt <- dt[,c('gini', 'population', 'mean_yrs_schooling', 'date', 'country')]
```

In the real world, data is rarely ready to go into a plot. That is one really good reason for you to master data manipulation and there are many more. This section showed how to retrieve data from the World Bank Data API and how to put different indicators together while keeping a minimal DataFrame. The next section using this data to build bubble plots and a map using different packages.

Crafting visualizations

Undoubtedly, plots are among the best ways to speak to an audience. Some would advocate that plots are so important that, before you start writing an article, presentation, or report, you should first design your figures. There are several advantages to adopting this plot-oriented writing:

- It speeds things up
- It enhances the chances of having self-explanatory graphics
- It improves the chances of holding your audience's attention

Learning how to draw neat graphics isn't easy and requires time and practice, but it does pay off. This chapter alone might not be enough to master such a skill, but it will certainly help.

R is not only famous thanks to its statistical capabilities, but also for its visualization tools. The `ggplot2` package was built based on a theory known as the grammar of graphics. Knowing this theory is not a requirement, but it might change the way you look at and design graphics.

You can make good plots so easily with `ggplot2` that I've heard of people migrating from Python to R for this package only. Let us kick-off this section by downloading `ggplot2`:

```
if(!require('ggplot2')){install.packages('ggplot2')}
```

Graphics are constructed in a very layered way with `ggplot2`. It feels as if you are summing methods together. The next code block demonstrates how to build a simple scatterplot using `ggplot2`:

```
library(ggplot2)
ggplot(data = dt) +
  geom_point(aes(x = gini,
                 y = mean_yrs_schooling))
```

Once the package gets loaded, initiate the plot with `ggplot()`. Name the dataset to be used in the `data` argument and keep two things in mind:

- For the sake of organization, `ggplot2` only works with DataFrames. The object addressed to `data` must be a DataFrame.
- It's possible to build a plot using more than one dataset.

The `geom_point()` function was called to add points to the plot. This function received `aes()` in order to map the aesthetics. The `gini` variable from `dt` was mapped in `x`, while `mean_yrs_schooling` was mapped in `y`. The result is displayed in the following diagram:

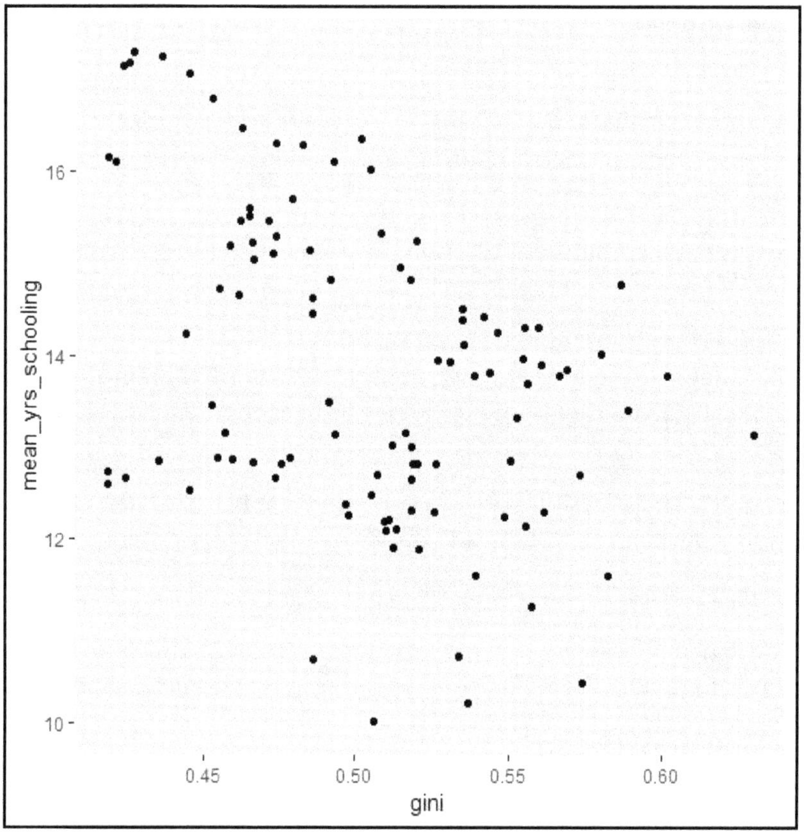

Figure 10.1: Simple scatterplot made with ggplot2

Figure 10.1 is not the bubble plot we are looking for yet. The aesthetic is `size` must be mapped:

```
ggplot(data = dt) +
  geom_point(aes(x = gini,
                 y = mean_yrs_schooling,
                 color = factor(country),
                 size = population), alpha = .4)
```

The last code block makes sure that the size of each point is related to the `population` variable. It also asks for different colors for each `country`. Notice how this last variable was set inside the `factor()` function. Color aesthetics generally go well with variables of the type factor.

The following figure displays the result:

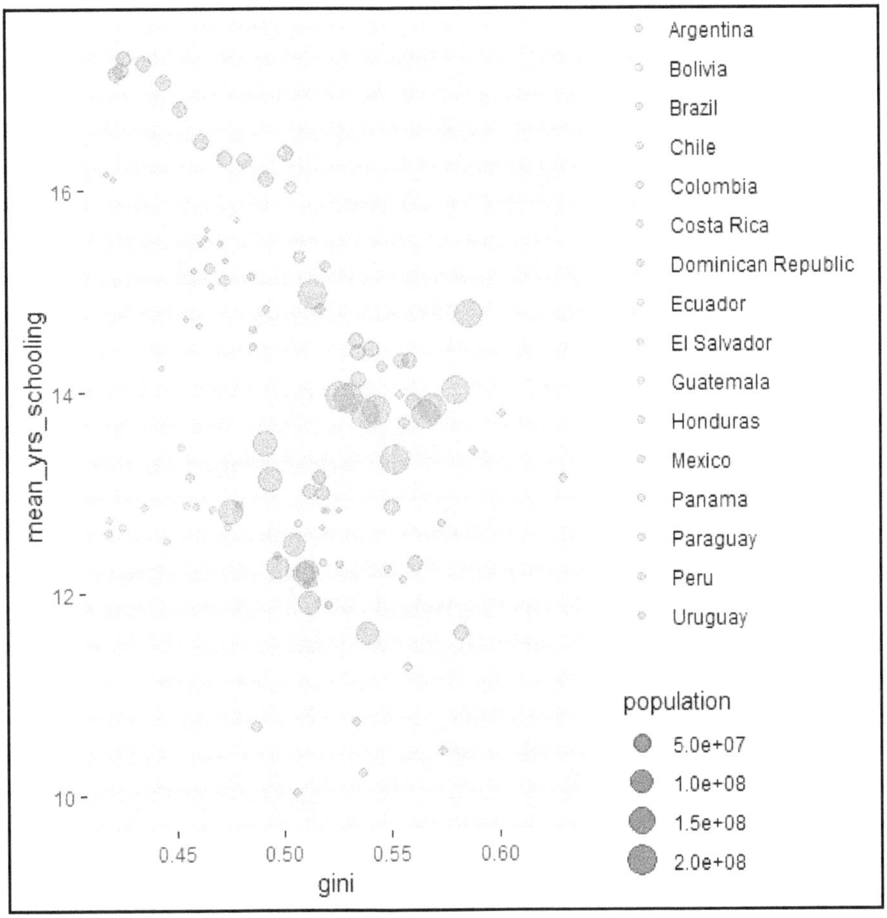

Figure 10.2: Bubble plot made with ggplot2

You might have perceived some transparency. This technique is meant to avoid a common problem known as over-plotting. Set the `alpha` parameter to add transparency to points. Values between 0 and 1 are accepted—0 means total transparency and 1 means no transparency.

Figure 10.2 could be considered good if it was intended as an exploratory analysis. This chapter won't go after a production quality plot. Nonetheless, it will elaborate on this `ggplot` a little longer. The following code block is renaming the axes labels, hiding `population` from the legends, and adding a new custom theme:

```
ggplot(data = dt) +
  geom_point(aes(x = gini,
                 y = mean_yrs_schooling,
                 color = factor(country),
                 size = population), alpha = .4) +
  xlab('Gini Index') +
  ylab('Mean years of schooling (25+)')+
  guides(size = F) +
  theme_classic(base_size = 16)
```

The vertical axis is renamed by `ylab()` and `xlab()` renames the horizontal axis. The `guides()` function used to hide the `population` variable from the legends. The last layer, `theme_classic()`, adds the classic theme and increases the base font size. The output can be seen in the following diagram:

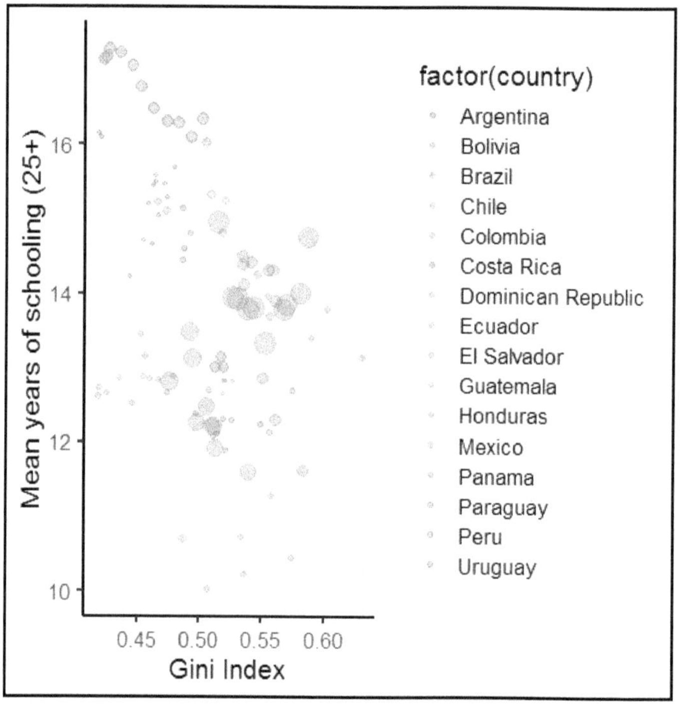

Figure 10.3: Bubble plot, classic theme

There are more things to do in order to get a production-grade plot. We could increase the number of ticks in the vertical axis, for example. Changing the fonts is always an option—Roboto Condensed is my favorite. Try the `extrafont` package to register and load new fonts into R.

> **TIP:** `ggplot2` is great. It can do a lot all by itself. Nonetheless, it has many supplemental packages, such as `ggthemes`, which may help you achieve even better results.

Interactive graphics are an ongoing trend. Although interactive plots can be crafted combining `ggplot2` and some other packages, such as `shiny`, the following paragraphs will introduce several packages that focus on interactivity.

Interactive graphics are not only a good fit for websites and applications of all kinds; many academic journals are encouraging writers to submit interactive plots. Enabling the audience to interact with plots is a powerful idea; it leverages the engagement to a whole new level.

There are several ways you can make a graphic interactive: tooltips, zoom (in and out), toggles, and the list goes on. This chapter won't dive into the nuts and bolts of building all of these features. Nevertheless, it will bring a demo from several packages, starting with `ggvis`. It can be downloaded from the `CRAN` repository:

```
if(!require('ggvis')){install.packages('ggvis')}
```

`ggvis` is very powerful, especially if combined with `shiny`. I personally enjoy the toggles that `ggvis` is capable of delivering, but this chapter is not aiming for that level of detail. Let's just try to make the bubble plot with it. The code is actually very simple and is similar to `ggplot2`:

```
library(ggvis)
dt %>%
  ggvis(~gini, ~mean_yrs_schooling, fill = ~factor(country)) %>%
  layer_points(size = ~population, opacity:=.4)
```

Instead of the plus signs used by `ggplot2`, `ggvis` uses pipes (`%>%`). Notice how the `~` symbol is used to indicate variables from the DataFrame. Also, `ggvis` has a very clever system that interprets differently the arguments based on whether it was set using `:=` or a single equal sign (`=`).

`ggvis::ggvis()` is analogous to `ggplot2::ggplot()`.
`ggvis::layer_points()` is analogous to `ggplot2::geom_point()`.

The `opacity` argument stands for transparency. Setting it with `:=` prevents the input from being rescaled—try to set `opacity = .4` to actually see what I mean. The result from the last code block is displayed in the following diagram:

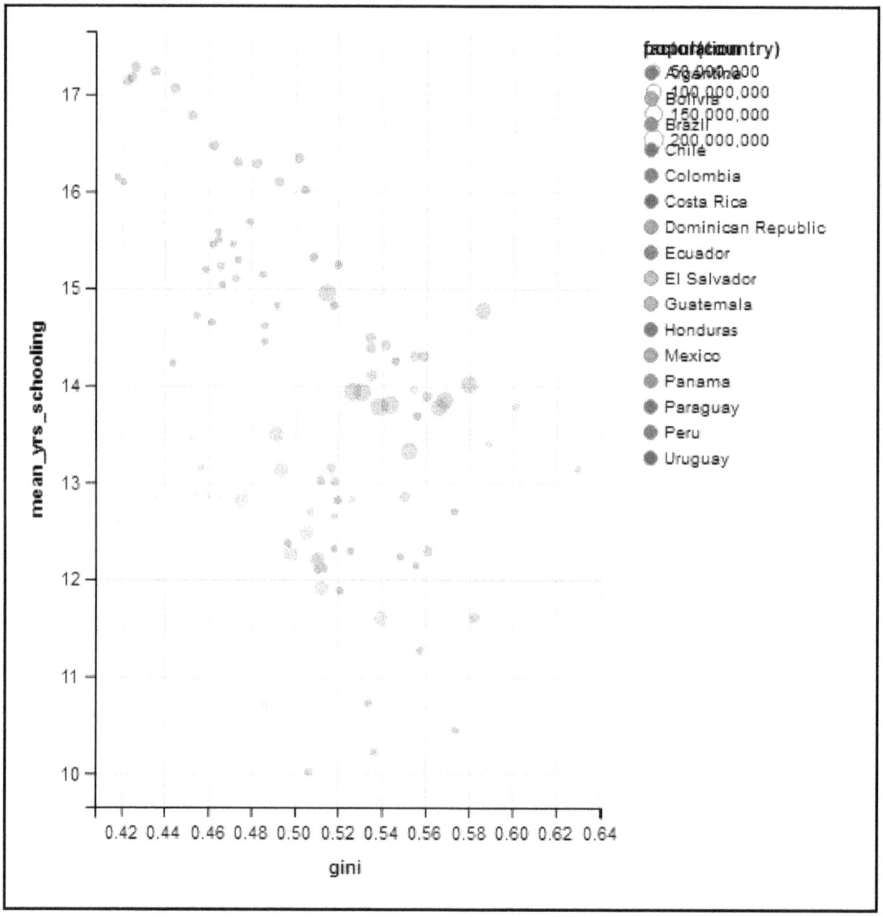

Figure 10.4: Bubble plot made with ggvis

There is still a lot more to do with `ggvis`. Toggles are not that hard to build. One of the strengths of `ggvis` is speed. Once the figure is rendered, it can dynamically change the information displayed very easily.

For the graphing library, try the `https://plot.ly/r/` URL—there are several examples you can dig into. `Plotly` is one of my favorites. I have a character in Tibia named after it. Plots made with it come with zoom enabled as a default. You can install `plotly` directly from `CRAN`:

```
if(!require('plotly')){install.packages('plotly')}
```

Graphics built with `plotly` can be constructed in a layered way too, just like in `ggplot2` and `ggvis`. However, I am going for a more direct approach and designing the whole graphic in a single function, `plot_ly()`:

```
library(plotly)
plot_ly(dt, x = ~gini, y = ~mean_yrs_schooling,
        type = 'scatter', mode = 'markers',
        color = ~country, size = ~population)
```

Plotly can try to smart guess which type of plot you're looking for based on the variables assigned, but picking the type by setting `type` and `mode` is frequently better:

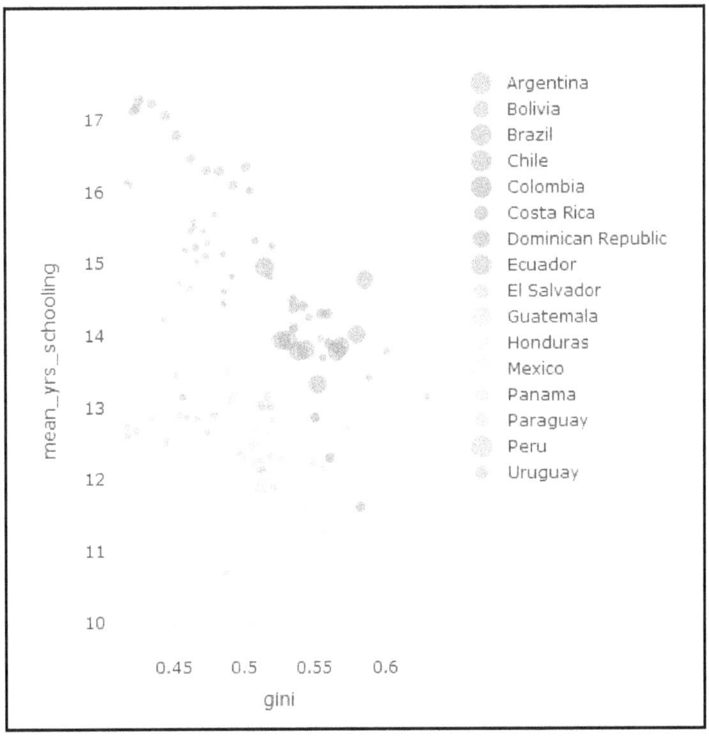

Figure 10.5: Bubble plot made with plotly

Even though the preceding figure is static (a print), the original code will output an interactive version where you can zoom and hover the mouse over the points to display information. Information displayed can be easily changed with a little tweak. Set the `hoverinfo` and `text` arguments to do so:

```
plot_ly(dt, x = ~gini, y = ~mean_yrs_schooling,
        type = 'scatter', mode = 'markers',
        color = ~country, size = ~population,
        hoverinfo = 'text',
        text = ~paste('<b>',country,' - ', date, '</b><br>Gini: ',
round(gini),
                      '<br>Population:', population,
                      '<br>Mean years of schooling:',
round(mean_yrs_schooling)))
```

Look at how HTML commands were used to format the tooltips—try it on your side and see how it works. Speaking for me, I love building dashboards with `plotly`. It's important to mention that `plotly` also goes very well with `shiny`.

TIP: It is possible to assign plots made with `ggplot2`, `ggvis`, and `plotly` to variables. If you choose to do so, they will only be rendered after being called.

`Plotly` can also be used to convert `ggplot` in to the interactive form. Try calling `plotly::ggplotly()` after you rendered `ggplot`. Don't forget to have it installed. You can find the reference manual for `plotly` at `plot.ly/r/reference`. It also has libraries for Python, MatLab, and JavaScript.

The next package will require `devtools` to be installed:

```
if(!require('devtools')){install.packages('devtools')}
```

Some packages may require you to have some software or another package already installed. For example, the next package we're looking for is `rCharts` and it requires the `yalm` package:

```
if(!require('rCharts')){
  if(!require('yaml')){install.packages('yaml')}
  devtools::install_github('ramnathv/rCharts')
}
```

With `rCharts`, you can build plots using several different JavaScript libraries. Versatility might be the biggest advantage of this package. That said, knowing a little JavaScript, JSON, and HTML notation can be very helpful here. The next code block crafts a visualization from `Highcharts`:

```
library(rCharts)
p1 <- hPlot(mean_yrs_schooling ~ gini,
                     data = dt, type = 'bubble',
                     size = 'population', group = 'country')
p1$chart(zoomType = 'xy')
p1$exporting(enabled = T)
p1$show()
```

The `hPlot()` function uses the `Highcharts` library. Crafting visualizations using `rCharts` may be a little bit different than what we've been doing until this point, but it is very layer-wise. The basic plot was assigned to an object called `p1`. Notice how a formula (`<variable 1> ~ <variable 2>`) was used to map points across the vertical and horizontal axis.

Next, methods were called to change features from the basic plot, `p1`:

- `p1$chart(zoomType = 'xy')` enabled zoom to happen both in the *x* and *y* axes
- `p1$exporting(enabled = T)` created a button to export the interactive plot as a static figure

By the end, `p1$show()` took care of rendering the final result. The original outcome was interactive, but the one printed as shown in the following diagram could not be:

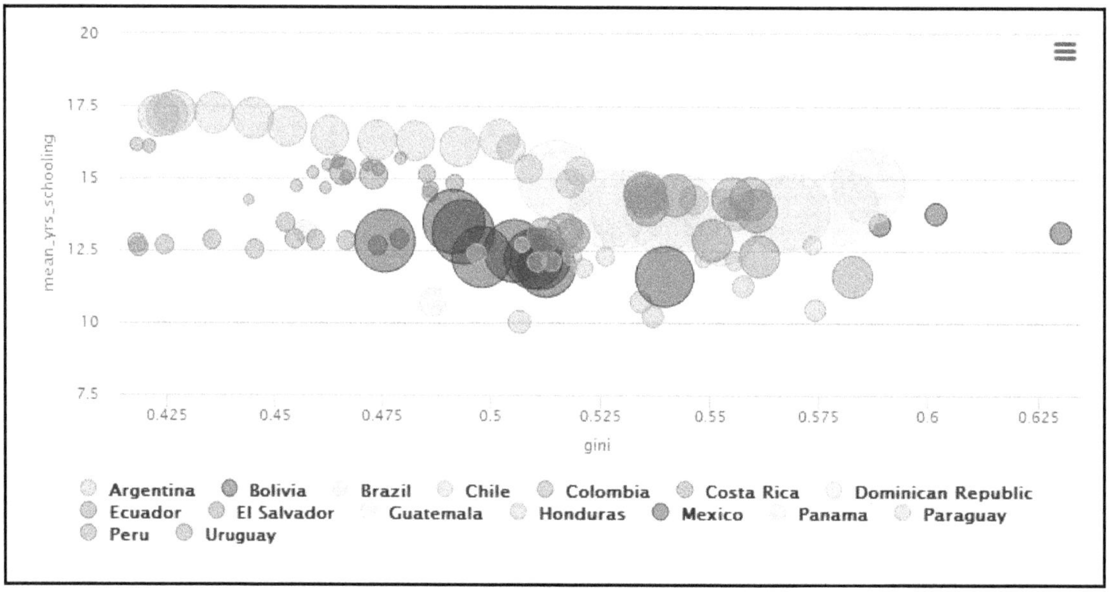

Figure 10.6: Bubble plot made with rCharts

The preceding diagram looks very different than the previous ones. The scale is different and the legend is displayed at the bottom. All of these could be easily changed. The code block ahead uses `$set()` to change scales and `$legend()` to move the entire legends. Additionally, `$tooltip()` was requested to change the tooltips:

```
p2 <- hPlot(mean_yrs_schooling ~ gini,
                    data = dt, type = 'bubble',
                    size = 'population', group = 'country')
p2$tooltip(formatter = "#! function() { return 'Gini :' + Math.round(this.x
* 100) / 100 +
           '<br>Mean years of schooling :' + Math.round(this.y * 100) /
100; } !#")
p2$legend(align = 'right', verticalAlign = 'top', layout = 'vertical')
p2$chart(zoomType = 'xy')
p2$exporting(enabled = T)
p2$set(width = 528, height = 528)
p2$show()
```

Many things had changed. The `$tooltip()` method used HTML and JavaScript to format the way texts are displayed when the mouse hovers a point. Pay attention to how simple quotation marks were used inside double quotation marks. This detail is very important.

Experiment with it. The actual result is very cool. The following diagram only displays a static version:

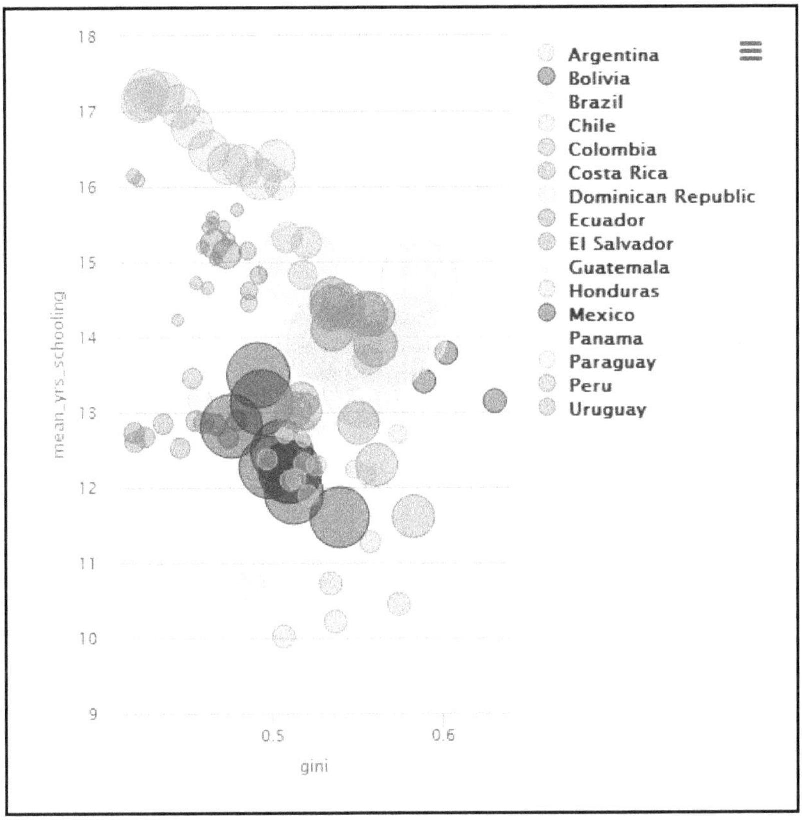

Figure 10.7: rCharts bubble plot rescaled

After rescaling and moving the legends, the final result is closer to the former ones. There is much more one can do with `rCharts`. Here is a list of JavaScript charting libraries that `rCharts` work with:

- Polly chart
- Morris

- NVD3
- xCharts
- Leaflet

Knowing how to work with JSON data, JavaScript, and HTML might be of great help whenever drawing with `rCharts`. Moving on, we have `googleVis`. It can be described as an interface between R and Google's Chart Tools:

```
if(!require('googleVis')){install.packages('googleVis')}
```

Once you're done with the installation, load the package and call `gvisBubbleChart()` to draw the bubble plot:

```
library(googleVis)
p3 <- gvisBubbleChart(dt, idvar = 'country',
                      xvar = 'gini', yvar = 'mean_yrs_schooling',
                      sizevar = 'population', colorvar = 'country'
                      ))
plot(p3)
```

After mapping each variable at the proper aesthetic, we've got the plot stored by `p3`. Call `plot()` to render it into your browser. Figure 10.8 shows a screenshot of it:

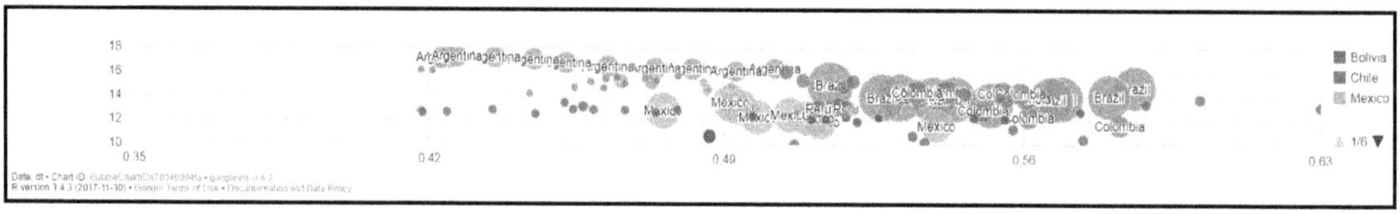

Figure 10.8: Bubble plot made with googleVis

Lots of defaults were used, which explains why the final result looks kind of weird. The code block in the sequence deploys some changes:

```
dt$id <- ''
p4 <- gvisBubbleChart(dt, idvar = 'country',
                      xvar = 'gini', yvar = 'mean_yrs_schooling',
                      sizevar = 'population', colorvar = 'country',
                      options = list(
                        width=600, height=600,
                        explorer= "{ actions: ['dragToZoom',
'rightClickToReset'] }"
                      ))
plot(p4)
```

First, it created a new column in the DataFrame; it's a character column carrying an empty string. Such a column was mapped as `idvar`, doing the trick of removing the names printed inside the bubbles. Next, it named the `options` argument. Setting it with a list enables us to tweak several things.

The latter argument was input with a list of length three. The `width` and `height` elements rescaled the whole plot. The `explorer` element received a string in the JSON format. Two actions were stipulated by such string: left-clicking and dragging will make the plot zoom-in; right-clicking will reset the zoom. The following diagram presents the print version of the output:

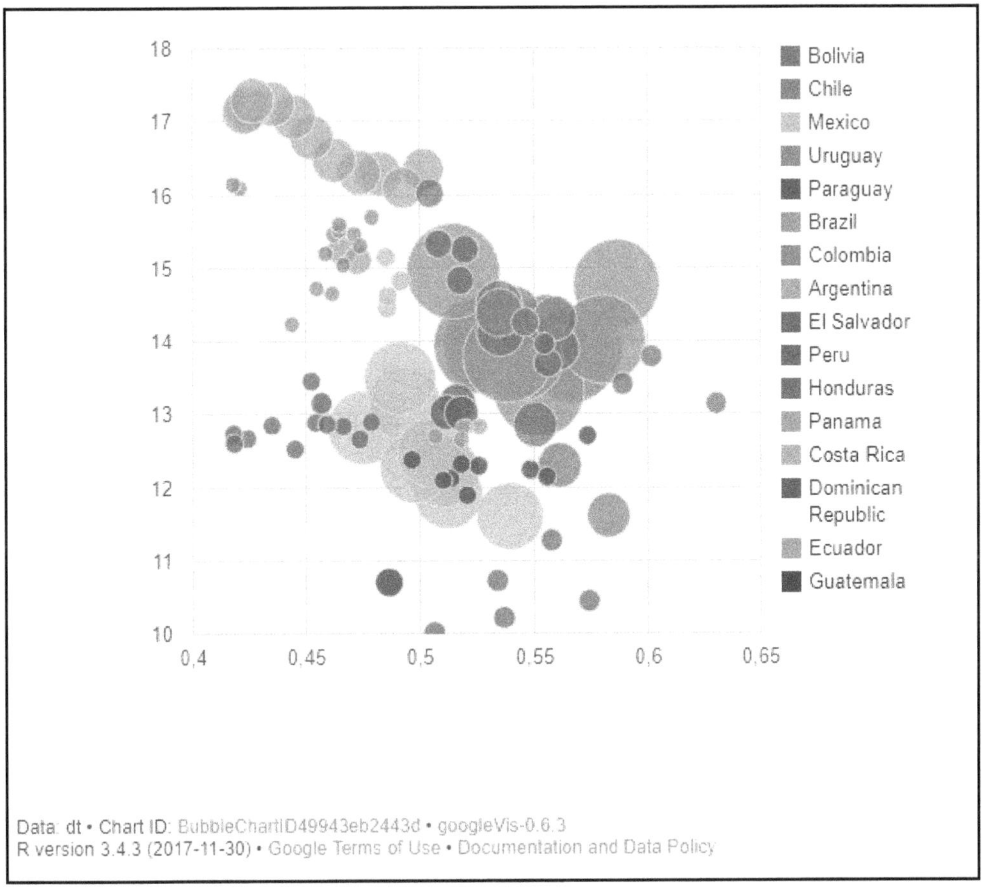

Figure 10.9: googleVis bubble plot

Reproduce it at your end to check the mentioned features working. There is a lot to be made with `googleVis`; choropleths are my personal favorite. Those are usually hard to build—data manipulation skills must be sharp to match geospatial data with whatever you desire to show.

In spite of that, building choropleths with `googleVis` is actually very easy. The packages abstract several steps that are usually mandatory. Additionally, choropleths made this way are interactive. These can be made with `gvisGeoChart()`:

```
map <- gvisGeoChart(dt_gini[dt_gini$date == '2008',],
locationvar='country',
                   colorvar='gini',
                   options=list(projection='kavrayskiy-vii',
                                backgroundColor = '#81d4fa',
                                region = '005'))
plot(map)
```

Given that the DataFrame has observations for many years, data input in `gvisGeoChart()` was filtered for the year 2008. The `locationvar` argument points to the variable holding the names for the locations in the map; `colorvar` tells which variable should be used to paint the map.

The remaining argument, `options`, sets a lot of things: projection type, background color, and scoped region. A static version from the output is displayed in the following diagram:

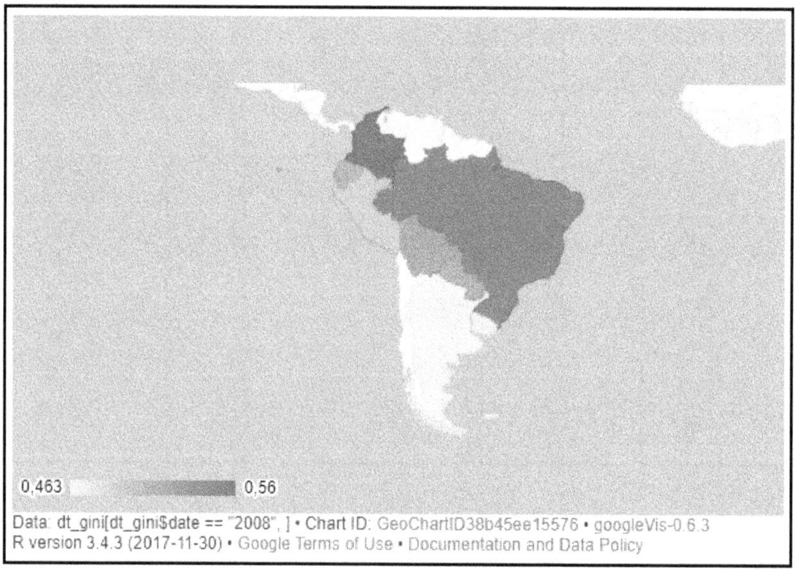

Figure 10.10: Choropleth made with googleVis

A great way to improve what you can do with `googleVis` is to check Google Charts' documentation and gallery:

- `https://developers.google.com/chart/interactive/docs/`

There is a section fully dedicated to maps:

- `https://developers.google.com/chart/interactive/docs/gallery/geochart`

Knowing how to build neat figures is not only a useful skill for data scientists but for anyone who needs to transmit information precisely. To this point, the reader was presented with several plotting libraries. The next section summarizes the entire chapter, while giving tips related to the discussed topics.

Summary

Lots of graphical packages were covered in this chapter: `ggplot2`, `ggvis`, `plotly`, `rCharts`, and `googleVis`. With `ggplot2` alone, you can easily draw high-quality plots. Combine it with other packages such as `shiny` or `plotly` to make interactive graphics.

The remaining packages—`ggvis`, `plotly`, `rCharts`, and `googleVis`—are specialized in making interactive graphics. These are great for applications of all kinds and web pages. Even academic journals are encouraging writers to craft and publish interactive plots.

This chapter drew bubble plots and a choropleth using the different packages. There are lots of kind of plots we could have drawn using these same packages. Some examples are as follows:

- Heatmaps
- Scatterplots
- Bar plots
- Lollipop plots
- Pizza charts

Crafting visualization is a great skill. Unless you are only dealing with databases—architecture and/or maintenance—this skill is a must-have. A safe path to take is to master `ggplot2` plus another package focused on interactive visuals. Practicing is the best way to improve. Drawing really pretty plots and tweeting them frequently is a great way to improve your skills while promoting yourself.

Quiz

1. **Quiz-tion**: There is a theory that strongly influenced the packages `ggplot2` and `ggvis`. This theory is known as:
    1. String theory
    2. Best polygon
    3. Grammar of Graphics
    4. None of the above
2. **Quiz-tion**: Pick the false statement about interactive graphics.
    1. They are appropriate for web pages
    2. They don't ever allow the audience to zoom in and out
    3. The `ggvis` and `plotly` packages allow users to build interactive plots
    4. The `rCharts` and `googleVis` packages allow users to build interactive plots
3. **Quiz-tion**: Which of the following statements is false?
    1. Overplotting can sometimes be softened by a technique called alpha transparency
    2. Data manipulation and preprocessing is never required before drawing a plot
    3. Plots made by `ggplot2` cannot be made interactive, not even with the aid of packages such as `shiny` or `plotly`
    4. Knowing HTML and JavaScript can sometimes be helpful while crafting interactive plots with `rCharts`

Answers—executing the following code will give you the answers to the quiz questions:

```
set.seed(10)
round(runif(3,1,4))
```

11
Going to Production with R

"Data is the new oil."

– Kevin Plank

In this chapter, we're going to introduce you to the package used to build an interactive app, or the Shiny app, which is how it is named. The first section explains what the `shiny` package is and the second section shows how to build a simple kind of Shiny app. The third section describes how reactive works and presents some reactive functions. In the next section, we create a Shiny app using data. And there is the last section, where we give a little advice about the `shiny` package.

In this chapter, we'll be cover the following topics:

- What is R `shiny` package
- Creating an R Shiny app for statistical modeling
- Best practices for Shiny

What is R Shiny?

The Shiny app package is basically a tool where you, with your R knowledge, build a web page and present the result of your R scripts to everybody, including people who don't know R. They can access the information without doing anything but clicking on a website. You, otherwise, need to know the scripts from the analysis you wish to make available.

The way that the `shiny` package works can be split into two parts: the user's interface and the `server` function. The user's interface is the website or **R Markdown** document that users interact with and spend some clicks on. The server can be your computer or a web server where the website is hosted—it must be a server running the R language. When the users request a new visualization, the Shiny app serves the web server with a new R script, then it runs the R codes and serves the new display to the Shiny app. If you configure your R app to be in the cloud, the user will be able to request others' information without your solicitude, but it requires a web page server with the cloud service available.

How to build a Shiny app

First, we need to install the `shiny` package. If you don't have it, make sure to run the following code:

```
install.packages("shiny")
```

To build a Shiny application with R, we need to construct the two structures we talked about before. The user's interface is a web page based on an HTML code, and, as the name says, it is an interface that users can interact with; it can be an interactive plot, texts, images, and so on. You don't need to worry if you don't know anything about HTML since we are going to use the `shiny` package to build it, though some knowledge about it can help you to build an improved app. The server, otherwise, must contain all information needed by the web server to provide the information requested by the UI. Run the following code if you want to see some examples:

```
library(shiny)
runExample()
runExample('01_hello')
```

A couple of things are happening now. A window with a histogram chart and a sidebar appeared (it is the UI), and your RStudio is still running the application (if you look at it, a `Listening on http://127.0.0.1:6931` message is shown in your R console). It happens because, by creating a Shiny application, an interface is shown based on the predefined codes. In this example, when the user moves the sidebar, interacting with the app, new code lines are requested. So, the Shiny app receives and sends them to the server. The server is going to process the new information according to what it was programmed to do, generating a new interface to be shown. This happens so fast that the user may not detect the information flow. To end the application, click the red stop sign in your R console, or close the UI window.

In the previous example, the code lines needed to build that application are shown too, and, if you analyze it, you may note that they have same structure as the following code. Because of the interaction between the `ui` function and the `server` function, the `shiny` package requests this kind of structure. I recommend you always use the same template, it will make it easier for you to understand your application. So, open a new R script and name it as app. R and write the following code:

```
library(shiny)

#The UI object
ui <- fluidPage()

#The server function
server <- function(input, output) {}

#Run the app
shinyApp (ui = ui, server = server)
```

The name of your app R script must be `app.R`. Otherwise, the `shiny` package won't recognize it as an application, and you will have trouble running your code. So, every time you need to create a new app, you will also need to open a new R directory and save a new `app.R` file inside it. If you want, you can create two R scripts, one for the `ui` function and another for the `server` function, but you must name them as `ui.R` and `server.R` respectively, remembering to keep them in the same directory.

If you run the code, a blank UI window will appear. This is the shortest kind of application that you can build. The `ui` object is where all of the elements needed to create the UI are stored and, hence, it contains what is going to be shown to the users. So, things like the web page name and the desired input and output are defined here. The `fluidPage` function is necessary to create the fluid page layouts; you can try `?fluidPage` in your console to learn more about it, but basically it is where you create the structure of your web page, define the input and output, and add the elements. The `server` function that receives the input from the UI, builds the R elements according to them (it can be a plot, a table, or anything else that is possible to do with R), and assembles it as the output required by the UI. You must build your app around the input and output using the following code:

```
library(shiny)

#The UI object
ui <- fluidPage(numericInput(inputId = "df", label = "Numbers between 1
  and 50:", value = 1, min = 1, max = 50, step = 1),
                plotOutput(outputId = "norm"))
```

```
#The server function
server <- function(input, output) {}

#Run the app
shinyApp (ui = ui, server = server)
```

Note that a number box with the number one inside it now appears, where you can choose any natural number between `1` and `50`, and a big blank space. The number box appears because of the input function inside the `fluidPage` function. There are many kinds of inputs, and they represent any possible interaction the user can do on a web page. You can choose one or more input function, according to your necessity. They are: `actionButton()`, `submitButton()`, `checkboxInput()`, `checkboxgroupInput()`, `dateInput()`, `dateRangeInput()`, `fileInput()`, `numericInput()`, `sliderInput()`, `passwordInput()`, `radioButtons()`, `selectInput()`, and `textInput()`. Inside the input function, we call the arguments required for that input to work properly. Each input has its own arguments, so type `?*Input` to look for them (change the asterisk for an input function; in our example, type `?numericInput` to see the arguments we wrote previously). The `label` argument is a textbox that will appear along with the input in our web page; use empty quotations marks if you don't want it. There is an important argument inside all of the input functions that we must talk about: `inputId`. It is an argument to name the respective input, and you can choose any character string nickname, but it needs to be properly specified because the server function uses it to read the user interaction.

Next, and separated with a comma, comes the output. Output is the thing you can do with R. It can be a plot, a text, an image, and so on. As the input functions, there are specific kinds of output functions according to what you want to be shown in your web page. They are: `plotOutput()`, `tableOutput()`, `textOutput()`, `htmlOutput()`, `imageOutput()`, `dataTableOutput()`, `uiOutput()`, and `verbatimTextOutput()`. While `output` is assembled in the `server` function, it needs to be specified here, so the UI can keep a space for it (it is the big blank space mentioned before). In addition, we need to name it as the `outputId` argument, just like we did with the input. We can create as many input and output as needed, just separate them with a comma.

The `output` object is built in the `server` function, so let's talk about it now.

The `server` function assembles `input` into `output`. You do this by inserting a list, such as an object that must be called as `output` and `$` plus `outputId`. Every time you need to refer to a specific `output` in the `server` function, use the `output$output_nameId` tag, where `output_nameId` is `outputId` chosen in the UI output function. The many output functions you have defined in the UI are listed here. Don't use commas to separate them; simply do it as is shown in the following but don't try to run the code, it is only an example:

```
server <- function(input, output) {
  output$output_nameId1 <- renderFunction({})
  output$output_nameId2 <- renderFunction({})
  ... )
```

Another important thing that must be specified and inserted in your code is the render function; it creates the type of output you wish to make. In the preceding example, I wrote `renderFunction`, but it isn't the right nomenclature. You need to choose the proper render function according to what will be displayed. The render functions are: `renderPlot()`, `renderPrint()`, `renderTable()`, `renderText()`, `renderUI()`, `renderImage()`, and `renderDataTable()`. Any R expression surrounded by the render function braces (`{}`) will be displayed in the UI, at the place specified by the output function.

So how do we create reactive objects inside the `server` function? The last important thing you need to know about the `server` function is to insert the inputs as variables inside the render functions, in the objects you desire the user to interact with. When you refer to the inputs in the `server` function, it follows the same standard as the output, so use `input$input_nameId` to call them. It must have this syntax. The following example would plot a sequence between 1 and any number set by the user in the input element:

```
library(shiny)

#the UI object
ui <- fluidPage(numericInput(inputId = "a_number",
                             label = "Numbers between 1 and 50:",
                             value = 1, min = 1, max = 50, step = 1),
                plotOutput(outputId = "a_plot"))

#the server function
server <- function(input, output) {
  output$a_plot <- renderPlot({plot(seq(0,input$a_number))})
}

#Run the app
shinyApp (ui = ui, server = server)
```

Let's get practical and build a useful app. Do you remember our plot about normal and t-distributions in Chapter 2, *Descriptive and Inferential Statistics*? Here is how to write an application for it:

```
library(shiny)

#the Users Interface
ui <- fluidPage(
  titlePanel("Difference between normal and t distributions!"),
                sidebarLayout(
                  sidebarPanel(
                    numericInput(inputId = "freedom",
                                                label = "Degrees
                                                of Freedom:",
                                                value = 1, min = 1,
                                                max = 50,
                                                step = 1)),
                  mainPanel(plotOutput(outputId = "norm")
                  )
                )
)

#the server function
server <- function(input, output) {
  output$norm <- renderPlot({
    x <- seq(-5,5,.1)
    par(lwd = 2)
    plot(x, dnorm(x), type = 'l', ylab = 'density',
         main = 'Prob. Density Distributions')
    lines(x, dt(x, input$freedom), col = '#e66101', lty = 2)
    legend('topright',
           legend = c('normal','t-student'),
           col = c('#000000','#e66101'), lty = 1:2)
  })
}
#Run the app
shinyApp (ui = ui, server = server)
```

Inside the `fluidPage()` function, the `titlePanel()` function was called to set the web page name. The `sidebarLayout()` function creates a Shiny app with a sidebar, and always needs two arguments: `sidebarPanel()` and `mainPanel()`. In the `sidebarPanel` function, we inserted the input, and, in `mainPanel` we inserted the outputs. This structure is the more common type of UI application built with the `shiny` package.

> **TIP**
> Yet, you can insert multiple HTML contents inside the `titlePanel`, `sidebarPanel`, or `mainPanel` functions, separating them with a comma if more than one is necessary. The `shiny` package will recognize it properly.

In the `server` function, I called the `output$norm` output, only because I named `outputId` as `norm` in the `mainPanel` UI output function. The `renderPlot` function was used to render a plot. So I just needed to write the plot code lines inside the braces of the render function. I want you to interact with the numbers of degrees of freedom, I changed the `df` argument inside the `dt()` function by the `input$freedom` input, as I named it with `inputId` on the `sidebarPanel` function. When you change the value in the numeric input, the Shiny app changes the plot and you can see that, the more you increase the degrees of freedom, the more the student distribution looks like the normal distribution. The following shows what the app looks like if you run the preceding code:

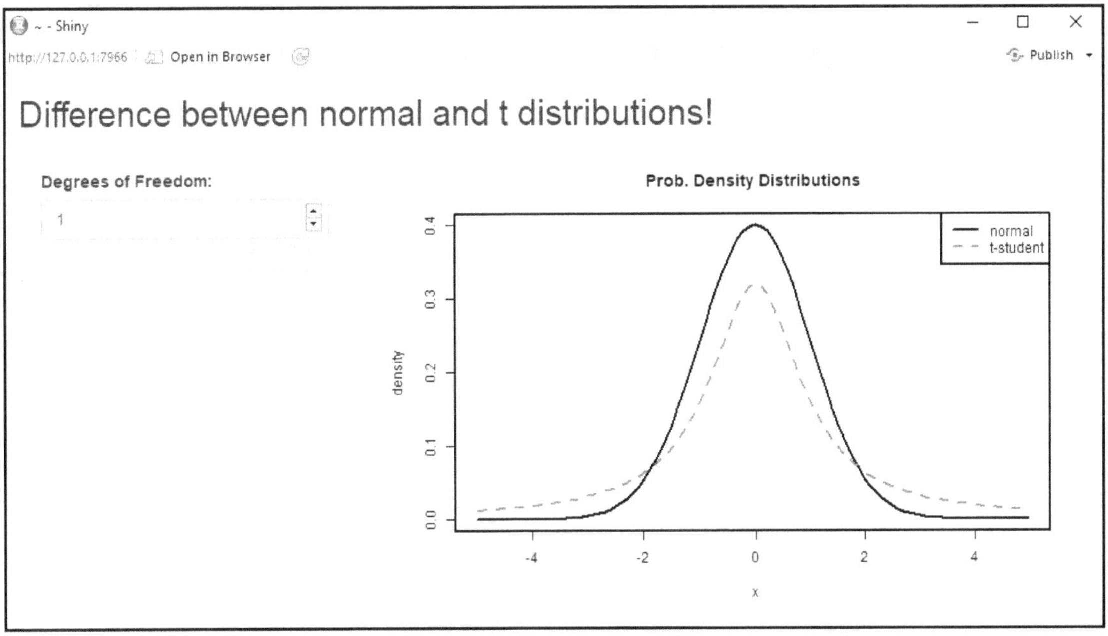

Figure 11.1: Probability density distributions application

It makes it much easier to view the interaction between the degrees of freedom and the t-distribution with our brand new app. So, let's learn a little more about the features required to build an app in the next section.

Building an application inside R

To build an application inside R, you need to understand how reactivity works. I'll explain it with an analogy using WhatsApp. Imagine your WhatsApp as the `input` object and you as the `output` object; any time a friend (the user) sends you a message, WhatsApp rings, alerting you about it, so you answer your friend with a new message based on what he/she wrote you. This is how reactive works in R's shiny package. Any time the user interacts and changes the value of an input, it alerts the server function that the output is outdated. So, the server function returns the code, pulling the new value inside the `input$*` variable, then returns the updated output.

It is important to know how it work mainly because there are situations where the `server` function can't rerun the code properly if a reactive expression isn't used. Reactive expressions are objects defined to alert the `server` function only when a specific interaction is executed; the interaction necessary to activate it varies according to the reactive expression used. We've already seen one kind of reactive expression, the render functions, which were used to display the output. Let's see other cases.

TIP

After requiring the `shiny` package in your R console, try to call `?reactive`. It will open the R documentation about the `reactive` function, and it can help you to better understand reactivity in Shiny.

The reactive and isolate functions

If you need to call an `input` argument inside many output objects, you must create a reactive expression using the `reactive` function. Let's see an example:

```
library(shiny)

#the UI object
ui <- fluidPage(numericInput(inputId = "number",
                             label = "A number between 1 and 50:",
                             value = 1, min = 1, max = 50, step = 1),
                textInput(inputId = "text", label = "A text box",
                          value = ""),
                tableOutput(outputId = "table_a"),
                tableOutput(outputId = "table_b"))

#the server function
server <- function(input, output) {
  the_number <- reactive({input$number})
  output$table_a <- renderTable(list(input$text, the_number()))
```

```
  output$table_b <- renderTable(list(the_number(),
                                      isolate({input$text})))
}

#Run the app
shinyApp (ui = ui, server = server)
```

This simple app creates a web page with two inputs and two tables. The first input is the numeric input as we used before, the second input is a textbox where the user can write any text. Both the number and the text are presented in `table_a` and `table_b` but in different orders. Note we used the `reactive` function to create a reactive expression called `the_number`; every time that we needed to use the expression inside the `the_number` object instead of calling `input$number`, we just called it as `the_number()` (you need to add the parentheses because `the_number` is an expression and not a variable). We called it twice, in the `output$table_a` object and in the `output$table_b` object. If you want to create a kind of list of reactive values, use the `reactiveValues()` function; it works similarly to the `reactive` function. Check the R documentation to see more about it (`?reactiveValues`).

If you pay close attention to the second output object, you'll see that we used the `isolate` function with the `input$text` object. If you run the code and try to insert a text in the textbox, you'll note that in the first table the text is actualized as soon as possible, whereas it is only actualized in the second table when you change the value in the numeric box. That is what the isolation function does: it saves the new interaction made by the user but doesn't call the `server` function to re-evaluate the code. It waits for another kind of interaction to trigger it, and when the `server` function is triggered and creates a new output, it pulls the newest value inside the isolated input element, and the output element is created with all of the values actualized. In our second table example, it happens when we change the numeric value.

The observeEvent and eventReactive functions

Suppose you want your app to react only under certain circumstances, such as when the user clicks a button. In these cases, you can use the `observeEvent()` or `eventReactive` functions. Both trigger when a specified event is fired. Let's work with our plot about the t-distribution:

```
library(shiny)

#the UI
ui <- fluidPage(numericInput(inputId = "freedom",label =
  "Degrees of Freedom:",
```

```
                                value = 1, min = 1, max = 50, step = 1),
                    textInput(inputId = "title", label = "Chart title:",
                              value = "prob. density distributions"),
                    actionButton(inputId = "upgrade", label = "Plot it!"),
                    plotOutput(outputId = "plot_a"))

#the server function
server <- function(input, output) {
  up <- eventReactive(input$upgrade, {
    x <- seq(-5,5,.1)
    par(lwd = 2)
    plot(x, dnorm(x), type = 'l', ylab = 'density',
         main = input$title)
    lines(x, dt(x, input$freedom), col = '#e66101', lty = 2)#input$freedom
    legend('topright', legend = c('normal','t-student'),
           col = c('#000000','#e66101'), lty = 1:2)})
  to_print <- observeEvent(input$upgrade, {print(list(input$title,
                                                      input$freedom))})
  output$plot_a <- renderPlot(up())
}
#Run the app
shinyApp (ui = ui, server = server)
```

A couple of things were changed in our app since the last time we saw it. We added a text input, an action button in the user's interface, and we used some new functions inside the `server` function. Once you run the code, at the first moment, there is no plot in the app. Click on **Plot it!** and it will appear with the number of degrees of freedom chosen in the numeric input and with the text input as the plot title. The `plot` event was delayed by the use of the `eventReactive` function, but how did we use it?

Calling the `eventReactive` function requires two elements: the trigger input and the expression to be executed when the trigger is fired. In our case, the first element is our button, or how we locate it: `input$upgrade`; the second element is all of the code necessary to build our previous plot. Note that we used the `input$freedom` and `input$title` tags on it, right in the places where we want the users to interact with the degrees of freedom from the t-distribution and with the chart title, respectively. So the `eventReactive(,{})` function was used with two elements. Before the button triggers, the second element inside the `eventReactive` function is treated as isolated; when you click on the button, the `input$upgrade` input value reacts, calling the second element, or the code to build our plot. Where will the plot be placed?

To set the plot in the right place, we called the `eventReactive` function in a new element, creating the `up()` reactive expression. So, the last thing we need to do is call the `up()` expression—remember to put the parentheses inside the proper render function in the output object designated for it, in our case, the `output$plot_a` element.

If you paid close attention when you clicked on the button **Plot it!**, the Shiny app, apart from inserting the plot in the web page, also prints the degree of freedom and the title chosen by the user in your R console, but this operation is not shown in the UI. The `observeEvent(,{})` function is responsible for it. The syntax is the same as the `eventReactive` function, so when its first element is triggered, the expression inside the second element is executed, but it is not shown to the users. So, basically, the `observeEvent` function creates a reactive expression to be triggered under a specific situation; when this situation happens, it forces the server to run the code expression in a second plan, not showing any results to the user. It is useful if you want to hide some executions from your users. The `observer()` function can be used similarly, but it uses the same syntax as the `reactive()` function.

Approach for creating a data product from statistical modeling and web UI

In this section, we are going to build an app with a dataset. Before we start with the construction of the architecture of our app, we need some open data to work with. I'm going to use the computer dataset that can be found in the `Ecdat` package, so make sure to install it by running `install.packages("Ecdat")`. A documentation about its variables is found at `https://vincentarelbundock.github.io/Rdatasets/doc/Ecdat/Computers.html`.

Once it was installed, if you type `class(Ecdat::Computers)`, you will see that it is a DataFrame. A lot of information is hidden inside this data, and our goal here is to present a couple of them in a Shiny application, publishing it in a web page. We are going to rearrange and group our dataset, so you'll need the `dplyr` package; make sure it is installed and run the following code:

```
library(dplyr)
dt <- Ecdat::Computers
dt <- dt %>% group_by(premium, ram, screen, hd)
dt <- dt %>% summarise(AveragePrice = round(mean(price), digits = 2),
                       AverageSpeed = round(mean(speed), digits = 0))
```

The first two lines are dedicated to select the columns we'll use and to group them by `premium`, `ram`, `screen` and `hd`. The `summarise` function was called to condense the values of the average price and the average clock speed of the grouped variables. Now that we have our data, let's start our app, step by step. First, we will define the page structure:

```
library(shiny)
library(ggplot2)
library(dplyr)

#you must insert the codes to call the dataset here, just the ones we used
above

#UI
ui <- fluidPage(
  titlePanel("Let's learn them all!", windowTitle = "Practicing"),
  sidebarLayout(
    sidebarPanel(),
    mainPanel(
      tabsetPanel(
        tabPanel("Plot", plotOutput(outputId = "plot")),
        tabPanel("Going further!")
      ))))
#server function
server <- function(input, output) {
  output$plot <- renderPlot({})
}
#calling shiny
shinyApp (ui = ui, server = server)
```

We started with the basic syntax of the Shiny app, that is, the `ui` object, the `server` function, and the Shiny app call. Inside the UI, we added a title with `titlePanel()`, divided the web page with `sidebarLayout()`, and kept the space for `sidebarPanel()`. Inside `mainPanel`, we created a tab panel with `tabsetPanel()`, with two tabs, using `tabPanel()` for each one. Note that the packages we'll use were written, and the place to set the code to call the dataset was defined, so copy and paste the codes for the dataset if you need. Now let's build the UI, adding the input, output, and a few HTML elements:

```
#the UI object

ui <- fluidPage(
  titlePanel("Let's learn them all!", windowTitle = "Practicing"),
  sidebarLayout(
    sidebarPanel(
      selectInput(inputId = "x_var",
                  label = "Choose the variable X:",
```

```
                  choices = c("Average Speed" = "AverageSpeed", "HD" =
                    "hd")),
        selectInput(inputId = "y_var",
                  label = "Choose the variable Y:",
                  choices = c("Avarage Price" = "AveragePrice",
                    "Average Speed" = "AverageSpeed")),
        radioButtons(inputId = "premium",
                   label = "Was the manufacturer a \"premium\" firm:",
                   choices = c("Yes" = "yes", "No" = "no"))
      ),
      mainPanel(
        tags$p("Hey there! I've learned a lot about shiny package,
          you should learn too, do it ",
              tags$a(href = "https://shiny.rstudio.com/", "here!")),
        tabsetPanel(
          tabPanel("Plot!", plotOutput(outputId = "plot")),
          tabPanel("Going further!", tags$h2("Tips"),
                 tags$p("There are many things to learn,
                  to go deep into shiny, check these ",
                      tags$a(href =
                        "https://shiny.rstudio.com/articles/",
                         "articles."))
                        ))))
  )
```

Inside `sidebarPanel()`, we added three inputs: they will be necessary for the user to interact with our plot. Selected inputs were used by calling `choice` and combining the display option with its value in the DataFrame. In `mainPanel()` and in `tabPanel()`, we used the tags functions to create some HTML codes. Use `names(tags)` to see all possible ways to set HTML codes; the syntax to call them is `tags$name`, and the elements inside them you'll need to explore by yourself. Each tag function has its own syntax, so spend some time there. In our case, we used `tags$h2` to add a title, `tags$p` to add a paragraph, and `tags$a` to add a link. Let's build our `server` function:

```
#the server function
server <- function(input, output) {
  output$plot <- renderPlot({
    data <- dt[dt$premium == input$premium,]
    ggplot(data = data, aes(x = get(input$x_var), y = get(input$y_var))) +
      geom_point(alpha = .5, stroke = 1.5) +
      geom_smooth(method = 'lm', se = F, show.legend = F) +
      xlab(input$x_var) +
      ylab(input$y_var) +
      theme_minimal()
  })
}
```

The `server` function was built with the unique output we've used. The dataset is separated by `premium` with `input$premium`. The `ggplot2` package is used to build the plot, and the `get` function is used with `input$x_var` and `input$y_var`, so the string sent by the input is read by the `ggplot` package as an object. Write the last line code by calling the Shiny app, using the following:

```
#the shiny app
shinyApp (ui = ui, server = server)
```

If you did everything right, you created the application shown in the following figure:

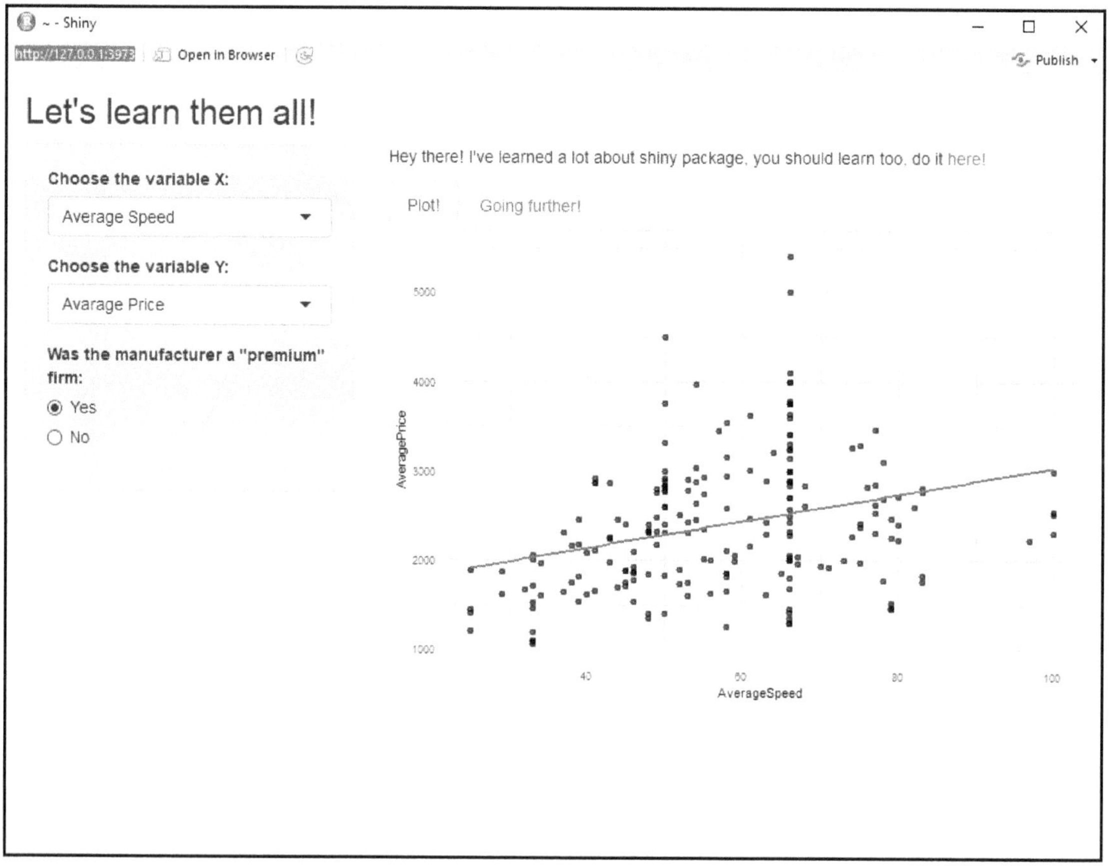

Figure 11.4: Our final app visualization

Don't forget to go further by yourself; there is a lot of stuff about Shiny to learn. In the next section, a couple of tips are given if you want to see more about the `shiny` package.

Some advice about Shiny

The `shiny` package requires a server running R. If you want see how to deploy an application online, I suggest you access `https://www.shinyapps.io/`, sign in, and develop your own app. The basic version is free to use, but it has limited resources, so you must go with a simple app. If you like it and want to improve, you can try the paid version or another data server. The Shiny RStudio gallery (`https://shiny.rstudio.com/gallery/`) can give you some inspiration and show you how people are using the Shiny app.

If your app is online, it will drain some resources from the server. It's good practice to keep all of the code you really don't need to run every time outside the `server` function. The code in the UI is executed only when the R section starts, but the codes inside the `server` function is executed every single time when the user interacts with your app, so any unnecessary code placed there can dry your server resources.

Summary

In this chapter, we introduced R shiny, which is an R package used to build interactive apps. We then created a simple Shiny app and later created an app showing how the `reactive` function works. Later, we created a Shiny app where we used data and, finally, we went through best practices for using the `shiny` package.

That's all in this chapter, folks. In the next chapter, we'll touch on another useful R package: `sparklyr`.

Quiz

1. **Quiz-tion:** Which package provides the primary functionality for R Shiny?
    1. `shinyserver`
    2. `shiny`
    3. `shinyus`

2. **Quiz-tion:** Which of the following options (functions) allow developers to create dynamic page layouts ?
   1. `fluidPage`
   2. `dynamicPage`
   3. `flashExtensions`
3. **Quiz-tion:** Which of the following are mandatory arguments for `eventReactive`?
   1. The IDs for all the reactive elements in the app
   2. The trigger input and the corresponding function (expression) to be run on trigger
   3. The trigger input only

Answers—executing the following code will give you the answers to the quiz questions:

```
set.seed(11)
round(runif(3,1,3))
```

12
Large Scale Data Analytics with Hadoop

"Without big data analytics, companies are blind and deaf, wandering out onto the web like deer on a freeway."

– Geoffrey Moore

Hadoop is an open source software developed by Apache for distributed computing, allowing analysis of big datasets in a secure way. It departs from the principle that every kind of machine has faults that happen often so they need to be cured by the software. Spark is a similar tool, being another kind of big data structure developed by Apache. But while the focus of Hadoop is secure data storage, the focus of Spark is data processing. They are different entities, but they mess things up, mainly because Spark is often used to process data held in Hadoop's filesystem.

In this chapter, we are going to learn about the `sparklyr` R package: a free and open sourced package developed by RStudio in conjunction with IBM, Cloudera, and H2O. Basically, `sparklyr` is a `dplyr` backend to Spark, and it provides an R interface to Spark's distributed machine learning algorithms, so we can handle large scale data using R.

Installing the package and Spark

To begin, you need to install a few packages and the Spark itself. To do it, call the following codes; it can take some time to download Spark:

```
install.packages(c("dplyr", "sparklyr", "DAAG"))
library(sparklyr); library(dplyr)

#installing Spark
spark_install()
```

The `DAAG` package contains the dataset we are going to use. So, let's start our learning. This chapter is divided into five sections plus this introduction. The next section teaches you how to manipulate Spark data using `dplyr` and SQL query. In the second section, we bring Spark data into R, for analysis and visualization. The third section shows how to use the Spark or the H2O machine learning algorithms. The fourth section presents the Spark API. Lastly, there is a final section to see the Spark connection on RStudio IDE.

Manipulating Spark data using both dplyr and SQL

Once you're done with the installation from this chapters introduction, let's create a remote `dplyr` data source for the Spark cluster. To do this, use the `spark_connect` function, as shown:

```
sc <- spark_connect(master = "local")
```

This will create a Spark cluster in your computer; you can see it at your RStudio, a tab guide alongside your R environment. To disconnect, use the `spark_disconnect(sc)` function. Keep connected and copy a couple of datasets from any R packages into the cluster:

```
library(DAAG)
dt_sugar <- copy_to(sc, sugar, "SUGAR")
dt_stVincent <- copy_to(sc, stVincent, "STVINCENT")
```

The preceding code uploads the `DAAG::sugar` and `DAAG::stVicent` DataFrames into the your connected Spark cluster. It also creates the table definitions; they were saved into `dt_sugar` and `dt_stVincent` objects. To read data into Spark DataFrames, just call the `spark_read_*` functions, where the asterisk must be the file type. Access the R documentation (`?spark_read_csv`, for example) to see the right syntax and arguments necessary. Now you can use the `dplyr` verbs with the tables object. For example, you can filter it this way:

```
dt_sugar %>% filter(trt == "Control")
```

What happens is that `dplyr` automatically translates your codes into SQL queries: it only needs to write the `dplyr` functions with the normal syntax. To see how translate is working, use the `show_query()` function to inspect it. If you are doing simple mathematical operations with R functions inside the `dplyr` functions, `dplyr` will translate the math operators into Spark SQL too.

Try to use another `dplyr` function; use `summarise` as an example, as they work in a similar way. Remember that you can combine many functions with the `dplyr`, `%>%` function.

If your objective is to use the SQL queries, you need the `DBI` package (`install.packages("DBI")` if you don't have it), calling its function `dbGetQuery()`. This function returns an R DataFrame and requires two arguments: the connection object (`sc` in our case) and the query (as quoted string). Try the following code as an example:

```
library(DBI)
dbGetQuery(sc, "SELECT trt FROM sugar")
```

To do this, some SQL query knowledge is necessary. Notice that a DataFrame is shown as a result of the last code. When we are using the `dplyr` functions to manipulate the table definitions, only they are changed; the dataset stays unaffected in the Spark environment, at least until you disconnect, then they are cleaned (if it is a local cluster).

Filtering and aggregating Spark datasets

To manipulate the table's dataset, we need to use the verb commands from `dplyr`. They will automatically be translated as SQL statements if you are connected to a DataFrame. I think here the best way to understand how it works is with an example, so let's run the following code:

```
mod_stvincent <- dt_stVincent %>% select(code, id, harvwt) %>%
  filter(harvwt > 15) %>% arrange(desc(id))
```

The `select` function is used to choose the `code`, `id`, and `harvwt` columns from our `dt_stVincent` table object. The `filter` function is added to the code to choose only the row lines where `harvwt` is bigger than `15`. In the end, `arrange` is used to set the order. You can also use `summarise()` as aggregators query and `mutate()` as operators query. `Dplyr` knows how to translate their mathematical algorithms to SQL. Run the `show_query(mod_stvincent)` code to see how the SQL translation works.

If you have paid enough attention, you will have noted that `mod_stvincent` isn't a DataFrame, but tables containing SQL queries. But don't worry, bringing Spark datasets into R is as simple as calling a function. Just use the `collect()` `dplyr` function and voila. Run the following code to make the (plot) magic happen:

```
mod1_stvincent <- collect(mod_stvincent)
plot(mod1_stvincent$id, mod1_stvincent$harvwt)
```

The `collect` function brings the datasets required, and it is manipulated by the `dplyr` functions to the R environment. Use `class(mod1_stvincent)` to see that it contains a DataFrame object. Now we can plot the variables from `dt_stVincent` easily. We only need to use our new `mod1_stvincent` object; we could use any R function we desire with it, too. If you try to build a plot directly with the `dt_stVincent` object or with the `mod_stvincent` tables (`plot(mod_stvincent$id, mod_stvincent$harvwt)`), the unique thing you'll get is a huge error message. If you want the same result using SQL query, try the next code:

```
mod1_stvincent <- dbGetQuery(sc, "SELECT *
  FROM (SELECT 'code', 'id', 'harvwt'
  FROM 'STVINCENT') 'tgssodfxtm'
  WHERE ('harvwt' > 15.0)
  ORDER BY 'id' DESC")
plot(mod1_stvincent$id, mod1_stvincent$harvwt)
```

You can see that the SQL query used is the same when you use `show_query(mod_stvincent)`. This is the `dplyr` package translate capability in action. If you are not a SQL expert, I advise you to keep with the `dplyr` package regular functions. They are easier to learn and apply by anyone who already knows R. If you need a specific function, you can look for it in the `dplyr` documentation, found at: `https://cran.r-project.org/web/packages/dplyr/dplyr.pdf`.

Using Spark machine learning or H2O Sparking Water

If your objective is to use Spark as a tool for your machine learning projects, this section will introduce you to how it is possible to do so within R. Spark contains its own machine learning library that can be accessed by `sparklyr`, so it's pretty simple to work your machine learning projects on Spark. The website `https://spark.rstudio.com/mlib/` provides a pretty good presentation about Spark Machine Learning library, so remember to visit it to discover the many available functions; they include an example workflow that is short and effective and shows how to sequence your project codes. We already talked about machine learning in `Chapter 6`, *Machine Learning with R*; in this section, I'm only going to develop the decision tree studies we did in that chapter, but now using the Spark machine learning library.

> TIP: The Spark machine learning package is a Spark package and not an R package.

First, let's call `sparklyr`. Start a connection and upload the `Chile` DataFrame from the `car` package into our Spark cluster:

```
library(sparklyr)
library(dplyr)
library(car)

#sc <- spark_connect(master = 'local') #Only if you aren't connected
dt_chile <- copy_to(sc, Chile, 'chile')
```

Now we're going to clean our data as we did before on `Chapter 6`, *Machine Learning with R*, but with `sparklyr`, and divide it into two partitions:

```
dt_chile <- na.omit(dt_chile)
partitions <- dt_chile %>% sdf_partition(training = 0.7, test = .3,
 seed = 50)

chile_training <- partitions$training
chile_test <- partitions$test
```

Pretty simple, right? It took less effort to remove the rows containing at least an NA value, which we did with a `na.omit()` function. To create a `test` sample with 30% of our observations was even easier. We just called the `sparklyr` function, `sdf_partition()`, to create and store the fractions in the `partitions` object. `Seed = 50` was set to make the example, reproduced with the same values. Let us check what we learned using the following code:

```
dt_chile_ML <- chile_training %>% ml_decision_tree(vote ~ ., seed = 50)
dt_chile_pred <- sdf_predict(chile_test, dt_chile_ML)
ml_multiclass_classification_evaluator(dt_chile_pred)
# [1] 0.5965722
```

The `dt_chile_ML` object was created with the `chile_training` data used with the `ml_decision_tree` function to train our data as a tree model. Then, we created the `dt_chile_pred` object to store the prediction result from calling `sdf_predict` upon the `test` dataset. In the end, we evaluate our results by calling the `ml_multiclass_classification_evaluator()` function.

If you want to work with the H2O distributed machine learning algorithms using `sparklyr`, you'll need the `rsparkling` package, so make sure you have it installed. The initial code is the same when you are using the Spark machine learning library, so copy and paste the previous code, adding the respective `library()` commands. The codes line with the following # symbol doesn't need to be rerun unless you started a new R session:

```
library(sparklyr); library(rsparkling)
library(dplyr); library(h2o)
library(car)


#only if you started a new R session since previous codes
#sc <- spark_connect(master = 'local')
#dt_chile <- copy_to(sc, Chile, 'chile')
#dt_chile <- na.omit(dt_chile)
#partitions <- dt_chile %>% sdf_partition(training = 0.7, test = .3, seed =
50)
```

When running the codes, you may find a compatibility problem. To solve it, install the right H2O version by calling the `install.packages()` code that is shown inside the message error and restart your R session. Then create the training and a `test` object with the following code:

```
chile_training_h2o <- as_h2o_frame(sc, partitions$training,
                                   strict_version_check = FALSE)
chile_test_h2o <- as_h2o_frame(sc, partitions$test,
                               strict_version_check = FALSE)
```

The previous `as_h2o_frame` converts the Spark DataFrame into H2O frame. We set `strict_version_check` to `FALSE` to not cross-check the version. Let's train the data with H2O machine learning functions:

```
dt_chile_ML <- h2o.gbm(y = "vote", training_frame =
  as.factor(chile_training_h2o) , model_id = "ModelTree")
dt_chile_pred <- h2o.performance(dt_chile_ML, newdata =
  as.factor(chile_test_h2o))

h2o.mse(dt_chile_pred)
# [1] 0.5894832
```

The `h2o.*` package functions are responsible for training and evaluating our data. The `h2o.gbm` function is used to train a tree model; we must use numerical, categorical, or factor data, so we called our training data with the `as.factor` function, and set `model_id = "ModelTree"` because we want this training model. Furthermore, `h2o.performance` was used to see our model performance with the `test` data, also as a factor. So, `h2o.mse` was used to show the performance result. Both the Spark machine learning library and H2O Sparking Water require their own function knowledge, so you have to explore it a bit by yourself. You can start here: `https://spark.rstudio.com/`.

Providing interfaces to Spark packages

API is an acronym for application programming interfaces and you can imagine it as a user interface application, but for software instead of humans. Saying it in another way, it could be seen as a tool for your programming. When you need it to insert a nail, you call a hammer API, and if you need it to remove a nail, then you call a plier API. Spark has its own toolbox API for R, which you can access here: `https://spark.apache.org/docs/2.2.0/api/R/index.html`.

Following our explanation, extensions are customized R packages created to provide an interface to any Spark package, or the Spark toolbox. There are many extensions already available, but you also can create your own extension to call any of these Spark APIs. One extension example is the `rsparkling` package viewed in the previous section; it is the `rsparkling` package that provides an interface to the H2O machine learning algorithms.

To access the Spark API available for R, you can call these functions: `spark_context()`, `java_context()`, `hive_context()`, and `spark_session()`. You must use your `spark_connect` object as an argument. To see the methods available, please check this site: `http://spark.apache.org/docs/latest/api/scala/#package`. Select one of the four functions and check the value member methods. To call them, use the `invoke(method = "any_value_member")` function. Let's create a simple and workable example:

```
library(sparklyr)
show_version <- function(sc) {
  spark_context(sc) %>%
    invoke("version")
}

sc <- spark_connect(master = "local")
show_version(sc)
```

The preceding code creates a function called `show_version`, and requires only an object (the Spark `spark_connect` object). The function calls the `spark_context` function to provide the `"version"` method from the Spark API. If you are not connected to a Spark cluster, remove the hashtag to start one, then call our function to see what your Spark version is. There are more examples presented in the `sparklyr` documentation, which you can see at `https://spark.rstudio.com/extensions/`.

Spark DataFrames within the RStudio IDE

Another simple way to start your Spark connections and browse your datasets is with the RStudio IDE. After you've installed the `sparklyr` package, it'll appear in the top-right part of your RStudio window, close to your R environment. If you aren't connected to Spark, it'll look like the following screenshot. If you are connected, call `spark_disconnect_all()` before continuing, so we'll be on the same page:

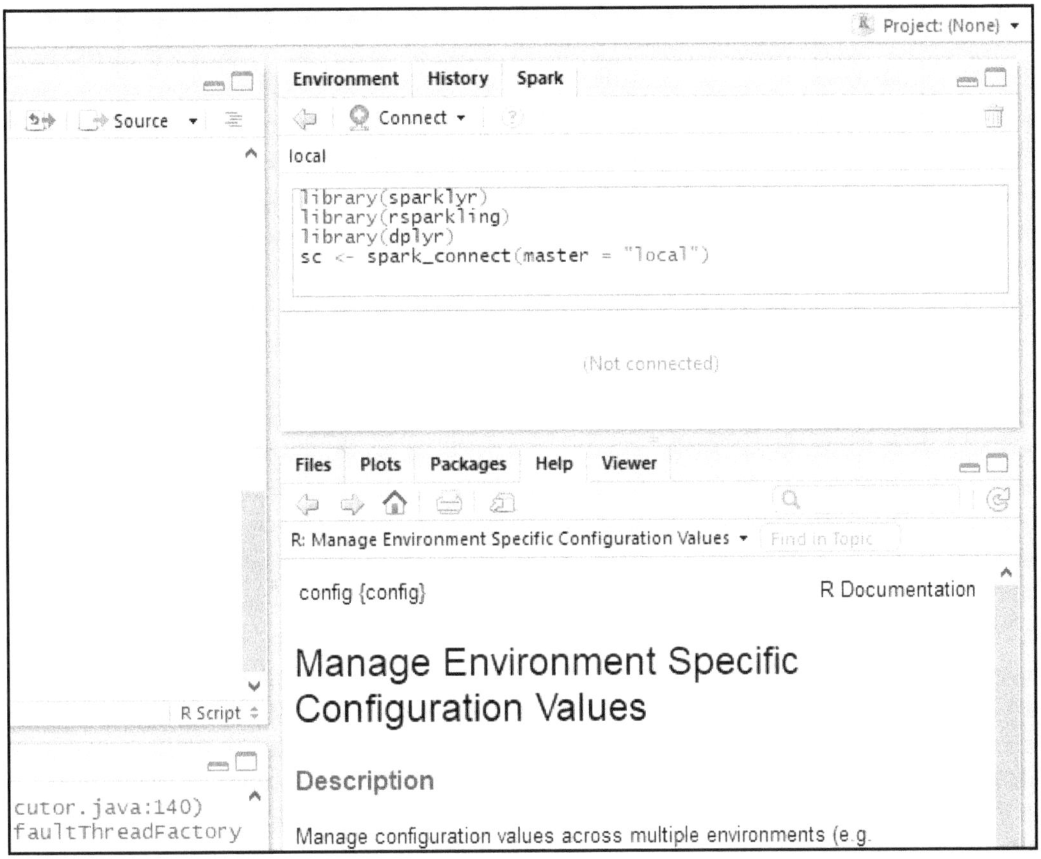

Figure 12.1: Spark shown in RStudio IDE

Click on the left arrow to see all connections, then click on the new connection button to establish a connection. A window will pop up where you can connect and manage Spark only with clicks:

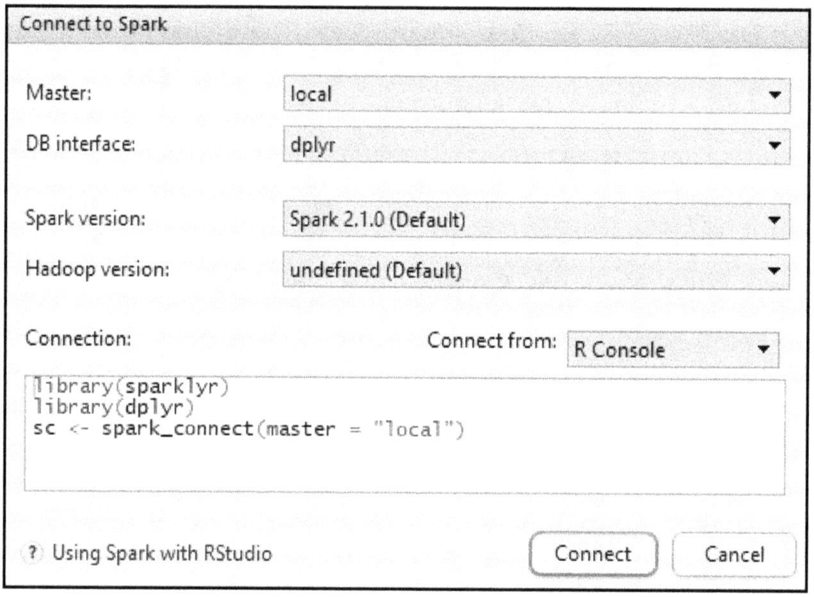

Figure 12.2: Spark connection guide from RStudio IDE

Once you upload a DataFrame into your Spark connection, you can browse it by selecting the file shown here, just as you are used to doing with your RStudio DataFrames. They will appear inside the connection IDE, shown in *Figure 12.1*.

All resources available in R can be used with Spark, it requires some extra time to learn how you can use them, more than these few pages here. Once that Spark is a great big dataset tool, if you are dealing with this kind of data, then I think the work hours are well paid. You should start by clicking on **Using Spark with RStudio** shown in *Figure 12.2*; there you will find a lot of information about it. I recommend you check the deployment examples.

Summary

In this chapter we saw the free and open source `sparklyr` package that provides an R interface to Spark and a backend to the `dplyr` package. Later, we created the `dplyr` data and SQL to manipulate Spark. We also used R to analyze Spark datasets to manipulate a table. We saw how we can use machine learning with Spark using R by Spark machine learning library and H2O Sparking Water. Later we created an extension application using Spark API and various Spark packages to browse Spark DataFrames within Rstudio IDE.

In the next chapter, we will see how we can use R on Azure Machine Learning Studio.

Quiz

1. **Quiz-tion:** Which of the following best describes sparklyr ?
    1. It is the R backend (package) for Spark
    2. It is the R backend for Spark and H2O
    3. It is a package in `tidyverse` used for Spark data analysis
2. **Quiz-tion:** How can you read a CSV file and create a Spark DataFrame ?
    1. Using `spark_create_csv`
    2. You cannot read CSV files in Spark directly
    3. Using `spark_read_csv`
3. **Quiz-tion:** What is MLlib?
    1. H2O machine learning library
    2. ML libraries in CRAN
    3. Spark machine learning library

Answers—executing the following code will give you the answers to the quiz questions:

```
set.seed(12)
round(runif(3,1,3))
```

13
R on Cloud

> *"Cloud computing is the third wave of the digital revolution."*
> *– Lowell McAdam*

Some computations, models, and analysis can be very hard to deal with through consumer grade (local) computers. Fortunately, even though the solution is rarely free, it's often inexpensive through the advent of cloud computing. Cloud computing is the paradigm that provides users with access to tailor-made (virtual) machines.

Benefiting from economies of scale, several companies are willing to provide consumers with cloud services in exchange for a fee. In addition to really understanding statistics, and knowing how to build and deliver very complicated models, mastering how to work in the cloud is a real game changer in the data science field and can lead you all the way to the big boys' league.

This chapter will give an introduction to cloud computing, using the Microsoft Azure Machine Learning Studio. We will discuss the following topics:

- Basic types of clouds
- Important aspects of clouds
- How to get started with Azure Machine Learning Studio
- R experience of clouds

Cloud computing

From my first year as an undergraduate student, there was this story a professor told us about top-notch computers taking weeks to fit a single linear regression model, back in her days as an undergrad student. I recall thinking, *It's lucky that today's computers can run it in no time*. This was naive though. As the history of computing shows, every time a faster horse is born, a more challenging track is built.

Computers have advanced a lot and so have the models—thankfully. In addition, our capacity to gather data has improved by teraflops. The first time I felt the need for cloud computing, I had designed a model so huge that I couldn't load it and the data simultaneously. It was either one or the other. Using a cloud service, this problem became manageable.

> TIP: Using distributed computing solutions, such as Hadoop and Spark, is another way out of this problem.

Speaking about a career, getting a cloud certificate and/or having some work done to show can help you through getting your first job, keeping your current one, or even getting you a promotion. The following sections deliver a brief discussion about which types of clouds there are, how data scientists use them, tips on picking a service, and what the advantages of Microsoft Azure Machine Learning Studio are.

Cloud types

What do cloud services really do? At the risk of oversimplifying, cloud services provide users with pools of shared computer resources to be operated remotely—often by the internet. This section will describe ways in which cloud services can be characterized and typical ways in which data community often uses them.

> Some cloud services are accessed through the Ethernet. These are mostly common to big companies that own one or more data centers of their own.

One very frequent way to characterize clouds is by the type of service they provide:

- **Software as a Service** (**SaaS**): Users have access to software through cloud computing. This tends to be less flexible but easier to use and understand.
- **Platform as a Service** (**PaaS**): Offers users a platform where they can develop their activities. It is very easy to master, plus it tends to be a little more flexible than SaaS.
- **Infrastructure as a Service** (**IaaS**): Usually through virtualization (virtual machines), users are granted access to computational resources. This tends to require a broader knowledge to operate but is far more flexible than any other option.

The best cloud companies available transcend the SaaS, PaaS, and IaaS classification, as they offer enough products for each of those categories. For example, Azure Machine Learning Studio could be well characterized as a PaaS, but, from them, you could also rent many E2s v3 instances, which are better labeled as IaaS.

Cloud providers can also be divided based on their nature—private, public, or hybrid. Speaking about individual cloud products, I tend to split them by what general tasks they are usually allocated for. Basically, data scientists might seek cloud services thinking about the following types of usage:

- **Store**: People are already used to cloud storage services such as Google Drive, Dropbox, and OneDrive, which are very good for storing personal files. High-level data science may require tons of data to be analyzed, but they have to be stored somewhere first. Storage clouds offer a specialized service that allows users to store huge amounts of data.

> A good example of a storage cloud used by data scientists is Amazon S3. Storing data on this type of cloud may give you the resources needed to handle big data (storage), facilitate team members to operate on the same database, and bring close the computational resources that will store and analyze data.

- **Compute**: Compute clouds are usually optimized for RAM memory, GPUs, or both. They are often required to carry out the heavy computations. Computer products tend to work well with storage ones and are a good option if either the local resources can't deal with the computations or there is a need for speed.
- **Hosting**: Eventually, computations will lead to an algorithm, an application to be deployed as a new service or with an existing one. An option is to rent clouds to host the application online (web hosting), which frequently offers auto-scaling tools that prevent you from being stuck with too few or too many servers.

Depending on how teams are arranged, a data scientist may be called to work only with one of these types or all of them at a time. If they work alone, the likelihood of working in all of them is far greater compared with the folks working in big companies, which may have specialized teams—data curators, hardcore data scientists, web developers—that will only work with only one or two of these types at the most.

> Based on usage, clouds could be split into more than three types. Nonetheless, the three-type division is both simple and very reasonable. Each of these three types could be directly associated with a verb: store, compute or host.

Each of these types of clouds comes with challenges of their own. For example, if you are storing data, you might worry about how to compress it to fit in less space while also being easy to recover, query, update, and maintain. While doing computations, you might care about efficiency and accuracy. Folks working with web hosting may be preoccupied with functionality and user experience. All of them should worry about security.

Throughout this chapter, we will explore the Microsoft Azure cloud using minimal examples. Before proceeding on to the practical stuff, let's discuss some important aspects to look for while picking a cloud.

Things to look for

How to pick a cloud? There is much to look for. The relationship between a data scientist and the cloud provider tends to be a long one, so it's better to choose carefully. Later in this chapter, we will be working with Azure, but you can pick any cloud you like. There is a three-stage process that I find very useful to decide on a cloud provider. Describing those in a few words:

- List resources
- Ask questions
- Compare prices

TIP

Even though many professionals get stuck with one cloud provider, there is no reason for you to go to the same one forever. After mastering one, jumping to the next one is very simple. Actually, the best practice would be to deploy multiple solutions over multiple providers, if you can afford to do that.

The very first things to look at are the computational resources. Does the service you are looking at offer all the resources you require? It's usually best to acquire both storage and computational power from the same place. If it does offer what you need, put the provider into a list for further consideration. Preferably, list several potential providers—this is the first stage.

For the ones that are in your list, check additional attributes. For each of the prospects, try to answer questions such as the following:

- How good is the environment they offer?
- Is it easy to work with?
- Does it work with tools that I am already familiar with?

- If not, how long will it take for me to master it? Do they offer help?
- Do they have good support? Is the service reliable?
- Is there any preconfiguration or additional features that will make your job faster or easier?

TIP

If a particular feature is essential to you, ask whether the provider offers it. Eliminatory criteria are helpful, unless they are not reasonable.

You can query any other aspect that you think is relevant. If you listed more than one provider, writing down the answers to your questions might give you a clearer understanding of how you like or dislike one provider over the others. Now that you know your preferences, it's time to price them.

Most clouds work with a pay-as-you-go format, and not knowing the prices can be costly. There is always a pricing page. Extensively research prices—this is very important. Once you are sure about prices, you have what you need to make your decision.

TIP

Clouds usually offer a type of free trial for first-time users, and this is wonderful for testing and learning. Be sure not to go over the boundaries allocated for free use, or you might be charged.

This section gave away generic tips about how to choose one cloud platform over others. Why should you stick with Azure Machine Learning Studio then? Well, a decision had to be made. I'm not sure whether you will agree with my motives, but you should definitely check them out under the next section.

Why Azure?

Over the first decades of the 2000s, competition has brought the best public clouds close enough both in terms of the products they offer and their prices. While I was writing this book, it was really hard to predict that a single public cloud would prove to be absolutely better than the others and overtake the market.

Clouds provided by Amazon (AWS), Google (GCP), and Microsoft (Azure) are all very good. Even though picking any of these would not be a mistake, this section is about to highlight the strengths of Azure while discussing why Machine Learning Studio is a good product to get yourself started with clouds.

First of all, Azure is provided by Microsoft, which means integration with a lengthy list of other products they provide. These integrated services are likely to play a very important role for medium-sized and large enterprises, usually as **Business Intelligence** (**BI**) tools.

If your business relies on Microsoft products, consider using Azure cloud. There are loads of compatibilities and synchronization tools that might help you a lot. Taking Microsoft's popularity into account, its ease of use may be a great advantage.

Being Windows-synchronizable might be a unique characteristic, but it's not the only one; compliance is another strong point. Updating data to a place where it shouldn't be can turn into a Godzilla-sized problem with huge consequences. Azure comes with many compliance certificates and attestations so that companies are more inclined to see it as a trustworthy data and application holder.

TIP: Avoid any problems. Always ask yourself whether your company, industry, or government allows data and applications to be featured in public clouds.

Counter to intuition, Azure also supports lots of open source tools besides the paid ones provided by Microsoft. You can launch a (virtual) machine set with CentOS as easy you can launch one based on Windows 10. Azure is not restricted to Windows' products at all.

All of this, combined with some other stuff I didn't mention, makes Microsoft Azure a very competitive cloud in general. Nonetheless, the current chapter won't discuss a lot of general aspects. It rather focuses on a single service called **Machine Learning Studio**.

Machine Learning Studio would be better labeled as a PaaS. Through a well-designed, intuitive platform, you can perform data science as easily as drawing diagrams. Machine Learning Studio works in a drag and drop system. With little technical knowledge and some theoretical understanding, preset operations such as load CSV, clean data, fit model, and export results can be chained together to form a whole data science work.

If you happen to know R, greater flexibility can be achieved because you can drag and drop and run R scripts there. Mastering Python is also good. Python scripts are also supported—iterating R and Python scripts is yet another option. The drag and drop interface is not only easy to use, it's responsible for the Machine Learning Studio's cool diagram layout.

Such a layout is great for a series of reasons. First, users can visualize how each stage is interacting to form the whole. Secondly, it favors organization and inspection, while allowing corrections and improvements to be deployed as fast as anything is spotted or imagined. Thirdly, this form is convenient for teamwork.

Colleagues can easily understand what has been done, take from it, and even promote discussions. Machine Learning Studio is a whiteboard where you and your team can design data science solutions with a pen and implement them as soon as you've finished drawing, by simply clicking a button.

Machine Learning Studio does support teamwork by allowing different users to work and interact across the same project within the same platform. I would not recommend it if a very sophisticated level of flexibility is required; otherwise, that is a great product both for lone workers new to data science and for experienced parties with a wide range of skills. The next section is meant to guide newcomers through the first steps into Azure.

Azure registration

From hereafter, we will be dealing directly with the Azure platform. While the current section will deal with registration, the next one will be a practical approach to Machine Learning Studio. Although I could do all of this without being charged a single penny, you could be if either the rules changed or you missed something.

If you are not confident about signing in and toying around Azure, feel free to just read the next steps and not put them into practice. We won't deal with big data and or heavy computation, so even for the full price, what this chapter will be teaching is unlikely to be expensive. On the other hand, mistakes do happen, and cloud mistakes can turn out to be uneconomical.

If you never used Azure before, that is great news. New users qualify to the free-tier usage. The free tier is not appropriate for large-scale production, but might be enough for learning and testing. Visiting the website is a good start: `https://azure.microsoft.com`.

On the home page, you can see a cool world map telling where they have data centers. If you scroll all the way down, you will see lots of renowned companies that trust Azure. At the bottom of the webpage, there is a menu where you can change language and currency on the bottom of the webpage.

If you have never joined Azure before, you can sign in for free by visiting the following link: `https://azure.microsoft.com/en-us/free/`.

Click **Start free** to begin, and then log into a Microsoft account—create one if you don't have one. To properly proceed with registration, a credit card will be needed. Don't worry; you may not be charged. Depending on the region you're in, your bank may charge a confirmation fee.

Once you sign in a Microsoft account, you can sign up for Azure. Registration is divided into four sections:

- **About you**
- **Identity verification by phone**
- **Identity verification by credit card**
- **Agreement**

As the bullet points suggest, you shall need a phone to complete the registration. The **About you** section will ask you for personal information. **Country** and **Region** is used for billing, and it may not be possible to change it later. Provide precise information and hit **Next**.

In the **Identity verification by phone** section, provide a phone number. Any phone that you have access to will do, but you insert a personal one. Choose whether to be texted or called. You will receive a call or message with the confirmation code. Make sure you got it right and click **Next**.

The third section is **Identity verification by credit card**. Azure won't charge you for this, but your bank can charge you a small fee depending on the region you're in. Additionally, be careful, because you can be charged automatically if you go over the limits set for the free tier.

TIP: If you are not willing to pay, be careful. Make sure not to go over the free-tier limits.

Last, but not least, there is the **Agreement** section. Read the terms, and if you agree with them, check the square that says that. You can also check the last square to receive offers and updates in your email.

After going through all these steps, a new user will end up with a brand-new Azure account free trial mode. The conditions for the free trial may change from time to time. By the time I was writing this chapter, a free trial came with 200,00 USD credit or one month's free experience, whichever came first.

TIP: Don't overestimate this initial credit. Costs can escalate really quickly, turning your credit into a huge debt.

Azure, like the majority of clouds, works in a pay-as-you-go system. At the end of the month, you will be automatically billed for whatever you have consumed. Save time to extensively research pricing. There are lots you could be charged for. Data transfer, data storage, pull requests, and running time are some examples.

Be cautious while working or learning in the cloud. Launching multiple instances, forgetting to terminate or pause a machine over a very long period or having your account stolen might culminate in a surprisingly expensive credit card bill. There are ways to avoid surprises and enhance security.

TIP Avoid any bad surprises by setting alarms to closely monitor costs.

The very first thing I did when I logged into my Azure account was to enroll on a live demo. By that time, the demo happened twice every Thursday. It lasted about an hour—really cool; you can send your questions and have them answered in real-time. Try to participate in one.

TIP There are lots of free contents you can learn from in Azure: live demos, webinars, tutorials, and documentation. Take advantage of those. If you don't feel like having enough, do not be afraid to contact support.

This section has provided a brief explanation regarding how to register in Azure. It also gave away some tips regarding pricing and learning. The next section is about to land some drills that are supposed to walk the reader through Azure Machine Learning Studio and teach them how to use R with it.

Azure Machine Learning Studio

Remember that you can recuse yourself from doing what this section is doing and simply pay close attention to it if you are afraid to be charged. Nonetheless, within the free trial, I was able to do the following, and even if you were charged full price, it's not likely to be expensive.

Visit the following link for more details about Azure Machine Learning Studio pricing: `https://azure.microsoft.com/en-us/pricing/details/machine-learning-studio/`.

You can check which **Free Trial** is on by logging into `https://account.azure.com` and then clicking **ACCOUNT** and subscriptions from the top menu. The following screenshot is highlighting the path:

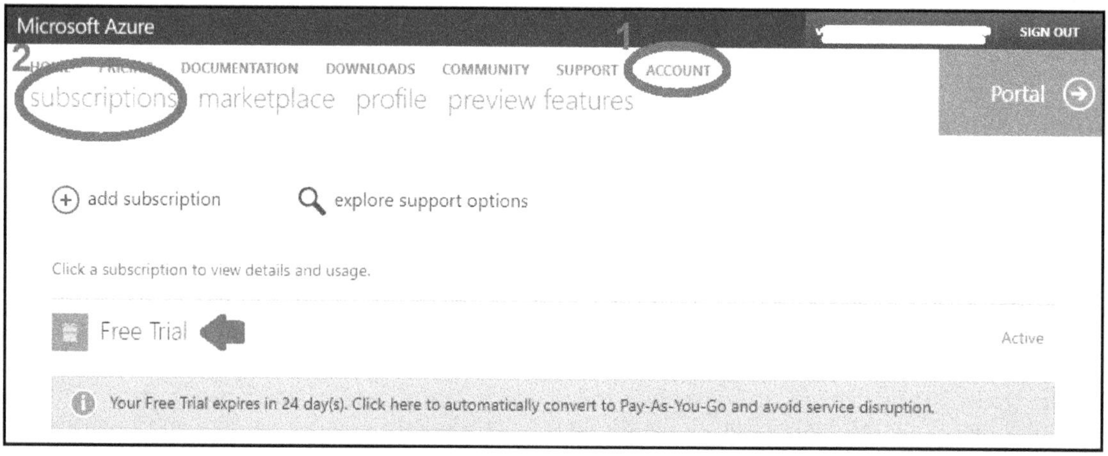

Figure 13.1: Account status

As you can see, free trial was still on with 24 days to go when I checked. The red circles show where you have to click to check it for yourself: **ACCOUNT**, **subscriptions**. Right next to **SIGN OUT** in the top-right corner, there is a blank space, and that is where the email is displayed.

The free trial can be terminated if either you go over the initial credit or the 30 days' limit, whichever is reached first.

Some billing information may be displayed if there is anything to be billed. Another way to check the billing information is by consulting the Azure portal. Access the portal through the following link: `https://portal.azure.com`.

After logging in, search for the topic **Cost Management + Billing** on the left menu, as shown in the following screenshot:

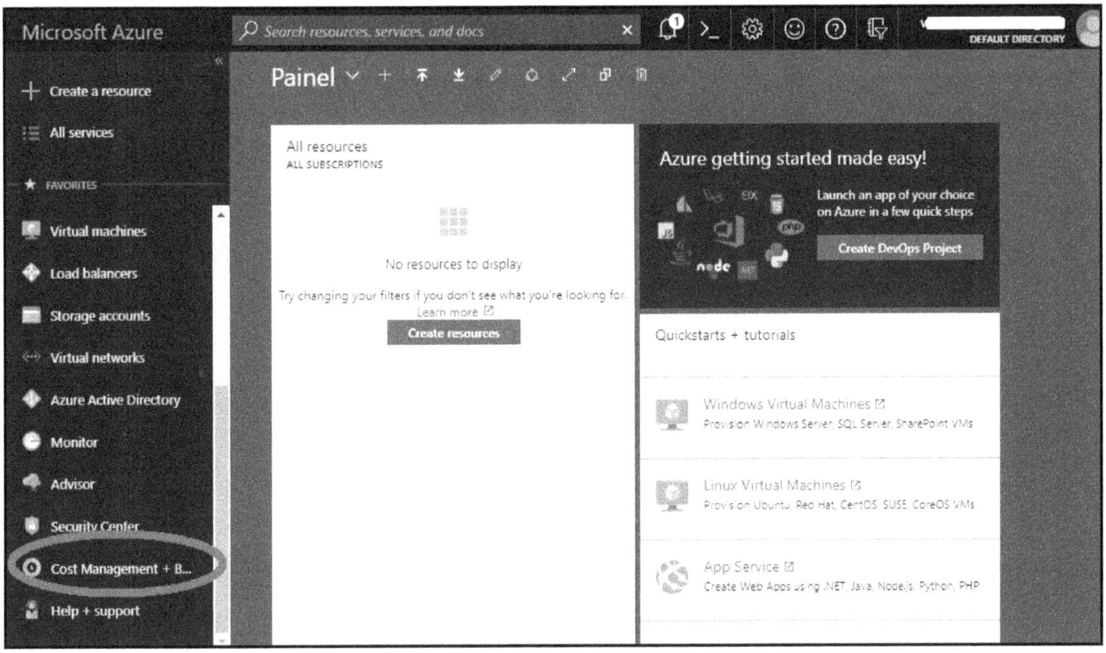

Figure 13.2: Azure portal

Azure portal displays this cool dashboard that you can modify at will—customization here is very cool. By clicking the icon circled in red (*Figure 13.2*), the user lands on a page with more detailed billing information. The following screenshot gives an example of what can be found in it:

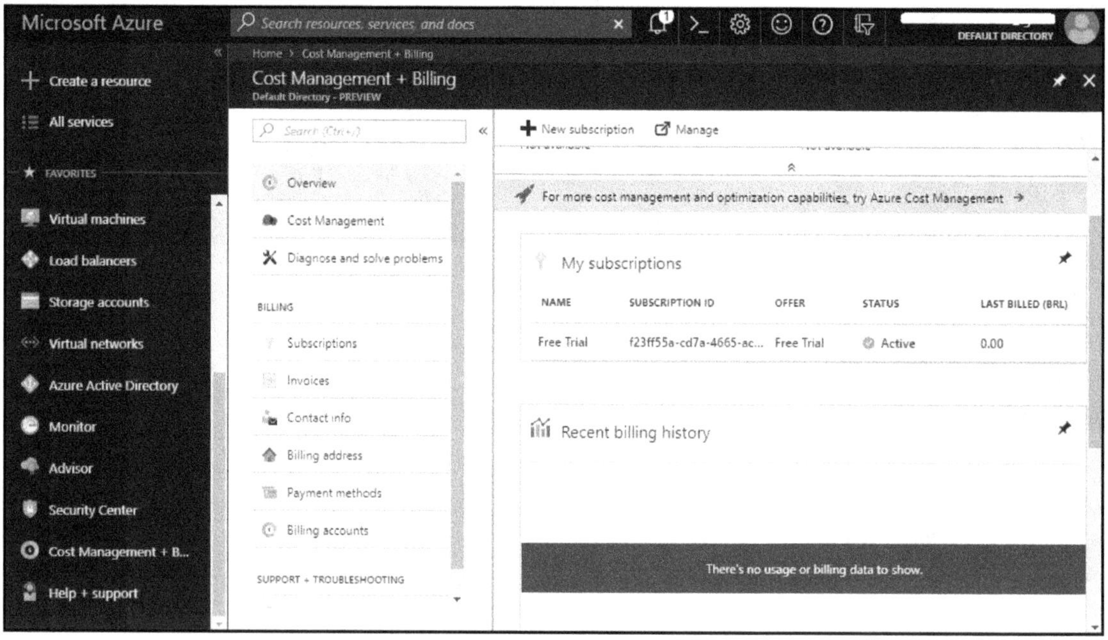

Figure 13.3: Azure portal billing tab

I was still in the free trial, so there wasn't anything to pay. Azure Machine Learning Studio can also be accessed through the Azure portal, which requires some extra steps when compared to directly accessing it through the following link: `https://studio.azureml.net`.

The home page may look like the following screenshot:

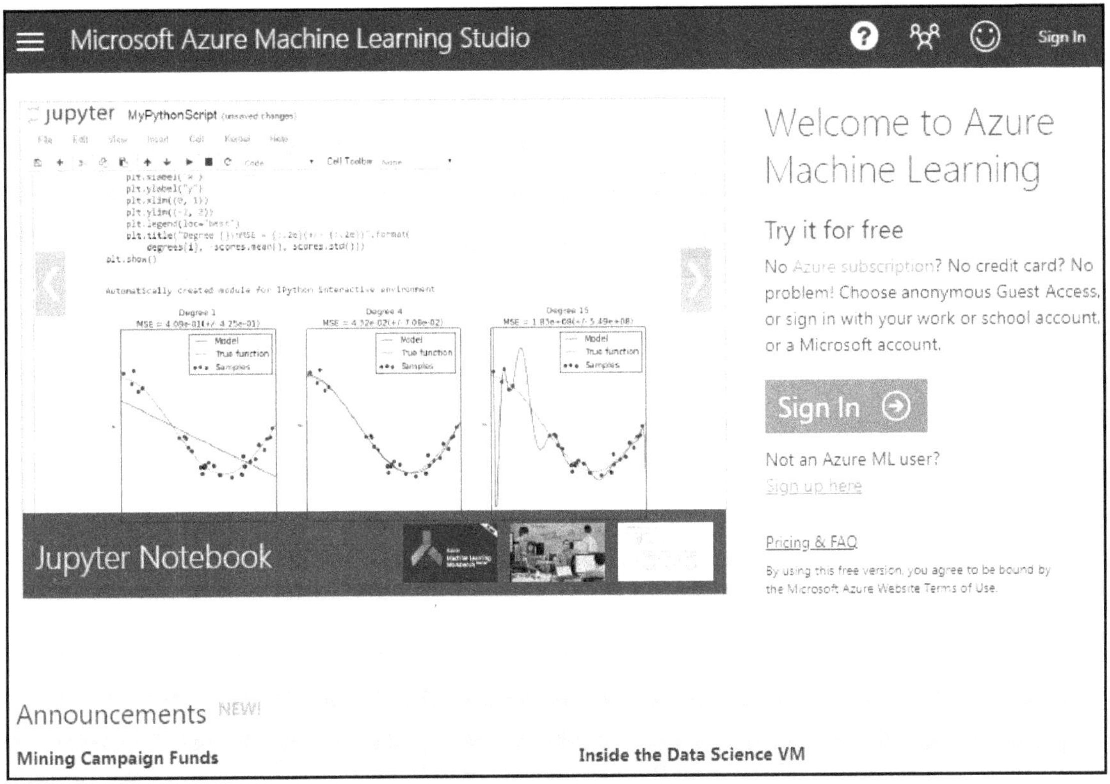

Figure 13.4: Microsoft Azure Machine Learning Studio home page

In the top-right corner, there is a **Sign In** button, click on it to reach for the platform. If you are already logged into Azure, you will be automatically taken to Azure Machine Learning Studio interface. If you are not, log in using your Azure credentials, and you will be led to the Machine Learning Studio interface.

> **TIP:** You can have daily billing reports sent to given emails. I recommend you check out the following URL: `https://docs.microsoft.com/en-us/azure/billing/`.

As soon you log into `http://studio.azureml.net`, you might see something such as this:

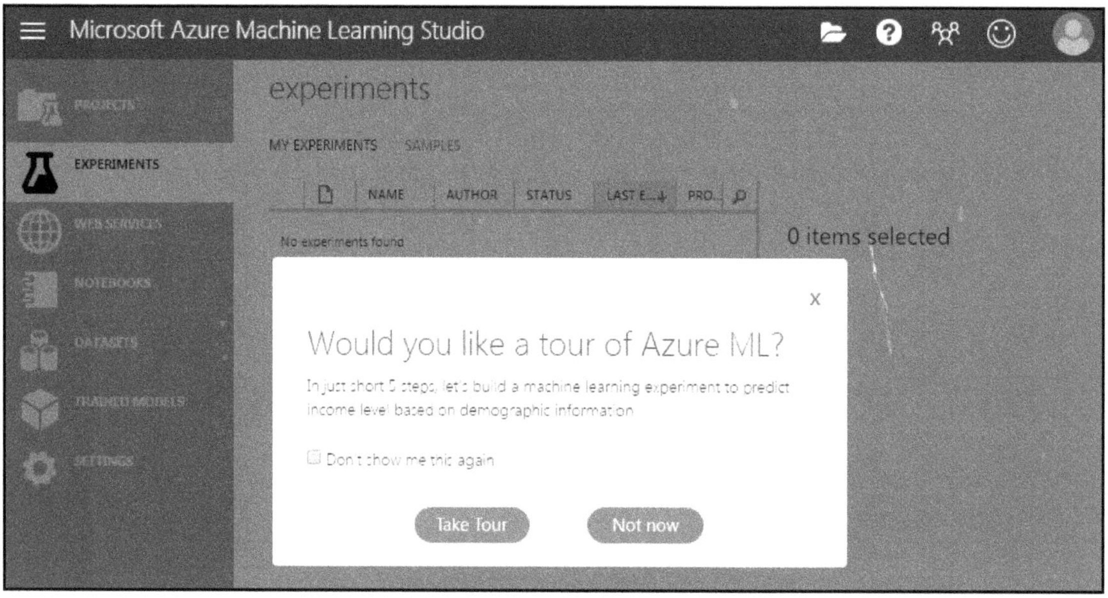

Figure 13.5: Azure Machine Learning Studio home page

By choosing **Take Tour**, the user will be guided to a brief quick-start tutorial. It will take around five minutes to complete. Take a break from reading and join the tour. You won't be introduced to R in Studio, but it will present the very same tool that this chapter will trust to deploy R code using Machine Learning Studio.

In the bottom-left corner, search for a plus sign next to the word **NEW**, written in uppercase, and select it. The following screenshot shows where to find the button:

Figure 13.6: Azure Machine Learning Studio, starting a new experiment

Clicking the singled-out icon will unleash a whole new blade with lots of options. A user can choose either to create a new **DATASET**, **MODULE**, **PROJECT**, **EXPERIMENT**, or **NOTEBOOK**. There is also an **X** button near the upper-right corner; click it to go back. This whole new blade is illustrated in the following screenshot:

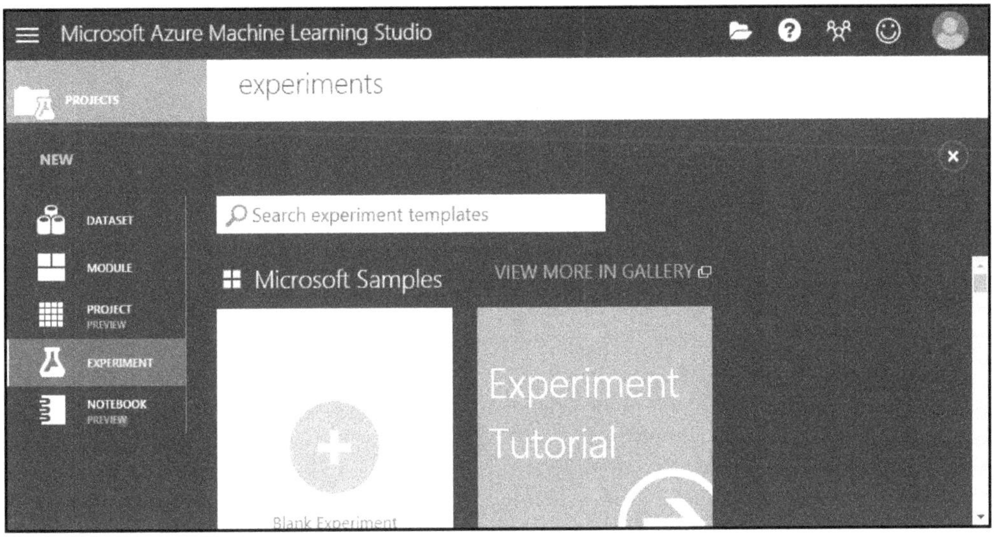

Figure 13.7: Azure Machine Learning Studio, experiment templates

As *Figure 13.7* demonstrates, to begin a new experiment, a user has to pick an experiment template. I am going with **Blank Experiment**, but, before you go on and select the same, take a quick detour and look at—only look—which other templates are available.

> Experiment templates can come from **Microsoft Samples** or **Gallery** (search for **VIEW MORE IN GALLERY**). Lots of cool templates are available, and there are some for R. They exemplify the practical tasks of data science—fraud detection, cleaning data, feature selection and creation, and so on.

After inaugurating **Blank Experiment**, you will be given a taste of the cool diagram-chart format that comes with the Azure Machine Learning Studio **Experiments**. Check the following screenshot for an example:

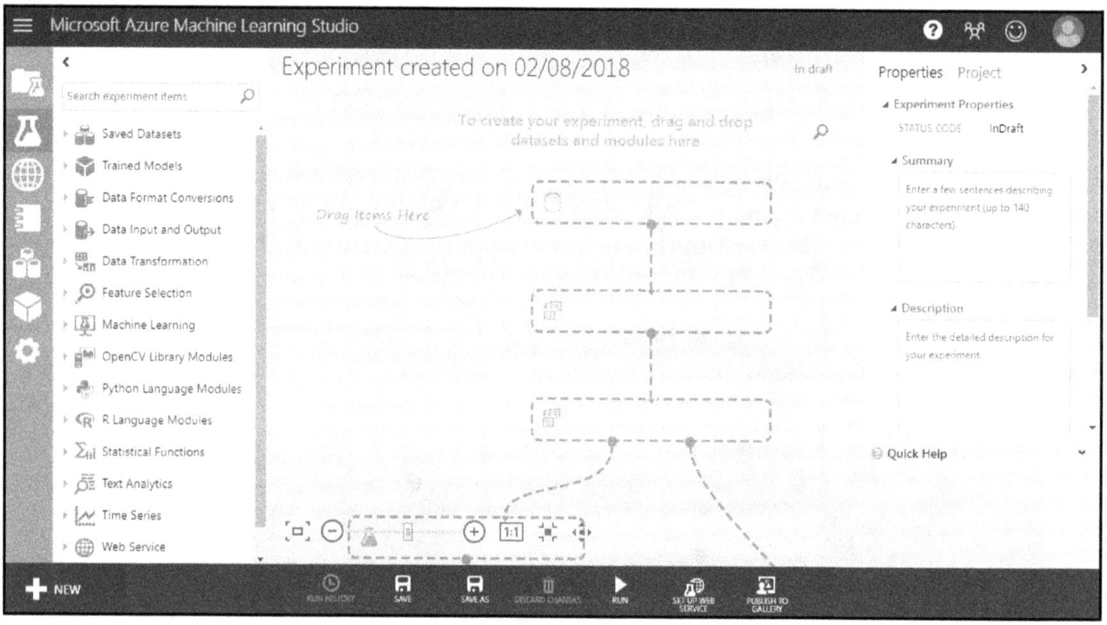

Figure 13.8: Azure Machine Learning Studio, blank experiment

Why craft wonderful visualizations for others to see and not have some cool stuff aiding us during work time? The **Experiment** interface helps data scientists to visualize the whole landscape of their work while not missing the connections between individual steps.

In *Figure 13.8*, there is a small text saying **Experiment created on 02/08/2018**. This is the experiment's title, and it can be tweaked by double-clicking and typing a new title.

On the left, there is a white blade with several topics: **Saved Datasets, Trained Models, Data Format Conversions,** and so on; there is even a topic for R language modules. Under each of these topics, there are one or more modules. **Experiments** are built by dragging, dropping, and connecting modules into the middle area.

Each module will handle one or more tasks. Some examples of tasks handled by individual modules are the following: loading data, converting data to a different type, splitting DataFrame, training models, making predictions, scoring, and evaluating models. By dropping and combining individual modules, complete data science models can be delivered.

TIP

Modules can be queried using the search bar. Look for the one near to the upper-left corner, with **Search experiments items** written in it.

On the right side (*Figure 13.8*), there is another blade. What you can do with it depends whether an active module is selected. When none is selected, a user can add descriptions about the experiment, which is a good way to document it. When a module is selected, users can change its options (parameters) if it has any.

Documenting your experiment is a good idea. Always seek the rightside blade to compose descriptions for the general experiment, or right-click a module to add comments to individual modules. Also use it to change parameters associated with individual modules.

Azure allows collaboration, and you may also want to visit your experiment later. For the sake of organization and understandability, do your best to keep objective and concise notes and comments—it pays well to do so in the long run. A particular worthwhile thing to remember with respect to Studio's **Experiments** is to know how modules work in general.

How modules work

To use a module, you have to pick one from the left-side blade and drag it inside the gray area in the middle of the window. That's not all. Each module has an output, which is supposed to either be the final product or to be fed as some other module as input.

To be strict about it, the white blade on the left side comes with both modules and datasets; nonetheless, this chapter is calling everything modules.

Except for a few, the majority of modules also need an input. Once a module is selected, it will be highlighted and you can see whether it requests one or more inputs, along with which kinds of inputs are needed, and you can also see how many outputs it has, along with each kind.

Inputs are represented by little circles on the top of the selected module. Outputs are represented by small circles on the bottom of the selected module. Details for both are shown when the mouse pointer hovers over a circle. Let's call the circles on the top of each module input circles, and the circles on the bottom will be called **output circles**. The following screenshot shows a module and its input and output-circles:

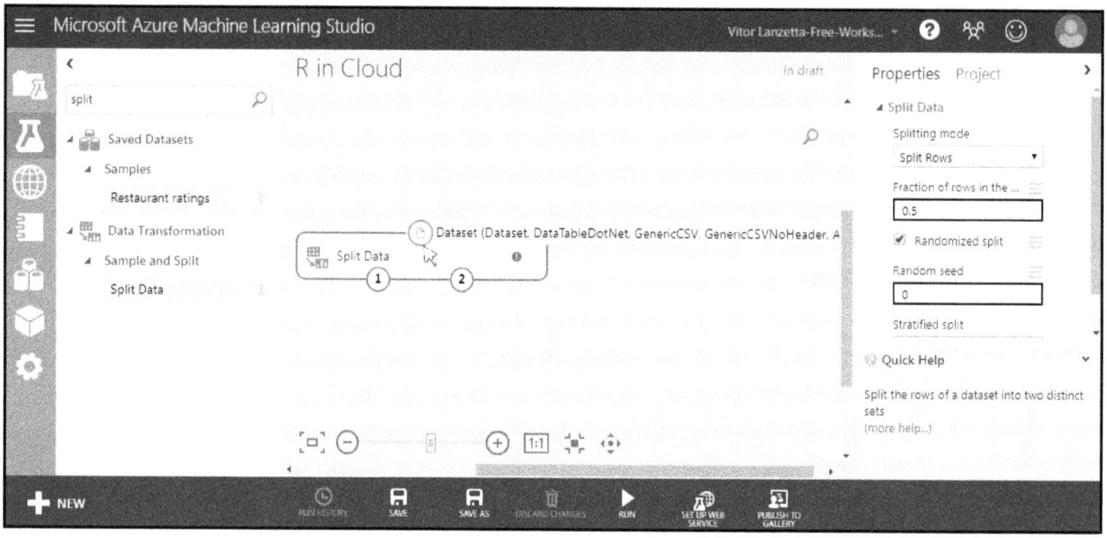

Figure 13.9: Azure Machine Learning Studio split Data module

Many things were done in *Figure 13.9*. First, the experiment was renamed to *R in Cloud*. The search bar in the left blade was used to search for **Split Data** module, which was dragged into the middle zone. Then the module was selected; it requests a single input and can have two outputs. By hovering the mouse pointer over the input circle, it showed the types of inputs accepted.

The red exclamation point inside the module indicates that it is not supplied with the input needed.

On the far right, inside the white blade, you can see the parameters related to **Split Data** module. They are **Splitting mode**, **Fraction of rows in the first output dataset**, **Random seed**, and **Stratified split**. There is even a small checkbox asking whether the split should be randomized or not.

In the end, all experiments can be described as a bunch of interrelated modules. To connect (relate) one module to another, all a user has to do is to click in the output circle of a module and drag the mouse to the output of the module you wish to connect to. Building data science models with Machine Learning Studio is as easy as that.

A module will be highlighted in red if you try to feed an input that is not allowed by it. A module will be highlighted in green if the type of input fed is acceptable.

Yet, you can make things slightly more complicated and flexible, by deploying raw codes as well. Skills in SQL, Python (both 3.x and 2.x), and R are welcome here. Let's put our knowledge of R and Machine Learning Studio together to build a complete experiment.

Building an experiment that uses R

Every meaningful data science starts with a question, a sense of purpose. What problems are you trying to solve? Who are you trying to save? What do you wish to accomplish with it? During play (learning) time, you can afford to be meaningless, since you are usually aiming at the technicalities. When playtime is over, seek meaning.

Once you have the big question, only then you reach out for data. Our goal here will be to develop a model capable of predicting whether a blood donor will donate again in a given month. For this, **Blood donation data**, made available by Microsoft Azure, will be used.

Clear some room by deleting any modules that may still be inside the experiment—select them and hit *delete* or right-click them and choose *delete*. Click inside the search bar on the left side and query **Blood donation data**. This module corresponds to a dataset, click and drag it to the grey area to start building the experiment.

Blood donation data can be also found under **Saved Datasets** | **Samples**.

Once you can see a module called **Blood donation data**, right-click it, drag and drop it into the middle area. Now the dataset is ready to be used, but, first things first, let's get started by visualizing it. Put the mouse arrow right over the dataset's output-circle, right-click it, and select **Visualize**, as shown in the following screenshot:

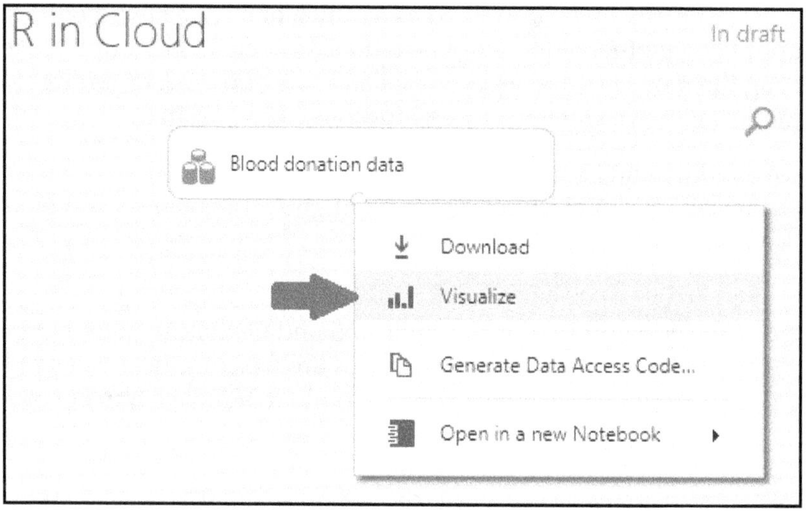

Figure 13.10: Visualizing a dataset

The first 100 rows will be displayed along with the number of rows and columns. If you happen to click a column, more information will be displayed about that variable. The following screenshot demonstrates the information displayed when the column **Recency** is selected:

Some data will require you to run the experiment before you're able to visualize it.

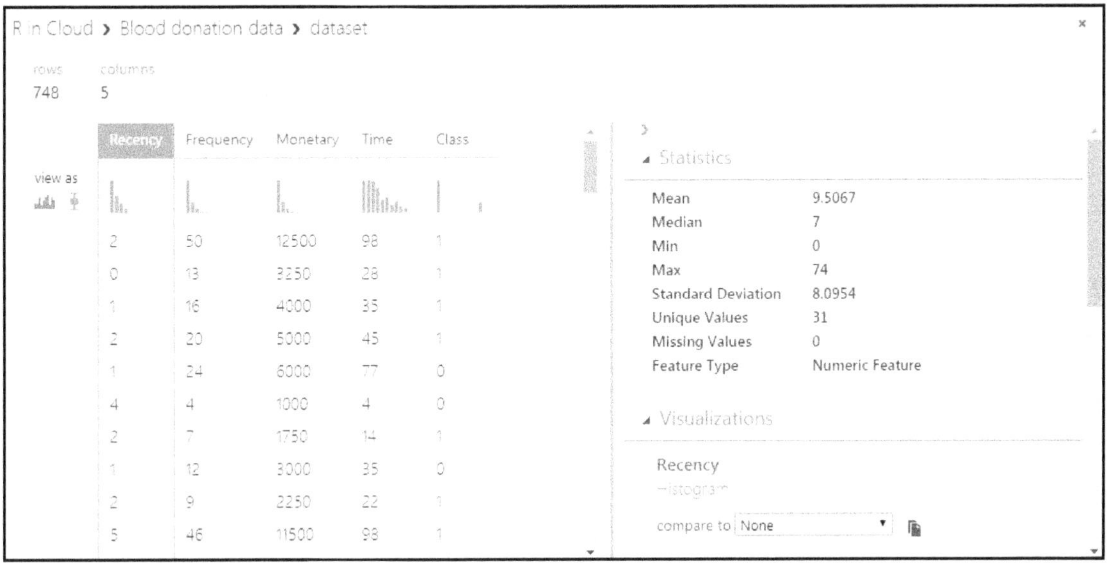

Figure 13.11: Information about the Recency variable

The **Blood donation data** module comes with 748 rows and five columns. The variables are as follows:

- **Recency**: Months since the last donation
- **Frequency**: Total number of donation
- **Monetary**: Total blood donated in cc
- **Time**: Months since the first donation
- **Class**: A binary where *one* means blood donation in March 2017 and zero means no donation

To check whether there are missing values is the least to do. Fortunately, this dataset has no missing values, so that is not something we will have to deal with. If it were, Studio has a module to handle missing values. Later, we will commit to a boosting model. Unless you feel that a principal component analysis may be needed, there is no reason for rescaling data.

The next step will be to split the data (training and test):

1. Search for the **Split Data** module on the left-side blade (**Data Transformation** | **Sample and Split**)
2. Drag it to the middle area, preferably under the **Blood donation data** module
3. Connect the output of **Blood donation data** to the input of the **Split Data** module

When you click the **Split Data** module, a set of options regarding this module might appear on the right side (**Propeties** pane); if they don't, search for the small arrow pointing left on the top-right corner right below the icon you click to **SIGN OUT** and click it. The following screenshot shows what it looks like:

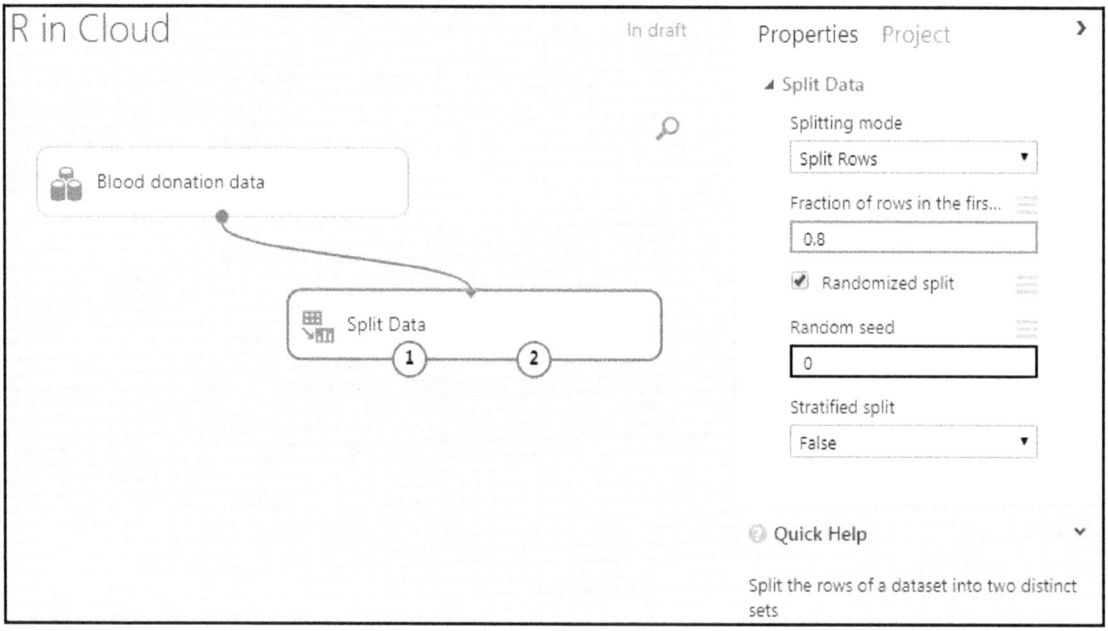

Figure 13.12: Split Data options

For the second option, a fraction of rows in the first output dataset, the default value is `0.5`, which means data is split *50/50*. Change this to `0.8` so that the data will be split *80/20*. The 80% of the dataset delivered by output will be later used for training; the other 20% handled by output will act during evaluation.

Training data can be handed to a module called **Train Model**:

1. Search for the **Train Model** module on the left-side pallette (**Machine Learning** | **Train Model**)
2. Drag and drop it into the central area
3. Connect the **Split Data** first output to the **Train Model** second input

The **Train Model** module will display an alert, a white exclamation point within a red circle. To properly function, the label column (some will recognize it as the target variable) must be pointed. Select the module. On the right side where the split rate was previously adjusted, **Train Model** will display an option for the label column. Hit the **Launch column selector** button to pick the label.

All the variables but the one chosen as the label will be considered features by the module. Our target here will be the binary variable called `Class`. Start typing `Class`, and soon this variable is displayed; pick it (as shown in the following screenshot) and click the check mark at the bottom-right corner:

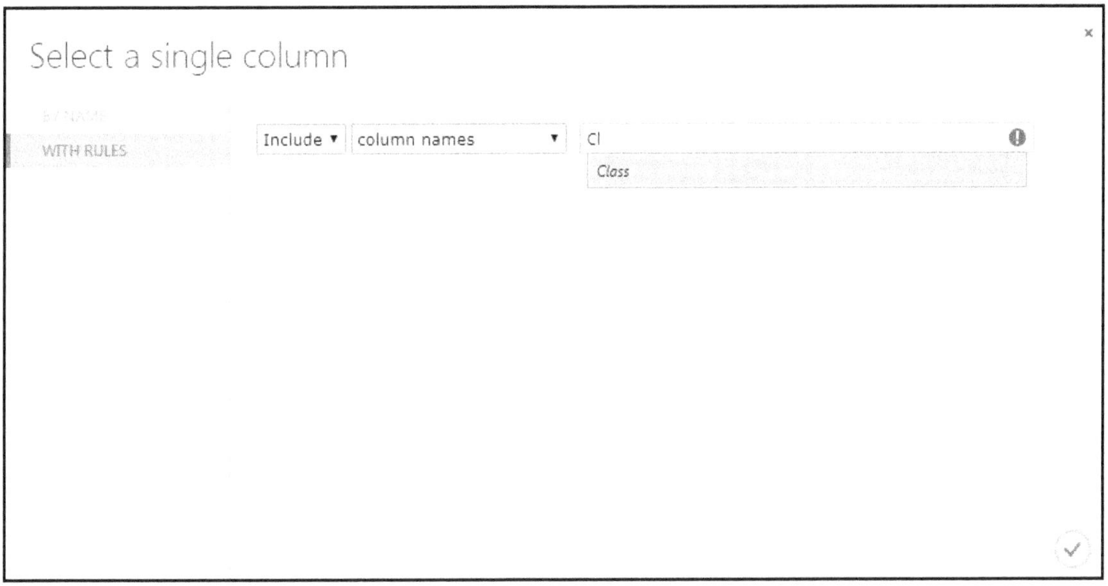

Figure 13.13: Selecting the label column

Even after the selecting the label column, the alert doesn't go away. **Train Model** needs another input. We're going for an R model:

1. Search for the module **Create R Model** on the left side (R language modules
2. Drag it to the central area
3. Connect the output of **Create R Model** to the first input of **Train Model**

In the **Properties** pane, the module **Create R Model** comes with two scripts: **Trainer R script** and **Scorer R script**. There is where the code must be deployed. **Trainer R script** is inputted with the dataset, the same one inputted into the related **Train Model** module, and must generate a proper model to be stored in a variable named `model`.

Detailed information on individual modules can be found in Azure's documentation. For example, detailed info about **Create R Model** can be found at `https://docs.microsoft.com/en-us/azure/machine-learning/studio-module-reference/create-r-model`.

The **Scorer R script** understands the variables, dataset and model. Its goal is to compute scores for the corresponding model while storing it in a variable called *scores*. Let's start with **Trainer R script**. Select the **Create R Model** module, and then click on the small stacked-windows icon right next to **Trainer R script** to open the editor, as shown here:

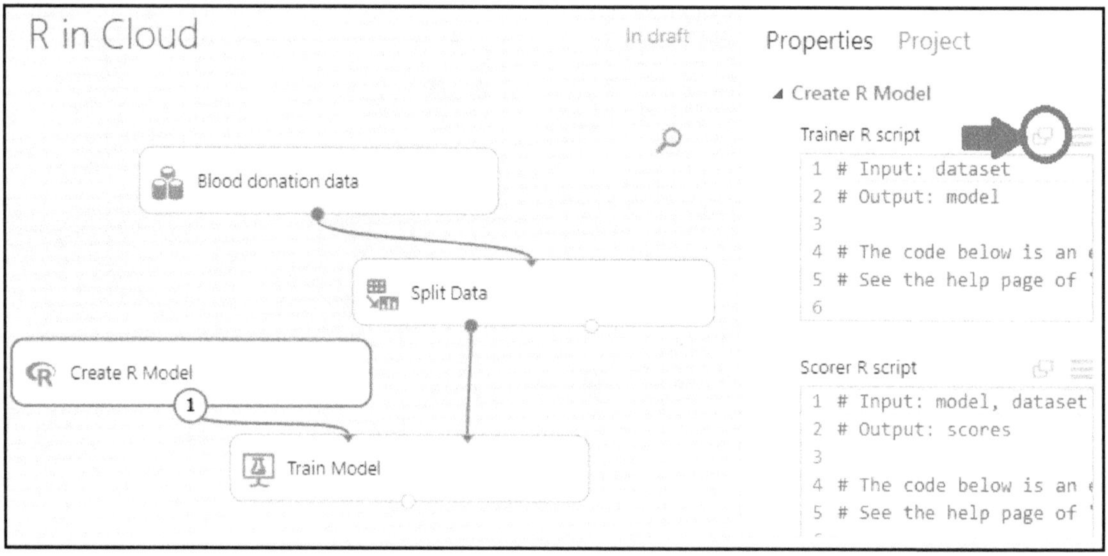

Figure 13.14: Opening the Trainer R script editor

After clicking the icon next to **Trainer R script**, a new window will pop up, where the R model can be designed. It comes with a sample code such as the following:

```
# Input: dataset
# Output: model

# The code below is an example which can be replaced with your own code.
# See the help page of "Create R Model" module for the list of predefined
functions and constants.

library(e1071)
features <- get.feature.columns(dataset)
labels <- as.factor(get.label.column(dataset))
train.data <- data.frame(features, labels)
```

```
feature.names <- get.feature.column.names(dataset)
names(train.data) <- c(feature.names, "Class")
model <- naiveBayes(Class ~ ., train.data)
```

First of all, it starts by loading the `e1071` package. Not all packages are supported by Machine Learning Studio. The following link contains all the supported ones: `https://docs.microsoft.com/en-us/azure/machine-learning/studio-module-reference/r-packages-supported-by-azure-machine-learning`.

There is a number of reasons for a package to not be supported, it goes from Java dependency, incompatibilities between package binaries and the sandbox environment to the requirement of direct internet access. The sample code is using a bunch of functions that are typical for Machine Learning Studio.

Recall that the module **Train Model** can distinguish labels (**Y**) from features (**X**) given that we selected the label column (**Class**); also, keep in mind that dataset is the variable name given to the actual data inputted to **Train Model**. Here is the explanation for some of the functions from the sample code:

- `get.feature.columns(dataset)` gets the columns from the dataset that are supposed to act as features
- `as.factor(get.label.column(dataset)` gets the column that is supposed to be a label (or target) from the dataset and makes sure its type is `factor`
- `get.feature.column.names(dataset)` gets the names from the columns that display features

Except for `as.factor()`, all these functions are particular to Machine Learning Studio and work very well in conjunction with **Train Model**. There are other ways of loading and arranging data, but the way the sample code did is actually very good and tends to avoid problems.

The last line is fitting a Naive Bayes model from the `e1071` package and storing it in a variable called `model`. This explains pretty much how **Trainer R script** is supposed to work: take `data` coming from `dataset`, handle it, and use it to fit a compatible model that must be stored in a variable named `model`.

Adapt the sample code so that it looks like the following:

```
library(gbm)
set.seed(13)
model <- gbm(formula = Class ~ .,
    data = dataset,
    distribution = 'bernoulli',
    n.trees = 3*10^4)
```

The drill that comes with the sample code is actually very good, but I prefer to stick with simplicity. You can use hashtags to document the code as well. The `model` variable is now storing a generalized boosted regression model fitted with over 30,000 trees. After running the modifications, again hit the check mark near the bottom-right corner.

It's time to adjust the **Scorer R script**. Click the icon right next to the words **Scorer R script**. The following is the code that comes by default:

```
# Input: model, dataset
# Output: scores

# The code below is an example which can be replaced with your own code.
# See the help page of "Create R Model" module for the list of predefined
functions and constants.

library(e1071)
probabilities <- predict(model, dataset, type="raw")[,2]
classes <- as.factor(as.numeric(probabilities >= 0.5))
scores <- data.frame(classes, probabilities)
```

The **Scorer R script** takes the variables `model`, from **Trainer R script**, and `dataset`, the one that will be later inputted into **Score Model** module, and must output a DataFrame named `scores`. Such a variable, as we will see later, will tag along with the dataset inputted to the **Score Model** module and is expected to bring the predicted values, but it could bring anything really.

> **TIP:** Be extra cautious while designing an **Scorer R script**. As almost anything can go through the score variable, and it is not that uncommon to mistake fails for wins.

Adapting the sample code for the `gbm` model, here is my suggestion:

```
library(gbm)
probabilities <- predict.gbm(model,
    newdata = dataset,
    n.trees = 3*10^4,
    type = 'response')
class <- as.factor(as.numeric(probabilities >= 0.5))
scores <- data.frame(Predicted = class, Probabilities = probabilities)
```

The preceding code uses the previously defined model to bear predictions. First, it scores the individual probability of a donor coming back, represented by the number *one*. Using a threshold of 50%, the actual class of an individual is also scored. Both `class` and `probabilities` are then gathered in a DataFrame named `scores`.

Scorers are meant to work with a specific module, the **Score Model** module, that is the one to set next:

1. In the modules menu (left-side menu), query for **Score Model** (it will be under **Machine Learning** | **Score Model**)
2. Drag and drop it in the center, preferably somewhere under the **Train Model**
3. Connect the output of **Train Model** to the first input of **Score Model**
4. Connect the second output from **Split Data** to the second input of **Score Model**

Done. Our experiment is loading the **Blood donation data**, splitting it into train and test (80/20), selecting the **Class** column as the label (target), training a model using the R `gbm` package, and scoring it through the test set. After connecting the dots and setting the parameters, the following screenshot shows how my experiment ended up looking:

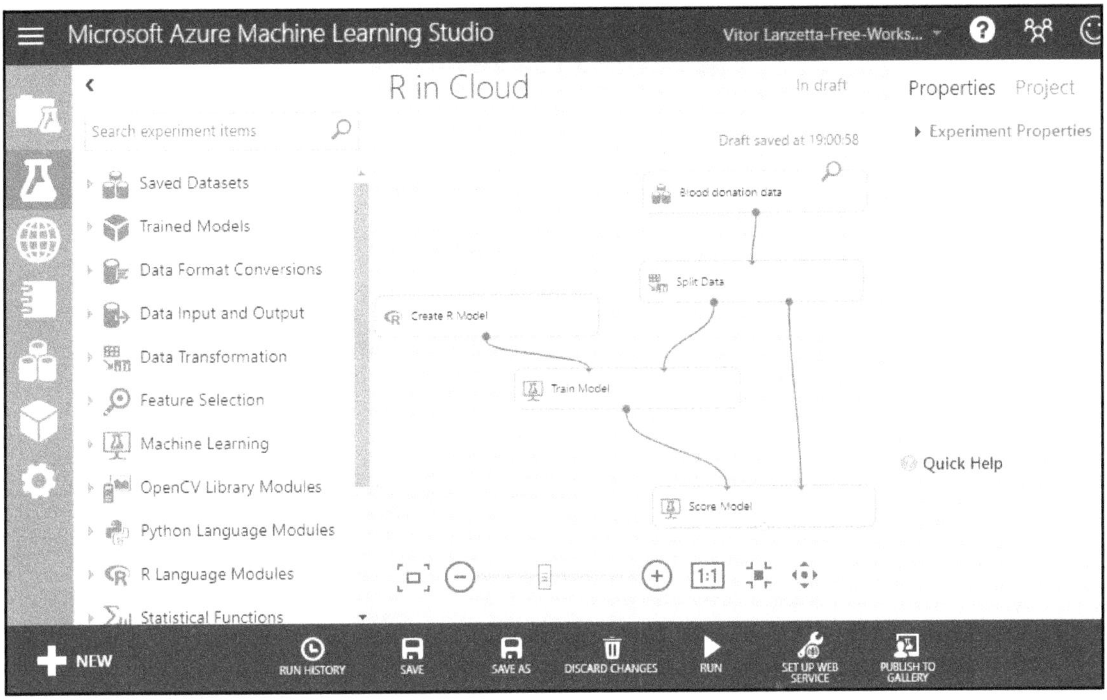

Figure 13.15: Azure Machine Learning Studio, experimental draft

We're not finished yet, but for an instance look for the **RUN** button in the bottom menu, hit it. You can run your experiment at any stage. A clock will sign modules in the query. Modules successfully processed will be marked with a green check sign. Failures will be marked with a red **X**.

Check whether everything ran OK. Right-click the output circle of **Score Model** module and select visualize to retrieve the predictions made with the test dataset. The result might look very similar to *Figure 13.16*, and predicted values are addressed to the **Predicted** column, while the **Probabilities** column is displaying each (estimated) probability:

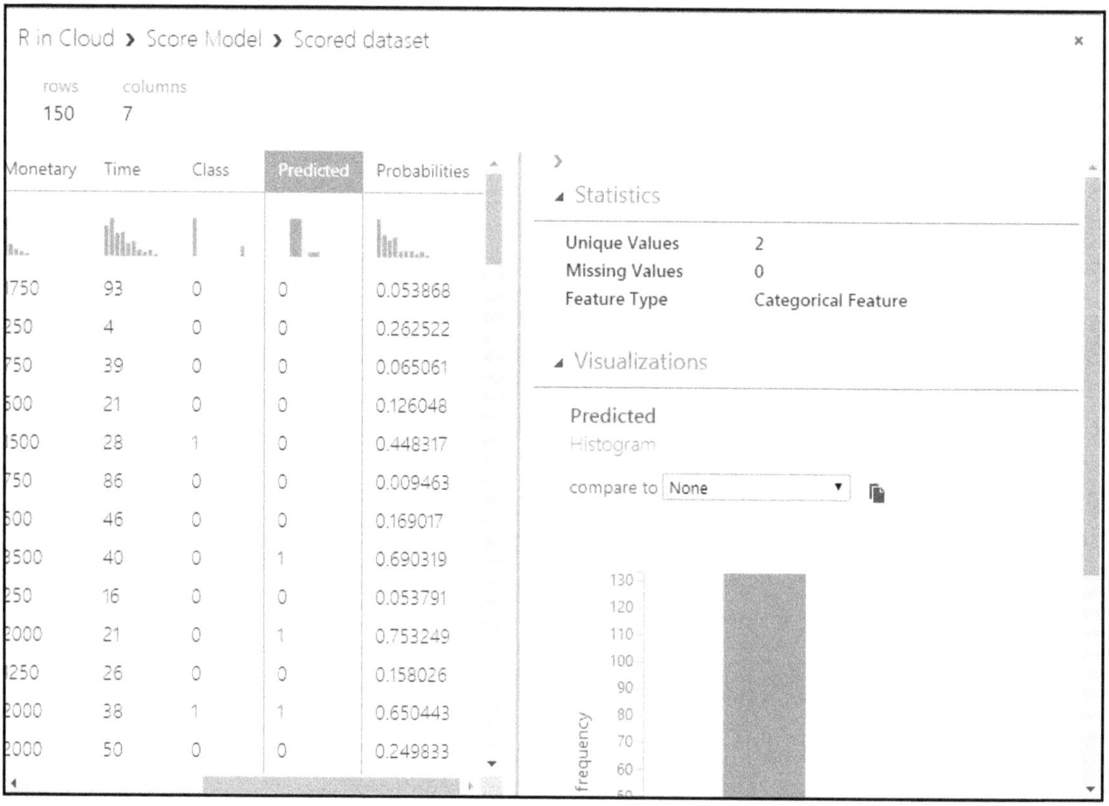

Figure 13.16: Predicted values for the test set

Usually, a module called **Evaluate Model** would come after **Score Model,** but, at the time of writing, the former wouldn't easily work with models designed by **Create R Model**. A solution would be to have the **Execute R Script** module in between **Score Model** and **Evaluate Model**. Instead, I prefer to demand and output the evaluation under **Execute R Script** itself, thus overcoming the need for the **Evaluate Model** module:

1. Search for **Execute R Script** under the menu on the left (R language modules)
2. Drag it into the central area, preferably under **Score Model**
3. Connect the output of **Score Model** to the first input (starting on the left) of **Execute R Script**

We have almost finished. The reason the output of **Score Model** must be connected to **Execute R Script** first input (from the left to the right) is that the code used assumes such a thing. Here is the code that I used to compute the hit rate for the test set:

```
test_set <- maml.mapInputPort(1)

hit_rate <- mean(test_set$Class == test_set$Predicted)
hit_rate <- data.frame(hit_rate)

maml.mapOutputPort("hit_rate");
```

After selecting the **Execute R Script** module in the experiment area, click the small **stacked-windows** icon right next to R script to modify the code. After running the experiment, the hit rate will be expressed as a dataset, which can be visualized by right-clicking the first output circle (starting on the left) of **Execute R Script**.

If all went well, the output of the sample hit rate should be around 84%. From there, you may want to deploy a few modifications to make an application out of it or to modify some of the parameters to improve the result. The following screenshot shows how my final diagram looked by the time I had finished with it:

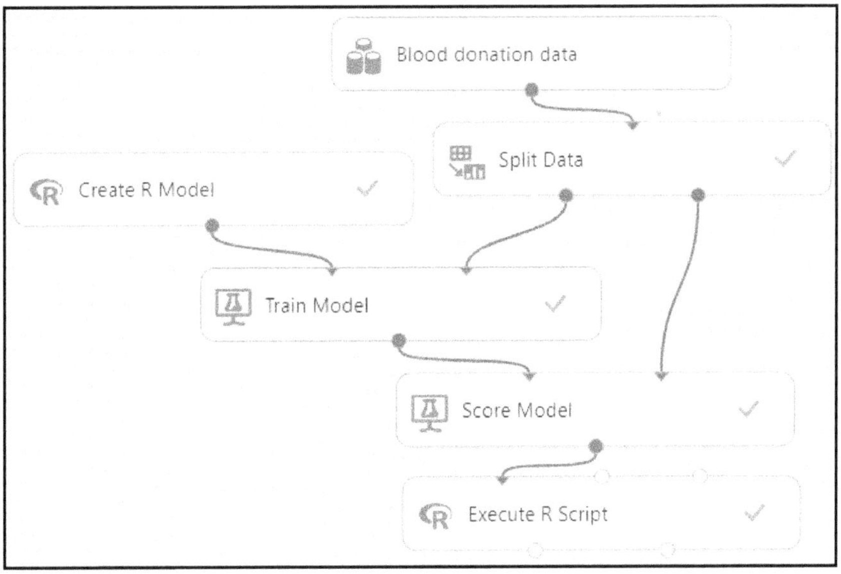

Figure 13.17: Experiment's final result

Simply saving the model is another option. It's important to highlight that the third input of **Execute R Script** takes files in the `.zip` format. This allows users to do lots of stuff, such as bringing more data, other R scripts, and even loading entire packages, although not every package is sure to be compatible with Azure Machine Learning Studio.

This section introduced a very minimal example especially drawn to walk the reader through R models in Azure Machine Learning Studio. There are two things I wish to emphasize: one, there is much more to learn about it—this small exercise was only meant to get you in touch with R in the Azure Machine Learning Studio. Two, such a platform was designed to deal with more complex problems, and gracefully enables teams to work very well together.

Before closing up this chapter with a quiz, I have some cloud-related tips to share.

First, try a small-scale local version of what you going to do in the cloud before actually performing any cloud operations. By trying them, you may anticipate problems that would only be noted on the fly; while local errors may only cost you time, cloud errors might cost time and money.

Second, always seek efficiency. Is the preprocessed data larger than the processed data? If the answer is yes, kindly consider preprocessing the data locally and only uploading it afterward. Being inefficient is costly both in the clouds and locally, but acting so in the former is more likely to lead you to bankruptcy.

Third, defensive programming. Notably, when the final goal is an application, being ready to deal with unwanted data types and exceptions pays off. Also, defensively programming combined with extensive documentation might prevent colleagues and you from making big mistakes, even if the final result is not an application.

Despite the fact that cloud computing is more challenging than local computing, it's a real thing, and knowing how to do it right is a game changer. Embrace the challenge.

Summary

In this chapter, we learned what cloud computing is and what cloud services do. We also saw which factors need to be checked before picking a cloud service. This chapter discussed the different cloud companies and the advantages of selecting Azure as our cloud service provider.

Some services provided by Azure were briefly introduced. The reader also saw a detailed process of registration. We learned about the Azure Machine Learning Studio and how it works, by implementing a modules work. We then moved to using R in the cloud. **Blood donation data**, Azure's built-in dataset, was adopted for our experimental purpose.

In the next chapter, we will discuss the paths in data-science career, ways to seek help and to improve your skills.

Quiz

- **Quiz-tion 1**: Formally, clouds are usually split into three different types, which of the following is not one of these types?
    1. IaaS: Infrastructure as a Service
    2. PaaS: Platform as a Service
    3. CaaS: Code as a Service
    4. SaaS: Software as a Service

- **Quiz-tion 2**: Which of the following modules can be directly used to code using R in Azure Machine Learning Studio?
    1. **Split Data**
    2. **Execute R Script**
    3. **Execute Python**
    4. **Blood donation data**

Answers—executing the following code will give you the answers to the quiz questions:

```
set.seed(13)
round(runif(2,1,4))
```

The Road Ahead

What's next? Which steps should a data science aspirant take next? You could hardly claim that there is only a single path to follow; nonetheless, some practices have proven to do good. This appendix's goal is to give away some helpful advice, guiding beginners into the next stages by aiding them through career decisions, growing new skills, and improving the skills they might already have developed.

Here is what we shall discuss in this appendix:

- Careers in data science
- Gathering data to practice with

Growing your skills

First of all, being a data scientist can mean a lot of things. There are several roles that data people can fit themselves into. For instance, you could grow a narrow and specialized set of skills so that you would mostly craft (wonderful) visualizations, as would an artist, or only handle and maintain datasets as a data curator, or mainly design and deploy very complicated models as a core data scientist.

The bigger the company, the more likely the data scientists are to be divided into specialized teams.

On the other hand, you can grow a very broad skillset and turn into a kind of full-stack data scientist. Each career path will request specific abilities and skills while coming with distinct challenges, rewards, and risks. Yes, *risks*. For example, a core data scientist in a small company may be replaced by H2O's Driverless AI; as ironic as it sounds—a visualization person in a top-grade magazine will hardly be replaced by software.

If you have read the whole book, you may have already figured out what you like the most, in other words, which role you would be most pleased to fill. Once you have decided, do a little research and discover what it's like to fill that role. Try to talk to people who are currently employed, but if you can't, I am sure Google and YouTube might help you with any questions.

What kind of companies are hiring for role A? What is the daily work like? How much could I expect to make? Ask yourself whether the career feels right for you. If not, research alternative career paths; otherwise, start planning from there. Even if you happen to hold all the skills needed but have zero or very little to show for it, it's time to get some practice and hopefully build a portfolio. The next step is looking out for data.

Gathering data

Gathering data is a must when practice time comes. Web scraping is a possibility. Doing it is both a way to get data and a way to tune-up your code skills meanwhile. You might be lead into mastering packages such as `rvest`; if you do so, you must likely improve your coding skills only by doing so. Also, web scraping goes along with knowledge of HTML, HTTP, and more, so, look for it if you are willing to cultivate a broader set of skills.

> **BEWARE!** Scraping the web is not always legally safe. Make sure that you're not breaking any laws or else doing something harmful with the information you scrapped.

If you are not into it, there is no need to go that far. Some R packages come with lots of datasets you can use. There is a web page that summarizes lots of them: `https://vincentarelbundock.github.io/Rdatasets/datasets.html`.

The web page, Vicent Arel-Bundock's repository, disposes of several useful pieces of information for every dataset. There, you will find the dataset name and the name of the package holding it, as well as the number of columns, rows, and available data types. Based on this kind of information, you can decide upon a data frame to use and download it directly from there, or load it using the related library:

Package	Item	Title	Rows	Cols	has_logical	has_binary	has_numeric	has_character	CSV	Doc
boot	acme	Monthly Excess Returns	60	3	FALSE	FALSE	TRUE	TRUE	CSV	DOC
boot	aids	Delay in AIDS Reporting in England and Wales	570	6	FALSE	TRUE	TRUE	FALSE	CSV	DOC
boot	aircondit	Failures of Air-conditioning Equipment	12	1	FALSE	FALSE	TRUE	FALSE	CSV	DOC
boot	aircondit7	Failures of Air-conditioning Equipment	24	1	FALSE	FALSE	TRUE	FALSE	CSV	DOC
boot	amis	Car Speeding and Warning Signs	8437	4	FALSE	TRUE	TRUE	FALSE	CSV	DOC
boot	aml	Remission Times for Acute Myelogenous Leukaemia	23	3	FALSE	TRUE	TRUE	FALSE	CSV	DOC
boot	beaver	Beaver Body Temperature Data	100	4	FALSE	TRUE	TRUE	FALSE	CSV	DOC
boot	bigcity	Population of U.S. Cities	49	2	FALSE	FALSE	TRUE	FALSE	CSV	DOC
boot	brambles	Spatial Location of Bramble Canes	823	3	FALSE	FALSE	TRUE	FALSE	CSV	DOC
boot	breslow	Smoking Deaths Among Doctors	10	5	FALSE	TRUE	TRUE	FALSE	CSV	DOC
boot	calcium	Calcium Uptake Data	27	2	FALSE	FALSE	TRUE	FALSE	CSV	DOC
boot	cane	Sugar-cane Disease Data	180	5	FALSE	FALSE	TRUE	FALSE	CSV	DOC
boot	capability	Simulated Manufacturing Process Data	75	1	FALSE	FALSE	TRUE	FALSE	CSV	DOC
boot	catsM	Weight Data for Domestic Cats	97	3	FALSE	FALSE	TRUE	FALSE	CSV	DOC
boot	cav	Position of Muscle Caveolae	138	2	FALSE	FALSE	TRUE	FALSE	CSV	DOC
boot	cd4	CD4 Counts for HIV-Positive Patients	20	2	FALSE	FALSE	TRUE	FALSE	CSV	DOC
boot	cd4.nested	Nested Bootstrap of cd4 data	999	2	FALSE	FALSE	TRUE	FALSE	CSV	DOC
boot	channing	Channing House Data	462	5	FALSE	TRUE	TRUE	FALSE	CSV	DOC

Vicent's repository

Loading a data frame directly from a package, which obviously can be downloaded using `install.packages()`, is time-saving. Of course, going into all the trouble of loading data from a file tends to be more realistic than doing it through a package, but sometimes saving time is just what you need. Speaking for myself, I tend to visit Vincent's repository when I just want to practice visualizations and nothing else.

TIP

If you have access to primary data, you can also build your own dataset and possibly make a living out of it.

If your idea is to browse data based on field/category, the UCI Machine Learning Repository is a good call: `https://archive.ics.uci.edu/ml/index.php`.

The repository *is a collection, domain theories, and data generators,* as the website defines it. Besides the data itself, readers might also find a brief description along with tips about how to use it, which algorithms to deploy, or which variable to predict; thus, you may not only have data but also an objective.

TIP

If you happen to own a dataset, you can donate it to the UCI Machine Learning Repository.

As the name suggests, the UCI Machine Learning Repository is optimal if you want to try machine- learning models. The home page displays the later datasets to come on board and the most popular ones. You can also click **View ALL Data Sets** to browse for more, or you can use the search bar:

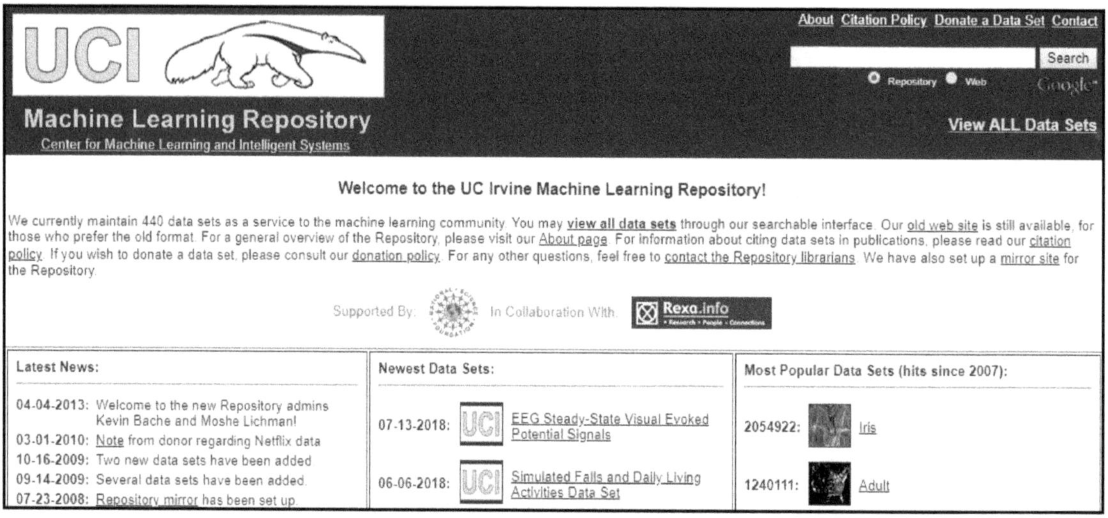

UCI Machine Learning Repository

Datasets can be also browsed by category. Be advised that you can use the dataset differently than what it is suggested for—set another target, test an alternative algorithm—but it feels nice to have an objective, doesn't it? Having a clear goal, plus being benchmarked while sometimes competing for money prizes might be a lot better—meet Kaggle: `https://www.kaggle.com`.

Kaggle is not exactly a data repository, but you can say that it has a data repository embedded in it. Mainly, Kaggle hosts data-driven competitions. They give the rules: a train and a test set. Using the train set, competitors have to fit a model to predict the targets for the test set.

> **TIP:** Couldn't find the data you were looking for? Try `reddit.com/r/data`, and ask users for help.

Sometimes, competitions will be featured by real companies trying to solve real problems and usually offering money prizes. It's quite a feat to score money in competitions such as that, but scoring high enough is likely to culminate in a job offer. From the companies' perspective, Kaggle is a storefront for data scientists.

Besides, even if you go directly to the lower ranks, you are likely to learn much if you can just keep an eye to the kernels and discussion boards. You might as well experience how feature engineering and fine-tuning can make a difference to real-world problems.

Expect to learn much from just testing yourself in a competition. Expect to learn even more if you consistently follow the kernels and discussions. From the data scientists' perspective, Kaggle is a storefront for models and best practices, and you might learn which algorithms are best at solving at some kind of problem.

> TIP: Many competitions allow users to join forces into teams at some stage. That's a great opportunity to learn from others, plus an opportunity for networking.

The data science field is evolving at a fast pace, and you got to stay updated, but how? The next paragraph will tell you something more about that.

Content to stay tuned to

There is lots of content that you can look at to stay tuned: job announcers, blogs, podcasts, social media, and academic journals. Through this section, expect to meet sources for all these kinds of content. It's up to you to decide which ones you will benefit from.

When it comes to methodologies, packages, and algorithms, a great place to see what the market is looking for is the R-users website: `https://www.r-users.com/`.

Jobs are announced on this web page. Announcers will tell visitors which kind of professional they are looking for along with which packages they wish them to already have mastered and much more useful information: what the company does, tasks related to the job, and so on.

Consistently tracking R-users and Kaggle will respectively give you the heads-up of what the top-performing practices/methodologies are and which abilities, skills, and libraries are most valued by organizations. Kaggle also has a blog where top scorers share how they were able to get there. Blogs are yet another source of knowledge.

TIP

Consider creating a blog of your own. Posting the learning process is not that hard, and it may help your career take off.

For those who wish to maintain blogs of their own, my tip is `blogdown`. There is great free material from which you can learn from: `https://bookdown.org/yihui/blogdown/`.

Whenever the topics R and blog come together, it's natural to think about R-bloggers. While I was writing this, the blog had over 750 contributors and countless tutorials. It's frequently updated, so you can keep up with what is going on in the R-world while learning a little something now and then: `https://www.r-bloggers.com/`.

News are also very likely to come up from RStudio's blog, so, here is a link to it: `https://blog.rstudio.com/`

RStudio is one of the reasons why R is so popular, not because they are disclosing the novelties but because they are the ones to bring them to life in the very first place. RStudio's folks are steadily improving the functionalities of R, either by maintaining important packages, developing new ones, or developing powerful tools, such as developing an absolutely incredible IDE.

My favorite blog by far is Bob Rudis's blog: `https://rud.is/b/`.

His work is amazing. There is another great blog that I highly recommend; it's called *Simply Statistics* or *Simply Stats* for short: `https://simplystatistics.org/`.

This blog is owned by three amazing guys: Jeff Leek, Roger Peng, and Rafa Irizarry. All of them are seasoned, capable biostatics professors. Not every post will be about R; nonetheless, expect to see lots of interesting things such as Peng's comments on an episode of *Law and Order*, or how Irizarry doesn't like violin plots.

TIP

Data science is not exactly new; statisticians were doing it well before R. While knowing how to code is crucial, lacking statistics will most likely destroy you, seriously.

If you're the kind of person who likes R, gaming, or sports, you may like to check my blog, *ArcadeData, R-Cade-Data*. I and my partner, Mr. Ricardo A. Farias, use data science to talk about games, sports, and e-sports: `http://arcadedata.org/`.

Building a routine to periodically check the blogs that you like is great. Yet another way to keep up with the blogs is to stay tuned to important R people in social media. Usually, there is a lot to learn from simply following good folks. I would never guess that I would learn as much from tweets as I did.

Here is a list of 10 R personalities (on Twitter):

- Bob Rudis (`@hrbrmstr`)
- Hadley Wickham (`@hadleywickham`)
- Mara Averick (`@dataandme`)
- Dr. Alison Hill (`@apreshill`)
- Renee M. P. Teate (`@BecomingDataSci`)
- Thomas Lin Pedersen (`@thomasp85`)
- Jesse Maegan (`@kierisi`)
- Jeff Leek (`@jtleek`)
- Roger D. Peng (`@rdpeng`)
- Rafael Irizarry (`@rafalab`)

You can find some of us there as well:

- Vitor Bianchi Lanzetta (`@vitorlanzetta`)
- Ricardo Anjoleto Farias (`@R_A_Farias`)

R users usually adopt the hashtag `#rstats`; consider deploying it the next time you talk about R on Twitter.

Do you enjoy listening to podcasts? You can listen to them and learn. These podcasts will talk about data science in general and eventually mention R, but they are all good:

- Not so standard deviation: `http://nssdeviations.com/`
- Talking machines: `http://www.thetalkingmachines.com/`
- O'Reilly data show podcast: `https://www.oreilly.com/topics/oreilly-data-show-podcast`
- Partially derivative: `http://partiallyderivative.com/`
- Data skeptic: `https://dataskeptic.com/`

Perhaps the best idea is to try a few episodes from each of these podcasts, selecting the ones that you like the most and then building a routine to frequently listen to those.

YouTube channels are also great to learn new things and answer any questions you may have:

- `https://www.youtube.com/channel/UCWN3xxRkmTPmbKwht9FuE5A`: Siraj Raval for tips and explanations related to data science
- `https://www.youtube.com/channel/UCk5tiFqPvdjsl7yT4mmokmg`: Data science tutorials for coding tutorials
- `https://www.youtube.com/user/keeroyz`: Two-minute papers for a summarized up-to-date research
- `https://www.youtube.com/channel/UC0e3QhIYukixgh5VVpKHH9Q` : Code bullet for comedy, tutorials, AI
- `https://www.youtube.com/channel/UCXuqSBlHAE6Xw-yeJA0Tunw` : Linus Tech Tips for reviews about hardware mostly

The last channel in the list, Linus Tech Tips, is not exactly about data science, but if you like, the idea of building and maintaining your own gear (PC) or a server all by yourself, Linus has your back, especially if you are a scientist by day and a gamer by night.

The last source of knowledge I want to talk about is academic journals. There is no rule, but you could expect novelties and breakthroughs to come first from journals. The following is a list of five journals I recommend reading:

- *The R Journal*: `https://journal.r-project.org/`
- *Big Data*: `https://home.liebertpub.com/publications/big-data/611/overview`
- *Big Data Research*: `https://www.journals.elsevier.com/big-data-research/`
- *Artificial Intelligence*: `https://www.journals.elsevier.com/artificial-intelligence/`
- *Computational Statistics and Data Analysis*: `https://www.journals.elsevier.com/computational-statistics-and-data-analysis`

Normally, people don't read all the articles from a journal. Checking the issues and picking one or two articles of your liking is more doable. Also, reading a scientific production can be hard sometimes if you're not used to it, but, believe me, it's only a matter of getting into the habit of doing so.

So far, we have discussed things such as distinctions between data scientists' roles, how to get data, how to discover what the organizations are looking for, which kind of materials can help you keep updated and learn even more. The paragraphs ahead are about to introduce the usage of **Stack Overflow**, a powerful platform responsible for uniting portfolio, clarification, and jobs all in one.

Meeting Stack Overflow

Stack Overflow is a powerful tool and, thankfully, learning how to use it is quite straightforward. This book is obviously focused on coding and data science, and so will be this introductory guide, but keep in mind that Stack Overflow can help you solve matters from practically any field of knowledge— cooking, grammar, literature, job interviews, chemistry... the list goes on and on.

There are basically three ways you can use Stack Overflow:

- You ask others for help—queries you may have or things that are troubling you
- You help others by solving their problems—answer their queries or overcome their bugs
- Seek a job

This book has a clear goal to teach practical machine learning with R; the next tips will be more directly related to programming and data science but can be generalized to other fields with some minor adjustments. If you are not registered yet, signing up is a good start: `https://stackoverflow.com/`.

It's also possible to log in using a Google or a Facebook account.

> TIP: Answering and asking questions might yield you reputation points—this is a real metric there. Try always to use the same account so you will gain a reputation and make a portfolio for yourself.

Let's say you have been experiencing a bug while you're coding. You have tried several solutions for many days now, and nothing seems to work. In this scenario, troubleshooting is giving you a hard time, so Stack Overflow is very likely to help you, right? That is accurate. Should you go out there and fire a question? The answer is *maybe*.

The very first thing to do is to check whether someone had already asked a similar question. Figure out what are the keywords related to your problem and search for those; warnings and errors are usually, but not always, helpful. Complement your search with the use of tags. Is your problem related to R? Add `[r]` to your query. Is it related to an external package, maybe `rvest`? Add `[rvest]` to your search.

> Tags can be indicated using brackets: `[ ]`.

If you find a similar question, and the question is well displayed so the problem is easy to understand, upvote the question to reward whoever wrote it and to make the question more visible. Next, check whether someone already answered the question in a satisfactory way. Upvote the answers/comments that really helped you.

TIP: You have limited upvotes per day, so don't waste them by just giving them one away to anyone.

During this stage, you may develop an even better solution. Don't be shy about posting it. Do not forget to link sources that may have helped you to come up with such a solution. Also, for questions, answers, and comments, it's very important to format it well. HTML and Markdown can help you through this. You can go to the following link to get tips about it: `https://stackoverflow.com/help/formatting`.

Sometimes, questions will remain unanswered because they were poorly written. There are mainly two ways out of this. The first one consists of editing the question for clarity, objectivity, and understandability. The ability to edit questions requires a lot of reputation points, which a new user may not have. Also, the question may be so badly written and/or downvoted that the effort outweighs the expected results, which leads us to the second way out.

The course of action for very badly written questions and/or highly downvoted ones is very close to the action for an as-yet non-existent question: ask a question. The only difference would be that for the former, you may get a feeling about what to avoid by reading the replies.

Click the **Ask Question** button to get started with yours. It may seem a trivial task, but asking really good questions takes time and effort. Doing it the right way will greatly increase the chances of you being answered while helping you to earn upvotes and reputation along the way.

Asking the right question is so important that Stack Overflow made several guides for it. I recommend you to at least visit the following link to have a look at one: `https://stackoverflow.com/help/how-to-ask`.

Nonetheless, based on this guide, I will sum it up in seven points:

- Pretend to be talking to a busy colleague; you usually are.
- Pay attention to spelling, punctuation, and grammar.
- Leave the title for last.
- What were you trying to do actually? Start with an intro.
- Produce an easily reproducible example.
- Include *relevant* tags.
- Read your question, and try out your sample code before actually posting.

These seven points will help you ask the right question. Make sure only to ask a question after ensuring there is no similar one around. Additionally, you can be on the other side answering other people's questions. By doing this you will most likely be dong the following:

- Exercising your communications and coding skills
- Gaining reputation points, and by doing so gaining more privileges under the platform
- Gaining badges, and by doing so growing a portfolio to show off your skills to employers

Search for questions using tags. My advice is to separate some time during the week to search and answer questions. Search especially for themes/packages/libraries that you are either using or studying a lot in your daily routine. Don't worry if you cannot answer any questions at first. Try to read and understand the proposed solutions.

By earning badges and points, a user grows their a portfolio, but this is not the only way Stack can help with the job thing. Stack Overflow actually has a job section that can be accessed through the menu on the left side or through the following link: `https://stackoverflow.com/jobs`.

Searching for a job then is very easy. You can use tags based on your skill set. It's also possible to adopt different filters—remote, location, background, and so on.

Taking the next on to data science may be difficult and as I mentioned before, there is no right or wrong. Still, growing some habits—participating in Kaggle's competitions, discussions, kernels, visiting blogs, listening to podcasts, reading journals, and using Stack Overflow—can help you on your path.

Other Books You May Enjoy

If you enjoyed this book, you may be interested in these other books by Packt:

Machine Learning with R Cookbook - Second Edition
AshishSingh Bhatia, Yu-Wei, Chiu (David Chiu)

ISBN: 9781787284395

- Create and inspect transaction datasets and perform association analysis with the Apriori algorithm
- Visualize patterns and associations using a range of graphs and find frequent item-sets using the Eclat algorithm
- Compare differences between each regression method to discover how they solve problems
- Detect and impute missing values in air quality data
- Predict possible churn users with the classification approach
- Plot the autocorrelation function with time series analysis
- Use the Cox proportional hazards model for survival analysis
- Implement the clustering method to segment customer data
- Compress images with the dimension reduction method
- Incorporate R and Hadoop to solve machine learning problems on big data

R Deep Learning Cookbook
Dr. PKS Prakash, Achyutuni Sri Krishna Rao

ISBN: 9781787121089

- Build deep learning models in different application areas using TensorFlow, H2O, and MXnet.
- Analyzing a Deep boltzmann machine
- Setting up and Analysing Deep belief networks
- Building supervised model using various machine learning algorithms
- Set up variants of basic convolution function
- Represent data using Autoencoders.
- Explore generative models available in Deep Learning.
- Discover sequence modeling using Recurrent nets
- Learn fundamentals of Reinforcement Leaning
- Learn the steps involved in applying Deep Learning in text mining
- Explore application of deep learning in signal processing
- Utilize Transfer learning for utilizing pre-trained model
- Train a deep learning model on a GPU

Leave a review - let other readers know what you think

Please share your thoughts on this book with others by leaving a review on the site that you bought it from. If you purchased the book from Amazon, please leave us an honest review on this book's Amazon page. This is vital so that other potential readers can see and use your unbiased opinion to make purchasing decisions, we can understand what our customers think about our products, and our authors can see your feedback on the title that they have worked with Packt to create. It will only take a few minutes of your time, but is valuable to other potential customers, our authors, and Packt. Thank you!

Index

D

E

F

G

H

I

K

L

M

N

O

P

R

S

T

U

V

W

X

Z

Printed in the USA
CPSIA information can be obtained
at www.ICGtesting.com
LVHW081939170124
768967LV00012B/416

9 781789 139402